DATE D

Clinical Approaches to
Sex Offenders and Their Victims

Wiley Series in

Clinical Approaches to Criminal Behaviour

Clinical Approaches to Violence
Edited by Kevin Howells *and* Clive R. Hollin

Clinical Approaches to Sex Offenders and Their Victims
Edited by Clive R. Hollin *and* Kevin Howells

Further titles in preparation

Clinical Approaches to Sex Offenders and Their Victims

Edited by

CLIVE R. HOLLIN
School of Psychology
University of Birmingham
and
Glenthorne Youth Treatment Centre
Birmingham

and

KEVIN HOWELLS
School of Psychology
University of Birmingham

JOHN WILEY & SONS
Chichester · New York · Brisbane · Toronto · Singapore

21672772
DLC

7-21-92

Copyright © 1991 by John Wiley & Sons Ltd,
Baffins Lane, Chichester,
West Sussex PO19 1UD, England

Other Wiley Editorial Offices

John Wiley & Sons, Inc., 605 Third Avenue,
New York, NY 10158–0012, USA

Jacaranda Wiley Ltd, G.P.O. Box 859, Brisbane,
Queensland 4001, Australia

John Wiley & Sons (Canada) Ltd, 22 Worcester Road,
Rexdale, Ontario M9W 1L1, Canada

John Wiley & Sons (SEA) Pte Ltd, 37 Jalan Pemimpin #05–04,
Block B, Union Industrial Building, Singapore 2057

Library of Congress Cataloging-in-Publication Data:
Clinical approaches to sex offenders and their victims / edited by
   Clive R. Hollin, Kevin Howells.
      p. cm. — (Wiley series in clinical approaches to criminal
   behaviour)
      Includes bibliographical references.
      Includes indexes.
      ISBN 0-471-92817-8 (ppc)
      1. Child molesting.   2. Sexually abused children—Mental health.
   3. Psychotherapy.   I. Hollin, Clive R.   II. Howells, Kevin.
   III. Series.
      [DNLM: 1. Child Abuse, Sexual. 2. Paraphilias—therapy. 3. Sex
   Offenses.   WM 610 C628]
   RC560.C46C58 1991
   616.85'83—dc20
   DNLM/DLC
   for Library of Congress   90-12609
                                                                          CIP

British Library Cataloguing in Publication Data:
Clinical approaches to sex offenders and their victims.
   1. Sex offenders. Psychotherapy
   I. Hollin, Clive R.   II. Howells, Kevin
   616.85830651

   ISBN 0-471-92817-8

Typeset by Inforum Typesetting, Portsmouth
Printed and bound by Courier International. Tiptree, Essex

CH To Martin Herbert, that rare combination,
scholar *and* gentleman

KH To Tony Black, for setting me on the right road

List of Contributors

ARNON BENTOVIM, *Hospital for Sick Children, Great Ormond Street, London, UK.*

LUCY BERLINER, *Sexual Assault Center, Harborview Medical Center, Seattle, Washington, USA.*

JON R. CONTE, *School of Social Work, University of Washington, Seattle, Washington, USA.*

DEBORAH DARO, *Center on Child Abuse Prevention Research, Chicago, Illinois, USA.*

GRAHAM DAVIES, *Department of Psychology, University of Leicester, Leicester, UK.*

MARY R. HAYNES, *The Health Science Center, Department of Psychiatry, University of Tennessee, Memphis, Tennessee, USA.*

CLIVE R. HOLLIN, *School of Psychology, University of Birmingham, Birmingham, UK.*

KEVIN HOWELLS, *School of Psychology, University of Birmingham, Birmingham, UK.*

DEREK JEHU, *Department of Psychology, University of Leicester, Leicester, UK.*

RICHARD I. LANYON, *Department of Psychology, Arizona State University, Tempe, Arizona, USA.*

BARBARA E. GERTH MARKAWAY, *Department of Psychology, University of Missouri – St Louis, Missouri, USA.*

WILLIAM D. MURPHY, *The Health Science Center, Department of Psychiatry, University of Tennessee, Memphis, Tennessee, USA.*

DEREK PERKINS, *Psychology Department, Broadmoor Hospital, Crowthorne, Berkshire, UK.*

PATRICIA A. RESICK, *Department of Psychology, University of Missouri–St Louis, Missouri, USA.*

EILEEN VIZARD, *Newham Child and Family Consultation Service, London, UK.*

D. J. WEST, *Institute of Criminology, University of Cambridge, Cambridge, UK.*

PATRICIA J. WORLEY, *The Health Science Center, Department of Psychiatry, University of Tennessee, Memphis, Tennessee, USA.*

Contents

Series Preface

This series around the theme of *Clinical Approaches to Criminal Behaviour* has its origin in a sequence of conferences we organized between 1984 and 1988. Our intention, both then and now, was to make some progress towards re-establishing an approach to changing criminal behaviour which has become unfashionable, unpopular and much maligned in recent years. It should be made absolutely clear that in the present context the term 'clinical' is not intended to imply a medical model, in which criminal behaviour is viewed as pathological, but to define an approach in which the focus is on the individual and on psychological methods of producing change. Having said that, we are not blind to the crucial importance of economic, political and social factors in crime and criminological theory. We agree that change is necessary at all levels to reduce crime, and have no wish to be seen as placing the spotlight of blame and responsibility exclusively on the offender to the exclusion of environmental factors. (As behaviourists, admittedly of differing persuasions within that broad church of theoretical opinion, how could we say otherwise?) However, we would also maintain that it is important not to lose sight of the individual, and it is here that the clinical approach comes into its own. The series is intended to serve two functions: to inform clinicians of developments in the clinical approach to criminal behaviour in its many forms, and to convince others that the clinical approach has a role to play in changing criminal behaviour. There is no reason why social reform and clinical change should be incompatible: others have written on the former approach, we now seek to re-assert the latter.

CLIVE R. HOLLIN
KEVIN HOWELLS

Preface

In the first volume in this series, *Clinical Approaches to Violence*, we aimed to set the tone for what was to follow. We encouraged our distinguished contributors to focus on three specific areas within their specialist fields: the empirical research; the theories built around the data; and, crucially, the practical application, both in terms of assessment and intervention, of this research and theory. Heartened by the response of the contributors to our blueprint, we have maintained the same format for this volume.

When selecting the topic for this second volume in the series we opted for sex offences for a number of reasons. Firstly, the topic is one which has seen a recent rapid development, both in terms of public and professional interest and involvement. While it is undoubtedly the case that sexual offences against adults, mostly women, and children have always been part of our society, it is perhaps only in the last decade that the true extent of the abuse has begun to be appreciated. In response to this growing awareness, researchers and practitioners from a range of professions, theoretical persuasions, and schools of clinical practice have become involved in working with sex offenders and their victims. While there are many advantages to this growth, a potential disadvantage is that the field may become increasingly fragmented. This fragmentation may be across professions, so that some aspect of sexual abuse is seen as the province of, say, social work, while another aspect is marked as the territory of, say, clinical psychologists. Thus our second reason for selecting sex offences as the topic for this volume was to make a statement that fragmentation is not inevitable: the contributors to this volume are from a range of disciplines—including psychiatry, psychology, and social work—and bring a range of theoretical views and styles of clinical practice. We think there is much to be learnt from this cross-discipline approach: indeed, as both editors and, of course, the first readers of this book, our immediate impression was that of realizing just how much is happening in the field, and how many unifying concepts can be perceived. In addition, through the work of the contributors our own knowledge base has grown considerably: this will benefit us greatly, and hopefully many other readers, in our roles of researchers, teachers, and practitioners.

The third reason for selecting the topic of sex offences, and which heavily influenced our choice of chapters and hence contributors, was to offer a book which would inform clinicians and researchers about offenders *and* victims. As the research base grows, so the number of specialist papers and books increases: while this increase in knowledge is vital, there is the danger that information on theories of sex offending, assessment methods, and clinical work with families, offenders, children, and adults becomes increasingly diffuse and inaccessible— perhaps especially so for hard-pressed clinicians. Therefore we have drawn together in this book theories, research, and practice relevant to both offenders and victims: the final product is, we believe, an unique overview of the field.

As in the preparation of any book, but perhaps especially so with edited books, we have accumulated a number of debts. We should like to thank Sheila Wesson, then later Rita Granner, for typing periodic deluges of letters, not to mention the occasional frantic burst of activity on the fax! We are grateful to our contributors for the high standard, in both presentation and quality, of their work which made our editorial task so much easier. Finally we would like to acknowledge the highly professional approach of our publishers at Wiley in Chichester: in particular Wendy Hudlass who chides us gently yet remains a veritable paragon of patience.

CLIVE HOLLIN
KEVIN HOWELLS

Sex Offenders and Victims: The Scope of a Clinical Approach

CLIVE R. HOLLIN and KEVIN HOWELLS
School of Psychology, University of Birmingham, UK

There is little doubt that the 1980s was the decade in which many people began to come to terms with two facts about sex offences. Firstly, that such crimes occur at a rate far in excess of the official figures: rape and sexual assault are not the isolated, statistically unusual events we might once have believed (e.g. Russell, 1982). Secondly, rather than fitting neatly into stereotyped caricatures, sex offenders and their victims are to be found across all strata of society. Thus, to pursue the latter point, it became more and more difficult to accept the stereotype of the sex offender as a lonely, frustrated old man: men who sexually abuse women *might* be old and disadvantaged, but they might also be young, affluent, socially competent, have committed other offences, and have long-term relationships (Alder, 1984; Davies and Leitenberg, 1987). In contrast to the popular image of the sex offender as mentally unstable (Hollin and Howells, 1987), most sex offenders are not clinically disordered; rather the motivation for the offence is to be found in other more 'normal' explanations such as the exercise of male power, or the expression of anger, or for social reward and peer acclaim (Groth, 1979; Scully and Marolla, 1985). Indeed, it is often the case that rape is portrayed as a violent, rather than sexual, act (e.g. Alder, 1984); although this is not a view which meets with unanimous approval (Palmer, 1988).

In the same vein the victim of sexual attack does not conform to the stereotype. Contrary to myths about rape (Burt, 1980), women victims do not 'ask for it', do not provoke hapless males to the point of no return, are not capable of resisting if they really wanted to, are not promiscuous, and do not have an unconscious wish to be violated. To a greater or lesser extent, women victims can

Clinical Approaches to Sex Offenders and Their Victims
Edited by C.R. Hollin and K. Howells © 1991 John Wiley & Sons Ltd

be young or old, black or white, single or married, mothers or childless, employed or unemployed (e.g. Ploughman and Stensrud, 1986).

While many people were appalled by the emerging picture of the true extent of sexual aggression against women, and the apparent 'normality' of the sex offender, the research on child sexual abuse gave rise to a quite different reaction. The first signs of disquiet came with research into the levels of sexual abuse of children: the estimates vary according to research methodologies and definitions of abuse, but figures in excess of one in ten children are not uncommon (Alter-Reid et al., 1986; Finkelhor, 1986). However, the findings of researchers such as Finkelhor (1984, 1986) that a great deal of child sexual abuse occurs within the family, that great bastion of civilization and stability, set in train a widespread reaction of disbelief and denial. A great many people simply refuse to accept that adults, including parents, can systematically and repeatedly sexually abuse children.

Given this controversy and denial, we decided to begin this second volume in the series Clinical Approaches to Criminal Behaviour with a discussion of the nature of sexual offences against children. In his opening page, Jon Conte makes the crucial point that the characteristic disbelief and denial serve as psychological mechanisms to cope with some unpalatable truths. However, as Conte continues, this disbelief also taints the thinking and practice of those professional groups concerned both with policy-making and delivering a service to the offenders and their child victims. To counter this disbelief and denial Conte offers an overview of the empirical evidence in order to paint as accurate a picture as possible of the true nature of sexual offences against children. In a chapter brimming with facts and insights, Conte discusses legal and clinical definitional issues and the extent and types of child sexual abuse, before considering the offender. In particular Conte challenges the myth that incest offenders do not sexually abuse children outside their own family: he cites the findings of Abel et al. (1988) that some incestuous fathers sexually abused children outside their own family and were involved in other sexual offences, such as rape, against women. While distinctions can be drawn between different types of child sex offenders, such as fixed and regressed offenders (Groth et al., 1982), the psychological mechanisms underpinning such taxonomies are altogether less clear. As Conte suggests, this should provide a target for future research: without an empirically based model of the agents and factors which lead to child sexual abuse, together with an acceptance of the scale of the issue, policy-makers and professionals are disadvantaged in attempting to understand, assess, and intervene to help and protect children.

Despite the fact that there are a myriad of empirical questions to be answered, a variety of theories have been put forward to explain sex offences. In the second chapter of the opening section on Offenders and Victims, Richard Lanyon presents a wide-ranging coverage of the theoretical perspectives which have been used to attempt to account for sex offences. Drawing parallels between theories of sexually deviant behaviour generally and sex offences specifically, Lanyon discusses psychodynamic, behavioural, and biological theories of rape and child molestation. In the final third of his chapter, and in sympathy with Conte,

Lanyon makes note of the recent rise of empirical, data-driven theories. In keeping with current preferences in psychology, Lanyon concludes that research must now focus on the role of cognition—specifically attitudes and fantasy—in the offender's behaviour. Increased awareness of these areas will, when integrated into existing knowledge, prove of benefit to the design of clinical assessment and intervention with offenders.

In the third chapter in the opening section Donald West considers the effects on victims of sex offences. He begins by casting doubt on the often expressed view that rape is a violent offence: although this should not be read as meaning that sex offences are not harmful. West discusses some of the short- and long-term physical, emotional and psychological effects of the sexual victimization of women, introducing the notion of post-traumatic stress disorder as a means of understanding the effects of sexual attack. West notes that the severity of this type of disorder is not uniform and its effects can vary from woman to woman in both duration and severity. Moving to child victimization, West considers both male and female child victims. After a discussion of prevalence rates, he considers both the initial and long-term effects of abuse. While these effects can be serious, West is at pains to point out, as have other writers (e.g. Widom, 1989), that the 'cycles of abuse' argument is hypothesis not fact. There is no clear evidence that adult problems, including sexual offending, are the inevitable consequences of sexual abuse in childhood. West concludes that we should beware of over-generalization of the effects of sex offences, and take time to consider fully the complexity of such behaviour and hence our response to it.

The second section of the book moves to assessment, perhaps the most thorny and difficult area, yet one which is crucial for theoretical understanding, clinical practice, and the detection of abuse in children. The first chapter, by William Murphy and Patricia Worley, looks in detail at the assessment of adult sexual interest. As did West, Murphy and Worley comment that there is continued debate whether sex offences are violent or sexual acts. While this debate has obvious implications for assessment, the matter is further complicated by the theoretical perspective of the practitioner making the assessment. The assessment of a rapist undertaken by a psychoanalyst would be very different from that made by, say, a radical behaviourist. In response to both these points, Murphy and Worley argue the case for the role of sexual arousal and sexual interest in sex offending; while they adopt a broad social learning theory approach by which to understand the assessment data. Using case material, Murphy and Worley discuss the practice of physiological and self-report assessment: they then move to the use of such assessments both to 'sort' adult and child offenders, and to inform clinical practice. While, as Murphy and Worley point out, there are limitations with this type of assessment, there is considerable consistency in the literature, suggesting promise for the future.

The next two chapters, by Graham Davies and Eileen Vizard respectively, were originally commissioned as a single chapter. After producing a first (joint) draft the authors suggested that their material would be better presented as two individual pieces. Our reading of the draft led us to the same conclusion, and Wiley were happy to accept our recommendation to lengthen the book by an extra chapter.

The reliability of a child's memory is crucial when that child has to give evidence in a court case: when the child is testifying about his or her own experiences of sexual abuse, the reliability of the evidence takes on a special poignancy. In his discussion of research on children's testimony, Davies begins with an overview of the psychology of memory, with an emphasis on developmental aspects of memory performance. Davies makes the observation that while the sophistication of memory performance might improve with age, contrary to common belief even very young children are capable of robust and accurate memory performance. In particular Davies points to the distinction between *available* and *accessible* material in memory (Tulving, 1983). The former is the information the individual is able to give spontaneously; the latter is the information which becomes accessible following cues or prompts. As might be expected, cued recall is generally more comprehensive than free recall. In the case of the child witness or victim, one of the roles of the interviewer is to build on the child's accessible memories so that, through cuing via questioning and the use of props such as anatomically correct dolls, additional facts become accessible. It may well be the case that younger children require a great deal more assistance and support to recall fully from memory. The danger, of course, is that the process of cueing introduces errors into the child's account of events. Davies discusses these issues in great detail and concludes that, given good practice and reasonable safeguards, children are capable of giving accurate testimony.

The process of conducting the interview with the abused child so as to effect maximum recall while minimizing the risk of introducing error is Eileen Vizard's concern in the following chapter. Vizard begins with a review of the literature on the contentious issue of the use of anatomical dolls in interviewing children suspected of being sexually abused. The use of such dolls can, as Vizard points out, be clinically revealing, but from a legal perspective the interviewer is open to charges of suggestibility. The same point applies to the type of questions the interviewer might use in order to prompt recall: the danger here lies in the use of leading questions which may gain valuable clinical information, but at the risk of an increased probability of introducing error and producing evidence which is not legally sound. In order to meet these points practitioners have devised a number of schedules and procedures for interviewing children suspected of being sexually abused. In what may well be the first review of its type, Vizard compares the utility of ten such interview protocols. The first draft of this chapter contained a case example but, serving to remind us all of the sensitivity of the topic, this was removed following legal advice. The 'ideal' case stands in its place as an example of the procedures.

The third and final section of the book is concerned with treatment and begins with a chapter by Derek Perkins on working with sex offenders in secure settings. We felt that this was an important beginning to the treatment section for two reasons: firstly to show that a clinical approach is viable even in the most difficult, even anti-therapeutic, settings; and secondly to emphasize that *offenders*, as well as victims, are of concern to clinicians. Perkins opens with a discussion of the key issues of the offender's denial of the offence, motivation to change, and cooperation in treatment. Rather than these issues being seen as obstacles to treatment, Perkins suggests that they should be seen as *targets* for treatment; aspects of the offender's functioning which should be as amenable to assessment and modification as the offending behaviour itself. Drawing on research into both the acquisition and maintenance of deviant sexual behaviour, Perkins discusses in detail the assessment and treatment of both the cognitive and behavioural aspects of offending. Throughout the chapter there is a careful consideration of the limitations imposed by conditions of security, together with a frank discussion of the arguments for and against clinical work with sex offenders.

It is undoubtedly the case that much sex offending takes place within families, suggesting that family therapy should play an integral part in a clinical approach to working with sex offenders and their victims. Arnon Bentovim discusses both the theory and practice of clinical work with families in which sexual abuse has occurred. He offers a conceptual model of abuse which draws together the individual, the family, and the society within which both function. Bentovim also suggests that the response to victimization can be seen in terms of a post-traumatic stress response, and the patterns of traumatic responding occur at both individual and family levels. Through the use of case material, Bentovim vividly describes the typical reactions—flashbacks, nightmares, sexual play, dissociation—found in abused children: further, Bentovim argues, if these responses are not dealt with, then family and societal systems can act to reinforce the responses and so maintain the abuse cycle. The family work advocated by Bentovim, again strikingly illustrated with case material, involves the four stages of *disclosure, separation, rehabilitation*, and *new family*. The essential practitioner skills and intervention techniques required at each of these stages is presented in detail. It is, we believe, fundamentally important to recognize Bentovim's point that there are families who are 'hopeless' as regards successful rehabilitation into the abusing family. Unpopular as the message may be in some quarters where to admit to hopelessness is seen as a sign of professional failure, there are strong arguments, as Bentovim points out, that it is in the child's best interest to plan for a permanent future in a new family.

While family work may be crucially important, there is also a strong case to be made for individual work with the sexually abused child. Lucy Berliner, in reviewing such individually-directed clinical work, also invokes the notion of the abusive event as a traumatic experience producing traumatic responses. Indeed, Berliner begins her chapter with a comprehensive review of the literature on the long-term effects of child sexual abuse. It is important to note Berliner's point that both the type and severity of these long-term effects differs significantly across children. However, two basic clinical targets emerge from the literature: the child's emotional and cognitive processing of the abuse experience. 'Successful' processing stems from the ability, together with a supportive social network, to talk about or be reminded of the abuse without experiencing undue distress. Where this successful processing has not taken place, then the child may develop maladaptive ways of coping with the cognitive and emotional impact of the abuse. Thus the child may have a set of avoidance strategies or generalized inappropriate responses in other areas of social functioning. Following Finkelhor and Browne (1985), Berliner suggests that the process of clinical assessment and intervention can be built around the four dynamics of *traumatic sexualization, betrayal, powerlessness,* and *stigmatization.* Each of these four dynamics is discussed in detail together with clinical strategies to effect change.

One of the facts of life is that children grow up, and that very often that process of growing can be marred and distorted by traumatic childhood events. The effects of being sexually abused as a child do not disappear with ageing, as Derek Jehu discusses in his chapter on clinical work with adults who were sexually abused in childhood. Jehu begins with a discussion of the, rather sparse, literature on men who were sexually abused as boys. The lack of a clinical literature—Jehu notes only one treatment programme (Bruckner and Johnson, 1987)—is surprising given the scale of the problem (Baker and Duncan, 1985), and the potential long-term effects both on psychological and social, including violent, behaviour. The prevalence rates among women are similarly high and the long-term effects equally serious. From a substantially larger literature Jehu is able to extract the principal long-term effects in women sexually abused as children: these include mood disturbances, self-injurious behaviour, stress disorders, and interpersonal and sexual problems. In a comprehensive review of both practice and outcome, Jehu discusses clinical programmes designed to ameliorate these long-term effects of childhood abuse.

Maintaining the theme of individually-directed treatment, the next chapter by Patricia Resick and Barbara Gerth Markaway is concerned with the clinical treatment of adult female victims of sexual assault. The chapter begins with a review of the cognitive, emotional, and behavioural reactions to rape. A typical pattern of reaction to assault is described in which the immediate effects of fear, shaking, and trembling gradually subside to be replaced by increased depression, fatigue, and restlessness. As time passes other adverse reactions, including interpersonal and sexual problems and lowered self-esteem, may also emerge. As in preceding chapters, the notion of post-traumatic stress is adapted to account for the effects of victimization. However, Resick and Gerth Markaway move on to discuss a number of theoretical perspectives—feminist theory, crisis theory, behavioural and social learning theories, and cognitive theories—which have been advanced to account for the traumatizing effects of rape. The assessment and intervention methods suggested by these different theoretical views are discussed in detail; a case study illustrates both the practice and outcome of a clinical programme.

While much of what has gone before has been concerned with accounts of the consequences of sexual abuse, the final chapter by Deborah Daro is concerned with prevention programmes. Daro begins with a number of statements, with which we would like to record our agreement: children have a right not to be molested; a child should not have to experience harm before services are made available; and children should be seen as entrusted into the care of parents and guardians rather than as the property of adults. Strategies to prevent sexual abuse have been drawn from psychodynamic, learning, and environmental theories: Daro reviews the contribution and styles of programme which follow each theory. The focus of prevention programmes, each discussed in turn, has been on strengthening children, and strengthening parents and caretakers, including educators. In a review of prevention programmes Daro examines the strengths and weakness, both practically and empirically, of these various approaches to prevention. She concludes with a blueprint for a comprehensive strategy for preventing sexual abuse: we believe this should be compulsory reading for everyone who lives, works, or is in any way responsible for the welfare of children.

Our contributors have covered a vast amount of ground to give, we think, one of the most comprehensive statements on sex offending yet collected in a single text. Our editing suggested a number of themes and issues running through the work and in the final chapter we identify these along with some suggestions for the future.

References

Abel, G., Becker, J., Cunningham-Rather, J., Mittleman, M., and Rouleau, J. L. (1988). Multiple paraphiliac diagnoses among sex offenders. *Bulletin of the American Academy of Psychiatry and the Law,* **16**, 153–68.

Alder, C. (1984). The convicted rapist: A sexual or violent offender? *Criminal Justice and Behavior,* **11**, 157–77.

Alter-Reid, K., Gibbs, M. S., Lachenmeyer, J. R., Sigal, J., and Massoth, N. A. (1986). Sexual abuse of children: A review of the empirical findings. *Clinical Psychology Review,* **6**, 249–66.

Baker, A. W., and Duncan, S. P. (1985). Child sexual abuse: A study of prevalence in Great Britain. *Child Abuse and Neglect,* **9**, 457–67.

Bruckner, D. F., and Johnson, P. E. (1987). Treatment of male victims of childhood sexual abuse. *Social Casework: The Journal of Contemporary Social Work,* **68**, 81–7.

Burt, M. (1980). Cultural myths and support for rape. *Journal of Personality and Social Psychology,* **39**, 217–230.

Davies, G. E., and Leitenberg, H. (1987). Adolescent sex offenders. *Psychological Bulletin,* **101**, 417–27.

Finkelhor, D. (1984). *Child Sexual Abuse: New Theory and Practice.* New York: Free Press.

Finkelhor, D. (1986). *A Sourcebook on Child Sexual Abuse.* Beverly Hills, CA: Sage Publications.

Finkelhor, D., and Browne, A. (1985). The traumatic impact of child sexual abuse: A conceptualization. *American Journal of Orthopsychiatry,* **55**, 530–40.

Groth, A. N. (1979). *Men Who Rape: The Psychology of the Offender.* New York: Plenum Press.

Groth, A. N., Hobson, W. F., and Gary, T. S. (1982). The child molester: Clinical observations. In J. Conte and D. Shore (eds), *Social Work and Child Sexual Abuse.* New York: Haworth Press.

Hollin, C. R., and Howells, K. (1987). Lay explanations of delinquency: Global or offence-specific? *British Journal of Social Psychology,* **26**, 203–10.

Palmer, C. T. (1988). Twelve reasons why rape is not sexually motivated: A skeptical examination. *Journal of Sex Research,* **25**, 512–30.

Ploughman, P., and Stensrud, J. (1986). The ecology of rape victimization: A case study of Buffalo, New York. *Genetic, Social and General Psychology Monographs,* **112**, 303–25.

Russell, D. E. H. (1982). The prevalence and incidence of forcible rape and attempted rape of females. *Victimology,* **7**, 81–93.

Scully, D., and Marolla, J. (1985). 'Riding the bull at Gilley's': Convicted rapists describe the rewards of rape. *Social Problems,* **32**, 251–63.

Tulving, E. (1983). *Elements of Episodic Memory.* Oxford: Oxford University Press.

Widom, C. S. (1989). Does violence beget violence? A critical examination of the literature. *Psychological Bulletin,* **106**, 3–28.

Part 1
Offenders and Victims

1

The Nature of Sexual Offenses Against Children

JON R. CONTE
School of Social Work, University of Washington, USA

The sexual use of younger persons by older individuals is a social problem witnessing a dramatic increase in research and knowledge development, public awareness, and clinical expertise. Many parts of the world are experiencing an increase in media reports of child sexual abuse and the ensuing hotly contested debates about the extent of the problem: how it is possible to determine 'true' from 'false' sexual abuse cases, whether sexual offenders should be treated in mental health programs or incarcerated in prisons, and numerous other issues involved in understanding and responding to these cases.

How is it possible for adults to overcome the strong social sanctions against the sexual use of children and repeatedly abuse children, often children to whom they are either related or with whom they have a relationship? This is a question repeatedly confronted by the public, policy-makers, and professionals engaged in providing health, social service, and mental health services to adult offenders and those victimized by them. It is my belief that until very recently many of the ideas used by the public, policy-makers, and many professionals to understand the nature of sexual offenses against children and those who commit them have the essential function of making it easier for the user of those ideas psychologically to cope with what the offender does, and that some of these ideas have little empirical support.

Within the field of child sexual abuse, it appears to many professionals involved in services to victims that it is the sexual offender, far more than the victims of sexual offenders, that receive the lions' share of funding, public attention, and even professional action. While this may or may not be an accurate perception, it reflects a schism within the field which serves artificially to segregate professional efforts. Most critically, it is my assumption that knowledge

Clinical Approaches to Sex Offenders and Their Victims.
Edited by C. R. Hollin and K. Howells © 1991 John Wiley & Sons Ltd

Table 1.1   Illinois revised statutes

Chapter 38
Criminal Law and Procedure
11–1 to 14

12–13.   Criminal Sexual Assault

12–13. Criminal Sexual Assault. (a) The accused commits criminal sexual assault if he or she:

1. commits an act of sexual penetration by the use of force or threat of force; or

2. commits an act of sexual penetration and the accused knew that the victim was unable to understand the nature of the act or was unable to give knowing consent; or

3. commits an act of sexual penetration with a victim who was under 18 years of age when the act was committed and the accused was a family member; or

4. commits an act of sexual penetration with a victim who was at least 13 years of age but under 18 years of age when the act was committed and the accused was 17 years of age or over and held a position of trust, authority or supervision in relation to the victim.

12–15.   Criminal Sexual Abuse

12–15. Criminal Sexual Abuse. (a) The accused commits criminal sexual abuse if he or she:

1. commits an act of sexual conduct by the use of force or threat of force; or

2. commits an act of sexual conduct and the accused knew that the victim was unable to understand the nature of the act or was unable to give knowing consent.

(b) The accused commits criminal sexual abuse if the accused was under 17 years of age and commits an act of sexual penetration or sexual conduct with a victim who was at least 9 years of age but under 17 years of age when the act was committed.

(c) The accused commits criminal sexual abuse if he or she commits an act of sexual penetration or sexual conduct with a victim who was at least 13 years of age but under 17 years and the accused was less than 5 years older than the victim.

12–16.   Aggravated Criminal Sexual Abuse

12–16. Aggravated Criminal Sexual Abuse. (a) The accused commits aggravated criminal sexual abuse if he or she commits criminal sexual abuse as defined in subsection (a) of Section 12–15 of this Code and any of the following aggravating circumstances existed during the commission of the offense.

1. the accused displayed, threatened to use or used a dangerous weapon or any object fashioned or utilized in such a manner as to lead the victim under the circumstances reasonably to believe it to be a dangerous weapon; or

2. the accused caused great bodily harm to the victim; or

3. the victim was 60 years of age or over when the offense was committed; or

4. the victim was a physically handicapped person.

(b) The accused commits aggravated criminal sexual abuse if he or she commits an act of sexual conduct with a victim who was under 18 years of age when the act was committed and the accused was a family member.

(c) The accused commits aggravated criminal sexual abuse if:

1. The accused was 17 years of age or over and (i) commits an act of sexual conduct with a victim who was 13 years of age when the act was committed; or (ii) commits an act of sexual conduct with a victim who was at least 13 years of age but under 17 years of age when the act was committed and the accused used force or threat of force to commit the act, or

2. The accused was under 17 years of age and (i) commits an act of sexual conduct with a victim who was under 9 years of age when the act was committed; or (ii) commits an act of sexual conduct with a victim who was at least 9 years of age but under

Table 1.1   Illinois revised statutes continued

Chapter 38
Criminal Law and Procedure
11–1 to 14

17 years of age when the act was committed and the accused used force or threats of force to commit the act.

(d) The accused commits aggravated criminal sexual abuse if he or she commits an act of sexual penetration or sexual conduct with a victim who was at least 13 years of age but under 17 years of age and the accused was at least 5 years older than the victim.

(e) The accused commits aggravated criminal sexual abuse if he or she commits an act of sexual conduct with a victim who was an institutionalized severely or profoundly mentally retarded person at the time the act was committed.

(f) The accused commits aggravated criminal sexual abuse if he or she commits an act of sexual conduct with a victim who was at least 13 years of age but under 18 years of age when the act was committed and the accused was 17 years of age or over and held a position of trust, authority or supervision in relation to the victim.

11–6.   Indecent Solicitation of a Child.

(a) Any person of the age of 17 years and upwards who (1) solicits a child under the age of 13 to do any act, which if done would be an indecent liberty with a child or an act of contributing to the sexual delinquency of a child; or (2) lures or attempts to lure any child under the age of 13 into a motor vehicle with the intent to commit an indecent act, commits indecent solicitation of a child.

development, policy formulation, and treatment can best be accomplished by a realistic understanding of sexual abuse of children and only then can meaningful actions at therapeutic and social policy levels be taken.

This chapter is written, in part, from the perspective of a researcher and therapist treating adult and child victims of sexual abuse in childhood. I identify this perspective from the outset because I will argue that what victims tell us about sexual offenses is critical in understanding the true nature of sexual offenses. This chapter is intended to provide an overview on sexual use of children by older persons. It is not possible to review comprehensively all victim and offender data and clinical experience here, so of necessity this chapter will paint a broad picture of the nature of sexual offending against children.

LAWS AGAINST CHILD SEXUAL ABUSE

In the United States every state has laws which make the sexual use of children illegal (for discussion see Bulkley, 1981). These laws include civil sanctions for a parent's abuse or failure to protect a child from abuse, and for abuse by a person acting in authority over a child (e.g. teacher or day care worker). Civil law has the goal of protecting the child and encouraging a parent (when the parent is an abuser or has failed to protect the child from abuse) to receive treatment and service. Sexual use of a child is also specifically prohibited in criminal law.

In recent years, many states in the United States have modified their laws, doing away with vague language about 'carnal knowledge,' 'indecent liberties,' or 'molestation' to define specifically the sexual acts which are prohibited. Many laws also specifically identify the age of the offender, the use of force, and the relationship between the victim and offender which make a behavior illegal. For example, some state laws provide for punishment when an offender is over a certain age, is a certain number of years older than the child, or is in a position of control or power over the child. State laws also often identify the degree of sexual contact, with intercourse resulting in a more serious punishment than fondling. As an example, the Illinois State law is outlined in Table 1.1.

The role of the justice system in child sexual abuse has been hotly debated from virtually the beginning of the rediscovery in many countries of child sexual abuse in the late 1970s. Currently there are few data which describe the operation of the justice system in these cases, the outcome of law enforcement handling of child sexual abuse on victims or sexual offenders—for data on effects of incarceration of offenders see Furby *et al.* (1989)—or which provide understanding about how the laws against sexual use of children are in fact being implemented.

Clinical experience suggests that cases drop out of the law enforcement system throughout its handling of these cases. Depending on where a victim lives, about 47% of cases are 'unsubstantiated' at the child protection investigation level (Westat, 1987). Prosecutors may decline to pursue criminal prosecution because insufficient evidence exists to support criminal charges, or for other reasons, sometimes valid (e.g. when witnesses will not cooperate), and often not valid (e.g. when the prosecutor uses idiosyncratic views about the age at which a child becomes a credible witness). No national data are currently available which report on the outcomes of prosecution.

Society has a vested interest in sanctions against sexual abuse of children. Efforts to protect children in family and family-like environments (e.g. schools or day care centers) and to protect society from sexual offenders would receive little opposition. The use of civil sanctions (e.g. court-ordered treatment of incest offenders or civil *no contact* orders which protect victims and their families from untreated sexual offenders), and criminal sanctions which can be used to encourage an offender into treatment and monitor his involvement in treatment long enough for treatment to have a chance to be successful, are not new ideas (Bulkley, 1981).

Unfortunately, it is not clear that the laws against sexual offenses against children are having their desired effect. The fear of criminal sanctions and public disclosure appears to have resulted in a significantly greater number of adults accused with sexual abuse choosing to fight prosecution. This has resulted in a plague of efforts to question the credibility of children to report abuse, to develop 'validation tests' which appear to be designed to get accused adults to be determined 'not guilty,' and generally to question professional practices and procedures which support children's disclosures of abuse.

Public and professional attention directed toward 'validating allegations' of abuse, the current mania surrounding professional procedures to investigate and support disclosure, and emphasis on legal processing of cases through civil and criminal justice systems diverts attention from policy questions essential to the prevention and recovery from sexual abuse. Do victims of sexual abuse receive treatment? Do sexual offenders stop sexual use of children? Does current policy change anything? While this discussion may at first reading appear a diversion in a chapter on the nature of sexual offenses, it is my contention that little else will really matter until public and professional attention is directed towards the development of a social policy which in fact protects both victims and society by constructing interventions and social responses which are likely to meet the goals of prevention and treatment of abuse.

CLINICAL DEFINITIONS

Clinical definitions of sexual abuse of children have involved several major approaches. In terms of defining sexual offenders who target children, the nomenclature of the *Diagnostic and Statistical Manual of Mental Disorders* (DSM III-R, 1987) is frequently used. Within the sexual disorders classification, pedophilia has as an 'essential feature . . . recurrent, intense sexual urges and sexually arousing fantasies, of at least six month's duration, involving sexual activity with a prepubescent child' (DSM III-R, p. 284). Table 1.2 presents the diagnostic criteria for pedophilia.

The use of sexual disorder diagnoses in practice has not been investigated but clinical experience suggests there are a number of problematic issues which limit knowledge about sexual offenses. Many mental health professionals report a reluctance to use a diagnosis, especially paraphilia, because of the stigma which may be attached to an individual who carries the diagnosis into his future. Even when an individual meets diagnostic criteria for paraphilia, the professional may prefer to use another diagnosis (e.g. Major Depression). Other professionals endorse beliefs about certain groups of offenders (e.g. incest fathers) which *a priori* rule out the sexual disorder diagnoses. For example, many professionals believe that incest is not a sexual disorder, rather that it is a family problem. This belief holds regardless of the incest father's sexual urges, fantasies, or arousal pattern (Conte, 1986).

Table 1.2   Diagnostic criteria from (1987) DSM III-R for Pedophilia

---

DIAGNOSTIC CRITERIA FOR 302.20 PEDOPHILIA

   A.   Over a period of at least six months, recurrent intense sexual urges and sexually arousing fantasies involving sexual activity with a prepubescent child or children (generally age 13 or younger).
   B.   The person has acted on these urges, or is markedly distressed by them.
   C.   The person is at least 16 years old and at least 5 years older than the child or children in A.
   Note: Do not include late adolescent involved in an ongoing sexual relationship with a 12- or 13-year old.
   Specify: *same sex, opposite sex, or same and opposite sex.*
   Specify: *if limited to incest.*
   Specify: *exclusive type* (attracted only to children, or nonexclusive type).

Additionally, there are few surveys of offender treatment samples which indicate the proportion of offenders with the various disorders. An important exception of this general point is the work of Abel and his colleagues (Abel *et al.*, 1987). Describing 561 sexual offenders, they report treating 224 non-incestuous pedophiles targeting female children, 159 incestuous pedophiles targeting female children, 153 non-incestuous pedophiles targeting male children, and 44 incestuous pedophiles targeting male children. The next highest number of offenders treated were 142 exhibitionists and 126 rapists. Their work is also important in understanding the diagnosis of sexual offenders. For example, they report that the patients they treated had an average of 2.02 paraphilias. Indeed, it was a rare patient who had only one diagnosis, e.g. female children other than relatives 15% of non-incestuous pedophiles targeting female children, and 26% of incestuous pedophiles targeting female children (Abel *et al.*, 1988). The implications of these data are of considerable importance in showing that the sexual problem for which the adult is referred or the initial sexual disorder diagnosis may well not be the only sexual problem the client experiences. Assessment of other potential sexual problems would seem critical to work in this area (see the discussion of Incest vs Pedophilia below).

Professionals working with victims have tended to define the sexual abuse of children along three dimensions: an *age difference* of five years or more between child and offender; *specific sexual behaviors*, such as exhibitionism, voyeurism, kissing, fondling, fellatio or cunnilingus, penetration of the vagina, anus, or mouth with sexual organs or objects, and photography (either taking pictures of the child or exposing the child to pornographic materials); and *sexual intent* wherein the intent of the behavior is the sexual gratification of the adult. It is assumed that a child cannot give *informed consent* to sexual contact with an adult because the young child does not know what s/he is consenting to, and that the child does not have the power to decline involvement (Finkelhor, 1979).

This approach presents no assessment problems in the majority of cases where there is little room for doubt (e.g. penile penetration of the vagina or anus). However, in some cases it can be quite difficult to determine the *intent* of the behavior. For example a young child provides a vague description of what sounds like her father's limited (a few times) touching of her labia (no penetration). The father indicates that he was checking for a diaper rash. It is not clear if this behavior has the intent of 'grooming' the child for more specific sexual behavior, does in fact serve as a form of sexual gratification, or is what the father says it is.

There is also little current information available about the range of sexual behaviors generally regarded as acceptable in families or how these vary by culture of sub-group. Certainly families vary in attitudes about nudity, privacy, touching, or kissing family members. In most cases of sexual abuse, these matters will be of little consequence since there is no doubt about the behavior (e.g. having a small child sit unclothed on an unclothed penis and rock back and forth). However, there are cases where these questions are of considerable importance in deciding whether the behavior is sexual abuse; inappropriate (perhaps even representing poor judgement); or variation within acceptable bounds.

The 'grey' area cases cannot be finally resolved here. It is important to note that defining behavior between adult and child as *sexual abuse* does, in some cases, require professional judgement. The professional making such judgements in these cases should be aware of the knowledge, attitudes, and criteria employed in rendering such judgements, and that each of these factors can influence the decision whether a certain behavior is abuse or not abuse.

HOW COMMON IS SEXUAL ABUSE?

In their comprehensive and thoughtful review of studies on the incidence and prevalence of child sexual abuse, Peters *et al.* (1986) report that estimates of the prevalence range from 6% to 62% for females and from 3% to 31% for males. As they point out, this variation may be accounted for by a number of methodological factors, such as differences in definitions of abuse, sample characteristics, interview format (e.g. in-person versus phone interview), and the number of questions used to elicit information about abuse experience.

There are a number of problems created by the variation and the magnitude of the problem as described by these figures. Even if one takes only the lowest estimates, it is clear that sexual abuse of children is a common experience of childhood and affects a large number of children. Indeed the numbers appear so large that they serve to create a sense of disbelief about the problem, making it easier for some to turn away from the problem as impossibly large. The variation in estimates and the resulting disagreement in professional and media reports on child sexual abuse, although potentially understandable due to methodological factors such as those discussed by Peters *et al.* (1986), also tends to create a sense of irritation in those who hear the varying estimates. This can serve to support further a sense that the problem may be overestimated or that there is too much 'hype' surrounding the problem. All these factors serve to support the denial which is inherent in abuse.

I know of no estimate of the number of sexual offenders in the general population. While on first thought it may appear impossible to get such an estimate because of subject fear of being identified, research with college students suggests that males will self-report violent behavior when appropriate safeguards are taken. For example, Demare *et al.* (1988) report that 27% of 222 men in a college sample, self-report likelihood of rape behavior. Such a research effort would appear well worth the effort as professionals seek knowledge about the extent of sexual abuse.

Abel *et al.* (1987) provide an innovative and eye opening estimate on the number of *sexual acts* committed by a sample of sexual offenders treated in their outpatient treatment program. The 561 sexual offenders committed a total of 291 737 acts. The lifetime number of victims were estimated for each of the major paraphilias represented in their sample of sexual offenders. The 224 non-incestuous pedophiles targeting female children had a total of 4435 victims; 155 non-incestuous pedophiles targeting male children a total of 29 981 victims; 158 incestuous pedophiles targeting female children a total of 286 victims; and 44 incestuous pedophiles targeting male children a total of 75 victims. As these data indicate, incestuous offenders targeting children related to them tend to commit more sexual acts per victim, and non-incestuous offenders targeting children not-related abuse more victims.

Victim data generally support the notion that sexual abuse of children often involves assault by more than one offender—in studies of child victims even samples of young children indicate that a proportion of victims have been abused by more than one offender. For example, 14% of the children studied by the Tufts New England Medical Center (Tufts, 1984) were abused by different offenders, and 10% of the child victims at the Seattle Sexual Assault Center were abused by more than one offender (Conte et al., 1986).

Studies of adults victimized in childhood confirm the notion that victims are often victimized by more than one offender. For example, in a large study of adult survivors ($N = 420$) of childhood sexual abuse recruited from treatment programs throughout the United States, only 30% of survivors were abused by one offender; 30% were abused by two offenders, 24% by three, 11% by four, and 5% by five or more offenders (Conte et al., 1989).

Answering the question, 'how common is it?' is not easily accomplished. As discussed above, estimates of the rate at which children are sexually abused indicate that it is a quite common experience of childhood. It appears that over childhood, many children are abused by more than one offender. Offender data suggest that sexual offenders targeting children tend to abuse more than one child. Since abuse continues to be under-reported (e.g. only 2% of incestuous and 6% of extra-familial cases in Russell's (1984) random sample of San Francisco households had ever been reported), it is simply not clear how many adults are in fact sexually abusing children at any one time—although it is clear that a large number of children are sexually abused.

RISK FACTORS

There has been considerable interest in whether some children are at greater risk for sexual abuse than are other children. Finkelhor and Baron (1986) conclude that it is currently not clear what factors increase children's risk for sexual abuse. It appears that girls are at greater risk, although boys are also victimized. Girls are more likely to be victimized if they have somehow been separated from their mohers (e.g. if they have ever lived away from their mother, or if their mother has been ill or disabled), or if they report poor relationships with their mothers. Although, as the authors note, these factors may be consequences of sexual abuse as much as risk factors.

Several studies have recently focused on how sexual offenders select and recruit children for sexual abuse. For example, Conte et al. (1989) interviewed a sample of sexual offenders treated in the community about the victimization process. These offenders claim the ability to identify and use vulnerabilities in a potential victim to gain sexual access to and maintain control over the child. Vulnerabilities were defined in terms of *status conditions* (e.g. living in a single parent family), *emotional characteristics* (e.g. needy, unhappy, shy), and *situational factors* (e.g. child was alone and unprotected, child was young). It is not clear if sexual offenders differ from other adults in that they have a special capacity to identify vulnerable children or if they are simply willing to use this knowledge against children (see also Budin and Johnson, 1989). The identification of factors which increase a child's risk for sexual abuse is of considerable importance in the design and implementation of organized efforts to prevent child sexual abuse.

WHAT IS IT?

Sexual abuse of children consists not only of specific sexual behaviors (e.g. vaginal intercourse) but also of actions which the offender employs to gain access and control over the child, what is said to the child during the abuse, and the child's perception of the abuse and abuse context (e.g. who the child thought knew about the abuse, why the child thought s/he was being abused, what the child thought would happen if the abuse was revealed). These components may vary quite dramatically across cases and are important not only because they describe the qualitative nature of the victims' experience, but also because many of these factors have been found to be associated with an increased risk for mental health problems resulting from sexual abuse (Wyatt and Powell, 1988).

Sexual Behaviors

The published literature focusing on the sexual offender has tended to employ either psychiatric diagnosis (e.g. pedophilia, non-incestuous, male target) or generally descriptive terms (e.g. incestuous child molester vs non-incestuous child molester). In this literature, there has not been much emphasis on describing different types of specific sexual behavior (e.g. anal vs vaginal intercourse). Erickson *et al.* (1988) do present relatively specific sexual behavior descriptions for a sample of 229 sexual offenders against male and female children. *Vaginal contact* occurred in 42% of female cases, *anal contact* in 33% of male and 10% of female cases, *offender oral* in 41% of male and 19% of female cases, *victim oral* in 29% of male and 17% of female, *offender fondle* in 43% of male and 54% of female, and *victim fondle* in 8% of male and 7% of female cases.

Fundamentally, in terms of understanding the etiology, maintaining conditions, and nature of sexual deviant sexual interest it is not clear what level of specificity is necessary. For example, it is important to know that a child molester preferring five year olds is more likely to favor anal intercourse over vaginal? It is currently not clear if this choice is significant in understanding the nature of the deviancy or how it is anatomically easier to have sex with a five year old.

The victim literature has tended to describe the specific sexual behaviors to which the child was exposed, although different studies have employed somewhat different definitions for the sexual behaviors examined. Kendall-Tackett and Simon (1987) in their description of 365 adults sexually abused in childhood, reports that 64% were *fondled from the waist up*; 92% were *fondled from the waist down*; 48% *oral sex*; 19% *attempted intercourse*; 10% *simulated intercourse*; 44% *intercourse*; 9% *anal intercourse*. Kercher and McShane (1984) describe the sexual behaviors a sample of 619 children were exposed to: 19% *exhibitionism by perpetrator*; 42% *fondling by perpetrator*; 39% *heterosexual intercourse*; 6% *homosexual intercourse*; 14% *oral sex on victim*; 14% *oral sex on perpetrator*; 8% *perpetrator masturbates self*; 2% *photographing child nude or in sexual act*; 2% *prostitution of victim*; 2% *sale/distribution of erotic material to victim*; and 3% *sexual performance by child*.

Table 1.3 presents the data on type of sexual abuse from the sample of 369 children reported by Conte *et al.* (1986). Children were exposed to an average of 3.5 behaviors (only 20% of children experienced one type of sexual behavior).

Sexual behaviors which are often thought of as 'less sexual' or 'less serious' tend to take place more often. It is not clear what to make of this fact. For example, in the case of the high frequency of fondling, it may be that fondling is

Table 1.3   Types of sexual abuse (*n* = 369 children)

Type of Sexual Assault:

A.   Victim Does to Offender

	%
Masturbate	21.1
Suck/lick penis	19.0

B.   Offender Does to Victim
(touches child's genitals or touches child with own genitals)

	%
Outside clothing	26.8
Inside clothing	62.1
Victim unclothed	31.2

Penetration (with penis/finger/object):

	%
Oral/penis	18.4
Anal/penis	8.9
Vaginal/penis	19.8
Oral/finger	0.8
Anal/finger	5.1
Vaginal/finger	25.2
Oral/object	0.3
Anal/object	1.1
Vaginal/object	2.4
Penetration attempted, but unsuccessful	13.0
Child swallow semen	2.7
Offender ejaculate on child	7.9
Offender took pictures of child	1.9
Victim forced to have sexual contact with others	3.3
Victim forced to watch pornography	3.3
Victim forced to watch sexual activity or offender expose self	8.4
Offender talked about sexual matters asked child to perform sexual act	26.0

part of the grooming process whereby offenders desensitize children to touch by gradually moving from non-sexual to sexual touch. More cases are identified at an early stage of the victim process than at a later stage when the child has been more successfully conditioned not to disclose. It may also be that cases in which one fondling took place are those in which an earlier disclosure prevented 'more sexual' behaviors from taking place.

A number of investigators have explored the association between the relationship between the victim and offender and the specific type of sexual behaviors constituting the sexual abuse. For example, using data on child victims, Kercher and McShane (1984) found significant differences for three of the nine sexual behaviors reported above. Intra-familial sexual abuse cases were more likely to include *fondling* and *heterosexual intercourse*, and less likely to include *exhibitionism* than extra-familial sexual abuse cases. (One wonders whether the lower reporting of *exhibitionism* in family cases reflects a greater tolerance for nudity in families than between non-related adults and children.)

In her sample of adults abused as children, Russell (1984) examined the degree of seriousness of the sexual abuse according to the relationship between victim and offender. *Very serious* included completed or attempted vaginal, oral, or anal intercourse, cunnilingus, and analingas; *serious* sexual abuse included completed and attempted genital fondling, simulated intercourse, and digital penetration; and *less serious* sexual abuse included completed and attempted acts of sexual touching of buttocks, thighs, leg or other body parts, clothed breasts or genitals, or kissing. Of incest cases 23% involved *very serious*, 41% *serious*, and 36% *less serious* abuse. Of non-incestuous abuse 53% consisted of *very serious*, 27% *serious*; and 20% *less serious* sexual abuse.

It is important to note that *severity of abuse* can be defined in many ways. Specific sexual behaviors may be grouped conceptually into categories such as those proposed by Russell (1984), alternatively the amount of force employed in the abuse may also be used to define severity. For example, Russell (1984) reports that 41% of incest cases involved the use or threat of force. Conte *et al.* (1986) report that 7% of victims were physically harmed/injured, 33% threatened with harm to victim or others; and 23% physically strained as part of the abuse. Of child victims studied at the Tufts New England Medical Center (Tufts, 1984) 48% were verbally threatened and 35% of victims exposed to aggression as part of the abuse.

There are a number of important issues surrounding the use of information about the specific sexual behaviors constituting sexual abuse. Symptomatic of the current mania about 'validating allegations,' Erickson *et al.* (1988) have suggested that 'by quantifying the relative frequency of different sexual acts in different circumstances, this information is intended as the beginning of an empirical criterion against which the statements of alleged child sex abuse victims can be weighed by medical experts, therapists, and those involved in criminal or custody proceedings' (pp. 77–78). Such a suggestion is without clinical, legal, or empirical foundation.

It is clear that the data indicate considerable variation in the sexual behaviors which constitute sexual abuse. Since fathers are more likely than strangers to engage in intercourse with their children, are we to disregard a child who describes intercourse during an abduction-rape by a stranger? Obviously not. Further, no other victim of a crime is subjected to a screening criteria to judge whether his or her crime fits the profile for that crime. If most home invasions take place between 8 a.m. and 4 p.m. when people are at work, are we going to be less likely to believe the adult who reports his home being burglarized sometime during the hours of 11 p.m. and 5 a.m? Again, obviously, the answer is no. The range of sexual behaviors is so great that the development of a 'profile of sexual abuse behaviors' which can be used to judge the credibility of children's reports of abuse will not be useful.

In a thought-provoking chapter, Plummer (1981) has made much of the data on the sexual behaviors that constitute sexual abuse. For example, he suggests that it is a 'stereotype that the sex act itself is damaging and dangerous and may even lead to such things as child murder' (p. 225). He then cites as evidence for this statement the high rate of occurrence of the 'less sexual (e.g. fondling) behaviors' and the low incidence of child sexual murders. As indicated previously in this chapter, this perspective ignores the feelings of victims who may find even 'less sexual behaviors' such as fondling or kissing painful, intrusive, and frightening.

In a similar manifestation of this perspective Plummer also suggests that it is a myth that 'the sex act is forced on the child and is uncontrollable' (p. 225). This may well be the perspective of the sexual offender or at least what his verbal behavior indicates he believes. However, simply on the face of it, such a proposition ignores the greater physical, intellectual, and experiential skills of the adult who selects, recruits, abuses, and then maintains the victim's silence with the abuse. Indeed, when offenders have been in treatment long enough to break down the distortions and denial which support abuse of a child, they are able to describe the ploys used to abuse children. Little they say would suggest that the act is not forced or, to any real extent, controllable by the child. For example, in the interviews reported by Conte et al. (1989), sexual offenders were asked if they had ever used force in abusing a child. While the majority responded to this question with a global 'No,' many then went on to describe situations where the child had witnessed them being violent with someone else (e.g. the child's mother), or where they restrained physically or otherwise demonstrated their superior strength to the child.

The point is not that all sexual abuse involves high levels of physical force or violence, but that many, perhaps most, incidents of sexual abuse of a child do involve specific actions and words in which an older person uses superior size, skill, knowledge, or resources to gain and maintain sexual access to the child. Verbal reports from sexual offenders about what they did, their intentions, and who is responsible for the sexual abuse are likely to be self-serving and biased. Understanding what constitutes sexual abuse and its nature requires information obtained from both offender and victim perspectives.

Other aspects of sexual abuse describe important characteristics or dimensions which make up the nature of the abuse. Victim data tend to describe the duration of the abuse: Russell (1986) reports that 43% of adults abused incestuously in childhood in her sample were abused only once. Conte *et al.* (1986) report that 24% of child victims in their clinical sample were abused once. The age and sex of the victim, the number of times the child was abused, and other variables describe the nature of the abuse from the victim perspective.

Other Components

In addition to the specific sexual behaviors (e.g. vaginal intercourse, making pornographic video tapes, digital penetration of the anus) which constitute sexual abuse of children, these behaviors take place in the context of a complex interaction in which children are recruited, groomed, and, often, maintained in sexual abuse situations. Such situations include what the offender says and does; the victim's perception, understanding, and reaction to what the offender says and does; the abuse itself; and the abuse context (e.g. the nature of the child's family at the time of the abuse, what the child thought would happen if the abuse was revealed, or who the child thought knew about the abuse). Table 1.4 presents selected aspects of the abuse and abuse context from a study of the effects of abuse on children (Conte *et al.*, 1989).

The non-sexual components of the sexual abuse of children have long been described in terms of global 'dynamics' or dimensions which describe the characteristics of sexual abuse from the victims' perspective. These include coercion,

Table 1.4   Selected aspects of the abuse and abuse context

Child accepts gifts and rewards in response to abuse
Child takes some part in initiating abuse
Child felt s/he would be believed if abuse was revealed
Child felt s/he would not be believed if abuse was revealed
Child feared negative consequences to self if abuse was revealed
Child feared negative consequences to others of abuse was revealed
Non-offending parent was supportive at time of disclosure
Child has a supportive relationship with sibling(s)
Child was coerced into abuse via threat of physical harm to self or others
Child was coerced into abuse via physical harm
During the abuse, the victim was physically restrained
During the abuse, child made effort to resist, escape, avoid abuse
Offender denies abuse took place
During the abuse, child passively submits, goes along
During the abuse, child pretends nothing happening
Child initiates report of abuse
Child was previously a victim of sexual abuse
Child believes that others in family knew about abuse and took no action to protect
Child perceives some responsibility in own abuse
Child has been pressured to recent abuse
Primary parent does not believe that abuse took place
Primar parent believes that abuse took place
Degree child perceives relationship with offender (other than abuse) is important
Child perceives no secondary gain from abuse
Number of family problems experienced by child's family
Child had a supportive relationship with an adult

---

manipulation, force and violence, ambivalence, secrecy, lack of control, isolation, betrayal, blame, and loss. The components of child sexual abuse, whether described in terms of the discrete actions or words of offenders, or the larger abuse context, or in terms of more global 'dynamics' or characteristics of abuse will vary across cases. In other words, not all children's experiences are the same. There are different opinions concerning how important it is to have information about these components in any given case. Some clinicians believe that these components describe the nature of the experience the child was exposed to and therefore it is important to have information about all the components and especially those which are most salient for the specific child. Other clinicians do not feel that it is important to have such detailed information. Currently, it is not clear to what extent these components are consistently associated with a more serious impact of sexual abuse, although some studies have found some to be significantly correlated with abuse impact (e.g. Wyatt and Powell, 1988).

However, as Conte and Schuerman (1987) have argued, current research methodology, especially the insensitivity of most measures employed to assess the impact of abuse, makes it extremely difficult to determine the effects of such relatively discrete factors as these on something as complex as child behavior. Perhaps more critically, given the multiple sources of variation on behavior, it would be somewhat surprising to find that time-limited and discrete behaviors, such as what the victim thought would happen if the abuse was revealed, or what the offender said to the child to maintain its silence, had a major impact on child functioning, as measured by broad, multi-item and multi-factor psychological instruments. Nevertheless, these components may have considerable impact on short-term functioning as evidenced in victims' reports of fear, anxiety, pain, and other distress during and immediately after the abuse. Consequently, to the extent that it is possible to obtain such information, it appears important in the treatment of victims to obtain information about the components of each victim's experience. Most critically, Conte (1989) has argued that the therapist's understanding of the victim's experience can, in part, be curative as a victim who feels misunderstood, out of control, isolated, and unable to express the pain and bizarre quality of life during abuse faces a therapist who by question and comment communicates an appreciation and understanding about the true nature of abuse. Denial of the victim's experience by a previous therapist who has failed to understand sexual abuse for what it is, as for example, by suggesting that the incest father was really trying to express fatherly love through the vaginal rape of his six year old daughter, is one of the most common complaints of adult survivors I see in therapy.

In terms of understanding the offender, information about the components of child sexual abuse is also important. Such information can be helpful in identifying a typical offense pattern which describes how children are identified, recruited, and maintained in abuse situations. Therapists working with offenders have used this information to help the offender prepare support persons in his environment who can help monitor and control his behavior until therapy can produce more stable and self-directed change. For example, during the time that behavioral interventions are targeted at modifying deviant arousal responses

(Abel *et al.*, 1984), individuals in an offender's environment who know that his typical offense pattern is to target neighbourhood playmates of his son can structure his son's play experiences so as to deprive the offender of easy access to his preferred sexual victim.

TYPOLOGIES

Although interest in sexual offenders who target children has only become wide-spread over the last decade or so, there have been a number of efforts to develop classification systems for these adults. Some of these systems have become so widely endorsed that they have been used to develop social policy regarding the preferred method of dealing with the various 'types' of offenders. Unfortunately, it now appears that many of these 'systems' or ideas were prematurely disseminated as they do not appear to be valid.

Personality Profiles

It is still quite common for mental health professionals acting as expert witnesses in legal proceedings in the United States to argue that an accused adult either does or does not fit the *profile* of a sexual offender. This information can have a powerful effect on the trier of fact since it comes from someone judged to be an expert and carries the apparent power of science. Recently such information has tended not to be admitted, or if admitted has been overturned on appeal, since an accused adult may have all of the characteristics of those individuals who have tended to commit a certain crime in the past, but the adult has not in fact committed the specific crime.

More critical to our discussion here is the fact that reviews of the existing empirical literature have failed to identify a consistent psychological profile or set of characteristics which discriminates between sexual offenders and others (Armentrout and Hauer, 1978; Langevin *et al.*, 1985; Quinsey, 1977, 1983).

Incest vs Pedophilia

There has been a longstanding belief that incest offenders represent a distinct and different clinical problem from non-incestuous offenders (i.e. pedophiles). This belief is at the foundation of current social policy in the United States which supports community based treatment for the incest offender who is regarded as not dangerous to society as a whole. Definitions of incest vary, but incest is generally recognized as sexual contact between persons who are biologically related (e.g. father–daughter, mother–son, grandparent–grandchild, or brother–sister) or between step-parents and step-children (e.g. step-father–daughter abuse). Much of the literature to date has focused on father or step-father and daughter abuse (Conte, 1985).

Although there is as much variation within *family oriented views* of adult sexual use of children as there is between *family and non-family views*, Conte

(1986) has suggested that all *family* views of the problem rest on two key assumptions: incestuous fathers and step-fathers do not act sexually outside the home, and that incest is the sexual expression of non-sexual needs. The belief that incest offenders do not act sexually outside the family is both a statement about the way things are in these families and a statement about the nature of incest. Incest is a family problem in which every member of the family contributes to the development and maintenance of the sexual relationship between father/step-father and daughter. This belief is at the basis for the assumption that incest offenders are not dangerous to children who live outside their homes and in most cases, can be left safely in the community (although, perhaps, not in the same house) during treatment.

Preliminary data have seriously challenged this core belief about incest. Abel *et al.* (1988) indicate that 49% of the incestuous fathers and step-fathers referred for outpatient treatment at their clinics abused children outside the family at the same time they were abusing their own children (18% of these men were raping adult women at the same time they were sexually abusing their own child). While replication of these data is critical in determining how generalizable they are, they do raise questions about the validity of the assumption that the initial referral diagnosis (e.g. father or step-father incest) has any significance in understanding the nature of the incest father or step-father's problem.

The assumption that incest is the sexual expression of non-sexual needs has led generations of professionals to direct attention toward non-sexual problems typically found in incestuous offenders (e.g. depression, poor self-esteem, difficulties in relationships with adult women). Virtually all sexual behavior may include sexual (i.e. tactical, physiological) and non-sexual (e.g. affectional or recreational) aspects. It is not clear why sexual abuse of children by a father or step-father should be regarded as a special or even different kind of *sexual* behavior.

Sexual Arousal

The assessment of the sexual arousal of incest fathers and step-fathers has been the subject of several empirical studies. For example, Quinsey *et al.* (1979) evaluated nine incestuous and seven non-incestuous child molesters and found that incestuous (father or step-father) offenders exhibited more appropriate (i.e. adult) sexual arousal than non-incestuous child molesters. Abel *et al.* (1981) found that incest offenders were sexually aroused to children. Marshall *et al.* (1986) evaluated 40 child molesters, 21 incest offenders, and 22 normal controls: the normal controls demonstrated minimal arousal to children (below 12), slight arousal to children 12–14, and a dramatic increase with substantial arousal to children 14 years and older; child molesters showed considerable arousal to children with the largest amount of arousal to 9 year olds, decreasing arousal to 11, 12, 13 year olds, and a gradually increasing arousal from 14–24 year olds. The findings that child molesters are aroused to children and adults is surprising and not consistent with other research. Incest offenders more closely paralleled normals, although they showed no dramatic arousal increase to children over 14 (as did normals). There were significant differences between normals and incest offenders in the magnitude of their arousal to 14–24 year olds, with the incest offenders showing less arousal to older persons.

The data regarding the extent and nature of incest fathers' and step-fathers' sexual arousal to children are contradictory and limited. There have been problems with some of the research on sexual arousal and incest. For example, as Marshall et al. (1986) point out, many studies have mixed natural fathers, step-fathers, and adoptive fathers in a single incest sample. It may well be that the level of arousal to children will vary across these sub-samples. Other problems in the studies of sexual arousal in incest and non-incestuous offenders include: small sample sizes, selecting non-representative samples or samples of unknown representativeness, the lack of raters blind to the hypotheses, and lack of control groups (Avery-Clark et al., 1981) Other factors which have not examined may also influence arousal to children. One wonders whether the length of time over which an individual has been involved sexually with children will influence and level of arousal? Do adults with only a few incidents over a short time period exhibit less arousal than adults who have abused many more children over a longer time period? Does subtle variation between the preferred victim (e.g. blonde five year olds) and the stimulus material (e.g. a brunette five year old) influence the level of arousal?

The answers to these questions and many more are yet to come from empirical research. It is currently not clear how many incestuous offenders are sexually aroused to children or what is sexually arousing about children. However, a method is available to answer this question, as illustrated by Abel et al. (1977) this method involves assessing differential arousal to sexual stimuli which vary along dimensions of interest (e.g. amount of violence). Thus Abel et al. (1977) demonstrated that rapists were physiologically sexually aroused to violence (i.e. a non-sexual dimension) against women. Recently, Quinsey and Chaplin (1988) reported that child molesters who have injured their victims are more sexually responsive in laboratory assessments to audiotape descriptions of violent sex depicting gratuitous infliction of physical violence than were child molesters who had not inflicted injury (see also Avery-Clarke and Laws, 1984). Hall et al. (1988) report that aggressive pedophilic stimuli are less arousing to child molesters than consenting pedophilic stimuli. Surprisingly, child molesters who used force against child victims were not more aroused to aggressive stimuli.

It would not be surprising to discover in the future that the components of sexual arousal to children can be identified and may include *physical features* (e.g. softness of skin, size and appearance of sex organs) and *emotional features* (e.g. domination, control, naivety). At the moment these are matters of clinical speculation. Future empirical evaluation of the extent and nature (i.e. what is sexually arousing about children) will be extremely important in understanding the nature of incestuous abuse.

While there is much yet to learn about the relationship between sexual arousal and sexual abuse of children, it is increasingly clear that consideration of this relationship is important in understanding the nature of child sexual abuse. The self-report of sexual offenders is likely to be unreliable (Abel et al., 1981;

Marshall and Christie, 1981; Quinsey, 1984; Quinsey et al., 1975). Although not all men respond sexually in the laboratory (e.g. 22% hild molesters and 34% of incest offenders in Marshall et al. (1986) and 80% of subjects in Hall et al. (1988) were able to inhibit sexual arousal), current available research suggests that many men respond differentially to various sexual stimuli, such as slides of sexual partners varying by age or sex, or audiotape descriptions of various sexual behaviors (see e.g. Abel et al., 1977; Quinsey and Chaplin, 1988). As outlined above, some studies have found that physiological sexual arousal measures can discriminate between violent and less violent offenders (Abel et al., 1977; Hall et al., 1988; Quinsey and Chaplin, 1988). In addition, child molesters respond differentially to adult and child stimuli, with more arousal to child stimuli (both male and female children), however a sample of normals selected from the community and non-sexual offenders responded only to adult, consenting stimuli (Quinsey and Chaplin, 1988).

Fixated or Regressed

Among the more popular notions about men who have sex with children is that there are two distinct types, *fixated* or *regressed* (Groth et al., 1982). The *fixated* offender has a primary sexual orientation toward children; this interest usually begins in adolescence, and there appears to be no precipitating event associated with the onset of the orientation, and male victims are primary targets. The *regressed* offender develops a primary sexual orientation to agemates, thus sexual involvement with a child is a clear change in interest and behavior, it comes about usually at a time of stress, may be more episodic, and female victims are primary targets.

While this topology may have been popular in the late 1970s and early 1980s to a practice field and a society trying to understand adult sexual interest of children, it appears to have lost much of its clinical value and a number of problems exist. It was primarily developed on an incarcerated sample of sexual offenders. Men in prison may be psychologically distinct from men with the same problem who are not imprisoned. To date no empirical evidence exists for the accuracy of the typology to classify adult sexual offenders. Indeed, community therapists report that many offenders have characteristics of both the regressed and fixated offender. It appears that the largest group of offenders is a *mixed* group combining certain of the characteristics of both fixated and regressed types. For example, in the sample of offenders described by Abel et al. (1988), 12% of the 159 incestuous offenders referred for sexual abuse of a daughter had abused non-related male children, 49% had abused non-related female children, and 19% had raped adult females.

To take a more functional view, it appears that many of the favorite concepts about incestuous offenders should be viewed cautiously as untested theories. It is premature to make assumptions about the number and sex of victims, the sexual or non-sexual nature of the interest which drives sexual abuse, or the associated features of the clinical problem based on an initial presenting problem of incestuous sexual abuse. Conte (1985) has suggested that this more functional view of the common clinical dimensions of adult sexual use of children be taken until additional research is available. Such a framework suggests that all offenders be assessed for the extent to which they present on the following dimensions which appear to be consistent with sexual abuse of children: denial, sexual arousal, sexual fantasies, cognitive distortions (e.g. 'it's OK for an adult to rub a child's genitals to make her more sexually responsive when she grows up'), social skill deficits, and other mental healh problems (e.g. drug abuse, depression).

Given the apparent lack of reliability of some of the concepts employed in clinical practice and policy formulation concerning the treatment of incest offenders, it is important for the clinician to be aware that these dimensions may be present in an offender who presents as an incestuous offender. For example, knowledge about the extent to which the adult is sexually aroused to children is vital information in helping the clinician understand what has to be done to help the adult control the behavior which places him at serious legal risk. Knowing the number, relationship, and location of an adult's victims not only tells the clinician what children are at risk, but can be helpful to the clinician and offender in structuring the offender's life early in treatment to help prevent a recurrence until therapy has a chance to be successful.

It should be generally recognized that sexual offenders, like many clients who exhibit negatively viewed behaviors, tend to minimize, rationalize, or distort reports of their behavior. It is increasingly clear that the first task of assessment is for the clinician to be aware of the possible dynamics and components of the problem which is to be assessed. It is unlikely that an offender will report behavior which the clinician does not ask questions about, seek information on, or otherwise try to elicit. In a study by Abel *et al.* (1983) offenders increased by 20% the number of types of sexual deviancy they described simply by being re-interviewed by experienced clinicians aware of the tendency for offenders to be involved in more than one type of deviancy. While these results are less than those obtained from the laboratory assessment of the nature of sexual arousal (62%), they do indicate the importance of the clinician's awareness of the nature of sexual offenses and the need to direct interviews to obtain from the client.

SUGGESTIONS FOR FUTURE WORK

Awareness that significant numbers of children are sexually used and abused by older persons, often older persons to whom they are related, is increasingly part of modern society, especially modern professional clinical practice. Understanding the nature of the experience of sexual use and abuse is not as easy as one might think. Strong social sanctions against sexual use of children, fear of punishment, and the psychological denial which is necessary for the adult offender to engage repeatedly in hurtful and illegal behavior make the adult sexual offender an informant of questionable reliability. The victim, who is aware of strong social reactions to victimization, the stigmatization which can result from disclosure, and who has spent many years using psychological defenses such as denial, repression, and minimization to tolerate the psychological and (sometimes) the physical pain and, in the case of child victims, may not have the developmental, intellectual, language, or psychological capabilities to remember or accurately report events and experiences, is often not in the best position to provide detailed information about the abuse. Professionals who embrace theories of sexual abuse which serve to minimize the behavior of their clients (e.g. sexual abuse is not about sex or incest fathers do not know how to express love) are not likely to be in a position to help clients report experiences or events which tend to challenge the professional's favorite theories.

Understanding the nature of sexual use and abuse of children requires both theory and knowledge that rest firmly on empirical grounds and incorporate both victim and offender perspectives. Given the steady and building body of research on sexual offenders, the easy part of understanding is that resting on empirical research. The material outlined above on the connection between sexual arousal and sexual abuse illustrates the availability and importance of such research. In terms of data dealing with the sexual arousal of adults engaged in sexual use of children, it is clear that the assessment and (if present) the treatment of deviant arousal is an essential component of treatment of sexual offenders. This is not to say that there are not many things still unknown about the development, nature, and effective reduction of deviant arousal patterns and, indeed, some of these research questions have been identified above.

What is more difficult, is the capacity to incorporate both victim and offender perspectives. This will require considerable effort over the short term. It calls both victim and offender researchers and therapists to engage in shared data collection and dialogue. There are a number of specific actions which would help with this process.

Offender Information about Specific Victims

It would be helpful if offender researchers and therapists systematically collected data about the victimization of specific children. Information collected from offenders about the selection, recruitment, abuse, and abuse context of specific victims would be beneficial in understanding the nature of sexual abuse. Information about the abuse context of the victim may not always be known by an offender but to the extent possible such information would be valuable in the development of a more complete understanding of sexual abuse, programs to prevent abuse, and treatment of both victims and offenders.

Victim Information about Offenders

With the exception of demographic or other basic classification data (e.g. relationship between victim and offender, age of victim, race of victim), victim studies often do not have information about the offender. In many circumstances data from the victim's perspective have been collected from public social service agency files (e.g. Child Protective Services) or victim-focused treatment centers (e.g. rape crisis centers) and much information about the offender is not available and cannot easily or legally be obtained. Efforts within communities to link victim and offender agencies and their records should be encouraged to deal with this problem.

Victims can also provide detailed and intimate information about the sexual offender's behavior. Little information has systematically been collected from victims about what offenders say prior to, during, and after the sexual acts. Some victims report being made to act our sexual fantasies or to say and follow specific instructions. While in many cases this information is very difficult for victims to report, it may be useful in understanding more about the nature of sexual abuse.

Common Nomenclature

Efforts would be aided by the development of common definitions for sexual behaviors. To date studies have varied in the specificity of the terms used to describe sexual behaviors (e.g. intercourse vs penile penetration of the vagina) or have employed somewhat different terms for what may or may not be the same sexual behavior (e.g. fondling vs fondling of clothed genitals and buttocks). Studies have not always reported information on the full range of sexual behaviors (e.g. the making or use of pornography) and even when mentioned (in the case of pornographic materials being shown to children) the acts depicted have not been described. There are obvious differences in the information available from offenders and victims. Thus within victim and offender studies a more common nomenclature would be helpful in developing a more representative and complete knowledge.

Policy Efforts

There has been virtually no serious, sustained, data-based discussion of social policy regarding the social response to child sexual abuse. As data become available it appears that many of the assumptions upon which social policy has been based are not valid. For example, that half of incest fathers abuse children outside their families or that, in at least some studies, incest fathers and stepfathers are more likely to use their daughters sexually in 'more serious' or 'more sexual ways' raises questions about the notion that incest fathers should be treated differently from other sexual offenders.

More fundamentally, it is not clear how sexual offenders should be treated at all. Virtually no national or international data are available on what after identification happens to adults accused of a sexual offense against a child. Anecdotal information suggests that cases 'fall out of the system' at various points from the identification to adjudication phases. There is currently considerable disagreement about the number of victims that actually receive service after the child protection interview. In a one-year follow-up in 1985 of 150 children seen at the Sexual Assault Center in Seattle, Conte and Berliner (unpublished) report that 15% of victims had received no treatment, 23% had received one month of service, and 15% two months. The average length of service was 3.6 months (between 12 and 16 sessions). These data suggest that most victims do not receive care over a long enough period for it to be helpful.

It is beyond the scope of this chapter to argue what social policy in sexual abuse should be, but such an argument is desperately needed. Policy can be articulated which recognizes the nature of sexual abuse, its effect on victim and society, and balances protection of society, recovery for victim, and treatment of offender so that he or she will stop the production of more victims. The technology is available to assist in the identification of offenders too dangerous to be treated in community settings (Abel *et al.*, 1977). Victim, offender and society have much to gain if both the victim and the offender are helped to move beyond abuse.

References

Abel, G., Barlow, D. H., Blanchard, E. B., and Guild, D. (1977). The components of rapists' sexual arousal. *Archives of General Psychiatry*, **34**, 895–903.

Abel, G., Becker, J., Cunningham-Rathner, J., Mittleman, M., and Rouleau, J. L. (1988). Multiple paraphiliac diagnoses among sex offenders, *Bulletin of the American Academy of Psychiatry and the Law*, **16**(2), 153–68.

Abel, G., Becker, J. V., Cunningham-Rathner, J., Rouleau, J., Kaplan, M., and Reich, J. (1984). The treatment of child molesters. Unpublished manuscript available from authors at SBC–TM, 722 W. 168th St. Box 17, New York, NY 10032.

Abel, G., Becker, J. V., Mittelman, M., Cunningham-Rathner, J., Rouleau, J. L., and Murphy, W. (1987). Self-reported sex crimes of non-incarcerated paraphiliacs. *Journal of Interpersonal Violence*, **2**, 3–25.

Abel, G., Becker, J., Murphy, W. *et al.* (1981). Identifying dangerous child molesters. In R. Stuart (ed.), *Violent Behavior: Social Learning Approaches to Prediction, Management, and Treatment.* New York: Brunner/Mazel.

Abel, G., Cunningham-Rathner, J., Becker, J. V., and McHugh, J. (1983). Motivating sex offenders for treatment with feedback of their psychophysical assessment. Paper presented at the World Congress of Behavior Therapy, Washington, DC.

American Psychiatric Association (1987). *Diagnostic and Statistical Manual of Mental Disorders* (3rd edn. rev.). Washington, DC: American Psychiatric Association Press.

Armentrout, J. A., and Hauer, A. L. (1978). MMPIs of rapists of adults, rapists of children, and non-rapist sex offenders. *Journal of Clinical Psychology*, **34**, 330–2.

Avery-Clark, C. A., and Laws, D. R. (1984). Differential erection response patterns of sexual child abusers to stimuli describing activities with children. *Behavior Therapy*, **15**, 71–83.

Avery-Clark, C., O'Neil, J. A., and Laws, D. R. (1981). A comparison of intrafamilial sexual and physical child abuse. In M. Cook and K. Howell (eds), *Adult Sexual Interest in Children*. Toronto: Academic Press, pp. 3–39.

Budin, L. E., and Johnson, C. (1989). Sex abuse prevention programs: Offenders' attitudes about their efficacy. *Child Abuse and Neglect: The International Journal*, **13**, 77–87.

Bulkley, J. (ed.) (1981). *Child sexual abuse and the law.* A report of the American Bar Association's National Legal Resource Center for Child Advocacy and Protection.

Conte, J. R. (1985). Clinical dimensions of adult sexual use of children. *Behavioral Sciences and the Law*, **3**, 341–54.

Conte, J. R. (1986). Child sexual abuse and the family: A critical analysis. *Journal of Psychotherapy and the Family*, **2**, 113–26.

Conte, J. R. (1989). An incest offender: An overview and introduction. Unpublished manuscript. Available from the author at School of Social Work, University of Washington.

Conte, J. R. (1990). The incest perpetrator: An overview and introduction. In A. Horton, B. Johnson, L. Rowdy, and D. Williams (eds), *The Incest Perpetrator: The Family Member No One Wants to Treat*. Beverly Hills, CA: Sage.

Conte, J. R., and Berliner, L. (unpublished). What happens to sexually abused children after disclosure. Unpublished manuscript. Available from the first author at School of Social Work, University of Washington.

Conte, J. R., Berliner, L., and Schuerman, J. (1986). The impact of sexual abuse on children: Final report. Available from the first author at the School of Social Work, University of Washington.

Conte, J. R., Briere, J., and Sexton, D. (1989). Mediators of long term symptomatology in women molested as children. Unpublished manuscript. Available from the first author at School of Social Work, University of Washington.

Conte, J. R., and Schuerman, J. (1987). Factors associated with an increased impact of child sexual abuse. *Child Abuse and Neglect*, **11**, 201–11.

Conte, J. R., Schuerman, J., and Berliner, L. (1989). The behavior of sexually abused children at intake and twelve months later. Unpublished manuscript available from the first author at 969 E. 60th St., Chicago, IL 60637.

Conte, J. R., Wolf, S., and Smith, T. (1989). What sexual offenders tell us about prevention. *Child Abuse and Neglect: The International Journal*, **13**, 293–301.

Demare, D., Briere, J., and Lips, H.M. (1988). Violent pornography and self-reported likelihood of sexual aggression. *Journal of Research in Personality*, **22**, 140–53.

Erickson, W. D., Walbek, N. H., and Seely, R. K. (1988). Behavior patterns of child molesters. *Archives of Sexual Behavior*, **17**, 77–86.

Finkelhor, D. (1979). *Sexually Victimized Children*. New York: Free Press.

Finkelhor, D., and Baron, L. (1986). High risk children. In D. Finkelhor (ed.), *A Sourcebook on Child Sexual Abuse*. Beverly Hills, CA: Sage, pp. 60–88.

Furby, L., Weinrott, M., and Blackshaw, L. (1989). Sex offender recidivism: A review. *Psychological Bulletin*, **105**, 3–30.

Groth, A. N., Hobson, W. F., and Gary, T. S. (1982). The child molester: Clinical observations. *Social Work and Human Sexuality*, **1**, 129–44.

Hall, G., Proctor, W. C., and Nelson, G. M. (1988). Validity of physiological measures of pedophilic sexual arousal in a sexual offender population. *Journal of Consulting and Clinical Psychology*, **56**, 118–22.

Kendall-Tackett, K. A., and Simon, A. F. (1987). Perpetrators and their acts: Data from 365 adults molested as children. *Child Abuse and Neglect: The International Journal*, **11**, 237–46.

Kercher, G., and McShane, M. (1984). Characterizing child sexual abuse on the basis of a multi-agency sample. *Victimology: An International Journal*, **9**, 364–82.

Langevin, R., Handy, L., Russon, A. E., and Day, D. (1985). Are incestuous fathers pedophilic, aggressive or alcoholic? In R. Langevin (ed.), *Erotic Preference, Gender Identity, and Aggression in Men*. Hillsdale, NJ: Erlbaum Associates.

Marshall, W. L., Barbaree, H. E., and Christophe, D. (1986). Sexual offenders against female children: Sexual preferences for age of victims and type of behavior. *Canadian Journal of Behavioral Science*, **18**, 424–39.

Marshall, W. L., and Christie, M. M. (1981). Pedophilia and aggression. *Criminal Justice and Behavior*, **8**, 145–58.

Peters, S. D., Wyatt, G. E., and Finkelhor, D. (1986). Prevalence. In D. Finkelhor (ed.), *A Sourcebook on Child Sexual Abuse*. Beverly Hills, CA: Sage, pp. 15–59.

Plummer, K. (1981). Pedophilia: Constructing a sociological baseline. In M. Cook and K. Howell (eds), *Adult Sexual Interest in Children*. New York: Academic Press, pp. 221–50.

Quinsey, V. L. (1977). The assessment and treatment of child molesters. *Canadian Psychological Review*, **18**, 204–20.

Quinsey, V. L. (1983). Prediction of recidivism and the evaluation of treatment programs for sex offenders. In S. N. Verdon-Jones and A. A. Keltner (eds), *Sexual Aggression and the Law*. Criminology Research Center: Simon Fraser University.

Quinsey, V. L. (1984). Sexual aggression: Studies of offenders against women. In D. Weisstub (ed.), *Law and Mental Health: International Perspectives*. New York: Pergamon Press.

Quinsey, V. L., and Chaplin, T. (1988). Penile responses of child molesters and normals to descriptions of encounters with children involving sex and violence. *Journal of Interpersonal Violence*, **3**, 259–74.

Quinsey, V. L., Chaplin, T. C., and Carrigan, W. F. (1979). Sexual preferences among incestuous and nonincestuous child molesters. *Behavior Therapy*, **10**, 562–5.

Quinsey, V. L., Steinman, C. M., Bergersen, S. G., and Holmes, T. F. (1975). Penile circumference, skin conductance, and ranking responses of child molesters and 'normals' to sexual and nonsexual visual stimuli. *Behavior Therapy*, **6**, 213–19.

Russell, D. E. H. (1984). *Sexual Exploitation: Rape, Child Sexual Abuse and Workplace Harassment*. Beverly Hills, CA: Sage.

Russell, D. E. H. (1986). *The Secret Trauma: Incest in the Lives of Girls and Women*. New York: Basic Books.

Tufts New England Medical Center. (1984). *Sexually Exploited Children: Services and Research Project*. Boston: author.

Westat (1987). Study of national incidence and prevalence of child abuse and neglect. Washington, DC: National Center in Child Abuse and Neglect.

Wyatt, G. E., and Powell, G. J. (eds) (1988). *Lasting Effects of Child Sexual Abuse*. Newbury Park, CA: Sage.

2

Theories of Sex Offending

RICHARD I. LANYON
Department of Psychology, Arizona State University, USA

The serious study of sexual deviations and sex offending is a recent pheno-menon. Sex offenders have traditionally been the object of society's fear, scorn, and ridicule, and have usually been placed squarely outside society's boundaries. Once safely removed, they have often also been the object of great curiosity. The original writings of Krafft-Ebing (1886/1965) and Ellis (1899/1942) reflected this attitude, and also reflected a definite theoretical position, namely, that such disorders were essentially a permanent part of the person and could not be changed. Freud took a similar position, viewing them as a product of the charac-ter disorder termed sexual psychopathology, and as extremely difficult to change. In everyday language, once a pervert, always a pervert.

A number of forces have converged over the past 40 years to permit the serious study of sexually deviant behavior. These include: (i) the pioneering work of Alfred Kinsey on the scientific study of normal sexual behavior, using classification procedures borrowed from zoology (Kinsey *et al.* 1948; Kinsey *et al.*, 1953); (ii) the discovery that sexually deviant behavior could sometimes be successfully eliminated by using certain behavioral procedures (see Langevin, 1983); (iii) the research of Masters and Johnson (1966, 1970) in studying the sexual arousal process and in developing therapeutic procedures for common sexual dysfunctions based on their work; and (iv) the human rights movement, particularly its long overdue focus on the rights of women and other victims of sex crimes. Regardless of whether the current interest in studying sex offenders stems mainly from a concern for potential victims or for the offenders them-selves, the attention is much needed; and it appears that potential offenders too will eventually come under the umbrella of the human rights movement through an unravelling of the causes of their behavior and the development of programs for the *prevention* of sex offenses. Thus, it is as an essential link in the chain of

Clinical Approaches to Sex Offenders and Their Victims.
Edited by C. R. Hollin and K. Howells © 1991 John Wiley & Sons Ltd

events leading to prevention that the topic of theories of sex offending assumes its greatest current importance.

SOME PRELIMINARY ISSUES

At the theoretical level, sex offending is more or less synonymous with the topic of sexually deviant behavior in general. Thus, the intention of this chapter is to review the theoretical literature on the major topics that are typically viewed as sexual deviations, including exhibitionism, rape, child molestation/incest, transvestism/transsexualism, and voyeurism. In preparing the review, it became readily apparent that most of the significant literature involves just two of the topics, rape and child molestation. Although it is intended that the review and the conclusions should embrace more than just these two factors, this unavoidable overreliance on two areas does limit the generality of the findings.

A second issue has to do with choosing an organizing scheme for the chapter. The choice of reviewing the literature by theoretical approaches, both globally and within each disorder, was made because it seemed the most manageable thing to do. The question of whether a different organizational scheme might have been preferable is addressed at the end of the chapter.

A third question is how to classify theoretical approaches. In addressing the same question ten years ago when reviewing theories of exhibitionism, the present author unhesitatingly chose the framework that most other reviewers would have chosen at that time; namely, psychoanalytic/psychodynamic; behavioral/learning; and physiological/biological theories (Blair and Lanyon, 1981). A category of 'descriptive characteristics' also was included at that time. However, the field has changed substantially in ten years, and much of the mainstream literature is no longer theoretical in this direct, obvious sense. Rather, researchers and theoreticians have taken a more empirical approach, casting a wide-ranging net that extends far beyond these traditional points of focus. The result is an active emphasis on developmental, interpersonal, personality, epidemiological, sociological, cognitive, and situational variables, together with attempts to develop explanatory models that are data-driven rather than theory-driven. In the present chapter, this fourth area is termed 'empirical theories,' and the other areas are termed psychodynamic, behavioral, and biological.

In deciding what to include in the present review, the term 'theory' was construed broadly. Thus, structures which impart a logical organization to a set of research findings or armchair speculations are included, as are taxonomies that are the empirical product of a multivariate data reduction system. Taking an overinclusive rather than an underinclusive approach maximizes the likelihood of identifying similarities among rather disparate ideas and sources of data.

It is beyond the scope of this chapter to examine fully the research literature in support of one theory or another. In general, there is little or no empirical support, either direct or indirect, for the psychodynamic theories (e.g. Kline, 1987); and the support for behavioral and biological theories tends to be unsystematic, and more indirect than direct. The situation with the empirical theories is, of course, different; the theories, though rudimentary, are based directly upon research data.

GLOBAL THEORIES OF SEXUAL DEVIATION

Any review of this nature must begin with the writings of Krafft-Ebing (1886/1965). Although Krafft-Ebing's avowed purpose was to classify rather than explain sexual variations, he made it clear that he viewed them as pathological and loathsome. He also offered a two-part causal explanation, tying them to hereditary factors and to masturbation. Interestingly, this theory does not appear to have been originated by Krafft-Ebing, but has been traced by Money (1984) to a French writer named Tissot in 1758. A rather different theoretical view was proposed by Ellis (1899/1942) in 1899. Ellis believed that sexual deviations should be viewed simply as normal variations of human impulses, rather than abnormal conditions.

Psychodynamic Theories

The theoretical view of sexually deviant behavior that has had the greatest impact on the field is that of Freud (1905/1953). Freud's view was that all sexually deviant behaviors are theoretically and etiologically similar, and that they represent a single type of psychopathology—specifically, a form of character disorder. The behaviors are viewed as highly resistant to change, and any serious attempt at treatment must be lengthy and based on restructuring of the character. In the author's view, it is this 'untreatability' aspect of the theory that has had the most profound influence on the beliefs and behaviors of professional workers for many years, a view that has been challenged only in the past 20 years by more recent views.

Freud used the term 'perversion' to indicate that either the *aim* or the *object* of a person's sexual desire had become diverted. He located the causes in early childhood development—the continuation into adult life of infantile sexual desires and practices (Rada, 1978). Subsequent psychoanalytic writers have expanded and elaborated upon this theory (e.g. Fenichel, 1945; Hammer, 1957). These accounts are complex, and there does not appear to be much agreement on the details. Typically, these explanations involve Oedipal conflicts, castration anxiety, repression of the Oedipal wishes, and regression into less mature behavior.

Behavioral Theories

A number of writers have offered global explanations for sexually deviant behavior within the framework of behavioral learning theory. Abel *et al.* (1978) presented a behavioral approach to the assessment and treatment of sexually deviant behaviors, based on an implied model of etiology that is also seen as underlying other disorders that are amenable to treatment through behavior therapy (e.g. Lanyon and Lanyon, 1976, 1978). In this model, it is assumed that the behavior itself is the disorder, and that there is no deeper underlying problem of which the deviant sexual behavior is a symptom. The problem is conceptualized as an inappropriate frequency of one or more events (behaviors, thoughts, or feelings), and this inappropriate frequency is thought to be maintained by the pattern of antecedents and consequences for the events. Such a framework is clearly treatment oriented, and provides the information that is needed for designing a treatment procedure. Not surprisingly, supporters of this position tend to offer treatment outcome studies using their model as evidence of the soundness of the etiological model itself.

Langevin (1983) has amplified the model by classifying deviant sexual preferences according to their stimulus and response characteristics. Thus, preference for an immature shape (child) is a stimulus characteristic, while preference for exhibiting is a response characteristic. This scheme is analogous to the Freudian view, in which either the object (stimulus) or the aim (response) preference of the person's sexual drive is perverted.

Also consistent with the behavioral model is an orientation toward the use of penile plethysmography to assess a person's differential arousal patterns (responses) to different sexual stimuli. The most recent reviews of this assessment technology are equivocal about its utility (e.g. Langevin, 1988; Travin *et al.*, 1988); however, the utility of the behavioral model is not dependent on these assessment techniques.

Another model which may be broadly construed as behavioral in nature has been proposed by Wolf (1985). This multi-factor model involves three main concepts. The first is that sexually deviant persons are said to have a disturbed developmental history, which includes 'potentiators' for later deviant attitudes and behaviors, and they must be diagnosable as having a personality disorder. The second concept includes the presence of disinhibitors, or situational factors which disrupt normal social controls against sexual deviance. The third concept lies in the importance of deviant sexual fantasy, which is said to be extensive, to reinforce positive associations to deviant sexual behaviors, and to desensitize the person's inhibitions. These factors are said to interact in a cyclical manner to develop and maintain the deviant sexual behavior.

A comprehensive behavioral learning model for the acquisition and maintenance of deviant sexual preference has recently been presented by Laws and Marshall (1990). These authors acknowledge the position that not all sex offenders necessarily have deviant sexual preferences. They divide their model into two parts, acquisition processes and maintenance processes, and present the model as a set of 13 general principles and 14 derived propositions. The individual principles of this model are plausible and in many cases noncontroversial, covering fully the many ways in which principles of learning can be applied to the etiology and maintenance of deviant sexual preferences.

Biological Theories

The idea that deviant sexual preferences have their roots in biological abnormalities in an attractive one, since it offers a degree of comfort in the belief that such men are not bad but ill, and it suggests the possibility of physical treatments to make them well again. Consistent with the strong advocacy by many professionals for the use of prescribed medications such as Depo-provera to control deviant sexual behavior, there is increased interest in finding a theoretical explanation for deviant sexual preferences that will be logically consistent with the use of this therapeutic tool.

A number of biological theories have been offered. In a review of studies of brain function related to deviant sexuality, Flor-Henry (1987) concluded that 'sexual deviations are, overwhelmingly, a consequence of the male pattern of cerebral organization' (pp. 78–9), and he pointed to specific findings in support of his position. Most of these findings involved either subhuman mammals or the disorders of transsexualism and exhibitionism. There is also literature on genetic and hormonal factors in human sexuality, but a recent review suggests that it is primarily relevant to the development of masculinity, femininity, and homosexuality (Goodman, 1987), rather than to the subject matter of the present chapter.

None of these theories appears to offer an adequate foundation for the basic premise on which pharmacological (antiandrogren) treatments for sex offenders is based; namely, that the offender's sex drive is out of control because his level of sex hormones, plasma testosterone is too high (e.g. Berlin, 1989; Bradford, 1985). The reasons for the hypothesized elevated plasma testosterone levels have not been systematically addressed, although the causes are assumed to lie in biologically based factors (e.g. Berlin, 1989). Successful reduction in sexually deviant behaviors as a result of antiandrogenic medication has been reported (e.g. Bradford, 1985; Bradford and Pawlak, 1987). However, it is only in the most aggressive of offenders that significantly elevated levels of plasma testosterone are reliably found (Rada *et al.*, 1983).

A general and moderate statement of a biological position has been offered by Berlin (1983), as follows: (i) some people commit sex offenses in response to intense, unconventional sexual urges; (ii) although the etiology of such interests is undoubtedly multiple, biological factors such as hormone levels or chromosomal makeup sometimes play a major role. Berlin's position is thus one of multiple etiologies, among which can be biological factors.

Other Global Theories

An ethological appraisal to the understanding of sexual deviation was proposed by Wilson (1987). Based on the single outstanding finding that sexual deviation is almost exclusively associated with the male gender, Wilson's theory involves the male's struggle for access to young, healthy females for reproductive purposes and the difficulties that may stem from the problems of managing sex drive among unsuccessful males. In this view, some sexually deviant behaviors are better viewed as inevitable, and should be tolerated rather than treated.

Money (1981) also wrote on the possible evolutionary origins of what he has termed heterosexual dysfunction. Rather than contributing a theory or explanation, Money identified phyletic components in eight general categories of sex related behavior and indicated possible ways in which paraphilias might develop.

More recently, Money (1984, 1988) presented a global theory of paraphilias involving predispositions that are set up during early childhood development. Money proposed the concept of a *lovemap*, referring to a person's personal template that depicts the ideal lover. Paraphilias are said to result from interference with the child's normal process of developing his or her lovemap, the particular paraphilia depending on the type of interference. No data are offered to support this theory, although there would seem to be considerable overlap with the Freudian view of the origin of perversions in early childhood development.

Two other global models deserve note. The first is the scheme for clarifying sexually deviant behaviors, or paraphilias, as presented in the *Diagnostic and Statistical Manual of Mental Disorders*, third edition—revised (DSM-III-R; American Psychiatric Association, 1987). Although this scheme is not presented as a formal theory or model, it unavoidably takes positions on several conceptual issues. For example, in order to warrant the term paraphilias, the problem must involve deviant urges and sexually arousing fantasies that are intense and recurrent, and which lead to overt behavior or to marked distress. It is also stated in DSM-III-R that individuals have an average of three to four different paraphilias (p. 280) and that such behavior is highly repetitive. Some persons are said to require triggering factors such as stress, while for others the behavior is more or less continuous, and situational factors may or may not be involved.

The DSM-III-R view thus involves a number of definite implications: that there is a common underlying basis for the paraphilias; that fantasy is a prominent aspect; and that the problem is continual in the person's life. It also implies the presence of underlying predispositions, but does not specify whether they are biological or developmental in nature.

Perhaps the most comprehensive attempt to present a global theory of deviant sexual behavior is that of Marshall and Barbaree (1990). In their view, biological factors cause for males a ready and unlearned propensity for sexual aggression. This propensity must be countered and overcome by the socialization process, which is expected to provide inhibitory controls over such behavior. Thus, the presence of poor parenting places the male at risk. Secondary risk factors include negative socio-cultural attitudes, including the use of pornography. Also important are situational factors, which serve as disinhibitors for the person who is already at risk to offend.

This model attempts to integrate the four groups of factors which are consistently presented as causal in sex offending—biological, early childhood development, socio-cultural, and situational. The model is limited in that it addresses only sexually deviant behavior in which aggression is involved. In so doing, the model presents a view which (although apparently unnoticed by the authors) bears considerable similarity to the early psychodynamic models of rape proposed by Cohen *et al.* (1971) and by Groth *et al.* (1977) (see below). Most striking, however, is the strong similarity between the basic premise of the model—sexuality and aggression as unlearned drives that must be socialized— and traditional psychoanalytic theory, which also holds that sex and aggression are life's basic driving forces, and that their appropriate channeling is the basic task in the socialization of children.

THEORIES OF RAPE

The next sections review theoretical frameworks or explanations that have been offered to explain specific sexual deviations. These explanations may have elements in common with global explanations, but they are also unique to a particular deviation. For example, global psychodynamic explanations of sexually deviant behavior have already been reviewed; below, psychodynamic explanations that are specific to rape are examined.

Psychodynamic Theories

Two psychodynamic typologies for rapists were proposed in the 1970s, and both have had a significant influence on subsequent theory and practice. The first was that of Cohen *et al.* (1971), which offered a three-way classification according to the aim of the act—i.e. whether aggressive, sexual, or sadistic. With an aggressive aim, the purpose of the behavior is to humiliate, dirty, and defile the victim. Such men are said to have a long history of difficulty in heterosexual object relations, and the women appear to be the victims of the offender's destructive wishes. There is body concern and body narcissism, together with intense rage that is related to sexual anxiety, and the victim is viewed as a substitute object for the original source of the findings, typically believed to be the mother.

With a sexual aim, the aggression is in the service of sexual wishes. The rapist has lived through the hoped-for scene many times in his fantasies, which involve great sexual skill on his part and the experience of intense pleasure by the woman. Such offenses are believed to be based in unacknowledged homosexual feelings, passive personality features, and feelings of interpersonal inadequacy. The failure of the act to fulfill the fantasy leads to its continual repetition. With a sadistic aim, the sexual and aggressive drives are fused, so that some degree of violence must be present in order for sexual excitation to occur. Such men are often believed to have a psychopathic character and to show a variety of such behaviors, such as impulsivity, stealing and lying. Psychodynamically, Cohen *et al.* stated that the sexualization of the aggression so overwhelms the ego when the aggression is aroused that the control and discharge mechanisms fail to function. Such offenders are relatively rare, and some of them are psychotic.

The second typology, analogous to the first, was proposed by Groth *et al.* (1977). In this scheme, rape motivation is believed to be dominated by either *power* needs or *anger* needs. In power rape, the 'rape is the means by which he reassures himself of his sexual adequacy and identity, of his strength and potency' (p. 1240). The assault may be 'preceded by an obsessional fantasy in which his victim may initially resist him but, once overpowered, will submit gratefully to his sexual embrace' (p. 1240). Groth *et al.* proposed two subtypes: *power-assertive*, in which rape is an expression of virility, mastery, and dominance; and *power-reassurance*, in which the offense represents an effort to resolve the offender's disturbing doubts about his own sexual adequacy and masculinity.

In anger rape, the offender's aim is to vent his rage on the victim and to retaliate for perceived wrongs or rejections he has suffered at the hands of women. Sex becomes a weapon, and the rape is the means by which he can use this weapon to hurt and degrade his victims. Such a person is often physically assaultive toward women in other contexts. Two subtypes were proposed: *anger-retaliation*, in which the rape is an expression of hostility and rage toward women; and *anger-excitation*, in which the rapist finds pleasure, thrills, and excitation in the suffering of his victim.

It should be apparent that these two frameworks are essentially similar. The categories of sexual aim and the power rapist are analogous, as are aggressive aim and the anger rapist. The third category of Cohen *et al.* (1971), sadistic aim, was conceptualized by Groth *et al.* (1977) as a subcategory of anger, the anger-excitement rapist.

This general psychodynamic scheme has exerted considerable influence in the literature, and is reflected in many subsequent writings which address both offender and victim issues. It has much intuitive appeal to mental health professionals, who often feel that it mirrors their accumulated practical knowledge. On the debit side, it has not led to significant advances in treatment and prevention, and it is as yet unsupported by research findings. Although Groth *et al.* (1977) reported that a sample of 133 rapists could all be classified according to their four-part scheme, the classification was done by the authors themselves, who presumably had a vested interest in the outcome. In that work, it was appropriately noted that aspects of more than one category can be present in any given rapist.

Behavioral Theories

There is little specific theoretical literature from a behavioral perspective on rape that is distinct from the behavioral literature on sex offenses in general. The behavioral assessment and treatment framework offered by Abel *et al.* (1978) for rapists has been identified above as a global framework, since it can also apply to other sexual deviations. The distinguishing feature in applying it to rapists lies in the use of physical force.

The findings from studies of physiological arousal to rape-related stimuli are relevant to an evaluation of a simple behavioral theory of rape. Based on a careful review of the empirical literature, Marshall (in press) concluded that rapists in general are less aroused by stimuli depicting forceful sex than by stimuli depicting mutually enjoyable sex. An exception to this finding involves the subgroup of rapists with the greatest amount of violence in their offense histories: these individuals are at least as aroused by forceful depictions as by mutual enjoyment depictions. Taken in conjunction with the generally accepted knowledge that most rapists do not lack for consenting partners, these findings do not support a simple behavioral model except for a small group, appropriately labeled sadists.

Biological Theories

Three types of biological explanations, or partial explanations, have been offered to explain rape. The first is that rapists frequently have brain dysfunction of a type that is consistent with impulsivity and the under-control of aggression. Hucker *et al.* (1988) recently reviewed this topic and conducted their own investigation, in which 51 sexually aggressive men and 36 control subjects underwent extensive neurological and neuropsychological examination. The results showed some subtle differences associated with sexual aggression, although not enough to regard such findings as a significant explanation for the disorder.

The second biological hypothesis, that rapists' sexual behavior gets out of control because their level of plasma testosterone is abnormally high, has been discussed above as global theory, although it is usually presented as most relevant to rape. The third biological approach has been through the study of violence, under the joint assumptions that (i) rape is essentially a disorder of violence or uncontrolled aggression, and (ii) there are physiological and genetic aspects to the propensity for violence (e.g. Money *et al.*, 1975). Considering the second and third approaches together, there appears to be sufficient evidence to suggest a constellation of factors, perhaps even warranting the term syndrome, that apply to a subgroup of rapists. In contrast to most rapists, who do not show sexual arousal in the presence of violent stimuli, this subgroup does so; in addition, it involves the most violent offenders. The origins of this extra violence are not yet understood; however, 'sadistic' or 'anger-excitement' concepts may be relevant here, and possibly genetic factors.

Empirical Theories

In the last ten years or so there has been a significant increase in empirical research on rape; such research has not been based in any particular theoretical approach other than a strong conviction that rapists *must* differ in important ways from other men. This research is characterized, for the most part, by methodological sophistication and a degree of patience in allowing the findings to develop rather than forcing them into a pattern. One might say that there is as yet no theory here, in the traditional sense of the word. Much of the work is consistent with the broad tenets of social learning theory, but it is the findings themselves that have guided further work, not the theory. The research areas tend to be developmental, cognitive, and social in nature.

The forerunners of this work were the early statements of writers such as Brownmiller (1975) and Medea and Thompson (1974), who stated that many men simply believe that they have the right to take sex from a woman if there is an opportunity to do so. In the words of Medea and Thompson, 'it is time . . . for women to stop thinking of rapists as crazy men. . . . The rapist is the man next door' (p. 36). Such a hypothesis, that rapism is in part a set of attitudes, has proven to be fruitful in guiding research activities.

The initial research efforts were focused around different unitary theoretical positions (Koss and Dinero, 1988), such as psychopathology, deviant arousal, attitudes supportive of rape, hostility toward women, heterosexual dating skills, marital adjustment, and victimization as children. For example, Seghorn *et al.* (1987) found physical and sexual abuse in the childhood histories of many rapists, usually embedded in a family system that would have been considered psychopathological even without the abuse. As another example, Scully and Marolla (1984) demonstrated that rapists showed attitudes that were supportive of rape behaviors. Such models, while insufficient when taken alone, have led to a substantial body of empirical findings that can be sorted and grouped in the hope of leading to new conceptual insights.

There now tends to be some tentative agreement as to what underlying variables are relevant. Thus, Malamuth (1986) formulated six 'predictor factors' for naturalistic sexual aggression—dominance as a sexual motive, hostility toward women, attitudes facilitating violence, antisocial characteristics/psychoticism, and sexual experience. In an empirical study, Malamuth (1986) demonstrated that these factors were additive in their success in predicting sexual violence, and that the inclusion of interactions in the predictor increased its success even more.

In a lengthy series of empirical studies, Prentky, Knight, Rosenberg, and their colleagues utilized multivariate procedures for developing and refining a classification system for rapists (e.g. Prentky et al., 1988; Rosenberg et al., 1988). Beginning with the Cohen et al. (1971) psychodynamic framework involving the interplay of sexual and aggressive drives, these researchers systematically incorporated data on psychopathology, substance use, criminal history, and offense data, plus information on family juvenile and adult history. The resulting classification scheme determines subtypes on three major dimensions: 'The meaning of the aggression in the rapist's behavior (expressive versus instrumental), the meaning of the sexual behavior (compensatory, exploitative, displaced anger, or sadistic), and the degree of general lifestyle impulsivity (low or high)' (Rosenberg et al., 1988, p. 169). Other variables, such as social competence, may also be relevant in further refining the system.

THEORIES OF CHILD MOLESTATION

Psychodynamic Theories

Until fairly recently, the most prominent theoretical explanation for child molestation has been psychodynamic in nature. Formalized by Groth (e.g. Groth et al., 1982), the essence of this approach is that the offender's underlying motivation is not basically sexual in nature, but involves the expression of nonsexual needs and unresolved life issues. Molestation is viewed as a 'pseudosexual' act—sexual behavior in the service of nonsexual needs. Groth et al. excluded from their definition of a child molester any person who uses or threatens physical force; they termed such persons child rapists, and considered them to constitute a very small minority of sexual offenders against children (although they may receive a disproportionate amount of publicity).

Another aspect of this model is the division of child molesters into two basic types according to the nature of their level of psychosexual motivation. The *regressed* offender has developed an age-appropriate sexual and interpersonal orientation, but under particular circumstances he may regress to sexual involvement with children. The *fixated* offender is one whose primary sexual interest is toward children, and who has never developed psychosexually beyond that level. Underlying motivations for both types may be various and complex, including the need to cope with feelings of powerlessness, attempts to process their own abusive childhoods, and misplaced needs for affection.

This theory essentially involves a two-way classification scheme plus some general statements about the etiology of the disorder. Apart from the position that it is primarily nonsexual needs that are being served, and that pedophilia is one of the possible consequences of child sexual abuse and neglect, Groth *et al.* (1982) have not offered much in the way of specific etiological hypotheses. Interestingly, studies of penile plethysmography tend to support the Groth *et al.* classification scheme, perhaps as a continuum rather than a typology. Thus, in a review of the literature involving the plethysmograph responses of child molesters, Marshall (in press) concluded that while molesters as a group were more aroused by sexual stimuli depicting children than adults, substantial proportions of them (37.5%, 55%, and 29% in three different groups) were more aroused by adult stimuli than by child stimuli.

Family systems theories can also be viewed as psychodynamic in nature, and are relevant to incestuous rather than nonincestuous child molestation. Such theories take the view that it is the psychodynamic interplay among family members that is of prime importance in the etiology of the problem (e.g. Meiselman, 1978; Mrazek and Kempe, 1981; Sgroi, 1982). The most typical aspects of this interplay are said to involve a father who either has a personality disorder or who belongs to subculture that is tolerant of incest, a mother who may have withdrawn from her sexual role in the marriage and may be passive, dependent, and masochistic, and a daughter who is gradually manœuvered by the situation into taking on some of the roles of the mother, including a sexual role.

Physiological Theories

There is no physiological theory that is specific to child molestation as distinct from sexual deviation. Hucker *et al.* (1986) compared child molesters with non-sex offenders on two neuropsychological test batteries and CT scans. Overall, the results showed more neuropsychological impairment in child molesters than in nonsex offenders, although the results of the three assessment procedures tended to be nonoverlapping. The composite pattern suggested more involvement with the left parieto-temporal lobe than with other lobes. Thus, the results suggested some degree of relationship between child molestation and impaired brain functioning, but not sufficient to have significant explanatory value for the disorder.

Behavioral Theories

There is no specific behavioral theory of child molestation that is distinct from global theories of sexual deviation. However, as with the theoretical literature on rape, behavioral concepts feature prominently in some of the empirically-based approaches (see below).

Empirical Theories

Parallel to their work on the classification of rapists, Prentky, Knight and their colleagues have developed a sophisticated empirical classification typology for child molesters (e.g. Knight and Prentky, 1990; Prentky *et al.*, 1988). Originating from a scheme proposed by Cohen *et al.* (1969), the current version of the typology, termed MTC:CM3, consists of two 'axes'. Axis I involves a dichotomous rating on two dimensions, degree of fixation and social competence, yielding four subtypes. Axis II refers to the amount of contact with children, and involves further sequential decisions according to the meaning of the context, the amount of physical injury, and the meaning of aggression to the offender. The scheme is reported to be reliable and to be based on stable traits which have identifiable roots in childhood. These researchers view their typology as defining stable subtypes among child molesters, which they consider to be an important first step in the design of research on etiology, treatment, disposition and prognosis.

As with theories of rape, in the last 12–15 years there has been a heightened interest in investigating the empirical relationship between molestation and a wide variety of psychological variables, including social-interpersonal, cognitive, childhood, family, and attitudinal factors. When combined with the sequential framework of mainstream behavior theory (i.e. a framework for explaining what leads to what), this approach has been fruitful in integrating a considerable array of research findings. The leading writer is Finkelhor (1984, 1986), who offered what he termed a four-factor psychological/sociological model for exploring child molestation. The model was presented as an interpretation of existing empirical research findings, and thus was considered to be based on data rather than theory.

In this model, four preconditions need to be met in order for child sexual abuse to take place. First, the offender needs appropriate motivation, of which there are three components: (i) the sexual abuse satisfies some important emotional need in the abuser; (ii) the child is a source of sexual arousal and gratification; and (iii) alternative sources of sexual gratification are blocked or inhibited in some way. Second, internal inhibitions against acting on these motivations need to be overcome. There are a number of possible disinhibitors: they may be specific to the abuser, such as senility, psychosis, or alcohol use; or they may be sociocultural, such as social toleration of interest in children or weak criminal sanctions against offenders.

The third necessary precondition involves factors that overcome external inhibiting factors. Examples of such factors are an absent or ill mother, unusual sleeping conditions, and an abused or over-dominated mother. The fourth precondition involves factors predisposing the abuser to overcome the child's resistance. Examples are coercion, a child who is emotionally insecure or deprived, and a situation of unusual trust between abuser and child.

Finkelhor (1984) also suggested the importance of two basic dimensions for classifying child molesters: the *strength* of the person's motivation to have sex with children; and *exclusivity*, referring to the percentage of the person's total sexuality that is involved with children. An adequate explanatory theory of child molestation should account for these two characteristics. Finkelhor considered his model to be more general than the family systems model, which might be regarded as one instance of the four-factor model.

The sex offender's cognitive processes, including fantasies, attitudes, and distortions, have recently received increased attention as relevant areas of inquiry. In an interesting and provocative paper, Abel *et al.* (1984) emphasized the importance of molesters' cognitive activity as it relates to their sexually deviant behavior. These authors offered the view that, among men who find themselves sexually attracted to children, some respond to this dilemma by changing the inner world in which they live through developing cognitive distortions that support their behavior. Common distortions include: 'A child who does not physically resist my sexual advances really wants to have sex with me;' 'Having sex with a child is a good way for an adult to teach the child about sex;' and 'Children do not tell others about having sex with a parent because they really enjoy the sexual activity and want it to continue' (pp. 88–9). Such cognitive distortions might also be viewed as internal disinhibitors within Finkelhor's (1984) framework.

OTHER SEXUAL DEVIATIONS

Exhibitionism

The problem of exhibitionism has received substantially less theoretical attention than either rape or child molestation, perhaps because it does not provide the same degree of physical and psychological danger and damage. Most theories of etiology are either psychoanalytic or behavioral.

Psychoanalytic explanations have been offered for many years. A frequent element in such explanations is the concept of castration anxiety; thus, exhibiting to young girls is thought to be a result of fear of castration by older, more mature women who may or may not resemble the exhibitionist's mother. According to Allen (1980), the exhibitionist suffers from disturbances in his psychosexual development with his earliest object relations. The culmination of distorted psychosexual development is the gratification of sexual and oppressive impulses through exhibiting, while at the same time defending against castration fears, narcissistic hurt, and gender confusion.

Behavioral theories have been offered more recently. The success of treatment procedures that are predominantly behavioral in nature (see Blair and Lanyon, 1981; Cox and Daitzman, 1980) has made the search for behavioral explanations especially attractive; however, none of the proposals offer much more than suggestions. For example, McGuire *et al.* (1965) offered a one-trial-learning model of etiology, involving the presence of 'a crucial, though possibly accidental, sexual experience' (p. 185). In contrast to recent research on rapists and child molesters, little or no attention has been paid to cognitive and attitudinal variables with exhibitionists, and it is likely that an adequate accounting of the development and maintenance of exhibitionism will require the prominent inclusion of these variables.

Although there is an impressive list of additional sexual deviations (e.g. Langevin, 1983; Tollison and Adams, 1979), the extant scientific literature is relatively sparse. There are a number of published case histories, some of which may include speculation about etiology, but systematic investigation is lacking. It is pointed out that most of these 'rarer' sexual deviations are not considered illegal, and thus do not constitute sex offenses in a legal sense. However, they are included here in order to identify conceptual similarities to those deviations that are illegal.

Transvestism and Transsexualism

Literature on these two disorders tends to be grouped together. Feinbloom (1976) utilized a sociological framework, viewing both problems as exaggerations or disruptions of normal social situations and expectations. The transvestite is viewed as attempting to make a statement about the degree of complexity involved in defining gender, and as seeking to loosen the rules in this regard. The transsexual is viewed as choosing to deny his or her biological reality as an accident of birth, and as choosing an identity with the opposite sex.

Feinbloom's formulations tend to be more descriptive than explanatory, although central to each is the basic importance of the person's attitude about himself/herself and about society. There is also the implication that transvestism and transsexuality might perhaps be more appropriately viewed as extremes on continua of normal behavior, rather than as abnormal conditions. Little attempt is made, however, to offer an account of how or why these problems may develop for particular individuals.

A comprehensive, five-stage theory for explaining these disorders was recently proposed by Docter (1988). Drawing on concepts and research findings from varied sources, Docter suggested that four constructs are central to transvestism and transsexualism and must have a basic role in an adequate explanation—sexual arousal and excitement, pleasure (i.e. affective considerations), sexual scripts (i.e. cognitive considerations), and cross-gender identity.

The first stage of Docter's theory deals with childhood antecedent developmental conditions, which are thought to include crises at particular stages of development, gender envy, and learned arousal to women's clothing. The second stage involves the development of fetishism involving women's clothing, while the third stage involves the development of complete cross-dressing. This stage requires the development of a cross-gender identity, or 'girl within'. In the fourth stage, most transvestites successfully integrate this identity with their primary identity and enjoy their transvestism. However, for a few there is a 'revolt-within-the-self', leading to transgenderism, or an oscillation back and forth from one gender role to the other. The fifth stage, for the latter few, is a reorganization of the self-system into a cross-gender identity, and the request is made for sex reassignment surgery. This condition is termed secondary transsexualism, and Docter believes it is far more common than primary transsexualism, or the stable belief that one has been assigned the wrong body from birth. Docter also emphasized the extreme length of time that is taken in moving through these stages (e.g. an average of 12 years' experience with cross-dressing before owning a complete outfit of women's clothing), sugesting the central importance of cognitive and attitudinal variables in the etiology and maintenance of these disorders.

Voyeurism

Voyeurism is often viewed as conceptually related to exhibitionism (Tollison and Adams, 1979), and it often occurs within the context of other sexually deviant behaviors. However, men who peep prior to attempting rape are viewed as rapists and not voyeurs (Langevin, 1983).

In psychoanalytic theory, the voyeur is believed to be fixated at the phallic stage of development, and various explanations have been offered for this state of affairs (e.g. Fenichel, 1945). Behavioral formulations tend to emphasize the voyeur's need for sexual arousal and gratification, together with his presumed anxieties, deficits in interpersonal skills, or other aversions related to the development and maintenance of normal sexual experiences. Tollison and Adams (1979) emphasized the great lengths to which a voyeur may go, considering the risks involved and the dangers of getting caught. These characteristics suggest that impulsivity and a need for danger-related excitement often accompany sexual arousal for such men. A noteworthy difference between voyeurs and rapists is the absence of physical coercion. In one sense, voyeurism represents the opposite of rape, since the voyeur's gratification is entirely solitary, usually without awareness on the part of the stimulus person.

INTEGRATION

What conclusions can be drawn about the current state of the art in theorizing about sex offenders and sexually deviant behavior? Before approaching this question, some comments can be made about the nature of the literature. First, the three 'traditional' theoretical approaches (psychodynamic, behavioral, and biological) have now taken a back seat to ideas based on the findings of research that is driven by data rather than by theory. Second, there are limitations in the scope of the available literature. The only disorders for which there has been significant research activity relevant to theories of etiology are rape and child molestation. Thus, any conclusions that are drawn refer to these disorders, although they can provide potentially useful research hypotheses regarding the etiology of other disorders.

What conclusions can be offered? There is a certain consistency throughout the literature in pointing to some broad conclusions for rape and child molestation. In particular, it seems clear that etiology involves multiple factors, that these factors may operate in different ways for different people, and that there is a great variation in what might be termed the 'severity' of the disorders.

There also appears to be agreement on the utility of an explanatory framework involving two kinds of factors, namely predispositions and triggering factors. Predispositions presumably develop over a number of years and could be a product of childhood environment. The role of biological factors in predispositions does not appear to be significant, except for occasional, unusual conditions, and for the contribution of violence (see below). The literature suggests the tentative conclusion that predispositions are largely cognitive (attitudinal and fantasy related) in nature. Triggering factors can be personal (such as alcohol, psychosis, or sexual needs), environmental (such as stress, stimuli related to a particular location, or the availability of a victim), or both.

The very fact of being able to offer a framework at all provides a partial answer to the question of whether there is a common core among the different disorders. The partial answer is in the affirmative: at the least, there appears to be a common framework within which further understanding can be sought. Further evidence on the 'common core' question has recently been provided by Abel *et al.* (1988). In a carefully conducted study of the histories of 561 male sex offenders, these authors found an average of four different paraphilias per man. Only 10% of their sample had a single diagnosis. It is noted that subjects were only included if they had recurrent, repetitive urges, and not if they had simply committed the behavior.

This framework is consistent with the widely accepted dimension of situational vs preference (or regressed vs fixated) in child molestation. Thus, a person with strong predisposing factors would be seen as falling toward the preference end of the dimension, while a person with few predisposing factors would be located at the situational end. For the latter person, the 'situational,' 'one-time,' or 'out-of-character' offender, strong and obvious triggering factors would presumably be required. Although there is little or no literature on the application of the situational vs preference dimension to sexual deviations other than child molestation, it is potentially applicable.

The literature suggests some tentative conclusions as to the role of violence in sexually deviant behavior. It would seem reasonable to experiment with the hypothesis that propensity towards violence or aggression is a characteristic that is separate from the sexual aspects of a disorder. There are some parallels between the literature on understanding and predicting violent behaviors (e.g. Monahan, 1980) and the literature on understanding and predicting sexually deviant behavior. Drawing on both literatures, one might hypothesize that the potential for sexually aggressive acts requires the presence of both sets of characteristics; namely, a predisposition towards violence and a predisposition towards sexually deviant behavior. Analogously, two sets of triggering factors would need to be present. If, in addition, aggression and sexual excitation interact and catalyze each other in a particular person, then there is the clear danger of serious physical injury or death.

It would seem appropriate to conclude that the importance of cognitive factors in the development and maintenance of sexually deviant behavior has been significantly underestimated. Whenever such factors have been studied, either empirically or in case reports, they appear to be essential ingredients in the problem. There are two major cognitive areas of relevance. One involves *attitudes*: toward one's rights and the rights of others, toward one's entitlement for sexual experience, and toward women (or children) in general. The other in-volves the role of *fantasy*: in contemplating the deviant act, or engaging in it in imagery together with the desired (imagined) consequences. The role of un-wanted deviant sexual fantasies as a source of distress has been virtually ignored in the literature. A significant exception to this statement is the DSM-III-R, in which paraphilias are *defined* in cognitive terms, as involving recurrent intense sexual urges and sexually arousing fantasies together with either overt behavior or subjective distress.

Some sexual deviant behaviors are episodic, while others are usually reflective of a lifestyle. Docter's (1988) model of the development of transvestism and transsexualism suggests a gradual progression toward the development of a life-style, as does Burgess's (1984) edited volume describing the child pornography community. The degree of similarity between the episodic vs continuous dimen-sion and the situational vs preference dimension is a topic for further study. It is possible that all sexually deviant behaviors have the potential for becoming continuous, but are subject to different degrees of legal, social, and normal sanctions.

As a final comment, the question of assessment is briefly addressed. The current state of theory and the supporting data clearly do not provide an ade-quate basis for the confident assessment of 'propensity' toward sexually deviant behavior, either in general or for a particular behavior. Such a basis can only come from a more systematic knowledge of predisposing factors and triggering factors than currently exists. Until that time, the most appropriate assessment strategy will continue to involve the collection of the broadest possible range of potentially relevant information, and its clinical integration by experts who are both familiar with the research literature and clinically experienced with sexually deviant persons.

References

Abel, G. G., Becker, J. V., and Cunningham-Rathner, J. (1984). Complications, consent, and cognitions in sex between children and adults. *International Journal of Law and Psychiatry*, **7**, 89–103.

Abel, G. G., Becker, J. V., Cunningham-Rathner, J., Mittelman, M., and Rouleau, J. (1988). Multiple paraphiliac diagnoses among sex offenders. *Bulletin of the American Academy of Psychiatry and the Law*, **16**, 153–68.

Abel, G. G., Blanchard, E. B., and Becker, J. V. (1978). An integrated treatment program for rapists. In R. T. Rada (ed.), *Clinical Aspects of the Rapist.* New York: Grune & Stratton.

Allen, D. W. (1980). A psychoanalytic view. In D. J. Cox and R. J. Daitzman (eds), *Exhibitionism: Description, Assessment, and Treatment.* New York: Garland.

American Psychiatric Association. (1987). *Diagnostic and Statistical Manual of Mental Disorder* (3rd edition, revised). Washington, DC: American Psychiatric Association.

Berlin, F. S. (1983). Sex offenders: A biomedical perspective and a status report on biomedical treatment. In J. G. Greer and I. R. Stuart (eds), *The Sexual Aggressor: Current Perspectives on Treatment.* New York: Van Nostrand Reinhold.

Berlin, F. S. (1989). The paraphilias and Depo-provera: Some medical, ethical and legal considerations. *Bulletin of the American Academy of Psychiatry and the Law*, **17**, 233–39.

Blair, C. D., and Lanyon, R. I. (1981). Exhibitionism: Etiology and treatment. *Psychological Bulletin*, **89**, 439–63.

Bradford, J. M. W. (1985). Organic treatments for the male sexual offender. *Behavioral Sciences and the Law*, **3**, 355–75.

Bradford, J. M. W., and Pawlak, A. (1987). Sadistic homosexual pedophilia: Treatment with cyproterone acetate: A single case study. *Canadian Journal of Psychiatry*, **32**, 22–30.

Brownmiller, S. (1975). *Against Our Will: Men, Women, and Rape*. New York: Simon & Schuster.

Burgess, A. W. (ed.) (1984). *Child Pornography and Sex Rings*. Lexington, MA: Heath.

Cohen, M. L., Garofolo, R., Boucher, R., and Seghorn, T. (1971). The psychology of rapists. *Seminars in Psychiatry*, **3**, 307–27. New York: Grune & Stratton.

Cohen, M. L., Seghorn, T., and Calmas, W. (1969). Sociometric study of sex offenders. *Journal of Abnormal Psychology*, **94**, 249–55.

Cox, D. C., and Daitzman, R. J. (eds) (1980). *Exhibitionism: Description, Assessment, and Treatment*. New York: Garland.

Docter, R.E. (1988). *Transvestites and Transsexuals: Toward a Theory of Cross-gender Behavior*. New York: Plenum.

Ellis, H. (1942). *Studies in the Psychology of Sex* (2 vols). New York: Random House. (Original work published 1899.)

Feinbloom, D. H. (1976). *Transvestites and Transsexuals*. New York: Dell/Delta.

Fenichel, O. (1945). *The Psychoanalytic Theory of Neurosis*. New York: Norton.

Finkelhor, D. (1984). *Child Sexual Abuse: New Theory and Research*. New York: Free Press.

Finkelhor, D. (1986). *A Sourcebook on Child Sexual Abuse*. Beverly Hills, CA: Sage.

Flor-Henry, P. (1987). Cerebral aspects of sexual deviation. In G. D. Wilson (ed.), *Variant Sexuality: Research and Theory*. Baltimore: Johns Hopkins University Press.

Freud, S. (1953). Three essays on the theory of sexuality. In *The Complete Psychological Works of Sigmund Freud* (Standard edn, vol. 7). London: Hogarth Press. (Original work published 1905.)

Goodman, R. E. (1987). Genetic and hormonal factors in human sexuality: Evolutionary and developmental perspectives. In G. D. Wilson (ed.), *Variant Sexuality: Research and Theory*. Baltimore: Johns Hopkins University Press.

Groth, A. N., Burgess, A. W., and Holstrom, L. L. (1977). Rape: Power, anger, and sexuality. *American Journal of Psychiatry*, **134**, 1239–43.

Groth, A. N., Hobson, W. F., and Gary, T. S. (1982). The child molester: Clinical observations. In J. Conte and D. A. Shore (eds), *Social Work and Child Sexual Abuse*. New York: Haworth.

Hammer, E. F. (1957). A psychoanalytic hypothesis concerning sex offenders. *Journal of Clinical and Experimental Psychopathology*, **18**, 341–60.

Hucker, S., Langevin, R., Dickey, R., Handy, L., Chambers, J., and Wright, S. (1988). Cerebral damage and dysfunction in sexually aggressive men. *Annals of Sex Research*, **1**, 33–47.

Hucker, S., Langevin, R., Wortzman, G., Bain, J., Handy, L., Chambers, J., and Wright, S. (1986). Neuropsychological impairment in pedophiles. *Canadian Journal of Behavioral Science*, **18**, 440–8.

Kinsey, A. C., Pomeroy, W. B., and Martin, C. E. (1948). *Sexual Behavior in the Human Male*. Philadelphia: Saunders.

Kinsey, A. C., Pomeroy, W. B., Martin, C. E., and Gebhart, P. H. (1953). *Sexual Behavior in the Human Female*. Philadelphia: Saunders.

Kline, P. (1987). Sexual deviation: Psychoanalytic research and theory. In G. D. Wilson (ed.), *Variant Sexuality: Research and Theory*. Baltimore: Johns Hopkins University Press.

Knight, R. A., and Prentky, R. A. (1990). Classifying sexual offenders: The development and corroboration of models. In W. L. Marshall, D. R. Laws and H. E. Barbaree (eds), *The Handbook of Sexual Assault: Issues, Theories, and Treatment of the Offender*. New York: Plenum.

Koss, M. P., and Dinero, T. E. (1988). Predictors of sexual aggression among a national sample of male college studies. In R. A. Prentky and V. L. Quinsey (eds), *Human Sexual Aggression: Current Perspectives (Annals of the New York Academy of Sciences*, vol. 528). New York: New York Academy of Sciences.

Krafft-Ebing, R. Von. (1965). *Psychopathia Sexualis*. New York: Putnam. (Original work published 1886.)

Langevin, R. (1983). *Sexual Strands*. Hillsdale, NJ: Erlbaum.

Langevin, R. (1988). Defensiveness in sex offenders. In R. Rogers (ed.), *Clinical Assessment of Malingering and Deception*. New York: Guilford.

Lanyon, R. I., and Lanyon, B. P. (1976). Behavioral assessment and decision making. In M. P. Feldman and A. Broadhurst (eds), *Theoretical and Experimental Bases of the Behavior Therapies*. New York: Wiley.

Lanyon, R. I., and Lanyon, B. P. (1978). *Behavior Therapy: A Clinical Introduction*. Reading, MA: Addison-Wesley.

Laws, D. R., and Marshall, W. L. (1990). A conditioning theory of the etiology and maintenance of deviant sexual preference and behavior. In W. L. Marshall, D. R. Laws and H. E. Barbaree (eds), *Handbook of Sexual Assault: Issues, Theories, and Treatment of the Offender*. New York: Plenum.

Malamuth, N. M. (1986). Predictors of naturalistic sexual aggression. *Journal of Personality and Social Psychology*, **50**, 953–62.

Marshall, W. F. (in press). Pornography and sex offenders. In D. Zillman and J. Bryant (eds), *Pornography: Recent Research, Interpretation, and Policy Considerations*. Hillsdale, NJ: Erlbaum.

Marshall, W. L., and Barbaree, H. E. (1990). An integrated theory of the etiology and maintenance of sexual offending. In W. L. Marshall, D. R. Laws and H. E. Barbaree (eds), *Handbook of Sexual Assault: Issues, Theories, and Treatment of the Offender*. New York: Plenum.

Masters, W. H., and Johnson, V. E. (1966). *Human Sexual Response*. Boston: Little, Brown.

Masters, W. H., and Johnson, V. E. (1970). *Human Sexual Inadequacy*. Boston: Little, Brown.

McGuire, R. J., Carlisle, J. M., and Young, B. G. (1965). Sexual deviations as conditioned behavior: A hypothesis. *Behavior Research and Therapy*, **2**, 185–90.

Medea, A., and Thompson, K. (1974). *Against Rape*. New York: Farrar, Strauss & Giroux.

Meiselman, K. C. (1978). *Incest: A Psychological Study of Causes and Effects*. San Francisco: Jossey-Bass.

Monahan, J. (1980). *The Clinical Prediction of Violent Behavior*. Rockville, MD: National Institute of Mental Health.

Money, J. (1981). Paraphilias: Phyletic origins of erotosexual dysfunction. *International Journal of Mental Health*, **10**, 75–109.

Money, J. (1984). Paraphilias: Phenomenology and classification. *American Journal of Psychotherapy*, **38**, 164–79.

Money, J. (1988). *Gay, Straight, and In-between*. New York: Oxford.

Money, J., Wiedeking, C., Walker, P., Migeon, C., Meyer, W., and Borgaonkar, D. (1975). 47,XYY and 46,XY males with antisocial and/or sex-offending behavior: Antiandrogen therapy plus counseling. *Psychoneuroendocrinology*, **1**, 165–78.

Mrazek, F. J., and Kempe, C. H. (eds) (1981). *Sexually Abused Children and their Families*. New York: Pergamon.

Prentky, R. A., Knight, R. A., and Rosenberg, R. (1988). Validation analyses on a taxonomic system for rapists: Disconfirmation and reconceptualization. In R. A. Prentky and V. L. Quinsey (eds), *Human Sexual Aggression: Current Perspectives (Annals of the New York Academy of Sciences*, vol. 528). New York: New York Academy of Sciences.

Rada, R. T. (ed.) (1978). *Clinical Aspects of the Rapist*. New York: Grune & Stratton.

Rada, R. T., Laws, D. R., and Kellner, R. (1976). Plasma testosterone levels, in the rapist. *Psychosomatic Medicine*, **38**, 257–68.

Rada, R. T., Laws, D. R., Kellner, R., Stivastava, L., and Peake, G. (1983). Plasma androgens in violent and nonviolent sex offenders. *Bulletin of the American Academy of Psychiatry and the Law*, **11**, 149–58.

Rosenberg, R., Knight, R. A., Prentky, R. A., and Lee, A. (1988). Validating the components of a taxonomic system for rapists: A path analytic approach. *Bulletin of the American Academy of Psychiatry and the Law*, **16**, 169–85.

Scully, D., and Marolla, J. (1984). Convicted rapists' vocabulary of motives: Excuses and justifications. *Social Problems*, **31**, 530–44.

Seghorn, T. K., Prentky, R. A., and Boucher, R. J. (1987). Childhood sexual abuse in the lives of sexually aggressive offenders. *Journal of the American Academy of Child and Adolescent Psychiatry*, **26**, 262–7.

Sgroi, S. M. (1982). *Handbook of Clinical Intervention in Child Sexual Abuse*. Lexington, MA: Heath.

Travin, F., Cullen, K., and Melella, J. T. (1988). The use and abuse of erection measurements: A forensic perspective. *Bulletin of the Academy of Psychiatry and the Law*, **16**, 235–50.

Tollison, C. D., and Adams, H. E. (1979). *Sexual Disorders*. New York: Gardner.

Wilson, G. D. (1987). An ethological approach to sexual deviation. In G. D. Wilson (ed.), *Variant Sexuality: Research and Theory*. Baltimore: Johns Hopkins University Press.

Wolf, S. C. (1985). A multi-factor model of deviant sexuality. *Victimology: An International Journal*, **10**, 359–74.

3

The Effects of Sex Offences

D. J. WEST
Institute of Criminology, University of Cambridge, UK

VICTIMS OF VIOLENCE

The behaviours labelled sex offending are so heterogeneous that it makes no sense to consider their effects without first taking into account the varied nature and circumstances of victimisation. A vast literature has appeared in the last two decades concerned with the effects of rape upon women. Rapes are by definition coercive or violent offences, but rapes constitute only a small proportion of the totality of sex offences. The 2471 rape offences recorded by the police in England and Wales in 1987 (although more than double the 1015 rapes recorded ten years earlier) still amounted to only 9.8% of the total 18 781 notifiable sex offences on record that year.

In spite of the currently fashionable assumption that rape is more a crime of violence than one of unrestrained lust, only a small proportion of victims sustain significant physical injury. According to one English survey (Wright, 1980), only 6% of victims sustained injury serious enough to require treatment and a majority suffered no physical damage whatsoever. Substantially similar findings emerged from a Scottish Office survey (Chambers and Millar, 1983). According to a recent Home Office analysis of reported rapes, the increasing number of incidents notified has not been accompanied by an increase in the proportion of cases involving serious physical violence. The proportion of rape victims investigated by American police who have been injured—especially in cities like New York that have a very high incidence of violent crimes of all kinds—is much greater than in England. In addition, the majority of English-language writings about rape derive from American sources.

The truth is that most sexual offences are not crimes of physical violence. A Home Office analysis some years ago (Walmsley and White, 1979) demonstrated that at least 43% of persons convicted of an indictable sexual offence had been involved only with consenting partners or 'victims'. Many sex offences do not

Clinical Approaches to Sex Offenders and Their Victims
Edited by C. R. Hollin and K. Howells © 1991 John Wiley & Sons Ltd

involve assault in any ordinary sense of the word. They are offences only because the behaviour is indecent (as in the common offence of indecent exposure or 'flashing') or because a participant is under age (as in unlawful intercourse with a girl under 16) or because the incident took place in public (as in homosexual indecency or importuning in or around men's lavatories). The majority of sex offences dealt with by the courts concern the involvement of children under 16 years of age. Among offences of this kind that are prosecuted as sexual assaults, actual physical violence is not typical; in many cases the young person has been at least superficially acquiescent or even an instigator, and the offenders are by no means always very much older than the victims.

The absence of serious physical violence in the generality of cases does not mean that sex offences are therefore harmless; they may do great psychological damage. Even fully consensual participation in sexual misbehaviour can lead to great anxiety and guilt and some would claim that it can cause socially undesirable sexual proclivities to develop. Moreover, the important minority of instances that do involve violence include some that are almost unimaginably horrendous. In her analysis of homicides in which the offenders were deemed to be of diminished responsibility Dell (1984) noted that 8% were associated with sexual attacks. Precise figures are unavailable, but of the 600 or so homicides recorded annually in England and Wales probably something in the order of 30 cases take place during or after a sexual attack.

STYLES OF VICTIMISATION

Victimisation is a combination of offender's behaviour and victim reaction. Some forms of victimisation are, like beauty, predominantly a matter of individual reaction. A group of amused young women joking with each other because they have noticed a 'flasher' trying to attract attention are arguably less victimised than the infuriated recipient of sexual innuendos from her boss. The man in the latter example may commit no crime and his behaviour would be considered less deviant than the flasher's, but nevertheless he may have a greater impact. Although much wronged and legally raped, a prostitute whose client has obliged her to submit to intercourse without the payment she had expected is differently victimised from the woman pounced upon by a nocturnal intruder into her home.

Where there is consensual participation, and where the persons concerned are of an age to appreciate what is happening and to know what they want and do not want, victimisation becomes a label bestowed by others. During a debate on the 'age of consent' staged by Robert Kilroy Silk on television in 1988, several young women voiciferously protested against outside interference with their sexual lives on what were to them the unrealistic grounds that they had not yet reached 16. Similarly, two men, prosecuted for acts of 'gross indecency' with each other inside a parked car, will feel themselves victims of the law rather than victims of sex.

Non-consensual victimisation is of a different order. It need not include actual bodily contact. Unwanted verbal propositioning, obscene telephone calls, genital exhibitionism, or exposure to pornography can all cause upset. These, however, are of a different order again from intrusive bodily manipulation. Here again, however, minor acts of indecent fondling are to be distinguished from serious assaults that proceed to forced anal, oral or vaginal penetration accomplished by brute force, or threats or the use of weapons. Injury or mutilation in the course of a sexual attack is about the worst imaginable type of victimisation a survivor can experience.

The relationship between victim and offender is another relevant variable. Assault by a boyfriend, called 'date rape' in America, may be less alarming or perceived as less life-threatening than being waylaid by a stranger whose actions are totally unpredictable. On the other hand, disillusionment occasioned by a breach of trust in the context of a close attachment can be very hurtful. If sexual misconduct disrupts an important ongoing relationship, with a relative, teacher or employer for example, this can prove more damaging than the sexual incident itself.

Victimisation takes on a different character when offender and victim are of the same sex, unless it happens that both are homosexually oriented. Unwanted approaches from one woman to another are perhaps less disturbing than those from one man to another, possibly because manifestations of female sexuality are less coarse or because heterosexual males feel their masculine self-image threatened by sexual attentions from another male.

A child who has been involved in supplying an adult with sexual gratification, even if he or she has been eager to do so, is almost universally regarded as seriously victimised, or 'abused' to use the current jargon. Be that as it may, it would be foolish to ignore the fact that incidents classed as child sexual abuse cover a wide range of acts. Distinctions relevant to victimisation of an adult—consent or non-consent, degree of coercion, relationship to the offender and whether the behaviour is homosexual or heterosexual—are equally relevant to the likelihood of damage when the victim is a child. Age is particularly important, and not just the age of the child and whether he or she is pre- or post-pubertal, but the magnitude of the age discrepancy between victim and offender.

Disorders observed in children or adults who have had sexual victimisation experiences are not necessarily caused by those experiences. Victims may have had some prior disturbance which explains their present condition or explains their reaction to the sexual trauma. In the case of children and adolescents who have been reared in generally disorderly, deprived or violent backgrounds the sexual incidents may be the least significant of the many forms of abuse to which they have been exposed. In assessing the effects of sexual incidents the context in which they occur is important, so the victim's circumstances and life style at the time need to be taken into account.

WOMEN'S VULNERABILITY

In demanding equal rights and autonomy for women, in sexual as well as in economic life, the feminist movement has done much to call attention to the sufferings caused by sexually assaultive males. Realisation that the needs of women victims were inadequately recognised or provided for in the male-dominated legal system led to the setting up of rape crisis centres. A spate of mainly American surveys have shown that rapes are many times more frequent than official statistics of reported cases might suggest. For example using a self-report questionnaire administered in classroom settings and returned anonymously, Koss *et al.* (1988) asked 6159 students about incidents of sexual victimisation that had happened since they were 14 years of age. The respondents came from a wide variety of institutions spread over the United States. The average age of the sample was 21 years. Only 91 persons (1.5%) failed to reply. As many as 15% of the women reported having been raped at least once and a further 12% had experienced attempted rape. Altogether over half of the women said they had been subjected to some form of sexual victimisation. Of the men, 4.4% admitted having committed acts amounting to legal rape. Over half of the rapes reported by the women took place on 'dates' and only a tiny minority of these were reported to police. Even more startling figures have been published: Russell (1984), who sampled a representative sample of households in San Francisco, employing sensitive female interviewers, estimated that 41% of wives had experienced attempted or completed rape by a man other than their husband, and 2.7% had had such an experience in the previous twelve months.

It is useful to know that a substantial proportion of the female population, at least in the United States, recall some serious sexual assault, for they cannot all have sustained permanent, noticeable damage. Studies of female sex victims have repeatedly detected severe and often lasting disorder in the majority of cases, but these researches are generally based upon selected samples of women who have gone to rape crisis centres or sought help from other agencies. Such women are likely to have reacted particularly badly or had particularly severe experiences.

Feminist literature rejects the view that rape is motivated by sexual attraction, preferring to regard it as primarily a crime of violence, an expression of aggression against women and a desire to subjugate and humiliate. Styles of attack are characterised as *blitz*, where the victim is quickly overpowered; *surprise*, when she is unexpectedly pounced on; and *con* when lured into a vulnerable situation. Assailants have been described by Groth (1979a) as seeking power and dominance in order to assert a macho image, compensating for some felt sexual inadequacy, expressing angry retaliation for supposed hurtful experiences with women, or finding sexual excitement through the infliction of pain or humiliation. These categories leave out of account offences committed through an excess of ardour, impatience or mistaken ideas of being 'owed' some satisfaction, which underlie many date rapes (Goodchilds *et al.* 1988). However, a victim who divines that her assailant is driven by one of the angry motives identified by Groth has good reason to fear serious maltreatment.

Undue emphasis on the nastiest and most dangerous varieties of sexual attack adds to women's fear of rape, a fear that is very common and very strong, even when in reality little risk is being taken (Warr, 1985). A Home Office national survey (Hough and Mayhew, 1983) found that 30% of all women, and 64% of women living on poor, council housing estates, were 'very worried' about being raped. Women of the older generation, although actually running a substantially smaller risk, are often even more anxious. The stricter codes of sexual morality prevalent during their formative years may still exert some influence, but those who are frail and living alone have some justification for feeling vulnerable to the housebreaker cum rapist, given the amount of publicity that the rare attacks on old people in such circumstances receive in the popular press. This pervasive fear can have devastating results when it leads to self-imposed restrictions, a miserable, housebound existence and an anxious preoccupation with protective devices (Davis and Brody, 1979).

Women whose fears revolve around the idea of death or mutilation may well be too scared to resist (Burnett *et al.*, 1985). Young and fit adults, unless set upon by a gang, can sometimes fight back. Doing so often lessens the chances of an attack succeeding, since assailants whose aim is to secure compliance with the least trouble to themselves will be discouraged or scared off. On the other hand, the anger-driven rapist is likely to be incited to further brutalities, even to the point of committing murder. In a study of rapists sent to a Massachusetts institution for dangerous sex offenders, together with their surviving victims (numbering 108 and 389 respectively), Carter *et al.* (1988) concluded that victim resistance was linked with a higher incidence of violence. This was only to be expected in view of the unusually violent and repetitive rapists under scrutiny, but the proportion of resisting victims who suffered severe brutality during the attack became very large, 80% or more, only when the incident was categorised as due to 'displaced anger' or 'sadism'. The investigators concluded that victims are better advised to look for ways of fleeing the situation, to try to reason with or discourage the offender verbally, or to display off-puting signs of distress, rather than to proffer retaliatory violence.

The severity of the trauma from an attack is partly determined by the woman's anticipatory attitudes and feelings. Apart from practical concerns about sexually transmitted diseases, unwanted pregnancy or criticism from angry lovers, parents etc.—what has been called the second assault (Williams and Holmes, 1981)—the victim may harbour illogical feelings of guilt, degradation, anger at failure to resist, or a distrust of all men. Pre-existing conflicts about sexual feelings or relationships will be aggravated and self-esteem and self-confidence reduced. Sexual acts carry enormous symbolic significance and the potential for psychological distress is much greater than the physical aspects of the assault might be expected to produce. Rape crisis centres run by militant women, who dislike the police and who exacerbate rather than calm down the victim's fear and distrust of men, are not always the best agencies to help.

RAPE TRAUMA SYNDROMES

Post-traumatic stress disorder is the formal clinical label for a common reaction which may follow any serious disaster or life-threatening crisis. According to the American definition in the *Diagnostic and Statistical Manual, III* (American Psychiatric Association, 1980) the determining features are as follows:

(1) The existence of a recognisable stressor that would evoke significant symptoms of distress in almost anyone.
(2) The re-experiencing of the trauma either through (a) recurrent intrusive recollections, (b) dreams, or (c) sudden feelings.
(3) A numbing of responsiveness or reduced involvement in the external world indicated by diminished interest in activities, feelings of estrangement from others, and constricted affect.
(4) In addition, at least two of the following set of symptoms need also to be present: hyperalertness, sleep problems, survival guilt, problems of memory or concentration, avoidance of activities, the intensification of symptoms when exposed to stimuli related to the traumatic event.

Burgess and Holstrom (1974, 1985) were among the first to identify a similar disturbance following sexual assault, which they named 'rape trauma syndrome'. In spite of the similarity, rape trauma is not directly comparable with classic post-traumatic stress disorder, which is a response typically associated with such extremely dangerous situations as wartime battles, natural disasters and gunpoint violence (Figley, 1985). Some near-homicidal sexual attacks equate well with these life-threatening situations, and are likely to produce the same effects, but that does not apply, for instance, to an offending boyfriend who refuses to comply with the limits on love-making which the victim has tried to impose. Symptoms fulfilling the DSM-III criteria are not to be expected and indeed do not occur following every unwanted sexual experience, or even following some really nasty assaults. Moreover, some of the most common sequelae of rape, notably sexual confusion and damaged self-esteem, are not prominent in classic post-traumatic stress disorder.

Although it does not happen invariably, women are often seriously traumatised by a sexual assault even when the incident was not especially brutal or life-threatening. Manifestations of rape trauma are both immediate and long-term. Initially, a state of shock may be accompanied by a numbing sensation and a feeling of unreality as if 'this can't really be happening to me'. Extreme fear can paralyse action and prevent resistance. For some women the rape situation is the realisation of a long-dreaded nightmare. The experience of helplessness, of inability to maintain personal integrity, of being defiled and perhaps infected with AIDS, shakes confidence and sets in train anxieties and self-questioning. The victim may be left in a trembling, distraught condition, unable to give a coherent account of the offence. Others appear to distance themselves from the event and to display a frozen calm and a superficial objectivity that conceals their inner turmoil and liability to subsequent psychological problems. Investigators conducting retrospective studies in which women are questioned about experiences of sexual victimisation can be surprised by the depth of emotion sometimes displayed during the recital of long past incidents that have been fretted over in secret for years without anyone having been told about them.

Burgess and Holstrom (1979) describe fear, both rational and irrational, as the emotion underlying most of the immediate post-rape distress. Nervous apprehension, 'jumpiness' and fears of going out alone, being followed or meeting strangers can amount to incapacitating phobias. A reliving of the event in flash-backs and nightmares, or an obsessive rumination about what has happened, may compete with ineffectual attempts to black out the painful memories. Loss of sleep and appetite, mood swings, crying fits, irritability, loss of concentration and other signs of heightened emotionality are common. Soreness or bruising caused by the assault, or nausea from hormones given to prevent pregnancy, can exacerbate hypochondriacal anxieties or provoke psychosomatic symptoms such as stomach pains, frequency of micturition or menstrual irregularity. Even in the absence of these overt signs of distress life styles may be seriously disrupted. Victims may become withdrawn, reluctant to resume work, uninterested in leisure activities and reserved with boyfriends. Loss of desire for or positive fear of sexual relations is very often reported.

Symptoms of trauma, even when severe, may not last long, so it is advisable not to treat victims as if they are necessarily going to become psychiatric patients. Common sense counselling and advice in coping with unfamiliar mat-ters, such as police questioning, compensation claims and trial procedures, are welcomed when deeper psychological probing is neither indicated nor desired. Substantial recovery often occurs in a matter of weeks or a few months. In their follow up study of cases dealt with by the emergency department of a Boston hostpial, Burgess and Holmstrom (1979) found that only 37% of rape victims recovered within a few months, but more recent research suggests more optimis-tic outcomes (Ellis, 1983).

Burt and Katz (1987), reviewing studies of recovery from rape, comment on the large number of antecedent influences, the highly variable outcomes, and the different forms of response to victimisation. The age of the victim, the duration of the assault and degree of violence, the sexual acts involved, the cultural and ethnic backgrounds of offender and victim, and whether the assailant is a stranger all have some effect, although not always the same effect upon different individuals. Older women, for example, tend to have fewer symptoms in the acute phase but recover more slowly than younger women. On the other hand, teenagers, among whom the risk of victimisation is especially high, sometimes suffer great distress from what might be thought to be less serious incidents, such as being pressed by too eager boyfriends into sexual activity that is short of penetration but more than what they wanted. Although immediate reactions of anger, guilt and embarrassment often subside quickly, in a minority of young victims symptoms such as depression or fear of going out alone appear to inten-sify over time. These long-term outcomes cannot be predicted from the circum-stances of the assault and are probably determined by extrinsic factors such as the victim's personality, previous history of trauma and family support (Ageton, 1984).

Whatever the age of the victim, persons close to her can add greatly to her distress if they react by withdrawal or by criticism or if they show more concern for vengeance against the perpetrator than for the victim's welfare (Foley, 1985). At the time when they are in greatest need of sympathy and support, some victims finds that they are no longer sharing an uninhibited exchange of feelings with their lover or husband (Miller et al., 1982).

Although few victims sustain lasting physical damage, the extent of bodily insult, arising from slapping, punching, gagging and so forth, affects recovery rate. Even years after a rape systematic psychological measures of self-esteem, anxiety or levels of depression and sexual adjustment often show some lasting impairment. The victim's prior level of psychological functioning is the most important determinant of ultimate outcome. The circumstances of the attack are more important in the genesis of immediate reactions. In the process of recovery, the development of self-assertiveness and self-esteem and the beneficial adjustments of work routine and social contacts to avoid stress and willingness to accept help are features linked to a speedier return to health.

CHILD VICTIMOLOGY

Whereas heterosexual offences against adults need to be actually assaultive before they are thought likely to be very traumatic, the mildest involvement of children in sexual acts is nowadays labelled 'abuse' from which bad and lasting effects are to be expected. Finkelhor (1988), a pioneer researcher in this field, identifies four elements which account for the traumatic impact on children. The first, 'traumatic sexualisation', is caused by premature and inappropriate sexual learning. Children often receive rewards for collaborating with adults in sexual acts. This encourages them to regard sex as a tool for manipulating people. From the way paedophiles talk and act in their company the children are liable to acquire distorted ideas of sexual morality and appropriate sexual conduct, and may begin to behave in sexual ways incongruent with their level of development. If sex becomes associated with memories of incidents that were unpleasant or anxiety-provoking, either at the time or in the retrospect, later sexual adjustment may be impeded. 'Betrayal', Finkelhor's second factor, occurs when, in the context of a trusting or dependent relationship, activities are introduced which the child finds subsequently to have been reprehensible and selfishly motivated. The third factor of 'stigmatisation' occurs through the furtive quality of the activity and the child's fear of being blamed if it is discovered. Finally, 'powerlessness' occurs most acutely when a child is coerced by force, threat or deceit to submit to unwanted and intrusive invasions of bodily privacy.

Finkelhor argues that behaviour exhibited by sexually abused children, both at the time and in later years, reflects these four types of trauma. Provocative and seductive demeanour with adults and aggressive sexual approaches to other children are signs of 'traumatic sexualisation'. Dependent clinging, or its opposites, angry distrust and avoidance of intimacy, are signs of 'betrayal'. Poor self-esteem, as measured by psychological tests, social withdrawal or joining up with marginal groups such as drug abusers, delinquents and prostitutes, are all signs of 'stigmatisation'. Anxiety, phobias, sleep disorders, depression, running away, school learning problems and, later on, sexual frigidity or sexual molestation of children can be attributed to the sense of 'powerlessness' instilled by early sexual abuse.

Assessments of the prevalence of offences involving children, like similar assessments of offences against women, are liable to sensational misinterpretations on account of the over-inclusiveness of some of the definitions of 'abuse' used in survey research (Wyatt and Peters, 1986). In a national survey conducted by the MORI organisation, 12% of British women and 8% of men reported that they had been sexually abused before reaching the age of sixteen (Baker and Duncan, 1985). The definition of abuse they used was 'when another person, who is sexually mature, involves the child in any activity which the other person expects to lead to their sexual arousal. This might involve intercourse, touching, exposure of the sexual organs, showing pornographic material or talking about things in an erotic way'. The reported prevalence of histories of abuse was raised by the inclusion of adolescents over 14, and by the inclusion of verbal indecencies and incidents with 'a peer who was sexually mature', which could mean another adolescent. Some North American surveys have gone further by counting as 'children' anyone under 18 (Wyatt, 1985). In a review of published survey statistics Peters *et al.* (1986) noted prevalence rates of child sexual abuse varying from 62% to 5% among females and from 30% to 3% among males. In a small survey of Cambridge women Nash and West (1985) found that 42% reported having had some sexual experience when they were under 16 with a person at least five years older than themselves. Discounting non-contact episodes, such as exposing and indecent talk, the prevalence was virtually halved. Of the minority who had experienced actual sexual intercourse this was sometimes with a male they regarded as a boyfriend and was naturally not thought of by them at the time as abusive.

One reason for the differences between survey findings is the way questions are put. Anonymously completed self-report questionnaires permit frank disclosure, but they are liable to be filled in without much searching thought and they allow scope for misunderstanding or misinterpretation, especially if the questions are not concrete and specific and couched in words in common usage. Face to face interviews with a sympathetic and sensitive inquirer have the advantage that good rapport encourages candour, helps clarify meanings and generally increases the level of reporting (Finkelhor, 1986).

Survey research reveals a wider range of incidents than those typically seen by clinicians who are dealing with the worst kinds of abuse. Social workers' concerns about sexual abuse centre upon intra-familial and incestuous situations, since these are likely to call for removal of the child from the parental home or for entry in an 'at risk' register. Surveys, however, reveal that incidents outside the home are at least as common, although they may be less often reported. In one research study in Boston (Finkelhor, 1984), in which parents with children aged 6 to 14 years of age were interviewed, 15% of mothers and 5% of fathers reported having been sexually abused in their own childhood and 9% of the parents said that a child of theirs had been the victim of actual or attempted sexual abuse. In regard to the children the perpetrators were said to have been non-relatives in 90% of cases, which was perhaps not surprising since the informants were their parents who could not be expected to admit having abused them. In the parents' own histories, however, instances of abuse by strangers or acquaintances were still in a majority of 68%.

A regular finding from surveys of adults is that many more incidents are recalled than were ever mentioned to parents at the time and fewer still were reported to police. In the survey of Cambridge women, 55% of those who re-called some relevant incident said that they had told nobody (Nash and West, 1985). The most commonly cited reason for this was fear that they would be blamed for what happened. Boys are even more reluctant than girls to tell parents about sexual incidents. Recent publicity and access to help lines for children may have changed the picture somewhat, but certainly it is still the case that many sexually abused children deal with their feelings about it in secret.

INITIAL REACTIONS TO ABUSE IN CHILDHOOD

Attempts to equate children's responses to sexual abuse with post-traumatic stress disorder have had even less justification than similar attempts in regard to women's reactions to rape. As Finkelhor had pointed out (1988), most child victims show no signs of the disorder and indeed would not be expected to do so since much of the abuse of children 'does not occur under conditions of danger, threat and violence', being more often a matter of 'abusers misusing their auth-ority or manipulating moral standards'. Most paedophiles are looking for a child who will accept them and show them affection. To resort to threat or force to overcome resistance would be for them counter-productive, unsatisfying and risk denunciation with all the dire consequences following from that.

Because paedophiles are generally tentative and persuasive rather than violent in their approaches, children can often extricate themselves from en-counters outside the home before unwanted activities have started or gone too far. Abel *et al.* (1985) questioned child molesters who were completely voluntary attenders as out-patients at the Sexual Behavior Clinic of New York State Psychiatric Institute. Their sample of 232 offenders admitted to a total of 55 250 attempted sexual molestations of children under 14, but only 38 727 were 'com-pleted'. In 30% of the remembered incidents the offender had desisted for one reason or another. If the incident is a one-off event, and if the importunate adult is a stranger or person with whom the child has no close tie, the incident may have little impact, save perhaps for some initial fright on realising the sexual intent. Children who have let themselves be lured into a continuing clandestine relationship which becomes burdensome of them, but which they are scared to break off for fear of attracting scandal or blame, are in a more stressful situation. They may have enjoyed for a time the unusual amount of attention and rewards from an adult, but they also suffer guilt feelings and fears of detection. Children who, together with some of their peers, have joined up with a so-called 'sex ring', participated in group sex and been introduced to pornography, can become identified with and surprisingly loyal to men whom outsiders regard as monsters. When the activities include pornographic photography children may discover that they are pressured into continuing involvement through fear of discovery (Schetky, 1988).

The greatest stress is experienced when a child is made to submit to unwanted sexual activity by force or threat or because the perpetrator is a parent or relative whose demands are difficult to refuse. The victim of parental abuse may feel hopelessly trapped in a miserable situation from which escape is impossible without bringing about the break up of the family and perhaps being committed to a children's institution. Children whose victimisation is discovered because their disturbed behaviour has attracted attention have usually been involved in these rarer but more stressful family situations. Their symptoms, other than sexual conduct inappropriate for their age, are similar to the symptoms displayed by children who have not been sexually abused but who are under stress in unhappy, rejecting or conflict-ridden families.

A girl victim may have good reason to suppose that her mother would disbelieve her if she accused her father or stepfather of molesting her or that the offender would retaliate for her attempt to betray him. Alternatively, and more commonly, she may want the sex activity to cease, but not at the cost of losing a father who, sexual misbehaviour apart, is loving and caring and a good provider. The child's ambivalence about disclosure under such circumstances is understandable, and he or she may well make subtle hints or half-hearted attempts at disclosure before finally making a full admission.

The events which follow upon disclosure or discovery can be extremely traumatic for the child victim or intra-familial abuse, including the arrest of the perpetrator or even his suicide (Wild, 1988), her own sudden removal from home, unpleasantly intrusive interrogations and medical examinations and signs of great distress or anger in mother and siblings. She may soon come to regret having made any statement and, even without improper persuasion from anyone, she may try to retract. The affair in Cleveland, when action was taken against an unusually large number of families, has brought home to many people the enormous suffering that can be caused by the action of the authorities in child sex abuse cases (Bell, 1988; Butler-Sloss, 1988). When action is taken on the basis of a third party's complaints or suspicions, and not through spontaneous, voluntary disclosure by the child, the victim is liable to the added torment of persistent, probing questions designed to elicit what must seem to her a reluctant confession with punitive consequences. When suspicions are vigorously disputed and families are split on the issue, the child's interests tend to take second place, particularly since public policy now demands the routine involvement of police in all cases.

The over-representation of intra-familiar situations among referrals to clinics dealing with sexually abused children is understandable in view of the disruption of the child's life which disclosure brings in these cases. Typical of the findings on children seen in mental health facilities who have been recently sexually abused are those reported by Conte and Schuerman (1988). Of 369 abused children (aged 4 to 17) 27% displayed four or more symptoms (according to a checklist completed by caseworkers). The most common symptoms were low self-esteem (33%) emotional upset (23%), and sleep disorders or nightmares (20%). Aggressive behaviour and problems in concentration were also prominent. The conclusion that fear and anxiety predominate in the initial symptomatology of children disturbed by sexual abuse accords with those of most previous observers (Browne and Finkelhor, 1986). Common sense dictates that where a child loses a parent and the security of its home, there will be long-term suffering. How serious subsequent disturbances is likely to prove, and how far it can be attributed to the sexual acts themselves or to the attendant circumstances, remain problematic and controversial questions.

LONG-TERM EFFECTS OF CHILD SEXUAL ABUSE

Retrospective inquiries into the histories of disturbed or behaviour disordered adults have revealed a high prevalence of childhood sexual abuse, very often abuse that was never disclosed at the time. From this it has been suggested that sex abuse victims are liable to all kinds of disastrous long-term outcomes. The conditions that have been implicated are remarkably various, including eating disorders (Root and Fallon, 1988), multiple personality (Bliss, 1986; Wilbur, 1984), impaired sexual responsiveness (Lindberg and Distad, 1985), promiscuity (McVicar, 1979), prostitution by females (James and Meyerding, 1977; Silbert and Pines, 1981) prostitution by males (Coombs, 1974; McCormack et al., 1986; McMullen, 1987), adolescent runaways (Janus et al., 1987), personality disorder (Herman and van der Kolk, 1987), general retardation of emotional and intellectual development (Gomes-Schwartz et al., 1985), and becoming a sexual abuser (Barnard et al., 1988; Goodwin et al., 1982; Groth, 1979b).

It is difficult to know what to make of this. Many of the reports fail to take sufficient account of the general prevalence of child sexual involvements in the milieux from which samples are drawn. Often the problems presented by the adult are the result of many different factors in addition to or other than sexual abuse. For example, many adolescent street prostitutes are runaways from disordered families in which sexual abuse has occurred, but often this is just one element, and not necessarily the most decisive, in a family situation that was fraught before sexual irregularities first began (Ennew, 1986).

There are particular reasons for scepticism towards the fashionable theory that sex offending by men is a consequence of sexual abuse in childhood. For one reason, it is too conveniently self-exculpatory. In one American study, of 83 men imprisoned for raping women over 17, 59% claimed that they had been sexually molested by women when they were boys, their average age at the time being just under 11 years with the majority of the incidents including sexual intercourse (Petrovich and Templer, 1974). Substantiation of such implausible claims is not possible. The theory that molestation of boys by men is a natural extension of their own boyhood experiences with molesters is not well founded, despite its popularity. The theory also carries the unfortunate implication that boy victims must be presumed to be potential offenders. Admittedly adult homosexual males more often recall boyhood sexual encounters with men than do heterosexuals (West and Woodhouse, 1990), but without themselves developing any particular interest in children. Homosexual interactions of boys with each other might be thought more likely to lead to pederasty, except that such behaviour is far too common to carry any such implication.

The evidence for long-term effects is strongest in the area of sexual adjustment. Indeed, victims themselves perceive by introspection a clear connection.

Surveys of non-clinical samples show a significant correlation between history of sexual abuse and sexual problems in adulthood. For example, Nash and West (1985) found that women who recalled abusive incidents in childhood, compared with women who did not, included a higher proportion without a hetrosexual partner (sexual inhibition) and a higher proportion who had started sexual intercourse at an unusually early age (sexual disinhibition). This agrees with other observers' findings of a link between childhood sexual abuse and both frigidity and promiscuity and also, more generally, with difficulty in emotional relationships with persons of the opposite sex. Absolute proof of cause and effect, however, is difficult to obtain. It has been said that some child victims are unusually attractive and seductive, so that precocious sexuality and subsequent promiscuity might sometimes be a cause rather than an effect of abuse. Another, more plausible, explanation that discounts direct cause and effect is that adults with sexual problems tend to remember and dwell upon childhood incidents that other people forget and to attribute spurious importance to them. In spite of these reservations, however, the volume of evidence, both clinical and statistical, for a link between sex abuse in childhood and a variety of neurotic and behaviour disorders in later life cannot easily be dismissed. It seems likely, however, that in most cases child sexual abuse contributes in interaction with other factors of personality and circumstance rather than itself being the prime cause of social or sexual pathology.

MALE VICTIMS

From the copious literature on life in American prisons it would appear that sexual bullying and taunting of the weak helps the more aggressive criminals to maintain themselves at the top of the inmate pecking order (Lockwood, 1980; Scacco, 1975, 1982; Weiss and Friar, 1974; Wooden and Parker, 1982). Rather than jeopardising their reputation with the taint of homosexuality, the recruitment of a personal 'sex slave', in return for protecting him from assaults by others, enhances the macho image. Victims of these situations not only suffer deep humiliation at the time, but after release they may continue to be affected, worrying about their ability to resume heterosexual relationships and blaming themselves for having been unable to resist (Sagarin, 1976).

Only relatively recently have homosexual assaults on men in other settings been thought sufficiently frequent to merit serious attention (Anderson, 1985; Forman, 1982; Goyer and Eddleman, 1984; Groth and Burgess, 1980; Kaufman et al., 1980; Mezey and King, 1987). Sometimes these incidents are more ferocious and involve considerably more violence than the average rape of a woman. Homosexual males are especially vulnerable: before the advent of AIDS, at least, they have been notorious for picking up strangers and thereby laying themselves open not only to robbery and occasional blackmail (Sagarin and MacNamara, 1975) but also to forcible or sadistic sexual acts which they had not anticipated. Male street prostitutes prepared to go back home with any man willing to pay incur still greater risks, including risk of what amounts to gang rape.

Regardless of sexual orientation, men subjected to sexual assault by other men, especially when forced anal penetration takes place, which can be extremely painful and cause significant injury, may suffer much the same trauma as do raped women. Moreover, they have less chance of receiving sympathetic consideration if they tell what has happened or report to the police. They fear criticism and contempt for having failed to defend themselves as a man should. If they are heterosexual they will fear being thought homosexual; if they are homosexual they will anticipate scant attention being paid to their complaint. A heterosexual male forcibly masturbated to the point of ejaculation is likely to feel confused and ashamed and any doubts or insecurities he may have had about his sexuality will be exacerbated.

Sexual molestation of boys is incomparably more frequent and a cause for more concern than unwanted homosexual approaches to adult men. Clinicians and social workers are not fully alerted to the diagnosis of sexual abuse in male children (Freeman-Longo, 1986). Risin and Koss (1987), in a survey of 2972 male students, found that 7.3% reported some childhood sexual experience meeting at least one of three criteria of 'abuse', namely age discrepancy between victim and offender, use of some coercion or sexual misconduct by an adult carer or authority figure. Findings from community surveys show that boys are more likely than girls to have sexual encounters with adults outside the home. In a student survey by Finkelhor (1979), 83% of the adults involved with boys were non-family members, compared with only 53% of those involved with girls. The proportion of boys seen in clinical work with sexually abused children has become substantial, up to a fifth or a quarter (Finkelhor, 1984), many of them being very young, less than 6 years old (Reinhart, 1987). In such samples the boys, more often than the girls, come from low income families and have also been subjected to physical abuse (Finkelhor, 1984). Complaints of anal penetration are especially common in the case of very young boys. Hobbs and Wynne (1986) examining a sample of 35 children injured by buggery, reported that 17 were boys, most of them very young.

The immediate effects of sexual molestation of boys are said to be much the same as in the case of girls (Rogers and Terry, 1984), especially when the offender is one of the family (Dixon et al., 1978; Porter, 1986). In the case of very young boys (average age 5 years) referred to a psychiatric facility Friedrich et al. (1988) found that unusual preoccupation with sex and frequent masturbation were the common complaints, as was aggressive behaviour and attempts to involve other children in sexual acts. In slightly older boys confusion about sexual identity, feelings of guilt and reluctance to talk about the experience have been noted (Leith and Handforth, 1988). As with abused girls, boy victims are believed sometimes to suffer severe after-effects in adult life. Dimock (1988), reporting on 25 men sexually abused as boys, found compulsive sex behaviour, that is excessive masturbation and promiscuity, sex orientation confusion, worries about masculine identity and unstable heterosexual relations.

Since persons identified as boy molesters are mostly men, the boys involved have in addition the homosexual element to cope with. Finkelhor (1984) found that male students who had sexual experiences with older men when they were boys were four times as likely as other male students to be currently involved in homosexual activity. This seems to confirm the fear expressed by many parents that sexual contact with an older male will lead to homosexuality, but as already pointed out, one suspects that boys vulnerable to these experiences may have been homosexually inclined in any event. Histories provided by adult male homosexuals suggest that in most cases awareness of homosexual arousal precedes actual homosexual experience (Bell *et al.*, 1981). The findings of a survey by West and Woodhouse (1990) of both students and men in the community revealed that recollections of sexual experiences with older males when they were boys were reported by about one in five. Most of the incidents were trivial and usually the boys had extricated themselves without much difficulty, but except for those who declared themselves currently homosexual or bisexual, their encounters were generally said to have been at the time unwanted and aversive rather than seductive. Even boys who are content to have protracted relationships with an adult paedophile tend to lose interest at puberty when attraction to girls assumes priority (Sandfort, 1987).

Sexual interference with young males by older women is rarely discussed but it undoubtedly occurs (Finkelhor and Russell, 1984). The West and Woodhouse (1990) findings suggested that experiences with women by pubertal boys under the age of 16 were quite common and recalled as pleasant initiation more often than traumatic. At younger ages sexual molestation by females is more likely to be anxiety-provoking. Adolescents, siblings or babysitters are often the culprits. In clinical samples sexual abuse of boys by their mothers is not uncommon, and is usually one sign among many of severe family pathology.

CONCLUSION

Sexual victimisation is an emotive topic that has lent itself to sensationalism, moral outrage and conflicting conclusions from methodologically insecure research. Whereas current thinking emphasises the serious effects of sex assaults and molestations, some authorities maintain that the supposed harm is often exaggerated. In relation to incest, which is one of the more extreme examples of 'abuse', doubts are still expressed that it is necessarily harmful (Henderson, 1983). In reality, incidents of sexual victimisation are so varied and the effects so dependent upon attendant circumstances and individual characteristics that any sweeping generalisation is certain to be fallacious.

The subject has benefited in some ways by capturing the attention of the media, of feminists and of professional journals. The importance of some hitherto largely concealed and neglected social problems has been recognised. On the other hand, undue emphasis on the worst possible prognoses is not always in the victim's best interest. In cases involving children excessive and over-hasty intervention may satisfy feelings of outrage at the cost of further damage to the victims. There is a great need for recognition of the diversity and complexity of 'victimisation' and for this to be followed by appropriately and discriminating responses.

References

Abel, G. G., Mittelman, M. S., and Becker, J. V. (1985). Sexual offenders: Results of assessment and recommendations for treatment. In M. H. Ben-Aron, S. J. Hucker and C. D. Webster (eds), *Clinical Criminology: Current Concepts*. Toronto: M & M Graphics.

Ageton, S. S. (1984). *Sexual Assaults among Adolescents*. Lexington, MA: Lexington Books.

American Psychiatric Association (1980). *Diagnostic and Statistical Manual of Mental Disorders*. 3rd edn, Washington: American Psychiatric Association.

Anderson, C. L. (1985). Males as sexual assault victims: multiple levels of trauma. In Gonsiorek, J. C. (ed.), *A Guide to Psychotherapy with Gay and Lesbian Clients*. New York: Harrington Park Press.

Baker, A. W., and Duncan, S. P. (1985). Child sexual abuse: A study of prevalence in Great Britain. *Child Abuse and Neglect*, **9**, 457–67.

Barnard, G. W., Fuller, A. K., and Robbins, L. (1988). Child molesters. In J. G. Howells (ed.), *Modern Perspectives in Psychosocial Pathology*. New York: Brunner/Mazel.

Bell, A. P., Weinberg, M. S., and Hammersmith, S. K. (1981). *Sexual Preference: Its Development in Men and Women*. Bloomington: Indiana University Press.

Bell, S. (1988). *When Salem came to the Boro*. London: Pan Books.

Bliss, E. L. (1986). *Multiple Personality, Allied Disorders and Hypnosis*. New York: Oxford University Press.

Briere, J., Evans, D., Runtz, M., and Wall, T. (1988). Symptomatology in men who were molested as children: A comparison study. *American Journal of Orthopsychiatry*, **58**, 457–61.

Briere, J., and Runtz, M. (1988). Symptomatology associated with childhood sexual victimisation in a non-clinical adult sample. *Child Sex Abuse and Neglect*, **12**, 51–9.

Browne, A., and Finkelhor, D. (1986). Impact of child sexual abuse: A review of the research. *Psychological Bulletin*, **99**, 16–77.

Burgess, A. W., and Holmstron, L. L. (1974). Rape trauma syndrome. *American Journal of Psychiatry*, **131**, 981–6.

Burgess, A. W., and Holmstron, L. L. (1979). *Rape: Crisis and Recovery*. Bowie, MD: Brady.

Burgess, A.W., and Holmstrom, L. L. (1985). Rape trauma syndrome and post traumatic stress response. In A. W. Burgess (ed.), *Rape and Sexual Assault*. New York: Garland.

Burnett, R., Templer, D., and Barker, P. (1985). Personality variables and circumstances of sexual assault predictive of a woman's resistance. *Archives of Sexual Behavior*, **14**, 183–8.

Burt, M. R., and Katz, B. L. (1985). Rape, robbery and burglary: Responses to actual and feared criminal victimisation, with special focus on women and the elderly. *Victimology*, **10**, 325–58.

Burt, M. R., and Katz, B. L. (1987). Dimensions of recovery from rape. *Journal of Interpersonal Violence*, **2**, 57–81.

Butler-Sloss, Lord Justice Elizabeth (1988). *Report of the Inquiry into Child Abuse in Cleveland*. London: HMSO.

Carter, D. L., Prentky, R. A., and Burgess, A. W. (1988). Victim response strategies in sexual assault. In A. W. Burgess (ed.), *Rape and Sexual Assault*. New York: Garland.

Cavaiola, A. A., and Schiff, M. (1988). Behavioral sequelae of physical and/or sexual abuse in adolescents. *Child Abuse and Neglect*, **12**, 181–8.

Chambers, G., and Millar, A. (1983). *Investigating Sexual Assault*. A Scottish Office Social Research Study. Edinburgh: HMSO.

Conte, J. R., and Schuerman, J. R. (1988). The effects of sexual abuse on children. A multidimensional view. In G. E. Wyatt and G. J. Powell (eds), *Lasting Effects of Child Sexual Abuse*. Beverly Hills, CA: Sage.

Coombs, N. R. (1974). Male prostitutes: A psychosocial view of behavior. *American Journal of Orthopsychiatry*, **44**, 782–4.

Davis, L. J., and Brody, E. M. (1979). *Rape and Older Women*. Rockville, MD: National Institute of Mental Health.

Dell, S. (1984). *Murder into Manslaughter*. Oxford: Oxford University Press.

Dimock, P. T. (1988). Adult males sexually abused as children. *Journal of Interpersonal Violence*, **3**, 203–21.

Dixon, K. N., Arnold, L. E., and Calestro, K. (1978). Father-son incest: Underreported psychiatric problem? *American Journal of Psychiatry*, **135**, 835–8.

Ellis, E. M. (1983). A review of empirical rape research. Victim reactions and response to treatment. *Clinical Psychology Review*, **3**, 473–90.

Ennew, J. (1986). *The Sexual Exploitation of Children*. Cambridge: Polity Press.

Figley, C. R. (ed.) (1985). *Trauma and its Wake: The Study and Treatment of Post-Traumatic Stress Disorder*. New York: Brunner/Mazel.

Finkelhor, D. (1979). *Sexually Victimised Children*. New York: Free Press.

Finkelhor, D. (1984). *Child Sexual Abuse. New Theory and Research*. New York: Free Press.

Finkelhor, D., Araji, S., Baron, L., Browne, A., Peters, S. D., and Wyatt, G. E. (1986). *A Sourcebook on Child Sexual Abuse*. Beverly Hills, CA: Sage.

Finkelhor, D. (1988). The trauma of child sexual abuse. In G. E. Wyatt and G. J. Powell (eds), *Lasting Effects of Child Sexual Abuse*. Beverly Hills, CA: Sage.

Finkelhor, D., and Browne, A. (1984). Initial and long term effects: A conceptual framework. In D. Finkelhor (ed.), *A Sourcebook on Child Sexual Abuse*. Beverly Hills, CA: Sage.

Finkelhor, D., and Russell, D. (1984). Women as perpetrators. Review of the evidence. In D. Finkelhor (ed.), *Child Sexual Abuse. New Theory and Research*, New York: Free Press.

Foley, T. S. (1985). Family and legal response to the victim. In A. W. Burgess (ed.), *Rape and Sexual Assault: A Research Handbook*. New York: Garland.

Forman, B. D. (1982). Reported male rape. *Victimology*, **7**, 235–6.

Freeman-Longo, R. E. (1986). The impact of sexual victimisation on males. *Child Abuse and Neglect*, **10**, 411–14.

Friedrich, W. N., Beilke, R. L., and Urquiza, A. J. (1988). Behavior problems in young sexually abused boys. *Journal of Interpersonal Violence*, **3**, 21–8.

Gomes-Schwartz, B., Horowitz, J., and Sauzier, M. (1985). Severity of emotional distress among sexually abused preschool, school-age and adolescent children. *Hospital and Community Psychiatry*, **36**, 503–8.

Goodchilds, J. D., Zellman, G. L., Johnson, P. B., and Giarrusso, R. (1988). Adolescents and their perceptions of sexual interactions. In A. W. Burgess (ed.), *Rape and Sexual Assault*. New York: Garland.

Goodwin, J., McCarthy, T., and DiVasto, P. (1982). In J. Goodwin (ed.), *Sexual Abuse: Incest Victims and their Families*. Boston, Mass.: J. Wright.

Goyer, P. F., and Eddleman, H. C. (1984). Same sex rape of non-incarcerated men. *American Journal of Psychiatry*, **141**, 576–9.

Groth, A. N. (1979a). *Men Who Rape: The Psychology of the Offender*. New York: Plenum.

Groth, A. N. (1979b). Sexual trauma in the life histories of rapists and child molesters. *Victimology*, **4**, 10–16.

Groth, A. N., and Burgess, A. W. (1980). Male rape: Offenders and victims. *American Journal of Psychiatry*, **137**, 806–10.

Henderson, J. (1983). Is incest harmful? *Canadian Journal of Psychiatry*, **28**, 34–9.

Herman, J., and van der Kolk, B. (1987). Traumatic antecedents of borderline personality disorder. In B. van der Kolk (ed.), *Psychological Trauma*. Washington, DC: American Psychiatric Press.

Hibbard, R. A., Brack, C. J., Rauch, S., and Orr, D. P. (1988). Abuse, feelings, and health behaviors in a student population. *American Journal of Diseases of Children*, **142**, 326–30.

Hobbs, C. J., and Wynne, J. M. (1986). Buggery in childhood—a common syndrome of child abuse. *Lancet*, 4 Oct., 792–5.

Hough, M., and Mayhew, P. (1983). *The British Crime Survey*. Home Office Research Study No. 76. London: HMSO.

James, J., and Meyerding, J. (1977). Early sexual experience as a factor in prostitution. *Archives of Sexual Behavior*, **17**, 31–42.

Janus, M. D., McCormack, A., Burgess, A. W., and Hartman, C. (1987). *Adolescent Runaways. Causes and Consequences*. Lexington, MA: Lexington Books.

Johnson, T. C. (1988). Child perpetrators—Children who molest other children: Preliminary findings. *Child Abuse and Neglect*, **12**, 219–29.

Kaufman, A., DiVasto, P., Jackson, R., Voorhees, D., and Christy, J. (1980). Male rape victims: Non-institutionalised sexual assault. *American Journal of Psychiatry*, **137**, 221–3.

Koss, M. P., Gidycz, C. A., and Wisniewski, N. (1988). The scope of rape: Incidence and prevalence of sexual aggression and victimization in a national sample of higher educational students. *Journal of Consulting and Clinical Psychology*, **55**, 162–70.

Leith, A., and Handforth, S. (1988). Groupwork with sexually abused boys. *Practice*, **2**, 166–75.

Lindberg, F., and Distad, L. (1985). Post-traumatic stress disorders in women who experienced childhood incest. *Child Abuse and Neglect*, **9**, 329–34.

Lockwood, D. (1980). *Prison Sexual Violence*. New York: Elsevier.

MacVicar, K. (1979). Psycotherapy of sexually abused girls. *Journal of the American Academy of Child Psychiatry*, **18**, 342–53.

McCormack, A., Janus, M. D., and Burgess, A. W. (1986). Runaway youths and sexual victimisation: Gender differences in an adolescent runaway population. *Child Abuse and Neglect*, **10**, 387–95.

McMullen, R. J. (1987). Youth prostitution: A balance of power. *Journal of Adolescence*, **10**, 57–69.

Mezey, G., and King, M. (1987). Male victims of sexual assault. *Medicine, Science and the Law*, **27**, 122–4.

Miller, W. R., Williams, A. M., and Bernstein, M. H. (1982). The effects of rape on marital and sexual adjustment. *American Journal of Family Therapy*, **10**, 51–8.

Murphy, S. M., Amick-McMullen, A. E., Kilpatrick, D. G., Haskett, M. E., Veronen, L. J., Best, C. L., and Saunders, B. E. (1988). Rape victims' self-esteem. A longitudinal analysis. *Journal of Interpersonal Violence*, **3**, 355–70.

Nash, C. L., and West, D. J. (1985). Sexual molestation of young girls. In D. J. West (ed.), *Sexual Victimisation*. Aldershot: Gower.

Peters, S. D., Wyatt, G. E., and Finkelhor, D. (1986). Prevalence. In D. Finkelhor (ed.), *A Sourcebook on Child Sexual Abuse*. Beverly Hills, CA: Sage.

Petrovich, M., and Templer, D. I. (1984). Heterosexual molestation of children who later become rapists. *Psychological Reports*, **54**, 810.

Porter, E. (1986). *Treating the Young Male Victim of Sexual Assault*. Syracuse, NY: Safer Society Press.

Reinhart, M. A. (1987). Sexually abused boys. *Child Abuse and Neglect*, **11**, 229–35.

Resick, P. (1986). Assessment of fear reactions in sexual assault victims: A factor analytic study of the Veronen–Kirkpatrick Modified Fear Survey. *Behavioral Assessment*, **8**, 271–83.

Rimsza, M. E., and Berg, R. A. (1988). Sexual abuse: Somatic and emotional reactions. *Child Abuse and Neglect*, **12**, 201–8.

Risin, L. I., and Koss, M. P. (1987). The sexual abuse of boys: Prevalence and descriptive characteristics of childhood victimisations. *Journal of Interpersonal Violence*, **2**, 309–23.

Rogers, C. M., and Terry, T. (1984). Clinical interventions with boy victims of sexual abuse. In I. Stewart and J. Greer (eds), *Victims of Sexual Aggression*. New York: Van Nostrand Reinhold.

Root, M. P. P., and Fallon, P. (1988). The incidence of victimisation experiences in a bulimic sample. *Journal of Interpersonal Violence*, **3**, 161–73.

Russell, D. E. H. (1984). *Sexual Exploitation*. Beverly Hills, CA: Sage.

Sagarin, E. (1976). Prison homosexuality and its effect on post-prison sexual behaviour. *Psychiatry*, **39**, 245–57.

Sagarin, E., and MacNamara, D. E. (1975). The homosexual as a crime victim. *International Journal of Criminology and Penology*, **3**, 13–25.

Sales, E., Baum, M., and Shore, B. (1984). Victim readjustment following assault. *Journal of Social Issues*, **40**, 117–36.

Sandfort, T. (1987). *Boys on their Contacts with Men*. Elmshurst, NY: Global Academic.

Scacco, A. M. (1975). *Rape in Prison*. Springfield, IL: C. C. Thomas.

Scacco, A. M. (ed.) (1982). *Male Rape, A Casebook of Sexual Aggressions*. New York: AMS Press.

Schetky, D. H. (1988). Child pornography and prostitution. In D. H. Schetky and A. H. Green (eds), *Child Sexual Abuse*. New York: Brunner/Mazel.

Silbert, M., and Pines, A. (1981). Sexual child abuse as an antecedent to prostitution. *Child Abuse and Neglect*, **5**, 407–11.

Tsai, M., Feldman-Summers, S., and Edgar, M. (1979). Childhood molestation: Variables related to differential impacts on psychosexual functioning in adult women. *Journal of Abnormal Psychology*, **88**, 407–17.

Walmsley, R., and White, K. (1980). *Sexual Offences, Consent and Sentencing*. Home Office Research Study, 54. London: HMSO.

Warr, M. (1985). Fear of rape among urban women. *Social Problems*, **32**, 238–50.

Weiss, C., and Friar, D. J. (1974). *Terror in the Prisons: Homosexual Rape and Why Society Condones It*. New York: Bobbs-Merrill.

West, D. J., and Woodhouse, T. P. (1990). Sexual encounters between boys and adults. In C. K. Li, D. J. West and T. P. Woodhouse (eds), *Children's Sexual Encounters with Adults*. London: Duckworth.

Wilbur, C. (1984). Multiple personality and child abuse: An overview. *Psychiatric Clinics of North America*, **7**, 3–7.

Wild, N. J. (1988). Suicide of perpetrators after disclosure of child sexual abuse. *Child Abuse and Neglect*, **12**, 119–21.

Williams, J. E., and Holmes, K. A. (1981). *The Second Assault: Rape and Public Attitudes*. Westport, CT: Greenwood Press.

Wooden, W. S., and Parker, J. (1982). *Men Behind Bars: Sexual Exploitation in Prisons*. New York: Da Capo.

Wright, R. (1980). Rape and physical violence. In D. J. West (ed.), *Sexual Offenders in the Criminal Justice System*. Cambridge: University Institute of Criminology.

Wyatt, G. E. (1985). The sexual abuse of Afro-American and White-American women in childhood. *Child Abuse and Neglect*, **9**, 507–19.

Wyatt, G. E., and Peters, S. D. (1986). Issues in the definition of child sexual abuse in prevalence research. *Child Abuse and Neglect*, **10**, 231–40.

Yates, A. (1982). Children eroticized by incest. *American Journal of Psychiatry*, **139**, 482–5.

Part 2
Assessment

4

Assessment of Adult Sexual Interest

WILLIAM D. MURPHY

MARY R. HAYNES

and

PATRICIA J. WORLEY
Health Science Center, University of Tennessee, USA

INTRODUCTION

Our understanding of sex offenders has in the past been hampered by two interrelated issues. The first has been a lack of theories specific to the etiology and maintenance of deviant sexual behavior (see Chapter 2). The second, because of a lack of sex offender specific theories, has been a limited number of assessment devices developed specifically for this population. However, over the last 20 years, we have seen changes in this situation. One theoretical notion that has led to specific assessment and treatment procedures is that deviant sexual arousal or deviant sexual interest plays a role in sex offenses. The purpose of this chapter will be to review both the theoretical rationale for assessment of sexual interest in sex offenders, the methods and procedures available for such assessment, and the research literature that currently supports the use of such procedures clinically.

Although this chapter is limited to the discussion of adult sexual interest, it is recognized that this is not the only domain of functioning that needs to be addressed in a comprehensive assessment of sexual offenders. Factors such as social competence, cognitive distortions, and attitudes toward women and aggression (Finkelhor, 1984; Murphy and Stalgaitis, 1987) may all play a role in the development and maintenance of offending behavior. These will be addressed in various ways in other chapters in this book.

Clinical Approaches to Sex Offenders and Their Victims
Edited by C. R. Hollin and K. Howells © 1991 John Wiley & Sons Ltd

THEORETICAL RATIONALE

The question of whether sex offenses are sexually motivated is one that continues to be debated among professionals. Historically, thinking regarding sexual offenders was heavily influenced by psychoanalytic concepts where the paraphilic behavior was seen as only a symptom of underlying, unconscious mechanisms such as castration anxiety or a failure to resolve the Oedipal complex (Hammer and Glueck, 1957; Karpman, 1954).

Psychoanalytic theorizing is less prominent in the sex offender area currently. However, a second major argument for sexual abuse being nonsexually motivated has come from the women's movement, which deserves a great deal of credit for bringing the significance of the problem of sexual aggression to the attention of the public and the mental health professional. Feminists have proposed that sexual offenses are crimes of aggression not of sexuality (Albin, 1977; Brownmiller, 1975). Rape and child molestation are viewed as the results of socialization and as such they represent extremes of generally accepted attitudes and standards, such as male dominance, traditional sex roles, and the view of females as sex objects.

This nonsexual motivation for sexual offenses has been integrated into clinical theories and typologies of sexual offenders, with probably the most dominant influence being Groth and his associates (Groth, 1979; Groth and Birnbaum, 1978). The Groth typology of rapists (the power, the anger, the sadistic rapist) and classification of pedophiles (fixated and regressed), has an underlying theme that sexuality is used in the service of some other psychological need. There is also some support for the role of various attitudinal factors such as rape myth acceptance, sex role stereotyping, and adversarial sexual beliefs, in predicting coercive sexual behavior in nonclinical samples (for reviews see Murphy *et al.*, 1986; Malamuth, 1984). However, most of these studies have used college student samples and the generalization of these data to sex offenders is unknown. In addition the variance accounted for by these types of variables, although being significant, is relatively small.

From the standpoint of the victim, redefining sexual offenses as aggressive rather than sexual has had a number of positive outcomes. The most obvious of these is that the woman's or child's behavior either before or during the sexual offense has been removed as an issue in legal proceedings. That is, it removes the placing of blame on the child or woman for the sexual offense. This is highly appropriate and no one can argue that victims should be blamed for the behavior of the offender. However, there are a number of arguments against totally removing sexual interest or sexual arousal as at least one of the factors motivating the offender's behavior. Palmer (1988) has critically reviewed the arguments against sexual motivation for rape, finding that the literature does not support a total absence of sexual motivations. Finkelhor (1984) also takes a more moderate approach, pointing out that most sexual behavior involves some nonsexual motivations. As Finkelhor cogently argues:

Even the most innocuous and socially conventional coupling behavior between a husband and wife is heavily motivated by nonsexual needs—needs for affection, needs for confirmation of masculinity or femininity, needs for assertion of allegiance and so on. Sex is always in the service of other needs. Just because it has been infused with nonsexual motives does not make child sexual abuse different from other kinds of behaviors we readily call 'sexual'. (p. 34)

The strongest voice for the role of sexual interest or sexual arousal in sexual offenses, and therefore the development of methods for assessing sexual interest, has come from behaviorally oriented clinicians and researchers. The major tenet of this approach is that deviant sexual behavior is learned in the same way as nondeviant sexual behavior and the same laws of conditioning apply (Howells, 1981; Laws and Marshall, 1990). Early accounts focused on the pairing of deviant sexual stimuli with masturbatory fantasies (McGuire et al., 1965), and laboratory classical conditioning studies (Beech et al., 1971; Langevin and Martin, 1975; Rachman, 1966; Rachman and Hodgson, 1968) or operant conditioning procedures (Quinn et al., 1970). However, it should be noted that these laboratory analog studies have not always been replicated (Herman et al., 1974; Marshall, 1974). Howells (1981) has also proposed the role of various social learning influences, such as modeling, and the development of appropriate heterosexual skills in both the development of deviant sexual interest and the maintenance of such behavior.

Laws and Marshall (1990) present a comprehensive and updated theory of the etiology and maintenance of deviant sexual interest. Not only do they propose the role of traditional learning concepts such as operant and classical conditioning, extinction, differential reinforcement and punishment, and stimulus generalization, they also introduce other important concepts. These include Seligman's (1970) theory on preparedness and Bandura's social learning theory (Bandura, 1977), including the role modeling plays in the development of deviant arousal, and the role of self-attribution in the development of deviant sexual interest. The advantage of the Laws and Marshall (1990) proposal is that it incorporates a variety of learning processes, details interactions between learning experiences, and presents these in terms of a series of testable hypotheses.

PHYSIOLOGICAL ASSESSMENT

Since Zuckerman's (1972) seminal review, which suggested that the direct assessment of penile tumescence was the most sensitive indicator of male sexual arousal, a number of studies have appeared applying this technique to sex offender populations. Because the majority of studies have focused on offenders against children and rapists of adult women, this will be the major focus of this section. We will attempt to review the general clinical use of psychophysiological assessment of sexual arousal, review supporting research, and review limitations of the use of the procedure. For more in-depth details of basic laboratory procedures, the reader is referred to Laws and Osborne (1983) and for more details of the research literature to Murphy and Barbaree (1988).

General Clinical Procedures

Assessment of sexual arousal in the laboratory setting requires a sensor or transducer to measure changes in penis size, a recording system, and some type of sexual stimuli. In the general procedure, subjects are seated in a comfortable chair and asked to attach the transducer in the privacy of the laboratory. Equipment and clinician or technician are usually in a separate room with clinician in verbal but not visual contact with the subject. Recording systems vary from multi-use physiographs, generally referred to as polygraphs, with erection responses recorded continuously on chart paper, to portable units designed specifically for recording erection responses to simple digital monitors.

The three most frequently used transducers to measure erection responses are the mercury and rubber circumferential strain gauge (Bancroft et al., 1966; Fisher et al., 1965), the metal band circumferential strain gauge (Barlow et al., 1970; Laws and Bow, 1976), and the volumetric device (Freund et al., 1965; McConaghy, 1974). The two circumferential devices measure only changes in the circumference of the penis while the volumetric device, which is composed of a glass cylinder enclosing the penis, measures total change in penile volume by measuring air displaced by penile change. Comparisons of the mercury and rubber gauge to the volumetric device (McConaghy, 1974) and the metal band strain gauge to the volumetric device (Freund et al., 1974) suggest that the volumetric device is more sensitive than either of the circumferential gauges. However, both these studies had limitations, with the McConaghy study being based on only four subjects; and in the Freund et al. (1974) study, 34 of the 48 subjects were excluded because of equipment failure. A more recent study (Wheeler and Rubin, 1987) failed to support this finding, showing little difference between the two devices, but reporting that the volumetric device was more sensitive to movement artifact. Laws (1977) found little differences between the recording characteristics of the two circumferential devices.

Users should be aware, however, that during early stages of the erection response, the volumetric device can produce responses opposite to that of the circumferential device. This occurs in situations where penis length increases while penile circumference either remains constant or decreases. Since the volumetric device measures total penile volume, it will show an increase in the erection response while circumferential devices may show a decrease in circumference. Because of the ease of use of the circumferential devices, their commercial availability, and the few differences found between circumferential and volumetric devices, the circumferential devices are more than adequate for most clinical and research situations.

The stimulus material most frequently reported in the literature has generally been of three types: videotapes, slide material, and audiotaped sexual scripts. Slide material has been used extensively to assess age preference and sexual preference among child molesters and audiotapes have been used more frequently to assess aggressive interactions in child molesters (Abel et al., 1981; Avery-Clark and Laws, 1984) and rapists (Abel et al., 1978). Clinical examples for patients recently assessed in our laboratory are presented in Figures 4.1

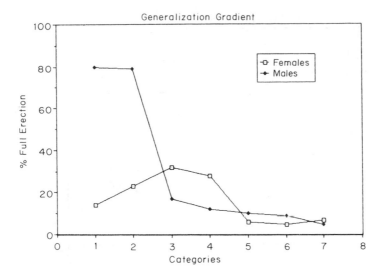

Figure 4.1   Sexual responding of a subject to male and female slides of various ages. Categories: 1 = 5 years old; 2 = 9 years old; 3 = 12 years old; 4 = 15 years old; 5 = 18 years old; 6 = 25 years old; 7= 35 years old

through 4.3. Figures 4.1 and 4.2 represent data from a 39-year-old homosexual pedophile who self reported an attraction to young boys since childhood and also reported that he had molested approximately 30 young boys. Figure 4.1 represents arousal to slides of males and females across varying ages while Figure 4.2 represents responses to two-minute audiotapes (Abel *et al.*, 1981) depicting sexual interactions between an adult male and 8- to 12-year-old boys

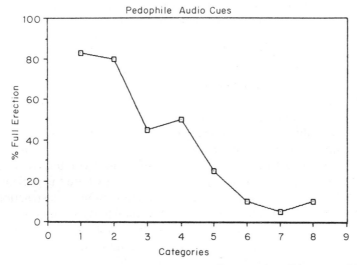

Figure 4.2   Sexual responding of a subject to audiotapes describing sexual interactions with children varying in level of aggression. Categories: 1 = Child Initiates; 2 = Child Mutual; 3 = Verbal Coercion; 4 = Physical Coercion; 5 = Sadism; 6 = Assault; 7 = Adult Female Mutual; 8 = Adult Male Mutual

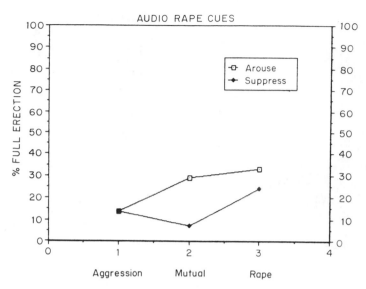

Figure 4.3   Sexual responding of a subject to rape cues under two instructional sets

varying in level of aggression. It can be seen that the patient showed his maximum arousal to boys in the 5- to 9-year-old age range, with more arousal shown
to nonaggressive stimuli than to aggressive stimuli, and almost no response to
any of the adult material of either sex.

   Although this patient's data are quite consistent with his history, Figure 4.3
represents an individual whose erection data were inconsistent with the initial
history. This patient was a 30-year-old male referred for the fondling of his
6-year-old niece on one occasion. The patient admitted this charge and assessment of sexual arousal indicated, as noted in Figure 4.3, that his maximum
response was to stimulus depictions of rape of adult women, with little arousal to
children noted on assessments similar to those depicted in Figures 4.1 and 4.2.
Later, during treatment, the patient admitted that he had raped his wife on a
number of occasions, had attempted to rape six other women, and had repeated
fantasies of raping.

   There are a number of other factors to be considered when using penile
tumescence procedures, either clinically or as a research tool. One such factor is
the type of instructional set used. In Figure 4.3, data are presented for two
instructional sets, one where the patient is asked not to interfere with his response (labeled arouse instructions), and a second set where the patient is asked
to try to control or suppress his response (labeled suppress instructions). This
allows the clinician or researcher to have some knowledge of the subject's ability
to control his responding. However, at the present time, there are few research
studies that document the meaning of responses under suppress instructions or
whether the responses under such instructions clearly give us a notion of the
patient's ability to fake responses.

   A second factor to be considered is the way such data are summarized and
interpreted. Since penile circumference varies widely from individual to individual,

there is a need to present information in a more standardized fashion. In Figures 4.1 through 4.3, data are presented as percent of full erection which is a method used in many clinical situations to standardize values across patients and across time. The full erection is usually established during the assessment procedure itself, based on the subject's self-report of full erection, or alternatively by measuring response to an explicit sexual videotape or having the subject self-stimulate himself to full erection. Using this method, most subjects can produce a full erection. Other methods include presenting data in terms of actual millimeters of circumference change, or converting data to z-scores based on the subject's responding to all the stimuli. For further details of the advantages and disadvantages of these various methods, the reader is referred to Earls et al. (1987). Clinically, how the data are interpreted is also of importance. In general, interpretation of whether a subject shows a deviant arousal pattern or not is based on contrasting responses of the subject to the deviant stimuli, i.e. to the molestation of a young child; and to the nondeviant stimuli, i.e. adult nonaggressive sexual interactions. This has led to the development of various indices which represent the ratio of deviant arousal to nondeviant arousal. For example, in Figure 4.3, the subject's rape index (arousal to rape divided by arousal to mutual) would be 1.13, suggesting more arousal to the rape material than to the mutual sexual interactions. There are few data available at this point to show whether the actual magnitude of the response is, in and of itself, a valid measure of the individual's sexual attraction pattern. For this reason, it is important in choosing or designing stimuli that one attempts to hold constant all confounding variables while only varying the component of interest. Thus, in developing materials to assess arousal to rape, it is important that the rape and mutual stimuli include the same sexual behaviors, the same environmental cues, and describe women of similar physical appearance; while varying only the degree of force by the male and/or the consent of the woman. If the material is not constructed in this fashion, then the data become much harder to interpret.

A final issue to be considered is what amount of change in the erection response is considered a true response versus error. It has generally been accepted in the clinical situation that if all responses are less than 20% of a full erection, the assessment should not be given much weight. However, in the research situation, subjects may not be excluded for low arousal so that data are more generalizable. In general, there are few data surrounding this issue to guide decision making.

Research Support

Studies have been basically of two types, the majority contrasting either rapists or child molesters with normals or other types of offenders. Early studies by Freund (1965, 1967a, b) clearly indicated that pedophile subjects could be differentiated from nonpedophile subjects using tumescence measures. This has now been replicated numerous times in different laboratories (Abel et al., 1981; Barbaree and Marshall, 1989; Freund and Blanchard, 1989; Marshall et al., 1988; Marshall et al., 1986; Murphy et al., 1986; Quinsey et al., 1979; Quinsey et al.,

1975). In fact, only one study could be found that did not show this general pattern (Hall *et al.*, 1988). However, in that study, a number of the subjects had been in treatment prior to the assessment and the subjects appeared as a group to show extremely low levels of arousal.

The second type of study in the literature is that which investigates the relationship of erection responses to certain aspects of the history of offenders. Both Abel *et al.* (1981) and Avery-Clark and Laws (1984) were able to separate more aggressive sex offenders against children from offenders who did not use physical aggression in the offense. Furthermore, Marshall *et al.* (1986) found a correlation of 0.40 between the degree of force in the offense and an aggression index, and a correlation of 0.66 between the number of victims and a pedophile index (arousal to children divided by arousal to adults).

It is also clear in the literature that not all child molesters show a deviant arousal pattern. This was initially described when contrasting incestuous versus nonincestuous child molesters. Using slide material, Murphy *et al.* (1986), Marshall *et al.* (1986), and Quinsey *et al.* (1979) have all shown that incestuous offenders show less arousal to child stimuli than nonincestuous offenders. In both the Marshall *et al.* and the Quinsey *et al.* studies, there were no significant differences between incestuous offenders and normal controls. With audiotaped stimuli, however, the data are slightly more mixed. Abel *et al.* (1981) and Murphy *et al.* (1986) found no differences between incestuous and nonincestuous offenders (neither employed a normal control group) while Marshall *et al.* (1986) again found that incestuous cases differed significantly from nonincestuous cases and were not significantly different from normals. The weight of the evidence would seem to suggest that many incest cases do not have deviant arousal patterns, but some do, and this can only be determined through adequate assessment.

A recent innovative study (Barbaree and Marshall, 1989) adds further support to the notion that offenders against children are heterogeneous in terms of their sexual interest. Barbaree and Marshall had three judges independently sort individual plotted age preference profiles (similar to those in Figure 4.1) into five categories. They then developed a computerized program that would optimally separate the profiles into these five categories. The five profiles were: (i) adult profile, with maximum responding to adults; (ii) a teen adult profile showing responses to 13-year-olds and older; (iii) a nondiscriminating profile in which subjects showed moderate responding to all age groups; (iv) a child-adult profile where subjects responded maximally to females 18 years of age and older and to female children 11 years and younger; and (v) a child profile where maximum responding was to children 11 years of age and younger. Of the nonfamilial child molesters, 35% showed the classic child profile with the rest being equally divided among the other four profiles. Similar data have been presented by Marshall *et al.* (1987) for offenders against males. It is likely in the future that more studies will be patterned after Marshall, Barbaree, and their colleagues. It is fairly well-established that child molesters differ significantly from normals but that there is a great deal of variability in this group. Future research will need to focus on this variability and how it might relate to offense characteristics, etiology, treatment needs, and treatment outcome.

The research literature with rapists at this point is not as consistent as that for child molesters. Early studies were fairly consistent in separating rapists from nonrapists using erection measures (Abel *et al.*, 1977; Abel *et al.*, 1978; Barbaree *et al.*, 1979; Earls and Proulx, 1987; Hinton *et al.*, 1980; Quinsey and Chaplin, 1984; Quinsey *et al.*, 1984; Quinsey *et al.*, 1981). However, at this point, three studies have now appeared that failed to replicate these results (Baxter *et al.*, 1986; Langevin, 1983; Murphy *et al.*, 1984). The reasons for these differences are not known at the present time. Different studies have used different stimulus materials which may account for some of the variability. There might also be differences in the characteristics of samples which are not clearly discernible from the method section of these papers. However, it is clear that more research is needed in this area. Approaches similar to Marshall and Barbaree's in developing various profiles might assist in better understanding the heterogeneity in this population. Also, clearer descriptions of stimulus materials are needed to determine whether variability in stimulus material is impacting on differences between studies. Until further studies are completed, interpretation of erection responses with rapists of adult women will have to be made with caution.

Limitation of Erection Data

There is reasonable scientific evidence and theoretical rationale for the application of penile tumescence measures in certain situations. However, there is also ample evidence to show clearly that such measures are not infallible and responses can be faked (Abel *et al.*, 1975; Freund, 1963; Laws and Holmen, 1978; Laws and Rubin, 1969; Quinsey and Bergersen, 1976; Wydra *et al.*, 1983). Therefore, a subject's failure to respond in the laboratory should not be considered evidence that the subject does not have a deviant arousal pattern and positive responses should be given more weight than negative responses.

At the present time, based on the research data, erection responses are most appropriate for use in research and clinical practice to determine treatment needs and to monitor treatment results. That is, subjects with a deviant arousal pattern may need specific behavioral treatments to reduce such arousal. In addition, within the clinical situations, patients' responses to deviant sexual material may be used to confront subjects who are denying their offenses or denying a deviant arousal pattern (Abel, Cunningham-Rathner, Becker, and McHugh, 1983; Marshall *et al.*, 1986).

However, erection responses should not be used as the sole means of making parole, probation, or other release decisions since there are limited data to relate such measures to recidivism. Also, erection responses should not be used within a legal situation to determine whether someone has or has not committed a sexual offense or fits the profile of a sexual offense which has occurred—at least in the United States. No psychological test can determine whether someone has committed a specific act and, as the literature indicates, there is no one erection profile for offenders. In addition, the majority of the research literature reviewed has been with individuals where there is relatively clear evidence of their guilt.

There is little evidence that similar results would occur in population where guilt of an offense has not been established.

SELF-REPORT MEASURES

Although there are a number of self-report instruments for assessing a variety of aspects of sexual functioning (Conte, 1984), there are few methods specifically designed for assessing deviant sexual interest patterns. A number of investigators and clinicians using psychophysiological assessment of sexual arousal also ask subjects to self-report sexual arousal following stimulus presentations (Abel *et al.*, 1978). Abel *et al.* found mean correlations between self-report and penile tumescence measurements of 0.74 with individual subject correlations ranging from 0.25 to 0.97. However, across studies, there appear to be a wide range of correlation values presented (Wormith, 1985). We know of no studies that looked at self-report sexual attraction to specific stimuli independent of arousal measures.

Because of the limited data with self-report measures of sexual interest, this section will focus on the few methods reported in the literature that are specifically designed for use with sex offenders. It is recognized that any patient can deny on self-report measures and they may have limited use in patients who are nonadmitters. However, there are few comparative data to determine whether self-report measures are more or less reliable than psychophysiological assessment procedures with the nonadmitter population.

Probably the most frequently used assessment method for adult sexual interest, although rarely discussed as such, is the clinical interview. A detailed history regarding the frequency of various deviant and nondeviant behaviors, the number of victims or consenting sexual partners, and the frequencies and types of sexual fantasies employed by the patient can give valuable information regarding the patient's or research subject's sexual arousal pattern. Of particular value in determining sexual interest may be the type of fantasies used during masturbation. For example, Murphy (1985) reported that child molesters who molested either males outside the home, females outside the home, or daughters/ stepdaughters reported respectively that 74%, 38% and 3% of their sexual fantasies during masturbation were deviant. Also for these groups, the offenders against males averaged 37 victims,, the offenders against female outside the home 5 victims, and the incest cases 1 victim. The difference between the incest and nonincest cases and percent deviant fantasies were consistent with the psychophysiological assessment literature in that nonincest cases appear to have more set deviant attraction patterns to children as a group than the incest cases.

There are also a number of structured instruments that reportedly allow assessment of sexual attraction. One such procedure is the Abel and Becker card sort which has been recently revised by Laws *et al.* (1988). The card sort consists of a series of brief descriptions rated on a 7-point scale (attractive to unattractive) of a variety of sexual behaviors. Included are scales for assessing pedophilia, rape, sadism, exhibitionism, voyeurism, and frottage. Laws *et al.*

found correlations ranging from 0.42 to 0.56 for self-ratings on the pedophilia scale of the card sort and physiological responses to the slides or audiotaped stimuli. It was also found that physiological responses to slide stimuli classified 43 of 48 pedophilic subjects' responses to audiotapes correctly, while the card sort correctly classified 38 of 42 pedophilic subjects. However, approximately 33% to 45% of the sample had to be excluded on the different measures for a variety of reasons. What these results do seem to suggest is that the card sort is as effective as psychophysiological procedures at classifying pedophilic subjects who are admitters. The effectiveness of the procedure with other diagnostic categories or other sexual interest patterns is unknown currently.

There are two other instruments, the Multiphasic Sex Inventory (Nichols and Molinder, 1984) and the Clarke Sexual History Questionnaire (Langevin *et al.*, 1983; Paitich *et al.*, 1977), that measure sexual interest mainly through sampling of specific sexual behaviors. The revised Clarke Sexual History Questionnaire (Langevin *et al.*, 1983) is a 225-item self-report questionnaire that covers a variety of deviant and nondeviant sexual behaviors. The scale was developed using Langevin's (1983) model of sexual behavior which involves both the concepts of orgasmic preference and the stimulus response matrix. Stimulus refers to the object of the sexual attraction, e.g. adult women, older men, immature children, etc., and response is the specific sexual behavior towards the stimulus (e.g. intercourse, exposing, digital penetration, etc.). The test samples a variety of nondeviant (adult heterosexual and adult homosexual) and deviant behaviors (pedophilia, hebephilia, voyeurism, exhibitionism, frottage, etc.). Also included are questions related to fantasies during masturbation, and questions related to whether the subject ever felt like or ever wanted to engage in a variety of sexual behaviors. The latter questions allow assessment of not only specific behaviours the patient has engaged in but also fantasies and urges they may have experienced. Normative data are provided for heterosexual controls and a variety of deviant samples (Russon, 1983). The test has good psychometric properties and a number of studies have now appeared to support the validity of this instrument (see Langevin *et al.*, 1983). The instrument appears to be a useful adjunct to psychophysiological assessment for both clinical and research purposes.

The Multiphasic Sex Inventory is a more recent instrument that samples not only a variety of deviant behaviors but also factors thought to be related to sex offenses, for example cognitive distortions, justifications, sexual knowledge, etc. Although the test includes scales for a variety of paraphilias, scales measuring child molestation and rape are the most well developed psychometrically. Little data are provided for scales tapping other paraphilias. Sample items for the child molest scales include such items as 'I have been attracted to boys sexually,' and 'I have reached orgasm while molesting a child.' Although the scales appear reliable, there are limited validity data associated with the scales. They do, however, appear to separate college students from known offenders. It should also be noted that this scale may be of limited use in looking at changes in sexual interest patterns following treatment. In fact, comparisons of treated and untreated offenders (Nichols and Molinder, 1984) found that scores on the child molest scale and rape scale increased following treatment. This finding is probably the result of the treated offenders' increased openness about their past behavior.

In summary, there is rather limited literature on self-report methods especially when compared to the more extensive data on psychophysiological methods. However, there are a number of methods that appear promising for use in both clinical and research situations. It is hoped that more validity data will begin to appear on a number of these instruments.

SUMMARY

We have attempted in this chapter to present a rationale for the assessment of adult sexual interest in sexual offenders and to provide some clinical methods along with supporting research for their use in addressing this aspect of functioning of sexual offenders. As with most areas of human behavior, more research is needed both in the area of developing methods for assessing sexual arousal and using such assessment procedures to understand better the etiology and development of deviant and nondeviant sexual interest. An example of such a use of sexual interest measures in Freund's (Freund and Blanchard, 1986; Freund, 1990) excellent work in using phallometric methods to investigate the theoretical notion of courtship disorders. Freund's studies clearly indicate a relationship between certain disorders, voyeurism, exhibitionism, toucherism, frottage, and rape. By understanding the relationship between these disorders, one may then be able to design studies that examine the etiology of this class of behaviours.

It is remarkable given the sensitivity of the subject being studied, human sexual interest, that there is as much consistency in the literature as there is. Although it is clear that our tools need to be refined, clinicians and researchers do have available to them some well-developed and promising methods for assessing sexual interest, at least in admitters.

References

Abel, G. G., Barlow, D. H., Blanchard, E. B. and Guild, D. (1977). The components of rapists' sexual arousal. *Archives of General Psychiatry*, **34**, 895–903.
Abel, G. G., Barlow, D. H., Blanchard, E. B. and Mavissakalian, M. (1975). Measurement of sexual arousal in male homosexuals: The effects of instructions and stimulus modality. *Archives of Sexual Behavior*, **4**, 623–9.
Abel, G. G., Becker, J. V., Murphy, W. D. and Flanagan, B. (1981). Identifying dangerous child molesters. In R. B. Stuart (ed.), *Violent Behavior: Social Learning Approaches to Prediction, Management, and Treatment.* New York: Brunner/Mazel, pp. 116–37.
Abel, G. G., Blanchard, E. B., Becker, J. V. and Djenderedjian, A. (1978). Differentiating sexual aggressives with penile measures. *Criminal Justice and Behavior*, **5**, 315–32.
Abel, G. G., Cunningham-Rathner, J., Becker, J. V. and McHugh, J. (1983, December). *Motivating sex offenders for treatment with feedback of their psychophysiologic assessment.* Paper presented at the World Congress of Behavior Therapy, Washington, DC.
Albin, R. S. (1977). Psychological studies of rape. *Signs: Journal of Women in Culture and Society*, **3**, 423–35.

Avery-Clark, C. A. and Laws, D. R. (1984). Differential erection response patterns of child sexual abusers to stimuli describing activities with children. *Behavior Therapy*, **15**, 71–83.

Bancroft, J., Jones, H. C. and Pullman, B. P. (1966). A simple transducer for measuring penile erections with comments on its use in the treatment of sexual disorders. *Behaviour Research and Therapy*, **4**, 239–41.

Bandura, A. (1977). *Social Learning Theory*. Englewood Cliffs, NJ: Prentice-Hall.

Barbaree, H. E. and Marshall, W. L. (1989). Erectile responses amongst heterosexual child molesters, father-daughter incest offenders and matched nonoffenders: Five distinct age preference profiles. *Canadian Journal of Behavioral Science*, **21**, 70–87.

Barbaree, H. E., Marshall, W. L. and Lanthier, R. D. (1979). Deviant sexual arousal in rapists. *Behaviour Research and Therapy*, **17**, 215–22.

Barlow, D. H., Becker, R., Leitenberg, H. and Agras, W. S. (1970). A mechanical strain gauge for recording penile circumference change. *Journal of Applied Behavior Analysis*, **3**, 73–6.

Baxter, D. J., Barbaree, H. E. and Marshall, W. L. (1986). Sexual responses to consenting and forced sex in a large sample of rapists and nonrapists. *Behaviour Research and Therapy*, **24**, 513–20.

Beech, H. R., Watts, F. and Poole, A. P. (1971). Classical conditioning of a sexual deviation: A preliminary note. *Behavior Therapy*, **2**, 400–2.

Brownmiller, S. (1975). *Against our Will: Men, Women, and Rape*. New York: Simon & Schuster.

Conte, H. R. (1984). Development and use of self-report techniques for assessing sexual functioning: A review and critique. *Archives of Sexual Behavior*, **12**, 555–76.

Earls, C. M. and Proulx, J. (1987). The differentiation of francophone rapists and nonrapists using penile circumferential measures. *Criminal Justice and Behavior*, **13**, 419–29.

Earls, C. M., Quinsey, V. L. and Castonguay, L. G. (1987). A comparison of scoring methods in the measurement of penile circumference change. *Archives of Sexual Behavior*, **6**, 493–500.

Finkelhor, D. (1984). *Child Sexual Abuse: New Theory and Research*. New York: Free Press.

Fisher, C., Gross, J. and Zuch, J. (1965). Cycle of penile erection synchronous with dreaming (REM) sleep. *Archives of General Psychiatry*, **12**, 24–45.

Freund, K. (1963). A laboratory method for diagnosing predominance of homo and hetero erotic interest in the male. *Behaviour Research and Therapy*, **1**, 85–93.

Freund, K. (1965). Diagnosing heterosexual pedophilia by means of a test for sexual interest. *Behaviour Research and Therapy*, **3**, 229–34.

Freund, K. (1967a). Diagnosing homo- or heterosexuality and erotic age-preference by means of a psychophysiological test. *Behaviour Research and Therapy*, **5**, 209–28.

Freund, K. (1967b). Erotic preference in pedophilia. *Behaviour Research and Therapy*, **5**, 339–48.

Freund, K. (1990). Courtship disorder. In W. L. Marshall, D. R. Laws and H. E. Barbaree (eds), *Handbook of Sexual Assault: Issues, Theories, and Treatment of the Offender*, pp. 195–208. New York: Plenum.

Freund, K. and Blanchard, R. (1986). The concept of courtship disorder. *Journal of Sex and Marital Therapy*, **12**, 79–92.

Freund, K. and Blanchard, R. (1989). Phallometric diagnosis of pedophilia. *Journal of Consulting and Clinical Psychology*, **57**, 100–105.

Freund, K., Langevin, R. and Barlow, D. (1974). Comparison of two penile measures of erotic arousal. *Behaviour Research and Therapy*, **12**, 355–9.

Freund, K., Sedlack, J. and Knob, K. (1965). A simple transducer for mechanical plethysmography of the male genital. *Journal of the Experimental Analysis of Behavior*, **8**, 169–70.

Groth, A. N. (1979). *Men who Rape: The Psychology of the Offender*. New York: Plenum.

Groth, A. N. and Birnbaum, H. J. (1978). Adult sexual orientation and attraction to underage persons. *Archives of Sexual Behavior*, **7**, 175–81.

Hall, G. C. N., Proctor, W. C. and Nelson, G. M. (1988). Validity of physiological measures of pedophilic sexual arousal in a sexual offender population. *Journal of Consulting and Clinical Psychology*, **56**, 118–22.

Hammer, R. F. and Glueck, B. C. Jr. (1957). Psychodynamic patterns in sex offenders: A four factor theory. *Psychiatric Quarterly*, **31**, 325–45.

Herman, S. H., Barlow, D. H. and Agras,W. S. (1974). An experimental analysis of classical conditioning as a method of increasing heterosexual arousal in homosexuals. *Behavior Therapy*, **5**, 33–47.

Hinton, J. W., O'Neill, M. T. and Webster, A. (1980). Psychophysiological assessment of sex offenders in a security hospital. *Archives of Sexual Behavior*, **9**, 205–16.

Howells, K. (1981). Adult sexual interest in children: Considerations relevant to theories of etiology. In M. Cook and K. Howells (eds), *Adult Sexual Interest in Children*. London: Academic, pp. 55–94.

Karpman, B. (1954). *The Sexual Offender and his Offenses: Etiology, Pathology, Psychodynamics and Treatment*. New York: Julian.

Langevin, R. (1983). *Sexual Strands: Understanding and Treating Sexual Anomalies in Men*. Hillsdale, NJ: Lawrence Erlbaum.

Langevin, R., Handy, L., Paitich, D., and Russon, A. (1983). A new version of the Clarke Sex History Questionnaire for Males. In R. Langevin (ed.), *Erotic Preference, Gender Identity and Aggression*. Hillsdale, NJ: Lawrence Erlbaum, pp. 287–305.

Langevin, R. and Martin, M. (1975). Can erotic responses be classically conditioned? *Behavior Therapy*, **6**, 350–5.

Laws, D. R. (1977). A comparison of the measurement characteristics of two circumferential penile transducers. *Archives of Sexual Behavior*, **6**, 45–51.

Laws, D. R. and Bow, R. A. (1976). Instrumentation: An improved mechanical strain gauge for recording penile circumference change. *Psychophysiology*, **13**, 596–9.

Laws, D. R. and Holmen, M. L. (1978). Sexual response faking by pedophiles. *Criminal Justice and Behavior*, **5**, 343–56.

Laws, D. R. and Marshall, W. L. (1990). A conditioning theory of the etiology and maintenance of deviant sexual preference and behavior. In W. L. Marshall, D. R. Laws and H. E. Barbaree (eds), *Handbook of Sexual Assault: Issues, Theories, and Treatment of the Offender*, pp. 209–30. New York: Plenum.

Laws, D. R. and Osborne, C. A. (1983). How to build and operate a behavioral laboratory to evaluate and treat sexual deviance. In J. G. Greer and I. R. Stuart (eds), *The Sexual Aggressor: Current Perspectives on Treatment*. New York: Van Nostrand Reinhold, pp. 293–335.

Laws, D. R., Osborne, C. A., Greenbaum, P. E. and Murrin, M. R. (1988, December). *Classification of sex offenders by physiological assessment of sexual arousal and a self-report measure of sexual preference*. Poster presented at the meeting of the Association for the Advancement of Behavior Therapy, New York City.

Laws, D. R. and Rubin, H. B. (1969). Instructional control of an autonomic response. *Journal of Applied Behavior Analysis*, **2**, 93–9.

Malamuth, N. M. (1984). Aggression against women: Cultural and individual causes. In N. M. Malamuth and E. Donnerstein (eds), *Pornography and Sexual Aggression*. Orlando, FL: Academic, pp. 19–52.

Marshall, W. L. (1974). The classical conditioning of sexual attractiveness: A report of four therapeutic failures. *Behavior Therapy*, **5**, 298–9.

Marshall, W. L., Barbaree, H. E. and Butt, J. (1988). Sexual offenders against children: Sexual preference for gender, age of victim and type of behavior. *Behavior Research and Therapy*, **26**, 383–91.

Marshall, W. L., Barbaree, H. E. and Christophe, D. (1986). Sexual offenders against children: Sexual preferences for age of victims and type of behaviour. *Canadian Journal of Behavioural Science*, **18**, 424–39.

McConaghy, N. (1974). Measurements of change in penile dimensions. *Archives of Sexual Behavior*, **3**, 381–8.

McGuire, R. J., Carlisle, J. M. and Young, B. G. (1965). Sexual deviations as conditioned behavior. *Behaviour Research and Therapy*, **2**, 185–90.

Murphy, W. D. (1985, September). *An overview of sex offenders against children* and *The clinical evaluation and treatment of sex offenders against children*. Workshops presented at the Training Conference on Child Sexual Abuse Evaluation and Treatment, Huntsville, AL.

Murphy, W. D. and Barbaree, H. E. (1988). *Assessments of sexual offenders by measures of erectile response: Psychometric properties and decision making* (Monograph Order No. 86M0506500501D). Rockville, MD: National Institute of Health.

Murphy, W. D., Coleman, E. M. and Haynes, M. R. (1986). Factors related to coercive sexual behavior in a nonclinical sample of males. *Violence and Victims*, **1**, 255–78.

Murphy, W. D., Haynes, M. R., Stalgaitis, S. J. and Flanagan, B. (1986). Differential sexual responding among four groups of sexual offenders against children. *Journal of Psychopathology and Behavioral Assessment*, **8**, 339–53.

Murphy, W. D., Krisak, J., Stalgaitis, S. and Anderson, K. (1984). The use of penile tumescence measures with incarcerated rapists: Further validity issues. *Archives of Sexual Behavior*, **13**, 545–54.

Murphy, W. D. and Stalgaitis, S. J. (1987). Assessment and treatment considerations for sexual offenders against children: Behavioral and social learning approaches. In J. R. McNamara and M. A. Appel (eds), *Critical Issues, Developments, and Trends in Professional Psychology*, vol. 3. New York: Praeger, pp. 177–210.

Nichols, H. R. and Molinder, I. (1984). *Multiphasic Sex Inventory*. Tacoma, WA.

Paitich, D., Langevin, R., Freeman, R., Mann, K. and Handy, L. (1977). The Clarke SHQ: A clinical sex history questionnaire for males. *Archives of Sexual Behavior*, **6**, 421–36.

Palmer, C. T. (1988). Twelve reasons why rape is not sexually motivated: A skeptical examination. *The Journal of Sex Research*, **25**, 512–30.

Quinn, J. L., Harbison, J. and McAllister, H. (1970). An attempt to shape human penile responses. *Behaviour Research and Therapy*, **8**, 27–8.

Quinsey, V. L. and Bergersen, S. G. (1976). Instructional control of penile circumference in assessments of sexual preference. *Behavior Therapy*, **7**, 489–93.

Quinsey, V. L. and Chaplin, T. C. (1984). Stimulus control of rapists' and non-sex offenders' sexual arousal. *Behavioral Assessment*, **6**, 169–76.

Quinsey, V. L., Chaplin, T. C. and Carrigan, W. F. (1979). Sexual preferences among incestuous and nonincestuous child molesters. *Behavior Therapy*, **10**, 562–5.

Quinsey, V. L., Chaplin, T. C. and Upfold, D. (1984). Sexual arousal to nonsexual violence and sadomasochistic themes among rapists and non-sex offenders. *Journal of Consulting and Clinical Psychology*, **52**, 651–7.

Quinsey, V. L., Chaplin, T. C. and Varney, G. (1981). A comparison of rapists' and non-sex offenders' sexual preferences for mutually consenting sex, rape, and physical abuse of women. *Behavioral Assessment*, **3**, 127–35.

Quinsey, V. L., Steinman, C. M., Bergersen, S. G. and Holmes, T. F. (1975). Penile circumference, skin conductance, and ranking responses of child molesters and 'normals' to sexual and nonsexual visual stimuli. *Behavior Therapy*, **6**, 213–19.

Rachman, S. (1966). Sexual fetishism: An experimental analogue. *Psychological Record*, **16**, 293–6.

Rachman, S. and Hodgson, R. J. (1968). Experimentally induced 'sexual fetishism': Replication and development. *Psychological Record*, **18**, 25–7.

Russon, A. E. (1983). Sex history questionnaires scoring manual. In R. Langevin (ed.), *Erotic Preference, Gender Identity and Aggression*. Hillsdale, NJ: Lawrence Erlbaum, pp. 307–28.

Seligman, M. E. P. (1970). On the generality of the laws of learning. *Psychological Review*, **77**, 406–18.

Wheeler, D. and Rubin, H. B. (1987). A comparison of volumetric and circumferential measures of penile erection. *Archives of Sexual Behavior*, **16**, 289–99.
Wormith, J. S. (1985). *Some physiological and cognitive aspects of assessing deviant sexual arousal.* (Report No. 1985–26.) Ottawa: Ministry of the Solicitor General of Canada.
Wydra, A., Marshall, W. L., Earls, C.M. and Barbaree, H. E. (1983). Identification of cases and control of sexual arousal by rapists. *Behavior Research and Therapy*, **21**, 469–76.
Zuckerman, M. (1972). Physiological measures of sexual arousal in the human. In N. S. Greenfield and R.A. Sternback (eds), *Handbook of Psychophysiology*. New York: Holt, Rinehart & Winston, pp. 709–40.

5

Research on Children's Testimony: Implications for Interviewing Practice

GRAHAM DAVIES
Department of Psychology, University of Leicester, UK

In 1983, Judy Johnson, a Los Angeles housewife with a history of mental problems, began to make a series of complaints to the police alleging that her 2 year old son had been sexually abused. Her initial allegations centred on a US marine who was also supposed to have sexually assaulted her dog. Later, however, her complaints focused on Ray Buckey, 29, the son of the proprietor of the McMartin nursery school which was attended by her child.

Faced with repeated allegations, the police reluctantly circulated a letter to the parents of 100 present and former pupils which mentioned Buckey by name and invited them to question their children regarding any sexual misconduct their children might have witnessed. As a result of this openly accusatory letter, several parents came forward claiming that their children had reported being party to satanic and bondage rituals, drug orgies and human sacrifice. A medical examination of Mrs Johnson's son revealed signs consistent with sexual abuse. As a result of these revelations, the local District Attorney eventually filed charges against not only Buckey, but also his 60 year old mother and seven other teachers at the nursery school.

The District Attorney referred a number of children for expert investigation to a Los Angeles-based child sex-abuse investigation and treatment centre and videotapes of these interviews were the main prop of the prosecution case. No physical evidence was found to link the school or the accused to the allegations and all the accused consistently denied any guilt. Preparatory and preliminary examination for the case took 17 months and was the longest and costliest in Californian history. In December 1986, the trial was further delayed following the death of Mrs Johnson from an alcohol-related illness. The State, meanwhile, changed its prosecutor after it was revealed that the original had

Clinical Approaches to Sex Offenders and Their Victims
Edited by C. R. Hollin and K. Howells © 1991 John Wiley & Sons Ltd

attempted to sell his exclusive story to a Hollywood script writer for development as a film.

The new prosecutor, Ira Reiner, decided to drop charges against all but Buckey and his mother and the trial finally commenced in July 1987. A total of 13 children were cited to appear for the prosecution. The defence, for its part, sought to discredit the children's statements, and in particular, the evidence from videotaped interviews. Buckey's attorney claimed that the tapes formed his best defence:

> They show the method by which these children were goaded and prodded into making incriminating statements . . . they are a perfect example of how not to conduct an investigative interview. . . . They assume guilt as a given and the function of the interview is not to find out what happened, but to force or cajole a child into making statements which the interviewer has already determined has happened. (*Los Angeles Times*, 13 July, 1987)

Subsequently, both Buckey and his mother were cleared of all charges. Sadly, the McMartin school case is not a unique example of a major child abuse investigation which has ended inconsequentially with both complainants and witnesses feeling aggrieved and victimised. Also in the United States, an enquiry in 1984 in Jordan, Minnesota, resulted in charges being laid against 24 adults. After extensive legal proceedings and repeated interviewing of the child witnesses involved (some as many as 30 or 50 times), all charges were dropped (Humphrey, 1985). In Cleveland in the United Kingdom in 1987 there was widespread concern when, in an eight-week period, some 202 children were diagnosed by a medical team as having suffered sexual abuse. Many of these children were subsequently interviewed repeatedly in an attempt to provide evidence supportive of the diagnosis. The number and style of these interviews were criticised in the public enquiry which followed the outcry (Butler-Sloss, 1988). The Report left open the question of the precise number of children who had actually suffered sexual abuse.

Such public humiliations for the helping professions do good to no one. Innocent adults are unjustly maligned. The genuine allegations of abuse made by individual children in all three cases were lost in the welter of accusation and recrimination which followed. Disputed medical diagnoses were clearly significant but much responsibility must rest on those who conducted the interviews with the children. If history is not to be repeated, interviewers must rapidly develop skills and techniques which maximise the elicitation of accurate and relevant information from youngsters while minimising error and invention. In this chapter, I try to show what cognitive psychology has to offer professionals seeking to develop their interviewing skills, while in a companion piece Eileen Vizard reviews existing interview techniques. We are convinced that only by a creative synthesis of theory and practice can interviewing move closer to a science than to an art.

This chapter begins by first considering the cognitive developmental background against which a child's statements and actions should be assessed, with particular reference to the minimum age at which reliable recall appears possible. It then goes on to consider experimental research on questioning style and interviewing technique with children, with special attention to the issue of suggestibility, one of the most contentious issues among researchers in the area. This leads on to a discussion of how the credibility of a witness, as opposed to their accuracy, may be reliably assessed. Finally, the implications of this research in the light of recent legal reforms are briefly considered.

DEVELOPMENT OF MEMORY

Experimental psychologists generally recognise three distinct stages in the memorisation process, each of which is potentially sensitive to improvement with increasing age and experience. *Encoding* involves the effective taking in of information from the environment and relating such events to existing knowledge and experience. *Storage* involves the retention of information over time and its accurate preservation in the face of conflicting information and suggestion. *Retrieval* involves the subsequent recovery of information, either autonomously by the observer (free recall) or with the assistance of external agencies (cued or prompted recall). Clearly, it is the final phase of memory which is in the hands of the interviewer, but what can be elicited is equally dependent upon the initial two stages.

Encoding

There is little doubt that the richness and completeness of children's spontaneous accounts of events shows a steady improvement with age. However, this improvement seems to owe more to increasing understanding of events observed—an informed perception—than any true growth in the capacity to process information as such. If we use the computer metaphor, the growth appears to be in the sophistication of the *software* of the memory system which improves with age rather than the *operating capacity* of the system (Brown, 1975).

At least three types of knowledge growth have been identified which contribute to the emerging capacity to remember in the child. The first of these is increasing *world knowledge*; older children simply know far more than their younger contemporaries and this knowledge informs their reports. Thus, an average 9 year old faced with a random display of common objects will recall far more than a corresponding 6 year old, the reason being that the older children's cognitive representation of these objects will be much richer and more elaborate than their younger counterparts. They can see a connection between, say, a golf ball and a rubber band (linked by their rubber content) and use this as a basis for effective recall, while the youngster must rely on more superficial cues or try to remember the item individually.

Normally, knowledge growth and increasing age go hand in hand, but it is occasionally possible to construct situations where the relationship is reversed and to observe the dramatic impact this has on the normal superiority of adult recall. Thus, Lindberg (1970) asked 9 year old children and 20 year old students to recall lists of words. Where the lists were drawn from conceptual categories in common adult usage (types of reading material, parts of a house), the expected superiority of adult recall was observed. However, when the words were derived from categories drawn up by the children's peers (films, cartoon characters), the 9 year olds' recall exceeded the adults.

A second area of memory growth concerns knowledge of *scripts*, events in the world which, while allowing some individual variation from instance to instance, nevertheless show a fixed sequence of steps or stages (Schank and Abelson, 1977). Such repeated sequences of action figure prominently in the lives of children: going to bed, having breakfast, dressing and undressing, are all examples. Prompting or anticipation by the child when a step is omitted or delayed is often the first manifestation of memory in the very young (Forbes, 1988). Scripts are a particularly significant concept in relation to sexual abuse which often follows a repeated stereotypical sequence. Both the range, flexibility and elaboration of scripts increases with age (Nelson, 1978).

A third area of memory growth concerns an increasing grasp of *encoding strategies*, techniques for taking in and retaining information over time. The earlier research of Flavell (1977) demonstrated that the improvement in memory performance with age on contrived memory tasks could be traced not to a biological unfolding of abilities, but rather to increasing mastery of memorising strategies. Such strategies include the use of category knowledge to organise items, strategic rehearsal and the use of imagery and spatial plans. The deployment of such deliberate acquisition strategies is of value only when the witness is aware at the time of the event that accurate recall will be required later.

Training programmes of 'street proofing' designed to protect children from abduction and abuse by strangers do include instructions on deliberate remembering. Such programmes have been shown to lead to improved recall among 10 year olds who viewed a film of a staged child abduction (Yarmey, 1988). In many instances, however, no preparation will be possible and the child must rely upon spontaneous memories of the event.

Generally speaking, the more involved the child is in the events, the 'deeper' the processing and the greater the likelihood of their subsequent recall (Craik and Lockhart, 1972). Thus, victims of real crimes are likely to produce more complete accounts of events than bystanders (Macleod, 1985) and events which are embedded in the context of the child's everyday experience are likely to be better recalled than arbitrary events divorced from daily rituals (Istomina, 1975).

Storage

This second stage of memory involves the preservation of what has been encoded over time. The effectiveness with which children can retain experiences over long time intervals is critical to their competency as witnesses, given the typical delays which occur between an initial complaint and appearance in court in abuse cases. What little is known about the spontaneous duration of memory in children as opposed to adults, suggests that much may depend on the quality and quantity of information initially encoded.

Mentally handicapped individuals were popularly supposed to be particularly poor at retaining information over time (Ellis, 1963). However, careful research which compared the performance of normal and handicapped subjects suggested that any difference was due to the initial quality of information encoded; when this was equalised through special instructions to the handicapped group, all differences were eliminated (Belmont and Butterfield, 1971). Laboratory research suggests that the same analysis applies to the memory capacity of young children. Given their more restricted encoding skills and world knowledge they may take in less about the events they experience than comparable adults and so their rate of loss of information over time will be accelerated in the manner of those with learning difficulties (Belmont and Butterfield, 1969). This provides a powerful argument for the early recording of statements of children on videotape and their admission in court, a point to which I will return.

Recent research by Brainerd and his colleagues confirms the generally faster forgetting rate of children for events experienced under laboratory conditions compared to adults (Brainerd et al., 1985). Brainerd, however, has gone on to show that children's memories for such material can be protected to a remarkable extent from the ravages of time by the actual process of being questioned about them. To be maximally effective, such questioning needs to be administered within one day of the incident concerned, implicating some kind of consolidation process (Brainerd et al., 1985). This kind of research has interesting implications for the 'inoculation' of child witnesses against forgetting but needs to be repeated using more naturalistic materials and settings (Brainerd and Ornstein, 1989).

Memory suffers degradation over time not simply because of delay but because of interference from relevant experiences encountered during the delay (Baddeley, 1976). The American psychologist Elizabeth Loftus has demonstrated how memories of adults for observed events can be systematically distorted by subsequent (or 'post-event') information. Thus, adults who observed a photograph of a man subsequently read a description of him supposedly written by another witness. The description was accurate in all save one crucial detail: the man would be described as having curly hair rather than straight, or as having a moustache where none existed. Subjects who read the erroneous details were 22% more likely to include the mis-information in their verbal descriptions, and 33% more ready to include it in an Identikit picture of the man compared to those who had read an accurate description (Loftus and Greene, 1980).

It is not difficult to demonstrate similar effects in children (e.g. Dale et al., 1978; Murray, 1988). Once again the relative susceptibility of children to such effects is important, given the frequency with which the child may be interviewed or exposed to statements or comments by significant adults. However, a survey of existing research found no clear relationship between age and susceptibility to misleading post-event information (Loftus and Davies, 1984). Once again, the issue may be confounded with how strongly the original events impressed themselves upon memory; a child who has been the victim of a repeated and stereotyped experience such as familial abuse may resist such effects much better than a peer who has been an innocent bystander to an isolated incident (Goodman et *al.*, 1987). Suffice it to note that interviewers have the power to cloud as well as clarify the products of a young child's memory.

One final aspect of memory longevity is the question whether the children themselves rather than external agencies may serve to interfere with memory by their own musings and fantasies. The claim that the young children's imagination may feed on the stored products of their memories leading to mischievous and misleading testimony is one of the oldest accusations against child witnesses (Varendonck, 1911). Research has been conducted which has compared systematically the ability of children of different ages to differentiate between externally produced experiences and sensations and internal ones generated by the child. This research has failed to show any kind of generalised deficit in this ability, at least for children as young as 6 years of age (Johnson and Foley, 1984).

Only one isolated instance of increased confusion has been uncovered which disproportionately affects the young: a markedly poorer ability to distinguish memory of simple bodily movements actually executed and imagined movements. This had led to speculation that children may be poorer at distinguishing intentions and actions (Lindsay and Johnson, 1987) but attempts to demonstrate this in a more forensically realistic setting have been unsuccessful (Davies and Baxter, 1988).

Early Memories

Much debate in the child witness area has surrounded the age at which a child can first report reliable memories. In the United States, a 3 year old was instrumental in successfully identifying her abductor (Jones and Krugman, 1986) while in Sweden a child testified to events about a murder which she had witnessed when she was 2 (*Daily Telegraph*, 9.3.1988).

Freud (1924) was struck by the apparent inability of his adult patients to recall events from their earliest years, a phenomena he termed 'infantile amnesia'. He contrasted this with his observation that children themselves seemed to recall events from their own younger lives. Freud explained this discrepancy by arguing that adults repressed early memories because these were too tainted with infantile sexuality and camouflaged them with more conventional and mundane recollections ('screen memories').

Actual studies of the content of an adult's early memories suggest, on the contrary, that they are frequently vested with strong emotion (the birth of a sibling; a personal accident) and more innocuous events are rarely reported (Dudycha and Dudycha, 1940). However, the truth of Freud's observation that young children can recall events from their earlier lives is borne out by modern research.

The very earliest spontaneous verbal memories shown by children appear to be prompted to external cues rather than being the result of direct questioning. Nelson and Ross (1980) asked parents of 21 to 27 months old children to keep diaries of memories demonstrated by their toddlers. The majority of instances were prompted by the sight of an event (48%) or person (32%) and only 5% came as a result of a direct question from the parent. Where memories could be dated, nearly 80% referred to events in the preceding month, though there were some isolated instances where memories dated from 18 months of age.

Children of 3 years of age show a marked improvement in dealing with questions about their past. Todd and Perlmutter (1980) observed groups of children aged approximately 3 and 4 years old at play and asked them questions designed to probe memory. Around half of their reported instances of memory still arose from spontaneous comments prompted by toys or friends, but their ability to cope with and understand questions markedly improved.

Memories concerning novel events such as a visit to the zoo or an aeroplane flight were much more easy to elicit than were more routine activities like a lunch at the nursery. Again, earliest memories related to events around 18 months with the majority from the preceding month. The children were poor at localising events in time, but when the accuracy could be ascertained from parents, some 80% were judged definitely true and only 3% pure invention.

A similar high accuracy in the recall of script-based memories has been reported by Nelson and Gruendel (1981) who examined the ability of children age 3 to 8 years to report routine events such as baking cookies or having lunch at nursery school. The elaborateness and richness of the narrative improved steadily with age but the order of the steps or sequences of an event were generally well recalled by even the youngest children. Moreover, they were consistent in their recall of such sequences when requestioned between one and four weeks later.

Retrieval

Memory theorists have long distinguished between the potential information about an event available in memory and that portion which is accessible to the individual on a given occasion (Tulving, 1983). This distinction is illustrated by the impact of prompts or cues on the amount recalled. In one laboratory memory study conducted by the author, 5 year old children were shown a series of common objects derived from conceptual categories familiar to a child of that age. Subsequent unaided recall averaged only 41% but when the interviewer mentioned the categories from which the items were drawn ('Do you remember any animals that I showed you? Any things to eat?', etc.), recall improved to 61% (Davies and Brown, 1978).

Clearly, the distinction between available and accessible information is of central importance to the interviewer. The goal for the interviewer is to build on the initial information which the child is able to provide (accessible memory) and to elicit through prompting, the additional facts which the child knows but cannot tell spontaneously (available memory). There is evidence from laboratory research which suggests that like encoding skills, the ability effectively to retrieve information from memory improves dramatically in the period between 5 and 10 years of age (Kobasigawa, 1974). It may be that younger children need a great deal more assistance and support to search their memories systematically and exhaustively than the average adult (Davies and Brown, 1978).

While the principles of cued recall can be demonstrated easily in the psychology laboratory, actually using this technique in real interview situations presents formidable practical problems. In the example above, the experimenter knew precisely what the child had seen and what questions to ask, a luxury denied to the investigator who must simultaneously build up an impression of what has occurred while trying to confirm his or her hypothesis through questioning. Clearly the opportunities for misunderstanding and the drawing of erroneous conclusions are always present. Yet, the interviewer must in practice always try to go beyond the normally sparse details of a child's initial statement. In the next section, the findings of research on children's testimony are considered, particularly as these relate to styles of questioning and aids to recall.

EXPERIMENTAL RESEARCH ON TESTIMONY

Unlike much of the experimental research on memory development, research on testimony generally attempts to simulate aspects of real witnessing situations. Concessions to reality can vary from the use of a slide or video sequence through a staged incident enacted in front of the child to explorations of actual events from the child's own life. Clearly, the latter can offer the strongest parallel to testimony in abuse cases, but the former offer advantages in terms of control and measurement (Davies, 1989). Taken together, such studies appear to offer some useful guidelines to the practitioner on both fruitful and counterproductive techniques for interviewing children.

Irrespective of method, laboratory research suggests that the child's initial unprompted account is likely to be the most reliable source of information. Furthermore, while the length and richness of this free account shows an increase with age, the proportion of erroneous detail stays low and remarkably constant across ages. In a typical study, Marin *et al.* (1979) had subjects aged from 5 years to adulthood witness a brief confrontation between two teachers over the occupancy of a room. When asked about the event later, the amount of useful information in the free account rose from around one item at age 5 years to over seven items for the adults, but the overall accuracy of statements (91%) was high across the whole age spectrum tested.

Once questioning begins, however, the situation reverses: now more information is made available by the subject, but at the expense of a higher rate of error. Dent and Stephenson (1979) secured accounts for children aged 10–11 years who had watched a film depicting a theft. Irrespective of type of questioning style, accounts based on questions were on average richer in information, but less accurate in content, than free accounts. Moreover, questions which asked for specific details ('What colour hair did the man in the white mac have?') produced higher rates of error than more general, open ended, questions ('Tell me as much as you can about what the man in the white mac looked like and what he was wearing'). Dent (1986) reported a similar pattern when she studied the free and prompted recall performance of developmentally delayed children of similar mental age. The errors witnesses commit are not randomly distributed. Errors are much more frequent in children of all ages when describing persons as opposed to events (King and Yuille, 1987; List 1986). Particular difficulties experienced by children include accurate estimates of height, weight or age of a person observed (Davies *et al.*, 1988). Among personal details, children seem particularly prone to misreporting hair colour, eye colour and clothing details (see Davies and Flin, in press, for a review). Davies *et al.* (1989) found some improvement in general accuracy of personal description from ages 7 to 10 years, but no major differences between the sexes.

Moston (1987) attempted to make children less ready to respond to questions with information of doubtful accuracy by explicitly reminding them that 'don't know' was a permissible answer. The children, aged 6–10 years, had seen a staged incident in their classroom and were questioned shortly afterward. Compared to uninstructed controls, the caution had no impact on accuracy of testimony; though the number of 'don't know' responses increased. He also reported that repeating the same questions, slightly rephrased within a session, led a significant minority of the children to change their answers in the wrong direction, this tendency being most marked among the youngest children. Moston interpreted this finding as reflecting a belief by the child that the repeated question could only have meant that the first answer was incorrect.

As the following chapter by Eileen Vizard makes clear, there is an extensive literature on techniques for interviewing abused children. Most of these procedures have been evolved by practitioners and are based on their often considerable personal experience. Experimental researchers have much to learn by scrutiny of these techniques: they represent an enormous source of research hypotheses concerning the accuracy of children's memory. By the same token, practitioners could gain from a more rigorous empirical evaluation of their approaches and the development of a more clearly articulated theoretical standpoint in relation to the mechanics of interviewing. One approach to interviewing adults which has been empirically validated and which has its origins in cognitive psychology is the 'cognitive interview'. The cognitive interview was originally developed by Geiselman and his colleagues as an aid for police officers interviewing witnesses to crime. It attempts to maximise recall of events by capitalising on principles of active memory retrieval derived from laboratory research on memory. Accordingly, witnesses are encouraged to: (i) recall all aspects of the event, however trivial; (ii) to view the events from different perspectives (the victim, the bystander), (iii) to recall the event repeatedly using different starting points; and most significantly (iv) to reinstate mentally the circumstances surrounding the incident by relaxation and visualisation. Relative to experienced investigative officers, civilian personnel trained in the cognitive interview have secured more information from adult witnesses to mock crimes (Geiselman *et al.*, 1986).

Geiselman and Pedilla (1988) report the results of a pilot study on a group of 7–12 year old children of an adapted version of the cognitive interview. Children in this age range seemed capable of employing the specific procedures necessary to use the technique and overall showed a 21% improvement in recall relative to uninstructed controls. However, the cognitive interview group also showed increased levels of confabulation, suggesting further development work may be necessary before advocating its use with children.

More generally, the physical and social setting of an interview appear potentially to have a strong influence on levels of recall. Young children's recall of events experienced in natural settings and embedded in their daily lives leads to much higher estimates of their memory competence than that based on artificial tasks learned in the laboratory (Wellman and Somerville, 1980). There is a great need for systematic studies of how environment and the nature of the questioner influence performance. Can mothers at home elicit more information about events than teachers in a classroom? (cf. Dent, 1982; Nide and Lange, 1987).

Children may also be able to capitalise on the physical cues of a familiar environment to improve the recovery of information from memory. Wilkinson (1988) took pairs of 4 year olds on a short walk around a local park during which a series of prescribed events took place. The next day the children were asked to describe these events, first in their own words and subsequently in response to a series of questions which became progressively more explicit if the child failed to respond. Questioning took place either in a room in the child's nursery or in the course of repeating the earlier walk. The presence of the contextual cues available on the walk increased total recall from the 48% recorded by the schoolroom group to an average of over 80%. No evidence was found that this dramatic increase in recall was accompanied by any increase in confabulation engendered by the presence of the cues.

One controversial use of physical cues concerns the employment of anatomically correct dolls in investigations of abuse. Some therapists had gone so far as to argue that the dolls should be banned on the grounds that they act as catalysts for the release of misleading and fantasy-based testimony (Yates and Terr, 1988). However, a recent review of the reactions of abused and non-abused children to such dolls revealed little evidence to substantiate this claim (Westcott et al., 1989a). In an observational study, Glazer and Collins (1989) examined the spontaneous play of 91 non-abused children when the dolls were both clothed and unclothed. The predominant form of play was feeding, bathing and putting to bed, and only five children showed any evidence of sexual interaction with the dolls. In three of these cases, a source of sexual knowledge was traced to the home.

A similar message emerges from an experimental study by Goodman and Aman (1987). The experimenters played nursery games with 3 and 5 year old children before asking them to recount what had occurred, either with or without the aid of anatomically correct dolls. No relationship was found between the tendency to resist leading questions implying possible abuse and the presence or absence of the dolls. Goodman and Aman, however, were unable to find support for the view that the dolls facilitated children's recall but the events the children described were innocuous games rather than explicitly sexual incidents where the anatomically appropriate nature of the dolls might well have facilitated communication between interviewer and child.

The impact of social facilitation as opposed to facilitation through the use of physical cues has been extensively explored by Moston and Engelberg (in press). This work challenges the view, widely held by lay persons and psychologists alike, that the presence and support of friends during the giving of evidence is likely to harm rather than facilitate accurate testimony. Children aged either 7 or

10 years of age interacted with a stranger who showed them how to use a tape recorder. Later, children were asked to recall the incident and to answer a series of questions about the event, some of which were leading. Having the opportunity to discuss the event with a fellow pupil who had not been present did not facilitate recall, nor did the presence of another pupil at the interview. However, a combination of prior discussion and the presence of the same pupil at the interview did significantly facilitate recall and also increased resistance to leading questions. The effect was present for both age groups. For the 7 year olds, the effects were particularly dramatic and actually eliminated the age differences in recall typical of research on testimony. Moston observed that the peer made little actual contribution to testimony presented by the actual witness. It appeared that recounting the events to a sympathetic colleague prior to interview and having that person present later helped to reduce any anxiety the children might normally have displayed with an adult questioner. His research provides empirical justification for the provision of social support for child witness giving evidence in court under the video link provisions of the 1988 Criminal Justice Act.

At the beginning of this section, it was noted that experimental studies showed a trade-off between the increased information produced by questioning and the decrease in overall accuracy. There are no reasons, however, for believing that this is an immutable law of nature. Some of the techniques described here, such as the use of cueing or social support, may serve to reduce inaccuracy to a minimum under experimental conditions. However, it is unclear to what extent such principles will transfer from research to the practical domain. Moreover, there may well be techniques, already in use in clinical practice, which are equally effective in maximising children's recall. However, one danger always present with any technique is that the law of diminishing returns will operate such that small increases in correct testimony will be accompanied by much larger rises in false or misleading information. The special problems which children are said to experience in differentiating fact from invention are one aspect of a more general allegation made against child witnesses: their suggestibility. This controversial area of research is reviewed in the next section.

THE SUGGESTIBILITY DEBATE

Suggestibility is sometimes viewed by lawyers and others as a trait or personal quality with which children are particularly imbued (e.g. Stone, 1984; Williams, 1987). Yet, as a recent review makes clear, there is little or no evidence for a unitary trait of suggestibility investing the recall processes of children. Not only do individual tests of suggestibility not intercorrelate significantly with each other, they also do not predict the degree of confabulation of individual children's reports. Suggestibility in children, at least, appears to be more a function of setting and task than a permanent state of mind (Baxter, in press).

Evidence that suggestibility may vary within and between situations comes from a series of studies by the American researcher, Gail Goodman. Goodman *et al.* (1987) examined the ability of children aged 3–4 and 5–6 years of age to recall a particularly painful and stressful personal event: a visit to a clinic to receive one, sometimes two, inoculations during which the child might have to be held down or secured on the parent's lap.

Up to nine days later, the children were questioned about their experiences, using a mixture of objective ('Did the nurse have spectacles?') and leading ('The nurse had black hair didn't she?') questions. Leading questions led to lower levels of accurate recall compared to the objective questions and the older children were generally more accurate than the younger. However, within the group of leading questions, those dealing with central events (the actions of the nurse and her appearance) were much more successfully resisted by children of all ages than those concerning peripheral events (the characteristics of the room). Goodman interprets these findings as suggesting that the central skein of the action was preserved in even the youngest children and showed resilience in the face of suggestive questioning.

The robustness and longevity of memories for such a stressful event appeared to support the view that children of such a young age could provide accurate accounts of abusive incidents and resist suggestion. Goodman *et al.* also included among their questions several of a kind frequently asked in the course of sexual or physical abuse investigations ('Did the nurse hit you? Did the nurse put anything in your mouth?'). Inaccurate responding on these 'abuse' questions was generally low. Moreover, when these same children were requestioned a year later, resistance, even among the youngest group, remained high (Goodman *et al.*, 1987).

It could be argued that those incidents, stressful though they appear to have been, were not of the type likely in reality to lead to enquiries concerning sexual abuse. Does resistance to such questioning extend to situations where the interaction between adult and child involves the actual touching of genital areas? Saywitz *et al.* (1989) examined the recall performance of groups of 5 and 7 year old girls who had taken part in a routine medical examination during which their genital and anal areas were touched and examined by the doctor. The memory performance of these girls was compared in turn with controls who had also attended for examination designed to detect back problems. Around 80% of the children who had been touched in the sexual areas failed to report it spontaneously or to demonstrate the relevant acts on a doll provided. However, all but a small minority admitted to the touching when questioned explicitly about it. Among the control subjects asked the same questions, only 3 out of 36 answered affirmatively, one of whom went on to claim that the doctor had placed a stick in her rectum. It is tempting to attribute such a response to childish fantasy, the claim frequently levelled against young witnesses (Stone, 1984). However, it may equally be a 'script memory' relating to some earlier interaction between a doctor and the particular child concerned: a confusion rather than an invention. Goodman's work demonstrates that across a variety of potentially stressful situations, non-abused children as young as 3 years of age will resist questions which imply sexual misconduct by an adult who has interacted directly with them. They do not, however, necessarily demonstrate that children are always resistant to suggestion under all circumstances. Nor, despite the great ingenuity shown by Goodman, can they successfully mimic the totality of the dynamics which operate on child witnesses exposed to abuse.

A recent series of experiments by Douglas Peters (1989) demonstrates a range of contexts in which younger children can be more suggestible than their older counterparts. Peter's initial study (1987) examined the ability of children aged 3 to 7 years of age to remember a visit to the dentist: a frequently traumatic event for adults, let alone children! All were on their first or second visit and their ability to identify the dentist and dental nurse, together with the room in which treatment took place, was tested by means of multiple choice recognition tasks. Recognition performance was tested on arrays which both included and did not include the relevant person or room. The inclusion of so-called 'target absent' arrays are now seen as an essential control in eyewitness identification studies as it cannot be assumed in reality that an abused child will always be faced with an array containing the transgressor. Peters reported a high rate of error on all target-absent arrays. In all, children made 71% false choices on such arrays compared to 31%, where the target was present. This tendency to choose even when instructions explicitly underline the fact that the person may not be present has also been reported by other researchers (King and Yuille, 1987; Davies et al., 1988) and needs to be taken into account when a young child's ability to recognise a stranger arises. However, the effect is not inevitable, especially in circumstances where there is extended perusal of the target (Davies et al., in press). It is notable that in an actual case in which a 3 year old was required to identify an abusing stranger, the child rejected a target absent array before going on successfully to identify the true abuser in a photospread containing his picture (Jones and Krugman, 1986).

In a second study (Peters, 1989), children aged between 6 and 9 years of age accompanied their parents to visit the researcher in a room at his laboratory. When they arrived, blood pressure and pulse rate recording apparatus was fitted to the child, who also played a card game with the experimenter. Shortly after this, experimental subjects heard a fire alarm go off, soon followed by the entry of a female accomplice who rushed into the room complaining of the smell of smoke, and acted out a brief conversation with the experimenter before leaving. After her departure the fire alarm was turned off and the experimenter moved to reassure the child that it was a false alarm. Subsequently, all children answered a series of questions, some of which contained misleading information ('Did the girl wearing a yellow sweater have brown hair?'—the girl was not wearing a yellow sweater). Finally, after a break, the children were asked a series of forced choice questions designed to test the extent to which they had absorbed the misleading statements ('Did the girl have a white or yellow sweater?').

The performance of these experimental subjects was assessed relative to controls who heard not a fire alarm, but a radio being switched on, and where the conversation between experimenter and the female accomplice made no reference to smoke. The clever design of this study enabled Peters not only to manipulate the stress levels experienced by experimental and control children, but also to confirm that stress had indeed varied by reference to the pulse and heart rate data.

When the responses of the two groups of children were compared, Peters was able to demonstrate a modest but statistically reliable fall off in performance for the high stress (fire alarm) group on both the objective and the misleading questions. Overall, the children resisted suggestion on over half (58%) of the information contained in the misleading questions. Peters' studies demonstrate some areas of potential weakness in children's testimony and the fact that stress in itself impairs rather than impoves memory. There is no question of the trauma of an incident enhancing recall. If Peters' results are representative of the levels of stress experienced in real abusive incidents, the contrary appears to be the case. However, two important provisos are in order.

First, in the studies described, no adults were included as controls, so there is no way of gauging the extent to which adults might also be susceptible to the same kinds of suggestions as the children. Certainly, research confirms that adults make more errors on target absent identification tasks (Malpass and Devine, 1981) and absorb information from misleading questions (Loftus, 1979). Second, although some children made errors or were taken in by misleading information, others were not; the results represent the statistical average of a group of children and in no way pre-empt or predict the performance of an individual child. These studies are thus pointers as to where special care or caution should be exercised in interviewing a child rather than a basis for dismissing or denigrating the testimony of an individual witness. The findings of Goodman on the one hand and Peters on the other have sometimes been interpreted as sharply discrepant and presenting alternative realities as to the nature of suggestibility in children (Raskin and Esplin, 1989). It is far too early to conclude that this is necessarily the case. The methods employed and the questions asked by these two experienced researchers are very different. Goodman has deliberately sought out naturally occurring stressful situations and asked the kinds of questions typical of abuse situations. Peters has generally chosen to manipulate the impact of differing stress levels on children's recall and to ask questions arising directly out of the events observed rather than to pursue explicitly abuse-oriented themes. Both researchers have concentrated on exploring relatively clearly structured events with objective questions from a neutral interviewer. This is by no means always the case in actual abuse cases, a reality acknowledged in the recent work of Clarke-Stewart *et al.* (1989).

Clarke-Stewart and her colleagues staged an incident for a number of 5 and 6 year olds where they observed a man posing as a janitor ('Chester the Molester'), tidying the toy area. Chester always picked up a doll, straightened its legs and cleaned and wiped its face, talking to the child as he did so. Half the children were given an explanation for his actions which centred on the importance of keeping the doll clean and tidy. For the remainder, Chester played with the doll in a malicious and suggestive manner ('Oh goodie, here's a doll. I like to play with dolls. I like to spray them in the face with water. I like to look under their clothes', etc. etc.). Some of the children who observed the 'playing' Chester were given sweets in return for not telling anyone about Chester's misdeads.

An hour later, each child met an experimenter posing as 'Chester's boss' and was questioned as to his actions with the doll. When the questions were objective and neutral in tone, the children were generally accurate, answering 14 out of the 17 questions correctly and maintaining that performance when requestioned a week later. However, such encouraging results need to be set against the performance of those children who were questioned in a manner deliberately designed either to incriminate the 'Cleaning' Chester or to exculpate the 'Playing' version. Fewer than half the children stuck to their story that Chester was cleaning after a series of comments from the Boss suggesting he had really been playing or vice versa, the remainder either switching to the questioner's view or alternatively suggesting he had both cleaned and played. Further, when these same children were requestioned by a different interviewer who pursued the same line of questioning as the first, only one out off 38 children involved stuck to their original interpretation of Chester's behaviour. Moreover, these altered views were perpetuated when the children were questioned at home by their parents a week later.

As to the impact of being bribed by Chester, only 5 out of 14 children admitted that he had played under orthodox questioning—and all of the bribed children went along with the line adopted by the questioned under the incriminating and exculpating conditions.

Clarke-Stewart's work underlines the importance of early interviews and an objective questioning style in interrogating children and the devastating impact of assumptions of guilt or innocence on the information elicited from a child of this age. The effects of such suggestion appear to be strong and maintained over time. It is not difficult to see the origins of misleading criminal testimony in a process of repeated questioning by committed interviewers. However, it would be dangerous to extrapolate these findings too far.

First, the results may well be specific to the 5 and 6 year olds tested in the main study. It may well be that older children would be more resistant to the biased and misleading questioning.

Second, the child was a bystander rather than a participant in an event of no special significance to him or her. Would the same results have been obtained if it was the child's own doll who had been cleaned or abused? Or the child itself?

Third, we have no way of knowing how deeply the new interpretation of events had been integrated into the child's memory, or whether more subtle questioning, perhaps with enactment or the use of cues (Wilkinson, 1988) might yet have elicited something closer to the truth. Clarke-Stewart's work continues and may well embrace these issues. In the meantime, there is no doubt of the importance of her research to our wider understanding of suggestibility in children.

In summary, the debate over children's suggestibility under questioning is far from complete. The idea that suggestibility is some kind of global trait invested in all children receives little or no support. On the contrary suggestibility appears to be a situational factor rather than a trait. Suggestibility appears at its maximum in ambiguous situations where the child is a spectator rather than a participant. It is exaggerated by post-event pressures where the questioner has strong reasons for shaping the child's recall pattern toward a particular interpretation. It is unclear whether a veridical account can still be recovered through the use of special interviewing techniques. Above all, they demonstrate the value of prompt interviewing by a neutral but not disinterested interrogator aware of the dynamics of suggestibility and compliance.

ACCURACY AND CREDIBILITY

Distortions in testimony can arise from factors other than the cognitive failings of the individual child. As others have warned (Raskin and Yuille, 1989), in interviewing children suspected of being abused the possibility of deliberate falsification can never be ruled out. The proportion of such false or malicious allegations is a continuing source of debate with estimates ranging from 2% (Jones and McGraw, 1987) to claims of over 50% in cases involving custody disputes (Raskin and Yuille, 1989).

There are major methodological difficulties in establishing reliable figures including the representatives of samples and the criteria employed in determining 'true' and 'false' allegations (Bulkley, 1989). One of the largest and most recent studies involved a sample of 1249 cases reported to the Departments of Social Services in North Carolina (Everson and Boat, 1989). The proportion of allegations judged palpably false by case workers varied from less than 2% in children aged under 6 years, to 8% in the adolescent group. Clearly, malicious allegations are a possibility which needs to be entertained by investigators, particularly among older clients.

Are there categories of appearance or behaviour which differentiate the true account from the false? Sadly, the cues employed by adults are not generally those which do effectively differentiate liars from truth tellers, at least, in experimental studies.

A review of such studies suggests that adults ascribe far too much significance to facial and bodily cues and far too little to more reliable indicators, such as speech hesitation, voice pitch and speech errors (De Paulo et al., 1985). Not surprisingly, the overall levels of accuracy achieved by adults in deciding which of their fellow adults is lying or telling the truth just exceed chance in most cases.

A similar rather pessimistic picture emerges from a study by Westcott et al. (1989b) which examined adults' ability to differentiate children who had actually experienced an event from those who had merely watched it on television. Such a distinction has important forensic ramifications where questions may arise in abuse cases as to whether children have taken part in sexual acts or merely viewed them in a pornographic video. In this experiment, interviews were videotaped of children aged 7–8 and 10–11 years answering questions concerning a school trip. Some of the children had been on the trip while others had merely seen the video. The tapes were then shown to adults who were instructed to identify those who had actually been on the trip. The adults' accuracy on this task exceeded chance and was higher for boys than girls and for the older group compared to the younger. When asked as to the cues upon which they relied, around a third of all judges identified confidence and composure as particularly important. However, recent experimental research points to the content of the child's statement as being by far the most reliable guide to truth or falsity.

Faller (1988), for instance, examined the characteristics of statements of 103 child victims of abuse where the allegation was corroborated by an admission from the abuser. She singled out three criteria which characterised these accounts. First, there was reference to the circumstances and place where the incidents took place, which was present in around 78% of all accounts. Second, there was reference to explicit detail of the sexual acts (81% of cases) and third, indications of a strong and appropriate emotional response on the part of the child (also 81%). Faller's study lacks an appropriate control group of children making false allegations, but it is notable that all three of her criteria are incorporated into the most developed system for assessing the credibility of children's testimony: Statement Analysis.

Statement Analysis was developed within the inquisitorial legal tradition of mainland Europe and emphasises the evaluation of testimony rather than the assessment of the moral worth or otherwise of the individual child. Different schemes of statement analysis have been developed by psychologists working in Sweden (Holgerson, 1988; Trankell, 1972) and Germany (Arntzen, 1982; Undeutsch, 1989) but all share a common theme: that true statements will show certain characteristics which may be objectively assessed. Steller and Koenken (1989) have synthesised the various individual systems into a comprehensive programme which they term 'Statement Validity Analysis' and it is the main features of this which will be briefly outlined.

Each statement is assessed on 19 separate counts which are grouped into five major categories of analysis. The first category, the formal structure of the statement, refers to the overall quality of the child's statement and takes in such aspects as internal coherence and consistency, spontaneity and amount of detail. Great emphasis is placed on the latter; it is held that a confabulator will be highly unlikely to furnish the range of sometimes irrelevant detail found in true statements.

The second category refers to the structural aspects of the statement: the anchoring of events to a particular time or place ('It happened at Uncle John's place the day after my birthday party'), is one example. It includes the presence of a clear sequence of development from an incident which arises from the child's normal daily life. The recounting of conversational ploys before and after the incident or unexpected complications ('He stopped doing it when the phone rang') are thought to be particularly telling signs under this heading.

A third category covers singularities in the content of what the child has to say. It includes such matters as the articulation of details of sexual acts which are not within the normal province of a child of that age or which may be wrongly interpreted (orgasm may be mistaken for sneezing). Unusual, distinctive or irrelevant details are scored under this heading as evidence of authenticity.

The fourth category covers evidence of motivational state as reflected in the child's testimony. Spontaneous corrections to the story or confessions of an inability to remember particular facts are included under this category, together with references to the witness's potential fallibility over particular details. False statements, it is alleged, will also not contain any suggestion that the witnesses themselves might be in part responsible for the incident or reflect ambivalent feelings toward the abuser.

The final category refers to telltale signs or details which clinical experience suggests are particularly frequent in sexual crimes of a particular kind. For paternal incest, these might include a pattern of progressive abuse starting with orthodox expressions of affection and only at a later age culminating in full intercourse. Steller and Koenken point out that this pattern is unlikely to be known by a young child or a parent seeking to persuade a son or daughter to give false testimony.

Raskin and Esplin (1989) report the encouraging results of a first attempt to evaluate Statement Validity Analysis by examining its ability to differentiate between statements derived from proven and disputed or doubtful allegations of abuse. Transcripts from 20 confirmed cases of abuse and a similar number from doubtful cases were evaluated by a clinician trained in the use of Statement Analysis but who was otherwise unfamiliar with the cases involved. She scored each statement on as many of the 19 criteria as were relevant and thus arrived at a total score representing the number of indices present. There was no overlap at all between the scores for the two groups of cases, indicating remarkably good differentiation between the two populations. The researchers went on to examine which criteria were particularly effective in differentiating between the two sets of transcripts. In all, 7 criteria were present in all the proven cases, with the presence of spontaneous corrections and unusual details differentiating particularly affectively between the two samples. Only 3 (details not understood; superfluous detail and doubts about one's own testimony) were not clear indices of reliability.

Clearly, such promising results will need to be extended and replicated: for instance, are the 3 ineffective criteria unreliable or did the small sample not include appropriate cases? Moreover, there are a number of issues on which development is required before Statement Reliability Analysis can become a practical forensic tool. Should scoring continue to be uniform across all criteria or should some particularly telling items receive extra weighting? Younger or developmentally delayed children are likely to produce statements which are shorter and less detailed than their more develolpmentally advanced counterparts. How can the scoring system take such factors into account in a systematic way? Finally, the statement itself is not a spontaneous product but the result of an interview which may be badly or skilfully conducted, producing more or less critical points depending upon the prompts which are offered. How can interviews be standardised to permit fully objective scoring? This being said, statement analysis does appear to offer the promise of an effective and objective method of assessing children's evidence.

CONCLUSIONS

In the last decade, more research has been conducted on the prowess and problems of the child witness than in the previous 50 years. An array of factual accounts have been supplied concerning both children's ability to recall staged incidents and the ability of adults to question them effectively. However, as this review emphasises, not all the facts are entirely consistent, nor is it clear the extent to which particular effects translate from the finely calibrated world of the laboratory to the robust conditions of the outside world. Potentially, there is much here, for the therapist or clinical interviewer, but future research needs to take more account of the social and motivational aspects of abusive incidents as well as the purely situational factors.

Perhaps the greatest contribution of experimental research has been to change the climate of debate over the cognitive competencies of child witnesses. Before the work of such pioneers as Gail Goodman and Helen Dent, children were perceived as uniformly poor and unreliable witnesses who were easily manipulated by parental pressures or courtroom ploys. Experimental research of the kind described in this chapter demonstrates that this is a distortion of the truth: there appear to be many situations and circumstances where child witnesses could provide valuable and accurate testimony. This reality has been acknowledged world-wide as legislatures have moved to abolish or modify the restrictions and prohibitions which formerly surrounded children's evidence.

Following an internal review of much of the research literature (Hedderman, 1988), the British government incorporated major reforms into the 1988 Criminal Justice Act. These included the abolition of the principle of corroboration for sexual abuse cases involving children and of the mandatory caution administered by judges in all cases involving the evidence of juveniles. In recognition of the new value placed on children's testimony, children are now permitted to give evidence away from the pressures of the courtroom in an adjacent room via a live video-link. However, the most controversial issue, that of the admission of pre-recorded video interviews involving allegations of abuse by children as young as 2 or 3 years of age, was left unresolved. A committee under Lord Justice Pigot has yet to report.

If, as seems likely, the Pigot Committee does recommend the introduction of such evidence under specified circumstances, this will place great responsibility on the interviewers involved to 'get it right'. They must balance the demand, on the one hand, to secure an accurate and full account from the child while, on the other, following the rules of evidence on the use of leading questions and hearsay. It was precisely the difficulties of interviewers in balancing that complex equation which contributed to the problems typified by the McMartin case and its lamented successors. Therapist interviewers have an unenviable task to perform; viewing, as I do from time to time, the results of their interviews on tape, I am full of admiration for the patience and ingenuity that they so often show in teasing out a child's story. Experimental psychologists cannot yet offer a complete or unequivocal answer to all of their problems but the research described here may help a little to ease the burden which our society has thrust onto their shoulders.

References

Arntzen, F. (1982). Die Situation der Forensischen Ausragepsychologie in der Bundes Republik Deutschland. In A. Trankell (ed.), *Reconstructing the Past: The Role of Psychologists in Criminal Trials*. Stockholm: Norstedt, pp. 107–20.

Baddeley, A. D. (1976). *The Psychology of Human Memory*. London: Harper and Row.

Baxter, J. M. (in press). The suggestibility of child witnesses: A review. *Applied Cognitive Psychology*.

Belmont, J. M., and Butterfield, E. C. (1969). The relation of the short-term memory to development and intelligence. In *Advances in Child Development and Behaviour*, vol. 4. New York: Academic Press, pp. 29–82.

Belmont, J. M., and Butterfield, E. C. (1971). Learning strategies as determinants of memory deficiencies. *Cognitive Psychology*, **2**, 411–20.

Brainerd, C., Kingma, J., and Howe, M. J. (1985). On the development of forgetting. *Child Development*, **56**, 1103–19.

Brainerd, C., and Ornstein, P. A. (1989). Children's memory for witnessed events. Paper presented at the Cornell Conference on the Suggestibility of Children's Recollections, Cornell University, Ithica, USA.

Brown, A. M. (1975). The development of memory: Knowing, knowing about knowing and knowing how to know. In *Advances in Child Development and Behaviour*, vol. 10. New York: Academic Press, pp. 103–52.

Bulkley, J. (1989). The impact of new child witness research on sexual abuse prosecutions. In S. J. Ceci, D. F. Ross and M. P. Toglia (eds), *Perspectives on Children's Testimony*. New York: Springer, pp. 208–29.

Butler-Sloss, E. (1988). *Report of the Inquiry into Child Abuse in Cleveland 1987*. London: HMSO.

Clarke-Stewart, A., Thompson, W., and Lepore, S. (1989). Manipulating children's interpretations through interrogation. Paper presented at the Society for Research on Child Development, Kansas City, USA.

Craik, F. I. M., and Lockhart, R. S. (1972). Levels of processing; A framework for memory research. *Journal of Verbal Learning and Verbal Behavior*, **11**, 671–84.

Dale, P. S., Loftus, E. F., and Rathbun, L. (1978). The influence of the form of the question on the eyewitness testimony of preschool children. *Journal of Psycholinguistic Research*, **7**, 269–77.

Davies, G. M. (1989). Children as witnesses. In A. M. Colman and J. G. Beaumont (eds), *Psychology Survey 7*. London: Routledge/British Psychological Society, pp. 175–93.

Davies, G. M., and Baxter, J. (1988). Children's ability to distinguish fact from fantasy. Paper presented to the NATO Advanced Study Institute on Credibility Assessment, Maratea, Italy.

Davies, G., and Brown, L. (1978). Recall and organisation in five-year-old children. *British Journal of Psychology*, **69**, 343–9.

Davies, G. M., and Flin, R. (in press). Children's identification evidence. In G. Koenken and S. L. Sporer (eds), *Identifizierung von Tatverdachtingen: Psychologische Erkenntnisse, Probleme und Perspektiven*. Gôttingen, German Federal Republic: C. J. Hogrefe.

Davies, G. M., Stevenson-Robb, Y., and Flin, R. (1988). Tales out of school: Children's memory for an unexpected event. In M. M. Gruneberg, P. E. Morris and R. N. Sykes (eds), *Practical Aspects of Memory: Current Research and Issues*, Volume 1. Chichester: Wiley, pp. 122–7.

Davies, G. M., Tarrant, A., and Flin, R. (1989). Close encounters of the witness kind: Children's memory for a simulated health inspection. *British Journal of Psychology*, **80**, 415–29.

De Paulo, B., Stone, J., and Lassiter, G. (1985). Deceiving and detecting deceit. In B. Schlenker (ed.), *The Self and Social Life*. New York: McGraw-Hill.

Dent, H. R. (1982). The effects of interviewing strategies on the results of interviews with child witnesses. In A. Trankell (ed.), *Reconstructing the Past: The Role of Psychologists in Criminal Trials*, Stockholm: Norstedt, pp. 236–43.

Dent, H. R. (1986). An experimental study of the effectiveness of different techniques of questioning mentally handicapped child witnesses. *British Journal of Clinical Psychology*, **25**, 13–17.

Dent, H. R., and Stephenson, G. H. (1979). An experimental study of the effectiveness of different techniques of questioning child witnesses. *British Journal of Clinical Psychology*,. **18**, 41–51.

Dudycha, G., and Dudycha, M. M. (1940). Childhood memories: A review. *Psychological Bulletin*, **38**, 668–82.

Ellis, N. R. (1963). The stimulus trace and behavioural inadequacy. In N. R. Ellis (ed.), *Handbook of Mental Deficiency*. New York: McGraw-Hill, pp. 1–32.

Everson, M., and Boat, C. (1989). False allegations of sexual abuse by children and adolescents. *Journal of the American Academy of Child and Adolescent Psychiatry*, **28**, 230–5.

Faller, C. F. (1988). Criteria for judging the credibility of children's statements about their sexual abuse. *Child Welfare*, **67**, 389–401.

Flavell, K. H. (1977). *Cognitive Development*. Englewood Cliffs, NJ: Prentice-Hall.

Forbes, D. D. S. (1988). A two-year old's memory observed. *The Psychologist*, **1**, 27–31.

Freud, S. (1924). *A General Introduction to Psychoanalysis*. London: Hogarth Press.

Geiselman, R. E., Fisher, R. P., and Mackinnon, D. P. (1986). Enhancement of eye-witness memory with the cognitive interview. *American Journal of Psychology*, **99**, 385–401.

Geiselman, R. E., and Pedilla, J. (1988). Interviewing child witnesses with the cognitive interview. Unpublished manuscript.

Glazer, D., and Collins, C. (1989). The response of young, non-sexually abused children to anatomically correct dolls. *Journal of Child Psychology and Psychiatry*, **30**, 547–60.

Goodman, G., and Aman, C. (1987). Children's use of anatomically correct dolls to report an event. Paper presented at the Society for Research in Child Development, Baltimore, USA.

Goodman, G., Aman, C., and Hirschman, J. (1987). Child sexual and physical abuse: Children's testimony. In S. J. Ceci, M. P. Toglia and D. F. Ross (eds), *Children's Eyewitness Memory*. New York: Springer, pp. 1–23.

Goodman, G., Hirschman and Rudy, L. (eds) (1987). Children's testimony: Research and policy implications. Paper presented at the Society for Research in Child Development, Baltimore, USA.

Hedderman, C. (1988). *Children's Evidence: The Need for Corroboration*. Home Office Research and Planning Unit, Occasional Paper No. 41. London: Home Office.

Holgerson, A. (1988). Formal structural analysis. Researchers in the History of Education and Theory of Interpretation, Report No. 6, Department of Education, University of Stockholm, Stockholm.

Humphrey, H. H. (1985). *Report on Scott County Investigations*. Office of the Attorney General, Minnesota, USA.

Istomina, Z. M. (1975). The development of voluntary memory in preschool age children. *Soviet Psychology*, **13**(4), 5–64.

Johnson, M., and Foley, M. A. (1984). Differentiating fact from fantasy: The reliability of children's testimony. *Journal of Social Issues*, **40**(2), 33–50.

Jones, D. P., and Krugman, R. (1986). Can a three-year old child bear witness to her sexual assault and attempted murder? *Child Abuse and Neglect*, **10**, 253–8.

Jones, D. P., and McGraw, J. M. (1987). Reliable and fictitious accounts of sexual abuse in children. *Journal of Interpersonal Violence*, **2**, 27–45.

King, M. A., and Yuille, J. (1987). Suggestibility and the child witness. In S. J. Ceci, M. P. Toglia and D. F. Ross (eds), *Children's Eyewitness Testimony*. New York: Springer, pp. 24–35.

Kobasigawa, A. (1974). Utilization of retrieval cues by children in recall. *Child Development*, **45**, 127–34.

Lindberg, M. A. (1970). Is knowledge-based development a necessary and sufficient condition for memory development? *Journal of Experimental Child Psychology*, **30**, 401–10.

Lindsay, D. S., and Johnson, M. K. (1987). Reality monitoring and suggestibility: Children's ability to discriminate among memories from different sources. In S. J. Ceci, M. P. Toglia and D. F. Ross (eds) *Children's Eyewitness Memory*. New York: Springer Verlag.

List, J. A. (1986). Age and schematic differences in the reliability of eyewitness testimony. *Developmental Psychology*, **22**, 50–7.

Loftus, E. F. (1979). *Eyewitness Testimony*. Cambridge, MA: Harvard University Press.

Loftus, E. F., and Davies, G. M. (1984). Distortions in the memory of children. *Journal of Social Issues*, **40**(2), 51–67.

Loftus, E. F., and Greene, E. (1980). Warning: Even memory for faces may be contagious. *Law and Human Behavior*, **4**, 323–34.

Macleod, M. (1985). Psychological dynamics of the police interview. Unpublished doctoral dissertation, University of Aberdeen, Scotland.

Malpass, R., and Devine, P. (1981). Line-up instructions and the absence of the offender. *Journal of Applied Psychology*, **66**, 482–9.

Marin, B. V., Holmes, D. L., Guth, M., and Kovac, P. (1979). The potential of children as eyewitnesses: A comparison of children and adults on eyewitness tasks. *Law and Human Behavior*, **3**, 295–306.

Moston, S. (1987). The suggestibility of children in interview studies. *First Language*, **7**, 67–78.

Moston, S., and Engelberg, T. (in press). The effects of social support on children's eyewitness testimony. *Applied Cognitive Psychology*.

Murray, S. (1988). Cross-modal integration in children's memory. In M. M. Gruneberg, P. E. Morris and R. N. Sykes (eds), *Practical Aspects of Memory: Current Research and Issues*. Chichester: Wiley, pp. 281–6.

Nelson, K. (1978). *Event Knowledge: Structure and Function in Development*. Hillsdale, NJ: Lawrence Erlbaum.

Nelson, K., and Gruendel, J. (1981). Generalised event representations: basic building blocks of cognitive development. In A. Brown and M. Lamb (eds), *Advances in Developmental Psychology*. Hillsdale, NJ: Lawrence Erlbaum, pp. 131–58.

Nelson, K., and Ross, G. (1980). The general and specifics of long-term memory in infants and young children. In M. Perlmutter (ed.), *New Directions in Child Development*, vol. 10. San Fransisco: Jossey-Bass, pp. 81–102.

Nide, R. E., and Lange, G. (1987). A note on young children's recall-memory proficiency with strange and familiar experimenters. *Journal of Psychology*, **121**, 567–74.

Peters, D. (1987). The impact of naturally occurring stress on children's memory. In S. J. Ceci, M. P. Toglia and D. F. Ross (eds), *Children's Eyewitness Memory*. New York: Springer, pp. 122–41.

Peters, D. (1989). The influence of stress and arousal on the child witness. Paper presented at the Cornell Conference on the Suggestibility of Children's Recollections, Cornell University, Ithica, USA.

Raskin, D. C., and Esplin, P. W. (1989). Assessment of children's statements of sexual abuse. Paper presented at the Cornell Conference on the Suggestibility of Children's Recollections, Cornell University, Ithica. USA.

Raskin, D. C., and Yuille, J. (1989). Problems in evaluating interviews of children in sexual abuse cases. In S. J. Ceci, D. F. Ross and M. P. Toglia (eds), *Perspectives on Children's Testimony*. New York: Springer, pp. 184–207.

Saywitz, K., Goodman, G., Nichols, E., and Moan, S. (1989). Children's memory for a genital examination. Paper presented to the Society for Research on Child Development, Kansas City, USA.

Schank, R. C., and Abelson, R. P. (1977). *Scripts, Plans, Goals and Understanding*. Hillsdale, NJ: Lawrence Erlbaum.

Steller, M., and Koenken, G. (1989). Criteria-based statement analysis. In D. C. Raskin (ed.), *Psychological Methods in Criminal Investigation and Evidence*. New York: Springer, pp. 217–45.

Stone, M. (1984). *Proof of Fact in Criminal Trials*. Edinburgh: W. Green.

Todd, C. M., and Perlmutter, M. (1980). Reality recalled by preschool children. In M. Perlmutter (ed.), *New Directions for Child Development*, vol. 10. San Francisco: Jossey-Bass, pp. 69–86.

Trankell, A. (1972). *Reliability of Evidence*. Stockholm: Beckmans.

Tulving, E. (1983). *Elements of Episodic Memory*. Oxford: Oxford University Press.

Undeutsch, U. (1989). The development of statement reality analysis. In J. Yuille (ed.), *Credibility Assessment*. Dordrecht: Kluwer, pp. 101–20.

Varendonck, J. (1911). Les témoignages d'enfants dans un procès de retentissant. *Archives de Psychologie*, **11**, 129–71.

Wellman, H. M., and Somerville, S. C. (1980). Quasi-naturalistic tasks in the study of cognition: The memory-related skills of toddlers. In M. Perlmutter (ed.), *New Directions in Child Development*, vol. 10. San Francisco: Jossey-Bass.

Westcott, H., Davies, G. M., and Clifford, B. R. (1989a). The use of anatomical dolls in child witness interviews. *Adoption and Fostering*, **13**, 6–14.

Westcott, H., Davies, G., and Clifford, B. R. (1989b). Lying smiles and other stories: Adult's perceptions of children's truthful and deceptive statements. Paper presented at the First European Congress of Psychology, Amsterdam, Holland.

Wilkinson, J. (1988). Context effects in children's event memory. In *Practical Aspects of Memory: Current Research and Issues*, vol. 1. Chichester: Wiley, pp. 107–11.

Williams, G. (1987). Child witnesses. In P. Smith (ed.), *Criminal Law Essays in Honour of J. C. Smith*. London: Butterworths, pp. 188–203.

Yarmey, A. D. (1988). Street proofing and bystander's memory for a child abduction. In M. M. Gruneberg, P. E. Morris and R. N. Sykes (eds), *Practical Aspects of Memory: Current Research and Issues*, vol. 1. Chichester: Wiley, pp. 112–16.

Yates, A., and Terr, L. (1988). Anatomically correct dolls—should they be used as a basis for expert testimony? *Journal of the American Academy of Child and Adolescent Psychiatry*, **27**, 254–7.

6

Interviewing Children Suspected of Being Sexually Abused: A Review of Theory and Practice

EILEEN VIZARD
Newham Child and Family Consultation Service, London, UK

Approaches to interviewing children suspected of being sexually abused are proliferating in England and elsewhere. This chapter will review existing literature in relation to interviewing children, the use of play adjuncts, such as anatomical dolls, and evidential issues, in relation to court proceedings. A review of current clinical practice—an attempt to organise the different interviewing protocols, according to parameters of structure, evidence gathering, and prescriptiveness—is followed by an 'ideal' case example, a discussion looking at common ground between various approaches to interviewing, evidential dilemmas, and finally possible ways forward.

REVIEW OF THE LITERATURE

Use of Anatomical Dolls in Interviews with Children

The use of anatomical dolls in interviews with children suspected of being sexually abused has been a source of concern amongst professionals since their introduction into clinical practice in England, around ten years ago. The existing literature on this subject has been reviewed by Westcott *et al.* (1989), with the conclusion that 'there seems no good reason to immediately remove the dolls from use in diagnostic therapeutic interviews with suspected child abuse victims' (p. 20). The need for further research into the specific psychological role of anatomical dolls in interview, and the need for caution in interpreting children's play with anatomical dolls, is stressed by the authors, who overall feel that, used in the right way, by properly trained professionals, the dolls may be helpful.

Clinical Approaches to Sex Offenders and Their Victims
Edited by C. R. Hollin and K. Howells © 1991 John Wiley & Sons Ltd

However, certain British clinicians have suggested that the use of anatomical dolls is in itself 'morally unjustified' (Family Law Reports, [1987], p. 337) and should be 'considered unethical' in cases of non-admitted child abuse (Family Law Reports, [1989], p. 288). In an article by Yates and Terr (1988) debating the use of anatomical dolls as a basis for expert testimony, Terr states that: 'The anatomically correct dolls make but one request—play sex' (p. 256). This view is echoed by others (McIver and Wakefield, 1987) who state that: 'Any information obtained from such [doll] interviews should be discarded. There is nothing to support their use as diagnostic or assessment tools' (p. 13).

In the context of contested civil court cases involving child sexual abuse allegations, legal and evidential issues were described in a special issue of the Family Law Reports [1987], in relation to cases involving the Great Ormond Street Interview Technique (Vizard and Tranter, 1988a) and the use of anatomical dolls. The majority of comments about the use of the dolls are negative, with some exceptions (see Swinton-Thomas, J., Family Law Reports, [1987], pp. 280–92). More recently legal practitioners (Enright, 1989), have seemed to accept that anatomically correct dolls can be used in interviews with suspected sexually abused children, but it has been suggested (Enright, 1989) that: 'There might be one or two interviews before the dolls are produced. . . . Certainly a child ought never to be introduced to the dolls by an interviewer who is effectively a stranger' (p. 77). This comment reflects the suspicion that the mere presence of anatomical dolls in an interview, particularly with a stranger-professional, may have undesirable but unspecified results.

In America, the affirmative side of the debate on pros and cons of the anatomical dolls has been put by Yates (Yates and Terr, 1988) who points out that:

> It would seem that the dolls are in the process of being accepted by the Profession. If we were to abandon their use because of the Courts' criticism, they could never be fully accepted by the Profession or introduced as evidence in Court. Above all, we need to continue to use the dolls, so that we may understand and further develop the technique. (p. 255)

Yates goes on to describe, with a certain irony, the fact that child psychiatrists have used anatomically absent dolls since the birth of their profession, and that this initial discrimination against dolls with genitals has led to a 'rather ludicrous position of being able to base an opinion on children's reactions to dolls, but not on dolls with genitals' (p. 255). Yates suggests that dolls with genitals should be part of the standard equipment in a therapist's room, hence allowing for the accumulation of clinical data about reactions of abused and non-abused children to dolls with genitalia.

Play with Dolls

The second area of contention in the literature relates to the meaning or otherwise of sexual play by children with anatomical dolls. Gabriel (1985) observed 16 children from a day care centre in a play session with anatomically correct dolls, and noted that half of these children showed an unusual interaction with the genitals of the dolls, and relevant associated play with the dolls. It was not clear whether this sample contained undiagnosed sexual abuse victims, since no efforts were made to exclude this possibility. Nevertheless, Gabriel suggests that sexualised play with the dolls may be seen as part of normal child development, where unconscious fantasies about infantile sexuality are enacted, using dolls with genitals. It is suggested that interviewers who use anatomically correct dolls may have a presupposition that abuse has occurred and may also be ignorant about the 'projection evoking properties of toys' (such as the dolls), so that later erroneous interpretation of children's play is then made.

Gabriel's study would suggest that such sexualised play is a normal response in young children, but this is not supported by other research; Glaser and Collins (1989) state: 'From our results, it appears that explicit sexual play with the dolls may well arise from the child's preoccupations which are based on previous exposure to explicit sexual information or activity' (p. 559). Of the 91 non-abused children between the ages of 3–6 years, given a play session with anatomically correct dolls, only 5 children who played with the dolls showed any sexualised quality in their play. In this study, the bulk of the children's play with the dolls involved day to day activities such as putting the dolls to bed, and feeding and bathing them. However, 35% of this sample of non-abused children showed reticence or avoidance towards the anatomically correct dolls, but familiarity with the dolls led to a wish to play with them again, and the authors conclude that the dolls were not regarded as unpleasant by the children.

In a larger scale study reported by Sivan et al. (1988), 140 young non-abused children aged between 3 and 8 years played with anatomical dolls as well as other play material: firstly with an adult interviewer present; secondly the child was observed playing alone; and thirdly with the adult interviewer returning, to encourage the child to undress the doll and name body parts, after which the adult left the child with undressed anatomical dolls. Given the choice of other play activities, children's behaviour involved the dolls less than 25% of the time, aggressive behaviour with the dolls occurred less than 1% of doll play—similar to other findings (Glaser and Collins, 1989)—and sexual play or discussion was not provoked in the children by the anatomical dolls.

Studies which compare sexually abused and non-sexually abused children's responses to anatomical dolls (Jampole and Webber, 1987; Templeton and Webber, 1985) suggest a significant excess of sexualised play responses in abused groups. This is supported by clinicians' accounts of sexualised play observed in interviews with children who were subsequently diagnosed as sexually abused, as compared to non-sexualised responses in referred children who were subsequently diagnosed as non-abused (Vizard and Tranter, 1988b).

In a study where the behaviours of 16 abused and 16 non-abused girls aged between 5 and 8 years were compared, the girls were firstly left alone with dressed anatomical dolls, and asked to change the clothes of the dolls, and were subsequently asked to tell the interviewer a story involving the dolls (August and Forman, 1986). It was noted that the non-abused girls showed significantly less aggressive behaviour with less reference to the dolls' genitalia than did the abused girls, some of whom spontaneously demonstrated sexual activity with the dolls, but others of whom showed higher avoidance of the dolls than the non-abused girls.

Overall, therefore, in relation to sexualised play of children with anatomically correct dolls, there is a strong consensus that sexually abused children may show more directly sexualised play with the dolls (Enright, 1989; Glaser and Collins, 1989; Jampole and Webber, 1987; Sivan et al., 1988; Templeton and Webber, 1985) and some evidence that aggressive doll behaviour may also be commoner in abused children (August and Forman, 1986). It is not clear whether significance can be attached to avoidant doll behaviour in either abused or non-abused children.

Consensus seems to have been reached on the advisability of presenting anatomical dolls clothed rather than unclothed to children (Boat and Everson, 1988; Vizard and Tranter, 1988c; White and Santilli, 1988); although it seems clear from other work (Glaser and Collins, 1989; Sivan et al., 1988) that whether clothed or unclothed, the dolls are not primarily used for sex play by children.

A recent study reported by Schor and Sivan (1989), looking at the names ascribed by non-abused children to the private parts of anatomical dolls, indicated that children in the older age groups were more accurate in labelling such parts than younger children. In addition, there was a sharp increase in children's understanding and ability to communicate about private parts, from age 5 years onwards. Because younger children tended to offer more labels per body part, and because such labels were incorrect, pressing young children for detail on such issues of labelling may not be helpful. Since children often proffer idiosyncratic labels to body parts that are different from parental labels, the advisability of checking the child's name for body parts (Yates and Terr, 1988) early in the interviews with children suspected of being abused is underlined by the Schor and Sivan study, which also shows that idiosyncratic body part names, different from parental labels, are not in themselves indicative of sexual abuse in the child.

Suggestibility, Memory and Dolls

Little research has been done on the interaction between suggestive leading questions and the use of anatomical dolls in the same interview. It has been suggested by Westcott et al. (1989) that the role of the dolls, whether as memory cues for past sexual events, or as sources of misleadingly sexualised statements or behaviours when coupled with suggestive questions, should be further investigated.

Goodman and Aman (1987) allowed 61 non-abused (screened to eliminate the possibility of sexual abuse) children aged 3–5 years to play games with a male adult, and subsequently questioned these children under three different circumstances: (i) with anatomical dolls; (ii) with non-anatomically correct dolls; and (iii) without dolls. The children were then asked to recall what went on in the play session with the male adult, and the children in groups (i) and (ii) were asked to demonstrate this with the dolls. Both non-leading and misleading or suggestive questions were put to the children, who were then allowed 5 minutes' free play. Results indicated that the presence of anatomical dolls did not lead to an increase in errors in replying to misleading questions (such as had the man kissed, touched or spanked the child?). These findings indicate that the anatomical dolls do not promote suggestibility in children, even when the dolls are used in conjunction with misleading, abuse-orientated questions.

In chapter 5, Graham Davies reviews the role of various cues to children's memory. It is acknowledged that whilst anatomical dolls may not provoke sexualised responses in non-abused children, even when used with suggestive questioning, nevertheless, there is no direct evidence that anatomical dolls specifically facilitate or cue memories of past abuse when used with abused children.

The possibility that contextual cues such as a familiar environment may be helpful to children in remembering a past event is borne out by research (Morton, 1990; Wilkinson, 1988), as is the facilitating effect of prior discussions with, and the subsequent presence of, a trusted peer, when 7 year olds are asked to describe an earlier event to an adult questioner (Moston and Engelborg, in press). Set against such research evidence is the persisting view of clinicians (Vizard and Tranter, 1988c) that it is often difficult to decide at the assessment stage whether a non-abusing parent (or relative from a family where sexual abuse has occurred) is a facilitator or an inhibitor for spontaneous child recall. The practice has therefore developed of allowing children an individual interview alone with a professional, such that 'ambiguous' familial cues are eradicated for a certain period of time. Indeed, while the possibility of child errors in describing adult personal qualities has been described (Davies *et al.*, 1988), it is not known whether the presence of an 'ambiguous' family member may not only inhibit a child's free recall of abuse, but might also possibly cue the older child into previously rehearsed false allegations against another adult. A more likely negative outcome for the presence of an 'ambiguous' family member in a child interview, is the false retraction of all allegations as part of a process of accommodation to an uncertain environment (Summit, 1983).

Recent British research by Glaser (personal communication) has indicated that previous facilitating discussion of possible abuse issues between a child and a skilled care worker or foster parent may significantly enhance the likelihood or later disclosure of sexual abuse in a formal interview. The role of a 'trusted' non-ambiguous extra-familial adult in an extended process of disclosure of child sexual abuse could, therefore, be relevant.

If a child's memory of traumatic events depends upon a sequence of encoding, storage and retrieval, then deficits can occur at all stages in this process. As Graham Davies (Chapter 5) points out, encoding involves the effective taking in of information from the environment, and relating such events to existing knowledge and experience. Many abused children have cognitive and developmental difficulties (Briere and Runtz, 1988). When this is taken in conjunction with abuser strategies in targeting, isolating, systematically confusing and entrapping children into sexual abuse (Salter, 1988), it seems possible that abused children become too confused about external reality properly to encode, subsequently store, and finally retrieve clear abuse memories.

Confusion, dissociation from reality and memory deficits are described in post-traumatic stress disorder (Lindberg and Distad, 1985), which is associated with unresolved child sexual abuse. Whilst spontaneous recall of abuse events is desirable both therapeutically and evidentially, with confused or inarticulate children memories of abuse may not be accessible for retrieval and recall. However, such memories may be repressed from consciousness although possibly betrayed by sexualised behaviour—described as a 'body memory' of the event (Vizard, 1988)—or by psychosomatic symptoms.

When abuse experiences are not available for retrieval and spontaneous description, it has been suggested that younger children, in particular, will need a great deal more assistance and prompting to search their memories for a response, and that in this sense, the interviewer must go beyond the sparse details in a child's initial statement (Davies and Brown, 1978). The fuller and still accurate recall of young children to specific-direct (leading, in legal terms) questions with a context cue, as compared to limited recall with generic questions, has been described in relation to non-traumatic experimental events set up during school-based research (Wilkinson, 1988). The facilitating effect of context as a cue to recall is noted particularly when non-verbal methods of recall are used, although it is not clear whether dolls or play materials are helpful as non-verbal cues. In trying to elicit information about the school-based events, Morton (1990) comments that: 'It is remarkable how one has to persevere in order to get some children of this age to speak' (p. 8).

The process of retrieval of affect-laden, abuse experiences may also be difficult for an anxious child victim: judicial initiatives which separate the child from the alleged abuser by a screen in court, or via a video link (Spencer, 1987) may prevent inhibition of the retrieval process. In clinical practice, retrieval and difficulties with recall are helped by a range of questions aimed at facilitating the child's capacity to respond.

Other Research Issues

False allegations of sexual abuse, once thought to be rare, are occurring more frequently in British courts in relation to custody and access disputes. Previous work has indicated that most false allegations are adult-instigated, although they may sometimes be child-articulated (Jones and McGraw, 1987). We do not know how often false allegations are made as a result of overzealous interviewing of suggestible children, followed by subsequent erroneous interpretation of interview material produced in this way. However, Jones and McGraw (1987) have also indicated that when professionals are biased by the belief that children never lie, then a suggestive questioning technique may be used, with the danger that the same bias will be brought to bear in later interpretations of the child's responses. Further research evidence is needed on these points, but bearing in mind that false allegations in a court context seem to be occurring more often, an overtly credulous approach towards believing children's abuse allegations should be tempered with caution. It has been suggested (Family Law Reports, [1987], p. 296), that a basic hypothesis that the child has *not* been abused should be disproved by the clinician using a range of non-leading questions to probe the truth. The ethical and technical issues involved in engaging with children during an interview, in such a frame of mind, have not yet been described.

British research (Vizard et al., 1989) has indicated that when abused but inarticulate children were interviewed, using some leading questions to facilitate communication, the children were rated as poor witnesses by lawyers, blind to other information, who subsequently viewed the videotaped interviews. The videotapes of inarticulate children were rated as likely to be of little evidential value, and interview technique was cited as the main reason for this judgement. By contrast, when either abused or non-abused children who were chatty and spontaneous were interviewed in the same way, also using some leading questions, the children were rated as good witnesses by lawyers; and the interviews were rated as more likely to be of evidential value, despite the presence of leading questions and facilitation. Other disciplines rating videotapes in this study were less affected by interview technique and more concerned with rating observed child behaviours as possible indicators of abuse. These other disciplines included professionals engaged in face to face interviewing of children, e.g. police and child psychiatrists. Although accuracy in rating the likelihood of child sexual abuse was equally good for non-abused children, across all professional groups, face to face interviewers were more consistent in rating children who had been abused, and were less likely than lawyers to rate as non-abused, those children who were in the 'probably abused' category.

However, a similar American study by Jensen et al. (1986) noted that blind ratings by psychiatrists, attorneys and social workers failed to distinguish between abused and non-abused children, videotaped in a semi-structured interview with anatomical dolls. This study showed all raters making false positive ratings for non-abused children.

It is possible, therefore, that lawyers without skills in face to face interviews may erroneously rate inarticulate, non-spontaneous abused children, and dismiss the evidential value of the videotaped interview. If this is so, there are implications for the training of lawyers and judges in relation to child development, speech, play and behavioural patterns, since incorrect perceptions of such behaviours could lead to false negative or positive 'diagnoses' by judges, with worrying results for children. A recent initiative by the Lord Chancellor (April 1989), in appointing a woman judge with an advisory role on judicial training, may lead to the further education of judges in relation to child development etc. as well as arresting adversarial attitudes now perceived as unhelpful by the judiciary (Judge Joyanne Bracewell, July 1989).

Leading Questions

Cross and Tapper (1985) define a leading question as one which: (i) suggests the answer desired; or (ii) assumes the existence of disputed facts to which the witness has yet to testify. (Category (ii), disputed facts questions, can also be described as improper rather than leading.)

However, the context also defines the leading nature of the question, so that 'Did you see any traffic?' which requires a Yes/No answer, might be a leading question for one witness, but not for another witness who has just said he was standing on the side of the road. Similarly, the question 'Did you hear what A said?' would be a leading and improper question if the presence of A in the witness's company, or the fact that A had said anything were in dispute. It is pointed out that it should never be forgotten that 'leading' is a relative, not an absolute term, and that therefore 'everything depends on the context'. If context is so important, it follows that the semantic nature of the question is less important than the questioner's assumptions about context. Therefore, semantic (what is a leading question), and contextual (when is a question leading), legal issues may be important when considering lawyer reactions to clinical interviews containing leading questions.

Returning to the issue of questioning which can help children to retrieve more information from memory, it can be seen that the semantic and contextual aspects of questioning are inextricably linked. Many clinically facilitating questions could be regarded as 'leading' in a legal sense. For instance, it could be objected that a preliminary question to a child, such as 'Tell me what happened', or even 'Tell me about it', contain both a suggested answer (that something/it happened), and a disputed fact (that something/it happened), in a context of alleged and disputed sexual abuse. On this basis, such questions should be regarded as improper and should, in legal terms, be disallowed, despite research evidence cited above that cues and prompts (leading questions) are needed to aid recall in certain young children.

Legal complexities in defining leading questions are matched by the paucity of clinical definition of such questions, which are proffered by only four groups (Bannister and Print, 1989; Jones and McQuiston, 1988; Vizard and Tranter, 1988b; White et al., 1987), and a typology of questions is suggested by one group (Vizard and Tranter, 1988c). This is surprising, since all other clinicians and groups are in complete agreement that (non-defined) leading questions should be avoided wherever possible.

Evidential Issues and Legal Opinion

Evidential issues in child abuse cases have been subjected to extensive legal challenge in the United States (Macfarlane and Krebs, 1986), and much information about victims' views has emerged from the work of American clinicians within the USA court systems (Berliner, 1987): experiences echoed in recent years by British clinical teams. In a special issue of the Family Law Reports [1987] judicial comments indicate disquiet with diagnostic interview techniques, involving children suspected of being sexually abused. One judge Hollis, J., (Family Law Report, [1987], p. 328) remarked in his judgement: 'The conclusions that I draw are these. First of all, there is no evidential weight to be attached to this so-called diagnostic interview whatsoever.' In the same issue of the Family Law Reports, Ewbank, J., states: 'I have doubt about its [the videotape] evidential standing. I have even more doubts about the evidential value of the technique. Of course, I remind myself that it is not intended to have evidential value. It is for clinical purposes and not, as I pointed out earlier, with a view to evidence' (p. 278). Such critical comments characterise this special issue of the Family Law Reports, but other judges have more constructive remarks to make. The view taken by a particular judge about the evidential value of such interviews may determine the extent to which that judge is prepared to ignore or override the conclusions of the interviewer, in relation to the possibility of sexual abuse having occurred. When a judge disapproves of a technique and the material elicited in such interviews, it is possible for the judge to make a legal 'finding' that abuse has not occurred, regardless of medical evidence or the expert evidence of the interviewer. There seems to be a question of who decides the 'truth' in cases of sexual abuse and, indeed, the notion of absolute truth or certainty in sexual abuse cases has been queried (Vizard, 1986). Judicial opinion is divided on this point, however, and in relation to another child abuse case, Waite, J., (Family Law Reports, [1987], p. 338) remarks:

> I have found the video recording helpful, but only insofar as it assists me to test the general probative value of the medical evidence. I do not see it as my function to draw any independent inferences of my own from what I have observed by viewing it. Like the evidence of the doctors itself, it is part of the evidential fabric and no more nor less than that.

Such a measured response to the evidential issues involved was little heard in the initial controversy which followed other judges' criticisms (Ewbank, J., 1986, in *The Times*) of the Great Ormond Street Hospital interview technique (see below). More recently, following the development of a semi-structured approach to interviewing children from Great Ormond Street Hospital (Vizard and Tranter, 1988c), judicial comments have been more favourable. Indeed, it has been said that the interviews now more closely approximate to the forensic needs of the court than in the early days of child interviews (Latey, J., Family Law Reports, [1987], p. 462). Nevertheless, recent legal publications continue to address concerns about interview techniques.

Enright (1989) notes a number of 'objectionable features' in the use of dolls, including the possibility that a preconception of abuse exists in the mind of the person interviewing a child victim, which combined with a 'pressure' interview— that is, one conducted in a driven way and combined with leading, multiple choice and hypothetical questions—could constitute a 'dishonest approach'. Enright suggests this is 'also potentially confusing to a child who might think "Is this a game?" ' (p. 80). The concern stated here is that children could be forced into false indications or allegations of sexual abuse, by partisan and pressure interviews, with subsequent gross injustice to the accused person.

Enright admits that:

> Hostility is particularly marked in cases where the evidence of abuse stems largely or wholly from diagnostic interviews conducted with the aid of anatomically correct dolls . . . not surprisingly some lawyers exhibit a degree of professional outrage over diagnostic interviews which may, and sometimes do, flout every convention governing the eliciting of evidence. Cross-examinations of clinicians tend, therefore, to be lengthy and hostile. It is, nonetheless, the best aid to an assessment of the evidence (p. 82).

Hence the child advocate or expert witness can expect rigorous cross-examination in relation to issues of technique, in a way which does not always seem constructive and which may cause professionals to back off from cases: this issue has been discussed from a clinician's perspective (Vizard, 1987). Criticisms of technique and practice have recently extended to the non-recording by an independent social worker of child interviews on videotape (Bush, J., [1988]a); and also to the use of leading questions in joint police/social worker interviews with children (Bush, J., [1988]b). However, a recent judgement, Waterhouse, J., in 1989 confirmed that child interviews should be videotaped, since the evidential material involved is helpful to the civil court in decision making.

A recommendation was made by Judge Pigot in 1989 that pre-recorded joint police/social work interviews with child witnesses can, under certain conditions, be accepted as evidence in criminal proceedings. However, it remains to be seen if recent guidance on police/social worker interviews with suspected abused children (Home Office, 1989) will allow for a child-centred, non-leading, yet evidentially sound method of interviewing to emerge on videotape.

A balanced review (Weyland, 1989) of legal and evidential issues in relation to the management of child sexual abuse cases within the civil courts has recently highlighted the awareness of lawyers that a conflict exists between 'judicial and psychiatric standards of evidence'. While enumerating deficiencies and strengths in certain psychiatric interviewing techniques, the author also raises the issue of judicial training: 'It is questionable whether judicial training and experience enable judges to draw inferences from diagnostic interviews which require for their interpretation a high degree of expertise' (p. 243). Weyland (1989) also emphasises the need for open mindedness and a willingness to revise hypotheses and theories, presumably desirable qualities for both the judiciary and expert witnesses.

INTERVIEWING CHILDREN—A REVIEW OF PRACTICE

In looking at the issue of how best to interview children suspected of having been sexually abused, the available approaches to this topic will be reviewed in order to tease out both points of difference and points in common. It is not intended to suggest that any one of these approaches is the correct one, or in any way the method of choice. Similarly, it is not intended to list every available interview protocol in relation to work with suspected sexually abused children since worldwide there are a substantial number of such approaches. However, at least ten different approaches are now recognised within British practice, including four American and one Canadian. These approaches are as follows:

(1) Great Ormond Street Team (Vizard and Tranter, 1988a,b,c);
(2) NSPCC (Bannister and Print, 1989);
(3) White *et al.* (1987);
(4) Jones and McQuiston (1988);
(5) Bray (1989);

(6) Statement Validity Analysis (SVA; Yuille, 1988);
(7) Boat and Everson (1988);
(8) MacFarlane and Krebs (1986);
(9) Glaser and Frosch (1988);
(10) Royal College of Psychiatrists (1988).

Apart from interview protocols as such, various official bodies in America and England have published statements (American Academy of Child and Adolescent Psychiatry, 1988), reports (Cleveland Inquiry Report, 1988; Standing Medical Advisory Committee, 1988), and guidance (Home Office, 1989) on the way in which interviewing child victims should be approached, and on the multidisciplinary assessment context.

It is important to remember that clinical work with children is a relatively recent phenomenon in the twentieth century, although a number of psychoanalysts such as Anna Freud (1962), Melanie Klein (1926/1975), and Donald Winnicott (1958) pioneered techniques for talking to non-abused children. Subsequently, psychiatric practice has evolved and the need for individual interviews with children presenting with a range of problems has been accepted. How best to conduct these interviews, however, has always been a matter of debate, with some clinicians suggesting a reasonably structured approach to talking individually with children (Hill, 1985), whilst others have suggested that children are equally well assessed in a family context (Hildebrand et al., 1981). Therefore, leaving aside the issue of possible sexual abuse, we can see that a lively professional debate exists within child psychiatry and psychotherapy with respect to the merits and demerits of different ways of talking with disturbed children.

This should help to put into context the peculiarly heated controversies which have arisen around different ways of interviewing suspected sexually abused children, some of whom are a client group for child psychiatrists and therapists.

The GOS Approach (Vizard and Tranter, 1988a,b,c)

In the early 1980s, the Great Ormond Street (GOS) Team in the Hospital for Sick Children, London, was one of the few agencies working with suspected sexually abused children in England. Within this group, a family-centred approach to assessing child psychiatric problems was initially the method of choice in relation to these new cases of suspected sexual abuse. Therefore, for some time, referred children were questioned about possible abuse experiences within a family context. This approach initially seemed viable, since the cases referred at that time were pre-pubertal and teenage children who were verbal and apparently able to discuss possible abuse within a family context. However, like other workers in this field in America in the late 1970s and in England in the mid and late 1980s, the Great Ormond Street Team learned on a trial and error base that even older articulate children could not necessarily talk freely about sexual abuse within a family setting. As a result, and in conjunction with the increasing numbers of young children being referred to the team, the practice was developed of interviewing separately all children suspected of being sexually abused. In addition such interviews were video recorded as, once again, video-taping clinical work was part of the ordinary practice of the hospital team at that time. The first individual interviews, conducted in the early 1980s by the GOS Team with children suspected of having been sexually abused, did not have a specific format or a particular approach, but relied on the clinical experience of the interviewer to decide how to pace the interview, and what questions, if any, to ask. The type of suspected sexually abused child being referred to the team was a child typified by psychosomatic symptoms (hence the hospital referral), chronicity of abuse (hence the mature age of the initial children referred), and anxiety or inhibition in talking about possible abuse experience (hence the refer-ral to a specialist team). This combination of qualities in many of the children referred meant that an intuitive clinical approach to talking with such children was initially developed by the team. This approach involved the use of a great deal of empathy, rapport building, and facilitative questioning, including a pro-portion of leading questions. Since many of these cases were involved in court based disputes about custody and access, any possible allegations made by chil-dren during such interviews became a matter of natural concern for the court. The coincidental fact that these interviews had been captured on videotape was not lost on lawyers representing the parents or the alleged abuser in such cases.

Considerable multi-disciplinary discussion followed the viewing of these con-troversial early videos, as a result of which the GOS technique was amended to a semi-structured format.

The GOS semi-structured approach to interviewing children suggests that certain stages in the interview can be followed by the clinician in a flexible way. The initial free play period allows the opportunity for a rapport to be established with the child in the early part of the interview, before moving on to more specific abuse related issues much later in the interview once the child's vocabul-ary for body parts has been elicited. The suggested stages are as follows:

(1) Free play period;
(2) Undressing dolls and naming body parts;
(3) Type of touching;
(4) Naming the dolls;
(5) Re-enactment of abuse;
(6) Recapping, reassurance and relief.

The need to put the emotional and therapeutic needs of the child first is stressed in this approach: guidance is given on how to recognise and avoid legally defined leading questions; and how to facilitate the child's spontaneous responses, which would in any event be more evidentially valid in court.

A typology of questions is suggested where open, closed, multi-choice and hypothetical questions are described and examples given. The interviewer is advised always to vary the questioning 'set' or order, so that children cannot learn or predict which type of question or alternative will follow. Thus the danger of the child trying to please the interviewer by predicting the 'correct' answer is minimised.

This approach also suggests that complex multi-choice or hypothetical questions (accepted to be leading in legal terms) should be omitted, or avoided if possible, and if they must be used then such questions should be reserved for the end of the interview. The need to avoid over-emphasising the importance of such interviews in the total assessment process is stressed where the family background and family functioning, risk factors for abuse, and medical and school reports will all form part of a full psychological assessment of the child concerned.

However, although the clinical experience of the GOS Team has suggested that a semi-structured approach to interviewing may be the best way forward, it is by no means clear, from a research point of view, that such an approach is any more valid than the initial GOS open ended clinical approach, or indeed, any of the other approaches listed above. Clinical research is currently being undertaken in relation to such videotaped interviews with suspected child abuse victims (conducted using this approach), in order to look at issues of validity and professional accuracy in rating the possibility of sexual abuse when looking at such interviews (Vizard et al., 1989). Early results suggest that, when conducted by skilled interviewers and subsequently rated by experienced clinicians, valid distinctions can be drawn between abused and non-abused children. It may be that further amendments to the suggested approach will be necessary as a result of these research findings.

NSPPC Approach (Bannister and Print, 1989)

This recently suggested approach to interviewing children has arisen out of the perceived need for National Society for Prevention of Cruelty to Children (NSPCC) workers to train to interview suspected child sexual abuse victims as part of the statutory work of that agency. The NSPCC model stresses the need for such interviews to be conducted sensitively, at the child's pace, and by a skilled, trained worker.

The approach is described as interactive, between child and worker, and play as a means of communication is stressed. Since the notion of a validation interview is presented, the implication seems to be that referral for some level of suspicion about child sexual abuse may be followed by an interview designated to validate (or invalidate) such a suspicion.

The proposed NSPCC model falls into three phases:

Phase 1—Reassurance;
Phase 2—Re-enactment;
Phase 3—Rehearsal.

In this model, the first phase is seen as an opportunity to make a non-threatening engagement with the child, to clarify family details, use play to understand the child's world, and to reassure the child so that a good rapport is established. Phase 2, re-enactment, is seen as the point in the interview where the focus may be more of possible disclosure of sexual abuse, with concurrent expression of feelings and anxieties by the child. In this phase, more direct play by the child and questions by the therapist may lead to disclosure with confirmation of details. The NSPCC approach suggests that the use of anatomically correct dolls may be helpful and guidance is given on how the interviewer can elicit the child's vocabulary for various body parts and so on. This approach also recommends the use of puppets, such as 'monster' and 'angel' puppets, to encourage interaction between interviewer and child, as well as the projection of worries on to the puppets themselves. In this way the interviewer is encouraged to enter fully into the child's play world, where the focus is the expression of worrying feelings, which might or might not lead on to disclosure of sexual abuse. More specific play with drawing or clay modelling is suggested as a method of encouraging disclosure: it is acknowledged, however, that in this approach to interviewing, more direct questions at the end of Phase 2 may be necessary with certain inhibited children. In Phase 3, rehearsal, it is suggested that the interview is concluded, with an opportunity for the child to express feelings about abuse if this has been disclosed, and for the interviewer to describe ways in which help can be offered to the child in future. It is pointed out in relation to Phase 2, that the abused child is likely to receive therapeutic relief if the interview goes well. Indeed, this is listed as the first purpose of conducting such an interview. Within the NSPCC model it is pointed out that for legal reasons leading and hypothetical questions should be avoided, and should only be used, if at all, at the end of Phase 2 re-enactment. However, it is conceded that in order to protect a child who may be at risk of further abuse, the use of leading questions or suggestions may in fact be necessary at this stage in the interview. No validation has yet been undertaken with this approach to interviewing.

White *et al.* (1987)

In this approach, the Sexually Anatomically Correct (SAC) Doll Interview protocol was developed for three reasons: (i) to provide data accepted as reliable and valid by professionals; (ii) to provide evidential data for court; and (iii) to show that objectively elicited data from pre-schoolers can be produced when using this protocol. The authors stress that the two basic guidelines used in this protocol are 'blindness' to any detail about the suspected sexual abuse, and the use of non-leading questions. Much emphasis is laid on the need for the interviewer to remain 'objective' and separate from the various parties involved in court proceedings; thereby showing 'external independence', as well as remaining 'blind' to background, so that all interviewer information is child-generated, thus ensuring 'internal independence'. It is also suggested that reliability ratings should be a standard part of training with the SAC protocol, so that interviewing expertise is maintained.

The clinical ethos of this approach to interviewing suspected abused children is forensic in nature. Whilst very precise advice is given on the quantity (very few) and the nature (specific) of the toys to be used during the interview, it is expected that the interviewer will be guided at all times by the need to produce evidentially valid, child-generated data for court. The Interview Protocol describes a free play session with the child, and suggests that this period should be used for making the child comfortable and relaxed and for building up a rapport with the interviewer,as well as allowing the chance for informal developmental assessment to occur. It is not clear to what extent, if at all, such a protocol expects the interview to have a positive or negative therapeutic impact on the child, since the child's feelings and emotional reactions are discussed only in the context of degree of cooperativeness.

Clear, firm advice is given to interviewers about the practicalities of conducting the SAC Interview: room and toy preparation is described, management techniques for child-parent separation and problems are shared, and it is stressed that 'the doll interview should NOT be done in the presence of the parent'. Whilst the possibility of more than two interviews with the child is mentioned, the expectation is that the experienced interviewer will complete the protocol and associated issues within two sessions.

The actual format of the interview is as follows:

(1) Free play period;
(2) Doll identification;
(3) Body parts identification and function;
(4) Abuse evaluation;
(5) Developmental issues;
(6) Termination.

The authors end with an 'admonition' that because of the speed with which the field of interviewing techniques is developing, it is vital for interviewers or 'evaluators' to keep abreast of legal, clinical and research developments. Interviewers are also encouraged to become more objective so that courts will more readily accept the data presented as evidence.

Although this structured approach to interviewing has not yet been validated, the authors claim that it is a reliable method of differentiating between the responses of 25 referred abused and 25 non-referred (probably non-abused children) who were interviewed using this method (White and Santilli, 1988). However, this study was not properly controlled, in that child sexual abuse had not been excluded in the non-referred group. Nevertheless, subsequent independent ratings of indicators derived from file reports, and from the SAC doll interview, confirmed that there were significant differences between the two groups of children, and that the SAC Interview Protocol could help in differentiating between these two groups. Methodological problems in approaching such a validation process are well described.

Jones and McQuiston (1988)

In this approach to interviewing suspected sexually abused children, the authors are aided by considerable experience in America, particularly in the Kempe Institute, where the approach was developed. Jones and McQuiston are emphatic that a 'cook book' style—i.e. a rigidly fixed format approach to interviewing—is not appropriate for cases of suspected sexual abuse. It is made clear that the interview in relation to sexual abuse should be put fully into a context of the child's development, family background, school, and so forth. Nevertheless, Jones and McQuiston suggest six possible sections or stages within the structure of the interview. These are as follows:

(1) Starting the interview;
(2) Inquiry about sexual abuse;
(3) Facilitation;
(4) Free play;
(5) Gathering of specific detail;
(6) The closing phase.

Within this format, guidance is given on the use of toys and play materials, including small doll figures, dolls' houses, puppets, larger dolls, anatomically correct dolls, line drawings, and the drawings of children themselves. Guidance is also given on therapist techniques, such as the avoidance of direct gaze at the child, the use of simple, developmentally appropriate short sentences in questioning, and the avoidance of leading questions.

Jones and McQuiston discuss the definition of leading questions, and ways in which the interviewer can reserve the option to use leading questions until it has been demonstrated that open ended questions are not helpful to that particular child. The point is made that one or two leading questions within an interview may perhaps be acceptable, but an interview which contained nothing but leading questions may be described as 'driven', and would not be acceptable either clinically or legally. In relation to possible error production using facilitation or leading questions, the point is made that certain research findings suggest that it may be interviewer style—e.g. aggressive, child hostile, driven—combined with non-stop leading questions which may lead to error production by child witnesses, rather than the use of leading questions *per se*. Jones and McQuiston stress the importance of adopting a relaxed yet purposive style, and with various caveats, describe methods of facilitation, which include the use of permission-giving statements, multiple choice (either/or format) questions, and hypothetical questions. It is made clear that hypothetical questions should be avoided unless absolutely necessary, and that if any of the facilitation techniques results in a spontaneous statement by the child, then the following question should be open ended to allow the child to elaborate in his or her own words.

Within the approach suggested by Jones and McQuiston free play is included as a possible stage in the interview, but the point is made that children should be allowed to play at any stage if it helps them to communicate, so that free play periods are interspersed with the general flow of the interview. The possibility is raised, with children who do not respond to facilitation, of a specific free play period being introduced in which the interviewer leaves the room to observe the child in free play through a one-way mirror. No tests of reliability or of interview validation of this approach have been published.

Bray (1980, 1989)

This approach, described by an experienced social worker, also acting as a *Guardian ad Litem* in court proceedings, is a child-focused, play-centred, and open ended method of talking with children suspected of being sexually abused. Little, if any, formal structure is suggested and Bray seems to suggest that in order to relate to the child as a person at the correct developmental level, any 'adult agendas' which might include preconceived ideas about issues to cover, and the pace of work, should be abandoned. Thus the child leads the interviewer at a pace and in a manner which is comfortable for the child concerned.

Aids to play and communication are described, including a toy box, where a whole range of types of play materials are provided, such as 'wiggly worms', animals with tongues which go in and out, and frogs which can jump on each other's backs. The point is made that these toys will seem innocent enough to non-abused children, but may have a special meaning for the abused child, and may act as a 'trigger point' in discussion with such a child, allowing mention of possible abusive acts. Within this approach the use of imaginative play is stressed, and the value of metaphorical statements is described, such as: 'This little sheep is sad inside his tummy—do you know anyone else who is so sad that he is crying?' This sort of statement is seen as facilitating and releasing for a blocked non-communicative child, whilst at the same time making it clear to the child that the therapist is empathic and understanding. Emphasis is put on the need for adequate time for such work, and on the importance of the adult interviewer learning how to speak in short, clear, child-centred sentences, in order to make sense to small children. In relation to anatomically correct dolls, it is pointed out that although the debate over the use of these dolls has often been heated, nevertheless, used with caution and sensitivity, the anatomically correct dolls can be of great assistance to children trying to put complex abstract memories of events into concrete demonstrations with three-dimensional dolls. It is pointed out that the interviewer's skill lies in collecting such concrete information from the child in a way which is uncontaminated by preconceptions, pressure or distortion, and this links to the need to work at the child's pace.

This approach to interviewing has not been validated through research, and given the necessarily free form of the approach it is difficult to see how this could be achieved.

Statement Validity Analysis (SVA; Yuille, 1988)

This approach to interviewing children grew out of collaborative work between researchers in Canada, the USA, and West Germany. Part of the ethos of the approach derives from the German experience of using a court appointed expert to interview suspected child victims, to evaluate all other evidence in the case, and then to present the court with an evaluation of the child's truthfulness.

The post-interview techniques of evaluating children's testimony developed by German and Swedish psychologists, and originally introduced by Undeutsch (1982), was described as Statement Reality Analysis (SRA). However, after systematic modification by Yuille (1988), it has become known as Statement Validity Analysis (SVA).

SVA has two main components—the interview procedure, and a statement analysis procedure. The interview procedure consists of four phases:

(1) Initial phase;
(2) Free recall phase;
(3) Specific question phase;
(4) Suggestibility check.

The initial phase is intended to allow assessment of the child's linguistic, cognitive, behavioural, and social skills. During the free recall phase, the pace of the interview is set by the child's need to pause or reflect, in a process of describing any event(s) of concern in their own words. If faltering or pauses are too long, facilitation to continue is offered by the interviewer, with phases such as 'and tell us what happened' (not, apparently, regarded as leading). Asking the child to repeat statements is also seen as a way of helping the interview to proceed, as well as supplying more evidential data for later evaluation.

In the specific question phase, the interviewer refers to notes taken during the free recall phase, and bases specific, open ended questions upon the issues that emerged earlier. Such specific questions may seek corroborative detail about the clothes worn by the child, the contents of the room, and so forth. No advice is given, in this phase, about how to broach the subject of possible abuse if this has not been spontaneously mentioned earlier by the child. In the last phase, the suggestibility check, the child is asked 'a few' leading questions about 'peripheral information', in order to check his/her susceptibility to suggestion. At some later stage in the interview the child may be confronted with discrepancies in the story which have emerged, but specific techniques for doing this are not described. The interview ends at this point with no specific closure or ending phase.

In relation to play adjuncts to be used in the interview, the authors concede that with younger children, aged under 5 years, 'it may be necessary to employ some aids during this interview' (p. 255). They suggest that drawings may allow the child to demonstrate body parts, whilst a doll's house may help the child to describe the environment in which abuse occurred. Part of the literature on anatomically correct dolls is reviewed, with the conclusion that such dolls are inherently suggestive of sexual matters of dint of their genitals. Since the authors believe that no agreement exists on either the method of use of the dolls, or on the interpretation of subsequently elicited play by the child with the dolls, their use is not recommended in SVA interviews.

It is suggested that the interview be conducted in a way which is 'supportive' for the child, whilst leading or suggestive questions are avoided. Other interview protocols which are too rigidly constructed (White and Santilli, 1988) are described, as are approaches which give details of questioning styles which should or should not be used. Although the SVA interview is more prescriptive towards the interviewer than other approaches, this specificity does not seem apparent to the authors. It is suggested that all SVA interviews should be videotaped to avoid repeated interviews of the child, and also to allow for accurate post-interview analysis of the data elicited.

In the second component of SVA, statement analysis or statement credibility evaluation, four stages are identified:

(1) Content criteria, or the systematic application of a set of criteria to evaluate the credibility of the content of the child's statement. These criteria cover general characteristics, specific contexts, peculiarities of context, motivation-related contexts, and offence-specific elements.
(2) In the second stage, a validity checklist examines statement-related factors, such as psychological characteristics, interview characteristics, and motivation.
(3) In stage three, various investigative questions, such as the medical and other evidence, are considered.
(4) In stage four, overall evaluation of the credibility of the child's statement is made.

In view of the extensive earlier use of SRA in German courts, and the positive feedback from such usage, it is felt that SVA is probably a reliable method of interviewing children and evaluating their evidence. Validity testing of the approach itself has recently started, and early results report good differentiation between abused and non-abused child statements, when the interview transcripts are subject to SVA (see Chapter 5, p. 110).

Boat and Everson (1988)

This model offers guidance for conducting a structured doll interview, particularly with children under 6 years of age where work with the anatomically correct dolls is seen as a major part of the suggested interview format. Boat and Everson stress that the initial part of the interview should be taken up with rapport building, assessing the child's understanding of key concepts, such as who, where, what and when as well as touch, asking the child to describe a recent memorable event such as a shopping trip, in order to get a sense of the child's language and memory, and so on. They then suggest ways of introducing the anatomically correct dolls which allow the child to identify them, and to name various body functions in an ordered way, with the dolls dressed and subsequently undressed.

It is then suggested that the interview may move on, through four different levels of escalation, to look at possible issues of sexual abuse.

Level 1 escalation—Critical Events Focus. At this point in the interview information can be gathered about critical events or times in the child's life when abuse is most likely to have occurred, such as around bathtime or bedtime. Questions may be asked, therefore, to establish who bathes the child, who takes the child to bed and so on. It is stressed that the interviewer should be relaxed and casual in style at this point.

Level 2 escalation—Critical Individuals Focus. At this stage it is suggested that the child can be asked in general terms about particular individuals or an individual who may be suspected of being an abuser. This will establish whether non-sexual play or domestic relationships are common with such an individual, i.e. details of games which may be played between the child and adult. Nothing sexual is mentioned at this point in the interview, and it is expected that the child should take the lead in providing information.

Level 3 escalation—Direct General Inquiry. At this point it is suggested that more direct questions about sexual abuse can be posed, perhaps using the anatomically correct dolls as reference points for the body parts already identified by the child. If the child replies 'No' to questions such as 'Has anyone touched your minnie?', then it is suggested that the interviewer begin to terminate the interview. However, if the child replies 'Yes', the interviewer may proceed to the following stage.

Level 4 escalation—Direct Inquiry about Specific Individuals. At this stage in the interview direct questions about identifying a person may be asked in relation to sexual abuse, such as 'Has daddy ever touched your minnie?'. It is pointed out that these are very leading questions and may be problematic with very young children, particularly if the questions are put in a suggestive manner, or in a way which may lead the child to wish to please the interviewer by giving a certain response. It is also pointed out that evidence obtained from questioning at this stage in the interview may not be admissible in court, and that in many ways the interviewers should be reluctant to escalate to Level 4, particularly with a very young child.

It is stressed that ending the interview is as important as beginning it, and that explanations should be given to the child and parents about what will be happening next; as well as the child being reassured that, for instance, placement in foster homes is not a punishment for his or her sexual abuse. It is pointed out that this structured model may not be adequate for assessing certain children who need longer to disclose: in such cases it is suggested that children are referred for an extended mental health evaluation. At present, no published data exist in relation to the validity or reliability of this approach.

Macfarlane and Krebs (1986)

This approach to interviewing and evidence-gathering is essentially unstructured in that no particular sequence of information gathering is suggested. however, a great deal of advice is given on the kinds of questions to ask and the relative valueof prompted or unprompted responses from the child.

It is pointed out that a common terminology has to be established between the interviewer and the child at the beginning of the interview, and that this applies to the nomenclature for body parts and sexual acts. At this stage in the interview it is suggested that anatomically correct dolls may be brought into the interview, possibly following on from a drawing of human figures, which can include sexual parts. It is suggested that clothed dolls are presented to the child, although there is a full discussion of the current contention over the use of anatomical dolls in American courts. It is made clear that the dolls themselves are not crucial in conducting an interview with a suspected child sexual abuse victim. The use of puppets and other toys as communication aids is discussed and questioning techniques are described to help interviewers elicit spontaneous material from children in relation to possible disclosures of abuse. Common defence patterns amongst blocked or frightened children are described, including the faltering acknowledgement by young children that abuse 'may' have occurred—described as the 'no-maybe-sometimes-yes' syndrome. As well as emphasising the need to proceed at the child's pace, the issue of allowing physical space and distance from the sexually abused child in the interview is discussed, in relation to children who are both physically avoidant and physically sexualised towards the interviewer. A list of various issues which may need to be enquired for during the interview is included, and suggestions are made about how to cope with avoidant or denying responses when such matters are broached.

Since the interview itself is not a structured interview, there is no clear guidance on how to close or complete the meeting with the child, but it is stressed that the child should be reassured that abuse, if it has occurred, was the adult's fault and responsibility.

Although these authors have interviewed a considerable number of children, no research has been undertaken to look at the reliability or validity of this approach.

Glaser and Frosh (1988)

An approach which falls somewhere between 'cookery book' listing and the less structured formats is offered by Glaser and Frosh. In this approach the process of the interview is seen to depend on its purpose, whether as a preliminary disclosure interview or as a later interview. It is stressed that the timing involved in raising certain listed issues will depend on the child's psychological position at various points in the interview. Glaser and Frosh therefore suggest that the interview should be child led, in the sense that no pre-fixed format can be rigidly followed.

However, although the list of relevant issues might suggest a lack of underlying structure, discussion of these issues shows that suggestions here and there are made about if, when, and how to broach such topics. Therefore, without adhering to a fixed structure on the one hand, or a totally unstructured approach on the other hand, Glaser and Frosh put forward a compromise consisting of the following possible sequence of issues: introduction; child's knowledge about purpose of interview; free play and names for anatomical parts; orientating the interview; full description of abuse; where abuse took place; whereabouts of other family members; who witnessed the abuse; who else involved; identity of abuser; timing and frequency; seeking details of the child's feelings about sexual contact; secrets; child's feelings towards abuse; definition of adult's responsibility; dealing with reluctance, anxiety and fears; checking account with child; telling mother; preparing for medical examination; evaluation.

It is made clear that spontaneous communications from the child should be encouraged and that using cues, involving issues from medical examinations, access visits, and so on, may provide links to take the child, in discussion, from an experience which is bearable to talk about to an account of possible abuse. Clinical judgement is still required to decide how and when to do such linking work, and the approach may, therefore, appeal to rather more experienced clinicians. No claims are made for the reliability or validity of this approach, and no research has yet been undertaken to look at these issues.

Royal College of Psychiatrists (1988)

This approach suggests that the child psychiatrist's perspective can complement that of other professionals, where the child psychiatrist has a primary orientation towards the recognition, prevention and treatment of psychiatric disorder in children. The point is made, by this group, that the notion of 'disclosure' interview is unhelpful since the term implies that there must always be something to disclose and does not allow for the possibility that a non-abused child may be interviewed. It is stressed that the interview should follow the same principles as a general psychiatric examination of a child, and should be of a duration which is appropriate to the child's developmental age, stage, understanding, and level of comfort.

The view is expressed that repeated sessions, probing the possibility of child sexual abuse, are unhelpful and may be harmful to the child. Whilst stressing that a rigidly pre-planned interview schedule is not recommended, this group goes on to suggest the possibility of a degree of structure as follows.

First stage: at this point in the interview a general assessment of the child's functioning is sought, including behaviour, emotions, relationships with peers, and adults, family relationships, and any possible traumatic experiences. A general rapport will be developed with the child. If grounds for suspicion exist, then the interviewer may move on to the second stage.

Second stage: 'helping the child to tell' (facilitation). At this point, it is suggested that the interviewer must steer a course between the extremes of overly leading questions on the one hand, and on the other hand being insufficiently enabling for the reluctant child. Toys, materials to cue memories, certain types of questions and the manner in which they are put, are suggested as ways in which the child may be assisted to talk about possible abuse. It is suggested that facilitation techniques should be reserved for the end of the interview. In relation to anatomically correct dolls, this group suggest that it is probably unnecessary to use them as a first stage of evaluation, but that the dolls may be useful as an adjunct to a facilitated second stage, particularly with children who are stuck for words. The point is made that these dolls should not be used by untrained professionals.

Third stage: a checking stage. It is suggested that at some point in the interview, checks can be made for the suggestibility of the child, the identification of the alleged abuser, and further details of any alleged abuse. It is pointed out that when checking with the child the interviewer has to avoid transmitting a sense of disbelief to the child which may cause much harm.

Fourth stage: closure stage. It is suggested that at the end of the interview, the interviewer should recognise any emotions with which the child has struggled, whilst at the same time avoiding the danger of congratulating the child for any disclosure which may have been made.

This recently formulated approach to interviewing sexually abused children has not yet been evaluated, in terms of either validity or reliability.

'IDEAL' CASE EXAMPLE

Jane was a 9 year old girl who made an allegation of sexual abuse by her natural father. When the allegation was reported to Jane's school teacher it was dealt with via the local child protection procedures. A sensitive medical examination of Jane confirmed that chronic vaginal interference seemed likely, and on subsequent interview of Jane by a trained police officer and social worker, Jane was able to describe spontaneously and with elaborated and idiosyncratic detail, a story of long-term sexual abuse by her father. This sexual abuse had increased in seriousness and frequency over four years, resulting in recent sexual intercourse, which was painful and eventually led Jane to disclose the abuse. Jane's mother believed her allegations, and Jane's father left the home on a voluntary basis pending police investigation. Since Jane's interview was videotaped, it was shown in part to her father, who broke down and confessed to the abuse, but denied actual sexual intercourse with Jane. A psychiatric assessment of Jane's father suggested that, like many offenders against children, he was in a phase of denial but that he was treatable. Since the police intended to prosecute, a recommendation was made for a non-custodial sentence with a probation order and a treatment order to a named psychiatrist for Jane's father. In the criminal proceedings, a videotape of Jane's interview was shown in court; Jane herself was carefully cross-examined on this videotaped statement, but was consistent in her evidence. Jane's father was found guilty of unlawful sexual intercourse, but the psychiatric recommendation was accepted: as part of a non-custodial sentence he was ordered to attend a treatment group, run by the Probation Service, with a condition of his residence outside the area where the family's home was located. Jane's mother was herself being supported by the local Social Services Department, who had interviewed Jane's two younger siblings as part of a wider assessment of parenting and child care within Jane's family. Group treatment was offered to Jane in the local Child Guidance Clinic, and a multi-agency plan was drawn up to assess the long-term possibility of rehabilitating Jane's father into the family, pending the outcome of both his court-ordered treatment and the social services' work with Jane's mother.

This 'ideal' case is far removed from the realities of clinical practice, where poor management of disclosure, a negative view of the clinical evidence in court, and variable post-court disposal and treatment often seem to be the norm for child sexual abuse cases in England. Great clinical concern is expressed by those working in the child abuse field in relation to court decisions which return clinician-diagnosed abused children to the home. However, although clinical follow up of some of these children indicates that abuse does recur, unless this can be redetected, reported again, and processed through court again (matters which are even less likely to occur coherently, the second time around), it is almost certain that the judge or magistrate, in wardship or care proceedings, will never get to hear of a possible error in his/her judgement and court orders. Because of the appropriate need for confidentiality in relation to children's cases, it is not possible to reprint here the clinical details of certain care and wardship cases which, sadly, support this contention. A major issue arising from such lack of follow-up feedback to magistrates and judges is the need for legal training in basic research methods, to demonstrate that outcome in past cases may indeed affect intervention (in this case the judgement and court orders) in future cases.

DISCUSSION

It may be helpful to look at those areas in relation to interviewing children where there is a consensus on practice issues and those areas where practice is still divergent.

Consensus Issues in Abuse Interviews

Most suggested approaches to interviewing favour a format which has some degree of structure, although all groups stress that a rigid structure which cannot adjust to the needs of the individual child is undesirable. The main exceptions to this would seem to be Statement Validity Analysis (Yuille, 1988) with its emphasis on data gathering for subsequent detailed evaluated, and White et al.'s (1987) approach with a forensic and legal emphasis. It could be argued that such approaches are more 'scientific' in some ways than play-centred techniques with children, and that spontaneous comments made by a child in such highly structured interviews could be taken very seriously by a court. However, the potential for rigorous scientific evaluation, inherent in such ordered approaches, has yet to be demonstrated with research findings which would confirm that more structure means more reliability.

It is not known what proportion of young victims could respond unaided to very structured, non-child-centred approaches to interviewing; although these might be suitable for older, more confident children. Courts and lawyers seem to favour a more structured approach to interviewing child victims, probably because such interviews can then be evaluated item by item as it were, rather than requiring lawyers to look at the overall evidential picture presented by the interview, a process which is much more complex. However, clinicians also seem to favour a traditional format in child abuse interviews (as in other psychiatric interviews), where an introductory phase is established, followed by middle and concluding stages. Whether such structure is described in terms of phases, stages, focuses, sections, or levels does not seem important, since an ordered approach to information gathering and enquiry is suggested by most groups.

An exception to this consensus on structure is the guidance suggested by the American Academy of Child and Adolescent Psychiatry (1988) in which no particular structure is proposed. Instead proscription and caution, in relation to the use of anatomical dolls, leading questions and coercive techniques is put forward. The interviewer is warned about the need to become familiar with the laws of evidence, in anticipation of subsequent legal scrutiny of interview techniques in court. A British approach (Bray, 1989) does not advocate any structure as such in child abuse interviews, and rather emphasises the use of play techniques in order to trigger spontaneous child responses.

Home Office (1989) guidance on joint police/social work interviews with suspected child victims, following the recommendations of the Bexley Experiment (Charnley, 1988), has been unable to suggest a firm format which might be followed in such interviews. However, it is agreed that an ordered approach to speaking with children is desirable, since the extra element of two interviewers working in parallel, and pursuing both evidential and therapeutic aims, is a novel approach where some sense of an agreed format could be helpful.

The Home Office guidance on interviewing stresses that although evidential requirements should be a major consideration for the interviewing police officer and social worker, the main purpose of such a joint interview is to provide some therapeutic outlet for the suspected child victim. The use of play materials, including anatomical dolls, is acknowledged as helpful, but training in the use of dolls is recommended.

Both the Cleveland Inquiry Report (1988) and the Standing Medical Advisory Committee Guidance to Doctors (1988) in relation to suspected child sexual abuse make the point that the notion of 'disclosure' interviews is not helpful since it seems to imply that there must be something to disclose. The Cleveland Inquiry Report suggests that the initial formal interview should ideally be conducted by a police officer and/or social worker, and that the purpose of this formal interview should be to listen to and hear what the child has to say. It is stressed that police and social workers interviewing in this delicate field must be experienced and skilled in working with children. Various play materials, including playdough, plasticine, and drawings, were suggested as being helpful in this initial interview. In relation to the anatomically correct dolls, the Inquiry Report urged extreme caution in their use, other than by those particularly qualified to do so. It is suggested that the use of the dolls as a routine prop in initial interviews with police and social workers seems highly undesirable.

The Inquiry Report pointed out that when certain children need help to tell, or when the assessment to date is inconclusive, there may be need for a second and different type of interview, using facilitation, play materials and possibly hypothetical or leading questions. It is pointed out that the facilitative techniques used in this second stage interview should not be incorporated routinely into the initial first stage interview, but should be reserved as a useful tool to be used sparingly by experts in certain cases.

There are advantages and disadvantages to both the more structured and the less structured approaches to interviewing. Firstly, clinicians may feel artificially constrained and pressured into using a partially structured approach when talking with children, in a way which may inhibit establishing a good rapport and the free flow of communication. It may also be genuinely difficult for some clinicians to adhere to an agreed format within an interview, since this may not be compatible with their individual clinical style. However, if such objections can be overcome, it is clear that more structured approaches to child abuse interviews are helpful from a research point of view, since comparisons can be made about issues which may have arisen during comparable phases or stages in interviews conducted according to a semi-structured format. Such comparative research data are urgently needed, and would seem to be a major disadvantage of the totally unstructured, free form approach to interviewing child abuse victims. It is possible that a huge number of idiosyncratic approaches to interviewing and techniques in working with children suspected of having been abused could develop, and perhaps have already developed, amongst clinicians. Thus different child-generated material, elicited in different ways, could continue to arise indefinitely, if a consensus on the elements of interviewing children was not agreed. Linking to the issue of structure in interviews, and perhaps proffered as a compromise by many approaches which do not wish to be identified with a rigid format, is the tendency to provide lists of issues which are either prescribed, and should be covered, or are prescribed, and should not be covered in such interviews.

Practical Issues

Approaches which list issues for the attention of the interviewer, (American Academy, 1988; Glaser and Frosh, 1988; Macfarlane and Krebs, 1986) are helpful in alerting the interviewer to major topics or difficulties which may be encountered in the interview with the child. There are basic issues to do with preparing the room, the child, and the therapist for the ensuing meeting, which need to be spelled out for novice interviewers. Similarly, a list of possible emotional reactions in the child, or indeed in the interviewer, may be helpful to the prospective interviewer in allowing the opportunity to plan possible responses in advance. Having said this, Jones and McQuiston (1988) disapprove of a 'cookery book' approach to interviewing, involving the endless listing of 'ingredients'. In reality, it could be argued that the anxious interviewer is still left with the dilemma of how actually to make this particular therapeutic cake—which 'ingredients' to put in first, in what proportion, and so on. Inexperienced therapists may therefore welcome the more structured interview approaches, where the therapeutic ingredients are apparently mixed and coordinated in a coherent manner. Of course it may not be apparent to the inexperienced interviewer that many of these appealingly predictable structured formats have not, in fact, been scientifically validated, as mentioned above.

Different approaches advocate differing degrees of facilitation with children at different points within such an interview, but no clear definition of 'facilitation' is offered by any group. There does seem to be consensus about the provision of toys and play materials for children to use during such interviews. But there is a range of opinion about the amount of such material which should be made available: some authors favour a limited amount of material, whilst others, usually those who favour a rather more open ended approach to interviewing, argue for the free provision of a large range of play materials.

In relation to the anatomically correct dolls, only one approach positively pro-scribes their use (Yuille, 1988), whilst most other approaches advocate the use of the dolls in conjunction with other methods. The Cleveland Inquiry Report and the Royal College of Psychiatrists urge caution in relation to these dolls, suggest-ing that they should only be used by trained interviewers; but not proposing any particular way in which they could then be incorporated into an interview. How-ever, since the publication of these reports a recent review of the use of anatomical dolls (Westcott *et al.*, 1989) suggests that they are not sexualising or suggestive to children when used appropriately (see p. 117). The groups which make the most structured use of the dolls are Great Ormond Street (Vizard and Tranter, 1988c), Boat and Everson (1988), and White and Santilli (1987). Jones and McQuiston (1988) also give guidance on use of the dolls but make it clear that the interview should not depend on the presence or otherwise of the dolls.

Two other controversies remain in relation to the dolls, the first being whether to present them to the child with the clothes on or off. Whilst there is consensus that the dolls should be presented with clothes on, there is less clarity about whether the child or the interviewer should undress the dolls, and if so at what stage. Secondly, there is no consensus on whether there should be any prelimin-ary inquiry about possible sexual abuse before the genitals of the dolls become visible to the child (since there is still controversy about whether they may or may not 'cue' a child into a false disclosure).

There seems to be consensus that the interview should not be longer than developmentally appropriate for the age of the child, and also that the gender of the interviewer is less important than the degree of experience of the person concerned in creating a rapport with children.

A consensus exists between certain groups (Vizard and Tranter, 1988c; White and Santilli, 1987; Yuille, 1988) on the value of an initial free play period in addition to play at other points in the interview. The rationale for this free play is to allow spontaneous child-generated play material, plus possible accompanying comments or disclosures about sexual acts, to emerge without interviewer press-ure. Clearly such child-generated material could be of later evidential value, but such material would also need expert interpretation.

There is no clear consensus on the number of interviews which it is desirable for children to experience, with a range of one (Bannister and Print, 1989; Vizard and Tranter, 1988c), to a possible series of interviews being suggested by certain workers (Jones and McQuiston, 1988).

There is some dispute on the amount of background information which it is desirable for interviewers to carry in their minds, whilst interviewing a child. For instance, the Great Ormond Street approach is in favour of comprehensive information gathering before the interview, so that the interviewer is alert to possible names of abusers, abusive situations, and so on. The SVA (Yuille, 1988) approach does not mention gathering background information on the family, but subsequent analysis includes medical reports and child psychological tests, as well as the material elicited during the interview alone. The NSPCC approach (Bannister and Print, 1989), perhaps confusingly, suggests that background infor-mation should be available to the interviewer, who should then try to ignore such information in the interview, for fear of developing a biased perception of the child's communications. Other approaches are even less clear: the American Academy of Child and Adolescent Psychiatry (1988), the Royal College of Psychiatrists (1988), and the Cleveland Inquiry Report (1988) all stress the need to put the sexual abuse inquiries within the interview into a wider overall context of background information. However, none of these groups clarifies how much of this information, if any, should be available to the interviewer at the time of talking to the child.

In relation to leading questions there is full consensus that such questions should be avoided if at all possible. This happy state of affairs vanishes, as discussed earlier, when definitions of leading questions are sought. The main point at issue seems to be under what circumstances should leading questions be introduced into an interview? Overall, there is a degree of consensus that such questions can be used when other questioning techniques have proved fruitless, and that ideally, this should be at the end of the interview. However, there is also the suggestion that in any sequence of questioning, at any point in the interview, the interviewer may if necessary progress through a sequence of more facilitation and leading questions to using hypothetical questions in order to elicit a spontaneous response from the child. The Great Ormond Street approach suggests this but points out that as soon as a spontaneous response is received from a child, the interviewer should revert to open questions. In this way there is a variation in the questioning style used throughout any one interview, and an avoidance of interviews which consist of a series of leading questions, delivered in a 'driven' fashion. There is some consensus (Jones and McQuiston, 1988; Vizard and Tranter, 1988c), that under very special circumstances with 'frozen' children, hypothetical leading questions may be used. Overall, there seems to be a tentative consensus about the advantages of using leading questions; and an overwhelming consensus about the disadvantages of using too many leading questions delivered in the wrong manner.

All English and American approaches now advocate the videotaping of the initial child interview(s), both to protect the child from repeated interview and in order to capture relevant evidential issues on videotape. Finally, it should be said that all interview approaches mentioned are in agreement about the need for subsequent expert interpretation of any material derived from children in such interviews. It is clear that clinicians and lawyers, who have experience in interviewing children, are aware that the material elicited from children, even in the most structured and evidentially correct manner, may need very careful later interpretation. The implications of this for legal training have been discussed. With two exceptions (White and Santilli, 1987; Yuille, 1988) all approaches emphasise the need for a therapeutic component for the child within such interviews.

In conclusion, the past decade in Britain has seen the emergence of a new clinical and forensic field in relation to the interviewing of children suspected of being sexually abused. Public and professional reactions to this new work have passed through an initial phase of rejection and confusion, have been followed by professional consultation and discussion about the clinical and evidential issues raised, and have resulted in the development of a range of approaches to interviewing, of which few have been subject to empirical research or validation. Future initiatives in this field should include training in child development and psychology for lawyers; evidential forensic training for clinicians; and long-term follow up of children whose videotaped interviews are admitted as evidence in court, in order to gather evidence about false negative and false positive legal findings. Research into the reliability and validity of existing interview protocols is urgently needed before professionals develop further approaches, and note should be taken of those clinical issues upon which consensus has already been reached. It is worth pointing out that unresolved disagreement in the field of child sexual abuse is not only professionally devisive and detrimental to child care decision making, but also obscures the areas in which progress has been made.

Author Note

I should like to acknowledge gratefully the advice of John Spencer in relation to legal and evidential issues. The following people also read the text and made helpful comments—Anne Bannister, Madge Bray, Graham Davies, Danya Glaser, David Jones, Marianne Tranter and Helen Westcott and Richard White. However, the opinions expressed are wholly my own.

References

American Academy of Child and Adolescent Psychiatry (1988). Perspective: Guidelines for the clinical evaluation of child and adolescent sexual abuse. Position Statement of the American Academy of Child and Adolescent Psychiatry 1988. *Journal of American Academy of Child and Adolescent Psychiatry*, **27**, 5, 655–7.

August, R., and Forman, B. (1986). Differences between sexually and non sexually abused children in their behavioural responses to anatomically correct dolls. Presented at a Symposium on the Use of Anatomically Correct Dolls in the Evaluation of Child Sexual Abuse at the 4th National Conference on Sexual Victimisation of Children, New Orleans, LA.

Bannister, A., and Print, B. (1989). Assessment interviews in suspected cases of child sexual abuse—an interactive model. Video training pack produced by the Joint NSPCC Greater Manchester Authority Child Sexual Abuse Unit.

Berliner, Lucy (1988). Children in court. Paper presented at an Advanced Training Conference on Child Sexual Abuse, 24 June. Nuffield Child Psychiatry Unit, Newcastle.

Boat, B. W., and Everson, M. D. (1988). Interviewing young children with anatomically correct dolls. *Child Welfare*, **67**, (4), 337–52.

Bracewell, Judge Joyanne, QC (1989). In on the act. Comments made at a conference on The Children's Bill in July 1989. *Family Law*, **19**, 337–338.

Bray, Margery (1980). Communicating with children who have been sexually abused. The use of non-directive play and selected play materials in disclosure. Paper given at the British Psychological Society Annual Conference, University of York, York.

Bray, Margery (1989). Communicating with children—communicating with the courts. In Allan Levy QC (ed.), *Focus on Child Abuse: Medical, Legal and Social Work Perspectives*. Over Wallop, Hants: Hawksmere.

Briere, J., and Runtz, M. (1988). Post sexual abuse trauma. In G. J. Powell and G. E. Wyatt (eds), *Lasting Effects of Child Sexual Abuse*: Beverly Hills, CA: Sage, pp. 85–99.

Bush, J. [1988]a. Re-Z (Minors) (Child Abuse: Evidence) 2 FLR 3.

Bush, J. [1988]b. Re-A (Minor) (Child Abuse: Evidence) 1 FLR30.

Charnley, Helen (1988). Child Sexual Abuse: Joint Investigative Programme. Bexley Experiment. London: HMSO.

Cleveland Report (1988). Report of the Inquiry into Child Abuse in Cleveland (1987). Inquiry chaired by the Right Honourable Lord Butler-Sloss, DBE. London: HMSO.

Cross, R., and Tapper, C. (1985). Cross on Evidence, 6th edn. London: Butterworths.

Davies, G., and Brown, L. (1978). Recall and organisation in 5 year old children. British Journal of Psychology, 69, 343–9.

Davies, G. M., Stevenson-Robb, Y., and Flin, R. (1988). Tales out of school: Children's memory for an unexpected event. In M. N. Gruneberg, P. E. Morris and R. M. Sykes, (eds), Practical Aspects of Memory: Current Research and Issues. Chichester: Wiley.

Enright, Sean (1989). Dolls as an aid to interviewing children: A legal view. In Allan Levy, QC (ed.), Focus on Child Abuse, Medical, Legal and Social Work Perspectives. Over Wallop, Hants: Hawksmere.

Ewbank, Mr Justice (1986). Reported in The Times, 16 July. Re-E. C., A minor, and G. C., A minor.

Family Law Reports [1987]. 1 FLR 269–346. Special Issue No. 4.

Freud, Anna (1962). Assessment of childhood disturbances. In The Psycho-Analytic Study of the Child, XVII. New York: New York International Universities Press, pp. 149–158.

Gabriel, R. M. (1985). Anatomically correct dolls and the diagnosis of sexual abuse of children. Journal of the Melanie Klein Society, 3, 40–50.

Glaser, D. (n.d.). Current research at Guy's Hospital—personal communication.

Glaser, D., and Collins, C. (1989). The response of young, non-sexually abused children to anatomically correct dolls. Journal of Child Psychology and Psychiatry, 30, (4), 547–60.

Glaser, D., and Frosh, S. (1988). The process of validation and decision making. In Child Sexual Abuse. Practical Social Work Series (BASW), Joe Campling (ed.). Basingstoke: Macmillan.

Goodman, G. F., and Aman, C. (1987). Children's use of anatomically correct dolls to report an event. Presented at a Symposium on Evaluation of Suspected Child Abuse: Developmental, Clinical and Legal Perspectives on the Use of Anatomically Correct Dolls. Held at Society for Research in Child Development Convention. Baltimore, MD.

Hildebrand, J., Jenkins, J., Carter, D., and Lask, B. (1981). The introduction of a full family orientation in a child psychiatric in-patient unit. Journal of Family Therapy, 3, 139–51.

Hill, P. (1985). The diagnostic interview of the individual child. In L. Hersov and M. Rutter (eds), Child and Adolescent Psychiatry—Modern Approaches, 2nd edn. Oxford: Blackwell, pp. 249–63.

Home Office Circular No 67 (1989). Joint training for police officers and social workers responsible for investigating child sexual abuse. Circulated to all Chief Officers or Police and Directors of Social Services in England and Wales.

Jampole, L., and Webber, M. K. (1987). An assessment of the behaviour of sexually abused and non sexually abused children with anatomically correct dolls. Child Abuse and Neglect, 11, 187–92.

Jensen, J. B., Realmuto, G., and Wescoe, S. (1986). Are there differences in the play with anatomically correct dolls: Abused vs non abused children. Paper presented to the American Academy of Child Psychiatry, Washington DC.

Jones, D. P. H., and McGraw, J. M. (1987). Reliable and fictious accounts of sexual abuse to children. Journal of Interpersonal Violence, 2 (1), 27–45.

Jones, D. P. H., and McQuiston, M. G. (1988). Interviewing the sexually abused child. The Royal College of Psychiatrists. Alden Press, Oxford, Gaskell.

Klein, Melanie (1975). The psychological foundations of child analysis. (An expanded volume of a paper, The psychological principles of early analysis, given in 1926). In The Psychoanalysis of Children, vol. 2 of The Writings of Melanie Klein, trans. Alix Strachey. London: Hogarth Press Institute of Psycho-Analysis, pp. 3–15.

Latey, J. [1987]. C v C (Child Abuse: Access) 1 FLR 462 and, subsequent note on this judgement in *Family Law*, July 1988, **19**, 255.

Lindberg, S. H., and Distad, L. H. (1985). Post-traumatic stress disorder in women who experienced incest. *Child Abuse and Neglect*, **9**, 329–34.

Lord Chancellor (1989). Announcement of the appointment of Her Honour Judge Joyanne Bracewell, QC, to assist with judicial administration and training. *Family Law*, 19 April, 132.

Macfarlane, K. and Krebs, S. (1986). Techniques for interviewing and evidence gathering. In K. Macfarlane and J. Waterman (eds), *Sexual Abuse of Young Children, Evaluation and Treatment*. New York: Holt, Rinehart & Winston, pp. 67–100.

McIver, W., and Wakefield, H. (1987). Behaviour of abused and non abused children with anatomically correct dolls. Unpublished Paper.

Morton, John (1990). The development of event memory. *The Psychologist: Bulletin of the British Psychological Society*, **1**, 3–10.

Moston, S., and Engelborg, T. (in press). The effects of social support on children's eye witness testimony. *Applied Cognitive Psychology*.

Pigot, J. (1989). Report of the Advisory Group on Video Evidence, 1989. Chaired by His Honour Judge Thomas Pigot, QC. London: Home Office, 19 December.

Royal College of Psychiatrists (1988). Child psychiatric perspectives on the assessment and management of sexually mistreated children. Paper prepared by a Working Group of the Child and Adolescent Specialist Section of the Royal College of Psychiatrists, December, 1988. *Psychiatric Bulletin of the Royal College of Psychiatrists*. **12** (12), 534–40.

Salter, A. C. (1988). Part III—Offender assessment and treatment. In A. C. Salter (ed.), *Treating Child Sex Offenders and Victims: A Practical Guide*. Beverly Hills, CA: Sage, pp. 84–182.

Schor, D. P., and Sivan, A. B. (1989). Interpreting children's labels for sex-related body parts of anatomically explicit dolls. *Child Abuse and Neglect*, **13**, 523–31.

Sivan, A. B., Schor, D. P., Koepple, G. K., and Noble, L. D. (1988). Interaction of normal children with anatomical dolls. *Child Abuse and Neglect*, **12**, 295–304.

Spencer, J. R. (1987). Child witnesses, video technology and the law of evidence. *The Criminal Law Review*, **1987**, 76–83.

Standing Medical Advisory Committee (1988). *Diagnosis of child sexual abuse: Guidance for doctors*. Prepared by the Standing Medical Advisory Committee for the Secretaries of State for Social Services and Wales. London: HMSO.

Summit, R. (1983). The child sexual abuse accommodation syndrome. *Child Abuse and Neglect*, **7**, 179–93.

Templeton, S., and Webber, C. (1985). An assessment of the behaviour of sexually abused and non-sexually abused children with anatomically correct dolls. Unpublished research report. Louisiana State University, LA.

Undeutsch, U. (1982). In A. Trankell (ed.), *Reconstructing the Past: The Role of Psychologists in Criminal Trials*. Stockholm. Norstedt & Soners, pp. 27–56.

Vizard, E. (1986). How certain can we be? *Family Law*, **16**, 313–14.

Vizard, E. (1987). Interviewing young, sexually abused children—Assessment techniques. *Family Law*, **17**, 28–33.

Vizard, E. (1988). Child sexual abuse—the child's experience. *British Journal of Psychotherapy*, **5**, (1), 77–91.

Vizard, E., and Tranter, M. (1988a). Recognition and assessment of child sexual abuse. In A. Bentovim, A. Elton, J. Hilderbrand, M. Tranter and E. Vizard (eds), *Child Sexual Abuse Within the Family—Assessment and Treatment*. Bristol: John Wright, pp. 59–83.

Vizard, E., and Tranter, M. (1988b). Helping young children describe experiences of child sexual abuse—general issues. In Bentovim *et al.* (eds), *Child Sexual Abuse Within the Family—Assessment and Treatment*. Bristol: John Wright, pp. 84–104.

Vizard, E., and Tranter, M. (1988c). Helping children to describe experiences of child sexual abuse—A guide to practice. In Bentovim *et al.* (eds), *Child Sexual Abuse Within the Family—Assessment and Treatment*. Bristol: John Wright, pp. 105–29.

Vizard, E., Wiseman, M., Bentovim, A., and Leventhal, J. (1989). Child sexual abuse videos—Is seeing believing? Paper given to the British Paediatric Association Annual Conference, York, 11–14 April.

Waterhouse, J. [1989]. R. v. Hove Juvenile Court. *Ex parte*, W. 2 FLR 145.

Westcott, H., Davies, G., and Clifford, B. (1989). The use of anatomical dolls in child witness interviews. *Adoption and Fostering*, **13** (2), 6–14.

Weyland, I. (1989). The response of civil courts to allegations of child sexual abuse. *Family Law*, **19**, 240–7.

White, S., and Santilli, G. (1988). A review of clinical practices and research data on anatomical dolls. *Journal of Interpersonal Violence*, **3**, 430–42.

White, S., Strom, G., Santilli, G., and Quinn, K. N. (1987). Guidelines to interviewing pre-schoolers with sexually anatomically detailed dolls. Unpublished manuscript.

Wilkinson, J. (1988). Context effects in children's event memory. In M. M. Gruneberg, P. E. Morris, and R. N. Sykes (eds), *Practical Aspects of Memory: Current Research and Issues*, vol. 1. Chichester: Wiley, pp. 107–111.

Winnicott, D. W. (1958). Child department consultations (1942). In *Collected Papers Through Paediatrics to Psychoanalysis*. London: Tavistock, pp. 72–84.

Yates, A., and Terr, L. (1988). Anatomically correct dolls: Should they be used as the basis for expert testimony? *Journal of the American Academy of Child & Adolescent Psychiatry*, **27**, (2), 254–7.

Yuille, J. C. (1988). The systematic assessment of children's testimony. *Canadian Psychology*, **29** (3), 247–62.

Part 3
Treatment

7

Clinical Work with Sex Offenders in Secure Settings*

DEREK PERKINS
Psychology Department, Broadmoor Hospital, Crowthorne, UK

SEX OFFENDING

Public information about sex offending comes from two main sources: first, the criminal statistics of offences known to the police, and secondly from surveys of the general community on experiences of having been a victim or a perpetrator of sexual offending. Sex offences known to the police in the United Kingdom have remained fairly stable over the last 20 years or so, but there is increasing evidence of under-reporting in many categories of sexual offence including rape and child sexual abuse.

It is now well established that under-reporting occurs in many classes of sexual offence. A British survey carried out in 1980 concluded that one in eight females and one in ten males are likely to suffer sexual abuse during childhood (BASPCAN, 1980). A general population survey in the USA found that 19% of female students and 9% of male students reported having experienced some sexual experience with an adult during childhood (Finkelhor, 1979).

It seems likely that this rise represents not only a greater willingness of those attacked to report offences to the police, but also a real increase in the prevalence of some, particularly sexually violent, offences. The 1988 Criminal Statistics—the most recent available at the time of writing—show an increase of 72% in crimes of violence over the last ten years. This compares with 18% for sexual offences and 143% for the offence of rape. In the case of rape this represents an average annual increase in reported offences of 17%.

*The views expressed in this chapter are those of the author and do not necessarily reflect those of the Special Hospital Service Authority.

Clinical Approaches to Sex Offenders and Their Victims
Edited by C. R. Hollin and K. Howells © 1991 John Wiley & Sons Ltd

Most convicted sex offenders are dealt with by non-custodial disposals but a minority, due either to the violence involved in their offending or because of its persistence, receive custodial sentences (Criminal Statistics, 1988).

Custodial disposals fall broadly into two categories, incarceration within the penal system (imprisonment, youth custody, etc.) or psychiatric hospitalization. This might be at a local psychiatric hospital, a regional secure unit or, if the offender is regarded as presenting 'a grave and immediate danger' to the public (Mental Health Act 1983), one of the three special hospitals in England and Wales (Broadmoor, Rampton and Ashworth) or the Scottish equivalent, the State Hospital Carstairs.

Of these two possibilities, imprisonment occurs more frequently. Most sex offenders are not mentally disordered under the terms of the Mental Health Act 1983. To be dealt with through the mental health system the offender must have been diagnosed as being mentally disordered (mental illness, mental impairment, severe mental impairment, or psychopathic disorder). The disposal, from out-patient treatment to special hospitalization, should be consistent with the degree of dangerousness which the patient represents.

Treatment for sex offenders in prison has taken place over many years but has tended, in the United Kingdom, to be confined to local initiatives within particular professional disciplines or establishments. Such initiatives are prone to arise and disappear depending on the interests and enthusiasms of particular staff in a post at any one time. Having said this, there are a number of centres where sex offender treatment has either continued over a number of years or else has resulted in the publication of new approaches to treatment or treatment evaluation research.

CONTEXT OF TREATMENT

The context in which treatment occurs can be as important in determining outcome as the therapy itself, and yet its influence is often overlooked in formal accounts of treatment. The key issues here are those of offender denial, motivation to change and cooperation in the process of treatment. These are all aspects of the offender's functioning which are just as amenable to analysis and modification as the sex offending behaviour itself.

The task with uncooperative or denying clients is to help them see as clearly as possible the options that lie before them with and without treatment, and to encourage involvement in treatments that will minimize their future risks of reoffending. In attempting to do this, however, the therapist treads a difficult line between legitimate discussion with, and sometimes persuasion of, the offender, and illegitimate coercion of the offender into adopting goals and carrying out procedures with which he disagrees. The term 'he' will be used throughout since, overwhelmingly, most sex offenders are male.

Many aspects of the justice system are inadvertently geared towards fostering offender denial. Upon apprehension offenders will typically attempt to deny or minimize their offending in the knowledge that unchallenged claims on their part that their offending was a spontaneous and isolated aberration—whilst the reality might be that carefully planned, multiple offending has occurred—will likely result in lesser degrees of punishment. Such denial or minimization is again reinforced at the stage of imprisonment where sex offenders in custody are typically subjected to verbal and physical abuse from other inmates.

Even the prison system's own schemes for minimizing assaults against sex offenders are indirectly encouraging offenders to disguise the true nature of their offences. They are moved from their local prison to more distant prisons for the purposes of maximizing their anonymity and thereby encouraging them to come off 'Prison rule 43' (segregation for own protection), which is often necessary in order to avoid victimization from fellow prisoners.

All of this represents a difficult if not impossible context in which to carry out effective treatment with sex offenders, a key element of which must be an acknowledgement by the offender of what he has done and some understanding of its impact on his victims.

In a long-term follow-up study of sex offenders being seen for treatment in prison and the community (Perkins, 1987), it was evident that for many sex offenders in treatment there is a gradual—although sometimes dramatic—shift in the information about themselves that they are prepared to reveal as treatment progresses. This was almost always in the direction of revealing more negative aspects of their past behaviour, and recognizing the risks of reoffending in the future: for example admitting deviant sexual fantasies and conscious control over their offending rather than statements that it had occurred out of the blue.

These shifts in information provided by the offenders seemed to be related to three events. Firstly, the increasing rapport between offender and therapist as treatment progressed. Secondly, the additional information that came to light as treatment progressed: for example the offender being unable to cope with social skills training and then going on to acknowledge something new about himself. Thirdly, the constructive tension in the treatment sessions which stemmed from the therapist having some direct input into the offender's achievement of important life goals outside the narrower confines of the therapy itself: for example keeping his marriage together, staying out of prison, or successfully completing a probation order.

The prison context to the treatment of sex offenders stands in contrast to that of the special hospitals and regional secure units. The function of these hospitals is to contain dangerous, mentally disordered individuals without limit of time, and to provide appropriate treatments until it is safe for the individual to be discharged from conditions of maximum security, and eventually if possible back into the community. Valid information about the offender-patient's needs, problems and past offending is central to his successful movement through the hospital and out into the community.

The fact that hospitalization is indeterminate and is geared primarily to therapy represents the major contextual difference from the prison system. Even the most uncooperative sex offender in a secure psychiatric hospital setting will come to learn that unless his problems are addressed he will not move on. Being confronted with the reality of this by the various members o the multi-disciplinary team responsible for his treatment—the nurse, psychologist, doctor, social worker, teacher and occupational therapist—eventually results in cooperation and attitude/behaviour change for most offenders.

Effective treatment for sex offenders depends on obtaining as full an understanding as possible of both the acquisition and maintenance phases of their offending (Feldman, 1977). Factors which lead to the acquisition of sex offending may be quite different from those factors which maintain the offending within the offender's current cycle of behaviour.

SEX OFFENCE ACQUISITION

Typical of factors associated with sex offender acquisition which appear to set the scene for later offending are sexual incidents which result in the subsequent sexualization of normally non-sexual stimuli (e.g. young children) or acts (e.g. violence). For some offenders these early sexual incidents might involve being the victim of sexual abuse but this is not necessarily the case. It should also be said here that only a small minority of those sexually abused as children go on to abuse others. Most sexual abuse results in a heightened risk of subsequent abuse and suffering for the victim (Finkelhor, 1986).

For other offenders, these sexual incidents in childhood or early adulthood do not involve the abuse of the offender. Offenders report a whole variety of early sexual memories which appear to have preceded the development of sexual deviations associated with subsequent offending. These range from the chance exposure to sexual imagery or activities, through to the development of a whole philosophy of interpersonal relationships in which sexual offending is seem as normal, harmless or justifiable.

Why then do some individuals become sex offenders and others, having had similar childhood experiences, not become so? As with more desirable adult characteristics and behaviour, such as becoming a champion tennis player or skilled scientist, the answer seems to lie in a complex mixture of early experiences. These events, in combination with chance factors and the vicious circles of cause and effect that follow, drive the individual into a flow of events over which, particularly for sexually motivated behaviour, he comes to feel that he has little control.

This is graphically illustrated in the Burgess et al. (1986) study of sexual homicides, in which interviews with 36 sexual murderers suggested causal relationships between early experiences, fantasy development and eventual sexual homicide. Examples are given of the relationships between early sexual abuse; the development of aggressive fantasies (of retaliating against others); play-acting of such retaliation (e.g. cutting the head off his sister's dolls when she annoyed him: he later beheaded his victims); the early sexualization of objects which would subsequently figure in the sexual murders (female underwear, shoes, rope, etc.); acting out sexual aggression against younger children; and finally committing sexually motivated murders.

Burgess *et al.* report a central theme of 'inevitability' within their sexual homicide group illustrated by the offender who said: 'All my life I knew I was going to end up killing'. Other perpetrators, from exposers to those having committed sexual homicide, seen in my own practice, have also often reported such feelings of being out of control, 'of being on a train that can't be stopped', or 'knowing that I had to continue until I was caught'.

From the sexual murderer to the repetitive indecent exposer similar patterns of offence acquisition are evident, from early, perhaps chance experiences, through experimentation in sexual behaviour—for some individuals this being subject to spontaneous or chance reinforcement—to the habitual recourse to sexual deviations or violence under certain setting conditions such as stress, frustration or low self-esteem.

SEX OFFENCE MAINTENANCE

Knowledge of a client's learning history is relevant to behavioural treatment in that it can identify both specific aspects of the offender's past which may have precipitated offending, and give information about habitual ways of responding to different situations which the offender may have developed over the following years. Such information is often what clients wish to discuss when they ask, as they not uncommonly do, why they have come to be as they are. However, as Peterson (1968) indicated, much of this historical information traditionally collected by therapists cannot be put to direct use in implementing behavioural treatment: Peterson's estimate was that threequarters of such data are unusable in treatment. As indicated earlier, factors which result in the development of

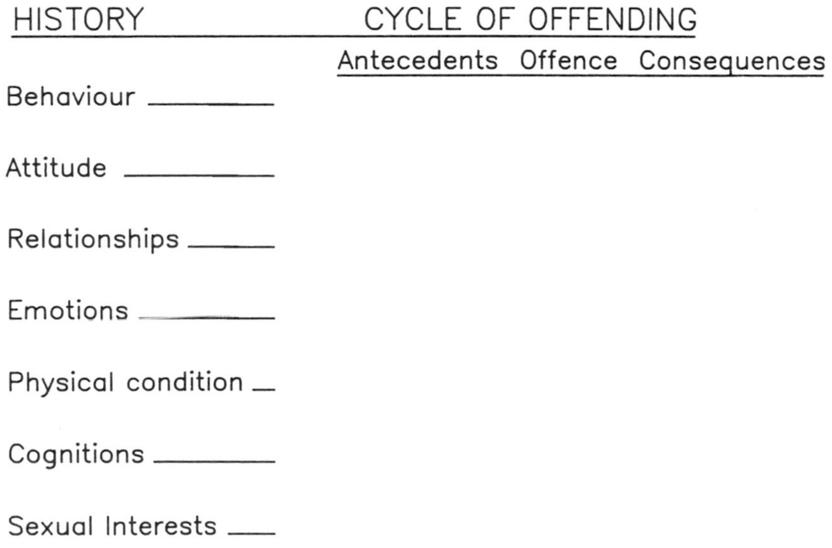

HISTORY	CYCLE OF OFFENDING
	Antecedents Offence Consequences
Behaviour _____	
Attitude _____	
Relationships _____	
Emotions _____	
Physical condition _	
Cognitions _____	
Sexual Interests ___	

Figure 7.1   Model for multi-modal analysis of sex offending. History and behavioural analysis

problem behaviours are not necessarily those which are responsible for maintaining them at the time the offender enters behavioural treatment.

For an understanding of the factors maintaining an offender's behaviour, the procedure of behavioural analysis is particularly relevant. The offender's deviant behaviour (B) is examined in terms of its antecedents (A) and its consequences (C). This analysis can yield information on various levels of the offender's functioning, along the lines of Lazarus's (1976) 'multi-modal analysis'. For sex offenders, particularly relevant levels of analysis which might be proposed are behavioural, cognitive, attitudinal, emotional, and physical condition (for example, drink or drug abuse, hunger and lack of sleep), as well as the state of personal relationships, sexual interests and opportunities for offending.

It is possible to use multi-modal analysis as a linking system between historical information about the offender's development (acquisition phase) and the cycle of offending represented in the behavioural analysis (maintenance phase). Some themes in the history, such as poor temper control, may become relevant in the maintenance of offending.

There is an appeal to this approach on the grounds of comprehensiveness and immediate therapeutic relevance. Figure 7.1 illustrates the kind of data system which results from this approach, linking historial themes (which may themselves require a therapeutic input—e.g. counselling for past abuses) with factors in the behavioural analysis (which will require modification if the offending behaviour is to be controlled).

Figure 7.2 illustrates the kind of analysis resulting from this system. Antecedents and consequences on the various levels of multi-modal analysis are identified, each representing a potential focus for therapeutic input. 'Vicious circles' in

ANTECEDENT ⟶ OFFENCE ⟶ CONSEQUENCES
(RAPE)

Deviant sexual fantasies	Sexual gratification
Sexual dysfunction	Tension release
Marital conflict	Marital conflict
Low self-esteem	Being ridiculed
Alcohol disinhibition	Heavy drinking
Opportunity	Fear of detection

Figure 7.2   Example of sex offence behavioural analysis

the cycle of offending can also be identified (underlined in Figure 7.2). For example, alcohol (which might precede offending as a result of its disinhibiting effects) might also become a consequence (with the offender using alcohol to cope with anxiety or guilt). Breaking into such vicious circles can be very effective therapeutically.

Such a representation is of course an over-simplification in that not all antecedents or all consequences occur simultaneously in time as implied by Figure 7.2. In reality, antecedents and consequences will themselves interrelate, and a flow diagram type of representation will convey matters more accurately, as in Figure 7.3. It may be, for example, that low self-esteem and heavy alcohol consumption can both develop without offending occurring, but their concurrence along with sexual abstinence beyond a critical period (with associated cognitive and physiological effects) and an opportunity to offend might predict that an offence will occur.

As the therapist strives to assemble data defined by this scheme, a number of advantages for therapy accrue, namely;

(1) The behavioural analysis identifies offence factors—antecedents and consequences—which might be amenable to change as a means of modifying the offender's offending;
(2) Attention is drawn to those areas where information is missing or uncertain, where further investigation and hypothesis testing are required, for example ascertaining what were the cognitive antecedents of the offender's offending—those thoughts passing through the offender's mind just before he offended;
(3) Offenders differ in the degree to which their offences can be understood in terms of one level of functioning rather than another, for example in

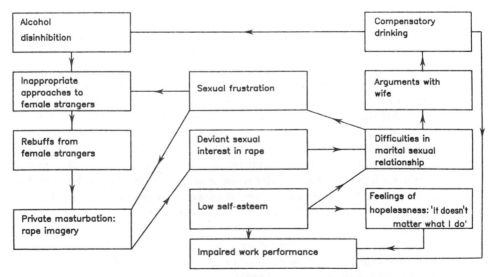

Figure 7.3 'Flow diagram' of the interaction between a sex offender's behaviour, attitudes, thoughts, feelings and sexual interests preceding commission of rape. (Reproduced from Perkins, 1988, by permission of the Open University Press)

terms of cognitive rather than emotional factors, and this can sometimes be ascertained from a behavioural analysis;

(4) It is not uncommon in behavioural analyses of offending to discover vicious circles of influence maintaining the behaviour in question, for example feelings of inadequacy both preceding offending and being one of its consequences—breaking into such vicious circles can often be an important therapeutic objective;

(5) Finally, a behavioural analysis is one means of evaluating treatment—that is, a means of judging at the termination of treatment how far the offender may still be at risk of reoffending—in terms of the number of antecedents and consequences of his offending which have remained unchanged.

DESCRIPTIVE AND TYPOLOGICAL RESEARCH

Knowledge of descriptive or typological research is of relevance not only in terms of knowing what might be expected from particular offender groups but also in answering offenders' not unreasonable queries about the likely factors behind their offending and the sorts of therapeutic procedures upon which they might need to embark. At the clinical practitioner level, the results of group-based researches provide what are in effect checklists of potentially relevant points to consider in working with the individual offender.

Some studies (e.g. Burgess et al., 1986; Cohen et al., 1971; Groth, 1979; Knight and Prentky, 1987; Prentky et al., 1987; Seghorn and Cohen, 1980) have explored the development of motivational models of rape and other sexually aggressive offences. From these studies certain motivational types or classifications have been proposed, the most common ones of which might be summarized as:

(1) *Compensatory*: here the motivation for the offence is primarily sexual. The offender is seeking sexual gratification from the victim and generally only uses as much force as is necessary to achieve this. Such offenders typically have social/sexual relationship difficulties which have resulted in normal sexual relationships being difficult for them to achieve.

(2) *Displaced Aggression*: here the offender is motivated by anger or hatred, the sexual aspect of the offence being simply one means of hurting or degrading the victim. Typically more force than is needed to commit the sexual act will be used and it may be directed towards a particular type of victim, such as prostitutes, older women or those perceived to be of higher social status. These offenders typically have histories of poor relationship with women and offending can be preceded by conflicts with females in their lives.

(3) *Sadistic*: here the motivation for the offence is again sexual but the offender derives sexual gratification by inflicting pain and fear on the victim. As with the 'displaced aggression' offender, the sadistic offender will use more violence than necessary to achieve sexual acts, but unlike the displaced aggression offender, the violence will appear more cold and deliberate. The

ultimately damaging expression of sadistic offending is sexually motivated murder.

(4) *Impulsive/Opportunistic*: these offenders typically have histories of various forms of anti-social behaviour and obtaining sex by force is yet another example of a generally impulsive and delinquent lifestyle. Sex offences are often committed in the course of some other activity such as burglary or non-sexual violence.

The work of Prentky et al. (1985) has attempted to extend such classifications further by developing a sub-classification system based on a sequential consideration for each offence of the following questions: (i) what is the meaning of the aggression in the offence? (instrumental or expressive); (ii) what is the meaning of the sexuality in the offence? (for the 'instrumentally aggressive' offenders, is it compensatory or exploitative?; for the 'expressively aggressive' offenders is it 'displaced anger' or sadistic?); (iii) finally for the four above sub-classifications, is impulsivity in the offender's history and life style 'high' or 'low'? This scheme produces eight sub-types overall.

Prentky *et al.*'s (1987) validation study had not at that stage confirmed the validity of these sub-groups, but they did report some relationships between a number of groupings and certain childhood factors. For example, exploitative offenders who typically used physical aggression after rape, had been drinking and committed offences around conventional social settings (e.g. bars), tended to have histories of non-intact parental marriages, childhood physical abuse, and juvenile penal histories.

Other studies have yielded complementary or overlapping motivational systems. Scully and Marolla (1985), for example, suggested five types of rape motivation, the first four of which might be summarized as sexually motivated, power motivated, revenge motivated, or incidental to other offences. These first four are similar to a number of other classification systems. The fifth motive was described as 'recreational' and based largely on adventure seeking, often in groups.

From some other studies indications of factors associated with offence escalation are gained. MacCulloch *et al.* (1983), for example, described how, for a group of sexual sadists, fantasy rehearsal of offences proved to be a common and important theme in the escalation of offending. Knowledge of these, and similar findings, can focus the therapist on areas of relevance in helping the client to change.

From the perspective of child sexual abuse, Finkelhor (1984) proposed a model of offender behaviour which, incorporating much of the descriptive research on the subject, involved a sequential system of four preconditions for offending to occur, each precondition representing a characteristic of the offender or offender-victim relationship. These four preconditions might be summarized as: (i) some motivation to abuse a child sexually; (ii) overcoming internal inhibitions against acting on that motivation; (iii) overcoming external impediments to committing sexual abuse; (iv) undermining or overcoming the child's resistance to the sexual abuse.

Each of these stages carries with it treatment implications. The first two stages imply treatment of the offender—sexual interests, disordered attitudes, poor impulse control—whereas the second two stages might involve interventions within the environments in which offending is liable to occur together with awareness education, assertiveness, and other forms of training for potential victims.

FROM ANALYSIS TO TREATMENT

Literature on the treatment of sex offenders can be broadly divided into: (i) that concerned with helping the offender gain insight into his offending; and (ii) that helping him to control or remove those influences which maintain the offending. Given the complex nature of sexual offence acquisition and maintenance, both approaches are important. Whilst treatment can be effective with only one approach or the other, more often than not attention will need to be directed to both approaches if the offender is to control his offending.

Approaches to sex offender treatment have been categorized in various ways, notably: (i) by treatment goals—e.g. modify deviant sexual interests, improve appropriate social skills; (ii) the type of therapeutic model being employed—e.g. psychoanalytic, behavioural, environmental; (iii) by the stages of hypothesized models of offender functioning (e.g. Burgess *et al.*, 1986; Finkelhor, 1984); or (iv) by the levels of functioning which may need to be addressed, along the lines of Lazarus's (1976) multi-modal analysis.

Reports of effective treatment for sex offenders are generally cognitive-behavioural in orientation. However, as Abel *et al.* (1976) have pointed out, this may simply reflect the greater degree of evaluative sophistication which has tended to be applied to cognitive-behavioural as opposed to psychotherapeutic techniques—the latter often being used in pursuit of offender insight development and coming to terms with past history.

It has been suggested that the effective treatment of sex offending requires the application of four areas of knowledge (Perkins, 1984), specifically knowledge of: (i) research into the particular classes of offending, e.g. rape, incest or exhibitionism, with which the offender presents for treatment; (ii) research into the efficacy of particular treatment methods, ideally as applied to the offender's own category of offending; (iii) the offender's learning history, including those factors which may have led to the acquisition and maintenance of offending; and (iv) behavioural analysis of the offender's current offence patterns.

Even with these notions to guide the assessment process, a full behavioural analysis of the offender's behaviour cannot always be generated at the outset of treatment. The offender may be unwilling or unable to reveal certain facts which will bear upon the behavioural analysis. Trust between offender and therapist may need to be built up over time, and new data, external to the process of assessment being carried out by the therapist working with the offender, may be needed to fill in some gaps in understanding.

It may be that prior to the commencement of treatment there is insufficient documentary or interview evidence to know precisely what happens when the offender offends. A comprehensive analysis might only be established after integrating within the preliminary analysis additional data stemming from many more interviews with the offender, including interviews conducted after further offences have occurred. The building up of an analysis in this way, as offences continue, although often implicit in the process of working with non-violent offenders in the community, is clearly not a process which could be advocated as part of an assessment strategy for violent sexual offenders. In reality, however, the same principle often applies when trying to understand why relapses have occurred and building this information into the analysis.

How to proceed from the stage of behavioural analysis to intervening with offenders so as to help them cease offending is not altogether straightforward. Offenders' motivation to change well-established patterns of behaviour may be mixed. There may be denial of certain aspects of their behaviour, and there may be many gains as well as disadvantages for offenders in maintaining their offence behaviour.

What then are the therapeutic skills in attempting to overcome these potential barriers to treatment? These might be said to fall broadly under two headings— the structure of the behavioural analysis and the context of the treatment.

Within the behavioural analysis itself can lie clues as to where treatment might most usefully be directed. There can be 'core influences' running through the analysis—sets of interrelated antecedents and consequences of the offending ('vicious circles')—into which therapy can sometimes inject a powerful influence. These might be internal to the offender, for example related to abnormally high emotional responses, or external to the offender, for example under-stimulation at work.

The task at this stage in treatment will be for the offender to be helped to grasp this, and to be motivated to try and tackle some of its aspects such that treatment can commence. For certain aspects of the analysis, for example attitudes about sexuality, it may be that the offender cannot or will not (it is not always easy to establish which) be able to work on this in the early stages of treatment. Particularly for imprisoned offenders, for whom involvement in treatment is not a requirement for their release, to push too hard too soon on all treatment goals may simply result in the offender opting out altogether.

This is not to say that difficult treatment goals should be side-stepped, but rather that they should be tackled in a planned way. It may be that the offender who holds views that men should always dominate women sexually or that women are not to be trusted, will need the experience of taking part, for example, in some more basic social skills training, the purpose of which he can grasp, before more complex attitudinal issues can be addressed.

TREATMENT TECHNIQUES

Whatever the theoretical orientation adopted in treatment and whatever 'within-therapy' goals are agreed, the ultimate aim of most reported work on sex offender treatment is a reduction in the severity or frequency of sex offending after treatment, compared with that which it would have been without treatment.

There are often several possible treatments for the same therapeutic goal (e.g. reducing deviant sexual interests) and some studies have attempted to isolate and evaluate the effectiveness of these individual treatments. Where such evaluation is extended to the measurement of reconviction rates, however, the results are generally disappointing (Howard League Working Party, 1985). However, this is perhaps not surprising, given the complexity of sex offending, and the unlikelihood of any such direct association between one treatment and reconvictions several years later.

Of the specific treatment techniques employed with institutionalized sex offenders, a broad distinction can be drawn between treatment goals related to deviant sexual interests, those related to deviant or inadequate socio-sexual behaviour, and those related to insight and associated problems of attitudes, beliefs and thinking.

Deviant Sexual Interests

Where offenders are sexually aroused by deviant acts (e.g. sadism), or by other than consenting adult partners (e.g. children), these deviant interests can be assessed by a combination of self-report, behavioural, and psychophysiological assessment. Typically an offender might be asked to indicate on self-report protocols his sexual interest in visually presented material or audiotaped descriptions of various sexual activities. His penile erection responses to this material can also be assessed by means of a penile phethysmograph (PPG). Abel *et al.* (1985) recorded how self-reported sexual interest and PPG results coincided in only 30% of offenders assessed, even when complete confidentiality was assured. When the remaining 70% of the offenders were confronted with this discrepancy, 70% of these (i.e. 49% of the total sample) revised their self-reports in the direction of the PPG assessment.

As well as helping the offender accept his sexual interest patterns prior to treatment, such PPG assessment can also be useful in monitoring treatment and, in combination with other data, provide some pointers to possible future risk factors.

Treatment at the level of sexual interests involves decreasing deviant and increasing non-deviant interests. Not all offenders will require this, however, and the distinction between those offenders who require such interventions to avoid future offending and those who do not is one of the most important considerations in designing therapy programmes.

Aversion Therapy

Aversion therapy, in which material depicting deviant imagery or prompting deviant thoughts is paired with unpleasant consequences, has been used in many treatment programmes for sex offenders. Developed originally from classical conditioning principles, the procedure has varied by paradigm (types and schedules of reinforcement), by the stimulus materials used (slides, video depictions or audio descriptions for example), and by the aversive stimuli used (electric shock, unpleasant smells).

Shame aversion therapy (Serber, 1970) also falls broadly in the aversion therapy paradigm. The procedure as described by Serber involved the offender acting out his deviant behaviour, in this instance exhibitionism, in front of thera-pist aides who were instructed to behave with ridicule or disapproval towards him. Serber and Wolpe (1972) reported the successful use of the procedure at six month follow-up with seven out of ten sexual offenders treated in this way. Obvious limitations, and possibly dangers, with this approach would arise with offenders who, in addition to deviant sexual interests, also had hostile impulses and/or negative self-images with respect to other adults.

Covert Sensitization

Unpleasant imagery has also been used, as in the covert sensitization procedure pioneered by Cautela (1967). Here the offender is helped to imagine a scene of relevance to his offending (e.g. walking to a school with the intention of finding a child to assault), following which he imagines some unpleasant consequence such as being arrested. Callaghan and Leitenberg (1973) found this procedure to be effective with a mixed group of exhibitionists, homosexuals and a paedophile; as did Barlow et al. (1969) with one homosexual and a paedophile. However, Christie et al. (1978) reported a failure of the procedure to modify the fantasies of a group of sexually aggressive offenders. It was hypothesized that this group may either have been poor in imaginal ability or immune to the imagined aver-sive consequences of their behaviour.

Recent reports on the use of covert sensitization have tended to emphasize the use both of negative imagined consequences for imagined offence behaviour and also of positive consequences for imagined alternatives to the offending (Salter, 1988). Salter describes how these positive imagined consequences of non-offending can be cognitive ('I made it. I can be in control'), social ('I'm home with my wife and family. I'm not afraid of anyone knocking on the door with something to tell them. I don't have anything to hide'), or material ('I'm having dinner in a restaurant and thinking "no more prison food for me" ').

All of these aversive procedures have the aim of modifying the arousal poten-tial of particular thoughts, acts or images to which the offender might be exposed after treatment and which without treatment might lead to his reoffending. Hallam and Rachman (1976) reviewed aversion therapy and concluded that it can indeed be helpful in this objective as measured by PPG and subjective assessments of sexual interest, but that its effects are more complex than condi-tioning alone and are likely to involve cognitive mediational factors.

A sex offender seen in my own practice on follow-up from prison into the community illustrates the point. He was attending weekly sessions which in-cluded aversion therapy and in the course of one visit mentioned that he had been in what he would previously have regarded as 'an ideal situation' to offend. He came across a woman alone at a bus stop, was tempted to offend in his usual fashion but 'the thought came into my mind—it's mad to do this while I'm going to the hospital for aversion therapy. It'll set the treatment back and ruin everything I've achieved'. He was clearly being influenced not only by any conditioning effects in the aversion therapy but also by the effects his commitment to the treatment had come to have on his thinking.

Enhancement of non-deviant sexual interests has been reported in some instances as having been achieved through the same aversive procedures used to suppress deviant sexual interests. Aversion relief is a procedure in which it was originally supposed that the relief experienced at the end of aversive stimulation, such as electric shocks administered during the presentation of deviant material, would become associated with the subsequent presentation of non-deviant material and hence reinforce arousal to this non-deviant material.

Barlow (1973), in a review of procedures designed to enhance sexual arousal, reported that aversion relief was the most commonly reported procedure at that time. However, in the few instances where its effects had been tested separately from those of other procedures, notably aversion therapy, it had proved to be ineffective, suggesting that it may be a useful adjunct to aversion therapy rather than a treatment in its own right.

Orgasmic Reconditioning

Marquis (1970) successfully introduced a procedure termed orgasmic reconditioning, also referred to as masturbatory conditioning, in which the offender replaces deviant with non-deviant masturbation fantasies. This positive reinforcement procedure was based on the association between early masturbatory imagery and subsequent sexual behaviour, as reported by McGuire et al. (1965). Successful results with the procedure have been reported by Abel et al. (1973) with a patient with sadistic fantasies; by Marshall (1973), using a combination of aversion therapy and orgasmic reconditioning with a group of child molesters; and by Marshall et al. (1977) with a group of incarcerated sex offenders.

Castration and Anti-libidinal Medication

The use of castration and anti-libidinal medication in the treatment of sex offenders has been reported over the years. Sturup (1968, 1972) reported a 1% reconviction rate for 900 sex offenders followed up for 30 years after castration, and similarly low reconviction rates have also been reported by Ortmann (1980). Oestrogen implants have also resulted in reports of reduced reconviction rates (Field and Williams, 1970). The main problems with these procedures are ethical, where the procedure is irreversible, and the probability of unwanted side-effects such as nausea, thrombosis and breast development.

The two forms of anti-libidinal medication in most common use are the anti-androgen cyproterone acetate and the tranquillizer benperidol (Bancroft, 1977, 1983). Unwanted side-effects are much less but long-term research on prolonged use of such medication is not yet available. Whilst there are cases where anti-libidinal medication can be helpful, given the offender's informed consent and ability to withdraw from the medication, it is unlikely that such treatment alone will meet all the treatment needs of most sex offenders. Many sex offenders commit their offences for motives other than sexual gratification, and simply reducing the libido of these offenders will not necessarily be sufficient to control their offending.

Case studies of two sexually motivated murderers with low levels of testosterone, reported by Raboch *et al.* (1987), indicate that decreasing levels of androgens alone is not necessarily any guarantee that sexually motivated offending will be prevented. Nevertheless, there are still cases where such medication used alongside other approaches can have a valuable part to play in, for example, reducing the more compulsive aspects of the offending, allowing a period of sexual 'quiescence' whilst other therapies are introduced, or helping the elderly offender for whom other forms of therapy may no longer be wanted or viable.

Socio-sexual Behaviour

Social skills

In addition to the deviant sexual interests which sex offenders may exhibit, they may also present with problems of social and sexual relationships and attitudes. Many offenders are either socially anxious, or lack the skills to function satisfactorily with other adults. Alternatively, they may possess attitudes and modes of thinking about relationships which propel them towards further offending and away from legal alternatives (Baxter *et al.*, 1986; Lipton *et al.*, 1987; Overholser and Beck, 1988). Both group and individual social skills training for sexual offenders have been reported. Rehearsal and feedback on role-played interactions relevant to the offender's behaviour patterns are the central feature of the approach. This is often supplemented by coaching and modelling by the therapists, other offenders undergoing the training, or via specially prepared training material.

Burgess *et al.* (1980) reported improved social skills as a result of a social skills programme for sex offenders in prison. Crawford and Allen (1979) reported on successful maintenance of social skills changes in a group of English special hospital patients over a two-year period. However, they pointed to the dual difficulties of determining precisely what constitutes appropriate social behaviour for each patient, and maintaining changes in the post-institutional environment.

There have been some attempts to tackle the issue of establishing appropriate social skills. Serber and Keith (1974), for example, engaged the services of the local gay community in the social skills training of homosexual child molesters. Perkins (1983), however, in reporting on a broad-based treatment programme for sex offenders, noted that there may be severe limitations to this approach— of attempting to establish accurately what would be the most useful and appropriate skills for each offender in the programme, given his particular social and geographical circumstances—on the grounds of the cost-effectiveness of the high level of input this requires.

Sexual skills

Other more direct approaches to developing appropriate sexual behaviour have been reported. Cole (1982), for example, reported that 'surrogate therapy', in which sexually inexperienced males were guided to successful sexual intercourse with therapist aides, had positive effects on social and sexual skills and confidence, which were maintained if the experiences were reinforced by real-life successes after treatment. Cole's sample were not, by and large, sexually deviant or sexual offenders, and there would remain reservations about this procedure with offenders who may be disordered on many more levels of a multi-modal analysis than Cole's subjects.

Sex education has been an issue addressed by a number of workers who have noted the lack of sexual knowledge of many sex offenders in prison (Woodward, 1980) and other residential settings (Wyre, 1989). It is also one of the major themes of assessment and treatment now addressed with sex offenders in special hospitals (Grounds et al., 1987).

Insight, Attitudes and Thinking

Group therapy

There have been various reports on the use of group therapy with sex offenders. Some groups in the USA have involved offenders being pressurized into attending on the basis that by so doing they would avoid police prosecution; see Mathis and Collins (1970) with indecent exposers and Hartman (1965a,b) with paedophiles. Hartman's approach emphasized group support, reality testing and controlling deviant sexual urges. Resnick and Peters (1967) carried out group-work with child molesters referred by the courts. The therapeutic elements in their approach again included peer support, together with exploration of relationships with women, attitudes towards authority, and self-esteem.

Costell and Yalom (1972) reported a group programme directed towards impulse control for sex offenders in a maximum security hospital. Reference was made to the problems involving the morale of long-term patients in treatment, and to the dual role of staff as therapists and agents of control—issues which are common to many treatment programmes in long-term custodial settings.

Wyre (1989) reported on the use of several parallel groups for sex offenders, first during his work in the prison system, and subsequently at Gracewell Clinic in Birmingham, England. Offenders attended the groups which were relevant to the main themes in their offending, such as sex education or attitudes towards women.

Psychotherapeutic groups for sex offenders have also been reported, particularly in North America. West et al. (1978) describe the Canadian Penitentiary Service's therapeutic community in which sex offenders engaged in group discussions about their offending in order to enhance insight and self-control. Similar principles underlie the group therapy regime at Grendon Underwood Prison in the UK, although this is not specifically geared to sex offenders.

Quayle (1989), at a secure hospital in England, reports on the use of a series of groups for young adult male patients diagnosed as suffering from 'psychopathic disorder', many of whom have committed sex offences or sexually motivated acts of violence. Patients progress from basic social skills training groups into groups within which they take part in 'family sculpting' to uncover and work on past family relationships, and reverse role-playing in which they come to see their past offending through the eyes of their victims.

In one part of the therapy, the patient faces the rest of the group, who play the role of his victim. Interestingly, Quayle reports that it is often through the offenders' identification with the victims of other ofenders' offences that they gain most insight into their own offences and the effects these are likely to have had on their victims (see also Grounds *et al.*, 1987, for a description of the ward in question).

THE PROCESS OF TREATMENT

In treatment, interventions of one kind can interact with others. For example, an offender in a group dealing with past behaviour might talk about the abuse he suffered as a child. From this, he might see the relevance of going on to participate in some direct assessments of his own sexual interests. At this point, discussion with him might uncover that he has quite different attitudes about the sexual abuse he has suffered and the sexual abuse he has himself perpetrated. Experimental work has also drawn attention to such interactions between different levels of functioning, and the fact that some aspects of functioning which have been assumed to be stable at a particular point in an individual's life, such as sexual interests, can vary with other aspects of functioning, such as cognitions. Yates *et al.* (1984), for example, found that male subjects exposed to mild insult from a female research assistant displayed a greater sexual responsivity to rape material than those subjects who had not received the insult.

At a clinical level, this might be exemplified by the offender who was not sexually responsive to paedophilic material when he was 'in love' with a woman, but showed significant responses to such material when he was not in love. Clearly, in this instance, it makes less sense to view changes in sexual interests as measured by the PPG in isolation from other factors but rather they should be seen as part of the kind of flow of interacting factors as illustrated previously in Figure 7.3.

Sex offender treatment is the focus of dramatically different points of view—indeed, the very phrase can arouse many different feelings. Some applaud such work, others are sceptical that changes can be brought about in such offenders; some are concerned with the potential for infringements of offenders' human rights which are inherent in some therapeutic approaches, and yet others see such work as undermining the interests, needs, or feelings of victims.

Particular methods rise and fall in popularity, often irrespective of evidence on efficacy. There is, for example, currently an ethics-oriented swing away from the use of aversion therapy on the grounds of its unpleasantness to the offender. However, in the absence of clear definitions of such factors, and a clearly balanced appraisal of options open to the offender requiring treatment, such a categorical position can be difficult to sustain. In the course of work in Birmingham (Perkins, 1983, 1987), for example, some offenders approached the prospect of social skills training or group therapy with greater apprehension, internal conflict and distress than they did aversion therapy. Whether or not this was because they could avoid unpleasant issues about themselves in the aversion therapy procedure more than in the social skills training was not always clear, but in any case this is a different issue. Simply in terms of the proposition that treatments which are too distressing should not be used, social skills training for some offenders would have figured worse than aversion therapy.

On another issue, Pacht (1976) has made the point that many sex offender treatments were not developed for that purpose but have been transferred in from other therapeutic settings. Howells (1986) has noted that social skills training approaches for sexual and violent offenders are often insufficiently linked to the analysis of the offence behaviour (we might simply be improving the social skills of sex offenders without reducing the probability of their offending), and that training is insufficiently linked to the issues of generalization beyond the custodial setting.

DENIAL AND MINIMIZATION

An issue so commonly associated with the treatment of sex offenders that it warrants particular emphasis and consideration is that of offender denial and minimization. This is the tendency for persistent offenders to deny that their offending was planned and repetitive, or even that they committed any offences at all; together with a tendency to underplay, distort or in other ways minimize their responsibility for their offending, its nature and its effects.

Once an offender has embarked upon treatment, the task is to help him achieve his therapy goals despite his own defences. In attempting to do this, however, the therapist treads a difficult line between legitimate discussion, and sometimes persuasion, as opposed to illegitimate coercion of the offender into adopting goals and carrying out procedures with which he fundamentally disagrees.

Even within this last proposition there are many imponderables: how do we really know what the offender's own treatment goals are? The therapist's own beliefs and moral judgements will no doubt be exercising their influence both subtly and in more direct ways. Therapists will generally exercise some limits over what they will be prepared to do and work towards with offenders: helping offenders cease offending will be acceptable but overcoming anxiety about committing offences or learning how to avoid detection will be unacceptable to most, if not all, therapists.

The context of treatment will also wield a powerful influence. An offender awaiting trial will generally express much more enthusiasm for treatment than an offender at post-trial who is free to opt into or out of treatment as he wishes. All of these influences on the offender are there; they exist whether the therapist likes it or not. The therapist can either chose to work with such factors, to guide the offender into treatment compliance and towards controlling his offending, or the factors can be ignored. Nevertheless, they will still exist to support or thwart the therapeutic effort at various points in the therapeutic process.

Any thought that these issues are the sole province of the behavioural thera-pists is misguided: they are equally applicable to other forms of psychotherapy than the behavioural variety. The key issues of client denial, motivation to change, and cooperation in the process of treatment are in themselves aspects of client functioning which are just as amenable to analysis and modification as the presenting problems of sex offending.

In any form of psychotherapy it is generally accepted that the client should give his/her informed consent to what takes place, that is that the therapist should: (i) be clear that the client is physically and mentally competent to give informed consent; and (ii) make the client aware of the advantages and dis-advantages of the proposed treatment, including its risks and alternatives.

This second point is a difficult but highly relevant one as far as behavioural psychotherapy with offenders is concerned. The way in which the therapist couches the options available to the client can play a central role in whether or not the offender agrees to treatment. Put more extremely, some offenders can sometimes be persuaded into treatment, even where there are no external pres-sures such as impending court cases or parole hearings bearing upon them, simply by the use of well-established techniques of persuasion.

In carrying out treatment work there is an interplay between the analysis of the offender's behaviour (acquisition and maintenance) and the process of gaining

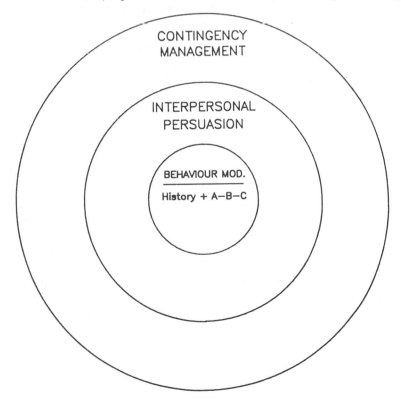

Figure 7.4   Levels of therapeutic intervention

his cooperation and overcoming denial. This might be represented diagrammatically as in Figure 7.4. The multi-modal analysis of the offender's history and cycle of offending is represented as the central 'core' of treatment. Around this is a process of persuasion based on the flow of interpersonal exchanges between the offender and the therapist. These exchanges might draw upon the various counselling and attitude change techniques related to the task in hand.

Represented as an outer circle in Figure 7.4 is another layer of influences upon which the therapist might draw. These involve the offender's current circumstances and the opportunities these provide for further enhancement of therapeutic cooperation and challenging of denial. Amongst these contingencies which the therapist may choose to highlight with the offender is the fact that a failure to change offence behaviour may result in imprisonment or loss of family relationships.

Discussions of such issues are not threats from the therapist, they are already facts in the offender's life irrespective of the therapist's actions. The therapist is simply drawing the offender's attention to these contingencies, discussing all possibilities with him and, ideally, offering constructive solutions which might be open to him to help him both control his offending and achieve his other legitimate aims. Bancroft (1979) alludes to such techniques in his paper on 'the nature of the patient-therapist relationship' in the behavioural treatment of offenders. Specifically, Bancroft lists the following nine ways in which the therapist can facilitate behaviour change in the offender:

(1) Helping the offender understand why he/she offends, one way of doing this being the joint construction of a behavioural analysis of the offending.
(2) Confronting the client with inconsistencies in his/her thinking.
(3) Revealing the therapist's values when they are in conflict with the client's.
(4) Teaching the client basic principles of problem-solving.
(5) Giving the client positive reinforcement for cooperating with treatment.
(6) Facilitating expressions of feeling.
(7) Facilitating communications both with the therapist and with significant other people.
(8) Eliciting 'externalization of intent', that is getting the client to make explicit his/her intention to act differently, so that this will be subsequently more difficult to evade.
(9) Fostering independence and discouraging dependence.

To these strategies, a number of others might be added, based upon experience in carrying out behavioural treatment with offenders in prison, hospital and the community (Perkins, 1984, 1986, 1987). Amongst those which have been most successful in engaging therapeutically with sex offenders are persuasion and contingency management.

Persuasion

There are a number of important points to note in effective persuasion.

(1) Establish common goals with the client: start from where the client is prepared to accept change, even if this means accepting a lesser level of commitment or insight than is ideal.

(2) Always keep the purpose of intervention in mind: guide interviews with 'open' questions (who, what, when, where, why, how) but pin down facts with 'closed' questions. Accept that not all facts will be elicited at once: be prepared to come back to potentially threatening topics.

(3) Clarify, but do not challenge the offender's beliefs too early: positively reinforce rather than punish revelations. Pick the right time to challenge offence-related thinking, i.e. once data gathering has been carried out.

(4) Reference to likely offence scenarios can help unblock offenders too anxious to describe details, e.g. 'There are often two main reasons why people have committed your sort of offence' (spell this out with examples as appropriate—e.g. sexual deviance versus social inadequacy explanations) 'Which do you think most applies to you?' Sometimes offenders will give clues to which might apply in their verbal and non-verbal responses to these descriptions.

(5) Often a casual approach to potentially threatening closed questions can be helpful, e.g. an off-the-cuff, low-key style of questioning, perhaps while looking away from the offender can sometimes work; subsequently, reflect back, question and, if rapport will allow, challenge inconsistencies in the client's attitudes or behaviour, perhaps with a style conveying genuine but good-natured incredulity at offence-related thinking.

(6) Do not persist with advice to argumentative or rationalizing clients. Rather, attempt to place them in the position of making suggestions for therapy, and reinforce good suggestions.

(7) Make sure that any particularly uncooperative client attributes as many good therapeutic ideas as possible to himself rather than to the therapist: the therapist can facilitate this by making references to, for example, 'Your good idea from last week's session', even if it was not quite all the offender's own idea.

(8) Stress the 'togetherness' of therapy with cooperative clients: use of terms such as 'we could' rather than 'I think' and 'you should' can help with this. However, be careful to avoid assuming personal responsibility for the offender's problems.

Contingency Management

As with persuasion there are a number of points to note.

(1) Provide the client with information relevant to the process of becoming committed to behaviour change, e.g. types of treatment options available, and the consequences of no treatment.

(2) Make the client aware of reinforcement contingencies operating outside the therapy situation: e.g. the likelihood of further imprisonment, divorce and loss of contact with children if offending continues.

(3) Capitalize on the principle of 'cognitive dissonance' (Festinger, 1957) by encouraging the client to believe that he is undertaking treatment with the minimum of external pressure: in this way genuine attitude change at the end of treatment is likely to be maximized.

(4) Capitalize on any short-term external reinforcers to treatment which might be available, e.g. improving relationships with relevant others in the institution or community, and taking time out from a boring routine in prison.

The way in which such processes can operate is illustrated by the following case example, which has been disguised in order to preserve the offender's anonymity. This life-sentence prisoner, convicted of rape of a young girl, when first seen admitted the offence, but maintained that any problems he might have had at the time had long since passed. The enormity of his crime, coming after a long history of previous indecent assaults on young girls had, he maintained, so shocked him that he would be deterred from any future offending. His main concern when first seen was the injustice, as he saw it, of his still being in custody five years after the offence. He compared his position with that of other sex offenders and saw in this comparison an unfairly harsh sentence for himself. He found it difficult to engage on the question of his risk to the community and maintained that treatment was not necessary.

Work with this offender began from the position of taking matters from his perspective, that is wanting to get out of prison. He accepted that the authorities would need to be convinced of his safety to the public and that this would require assembling a good deal of information about his past offending and his current propensity for offending. It proved easiest to engage him initially on his own childhood, including the various abuses and disappointments he had suffered. By responding to this in an understanding way and by acknowledging how such a disturbed childhood could well have led on to his own offending, it became possible to elicit further details about his cycle of offending which could be addressed at subsequent points in treatment. The therapeutic process was, at this stage, focusing on the acquisition phase of his offending. He proved to be amenable to discussion about his past life and gained some insight into the reasons for his offending.

However, he still maintained that he had no problems currently although a sufficient crack in his defences had been achieved such that he acknowledged past deviant sexual fantasies concerning young girls, including sadistic elements, together with an inability to relate emotionally or sexually to adults, a pretence he had previously vigorously maintained. Discussion about his past sexually deviant interests and masturbation fantasies involving both young females and a degree of sadism led to the issue of how any changes in these features of his makeup might be demonstrated to the authorities. After much weighing of the pros and cons, the offender took part in an auditory PPG assessment, which clearly indicated the presence of very strong sexual responses both to young females and to certain sadistic acts.

Almost immediately upon discussion of these results with the offender, he acknowledged with evident distress the continuing presence of the fantasies without any further reference to his previous denials. The point had been reached where the beginnings of treatment for the sexual deviation aspect of his offending could be addressed for the first time. The PPG had in effect been both an assessment measure and, perhaps more importantly, a therapeutic device in creating and working through his anxiety and denial about his sexual interests.

EVALUATION

Rutter and Giller (1983) draw attention to a number of pitfalls in the evaluation of treatment programmes for offenders which have a bearing on judgements about the success or otherwise that interventions with sex offenders have achieved. These pitfalls concern the adequacy of sample sizes and subject matching, the inclusion of control groups, types of outcome measures, lengths of follow-up, and the statistical evaluation carried out. In addition to these there is the question of the quality of the treatment itself, and Rutter and Giller highlight the fact that in many instances the planned interventions have not actually been carried out.

In reviews of behavioural treatment techniques used with offenders, Burchard and Wood (1982) and Rutter and Giller (1983) examined evidence on the effectiveness of treatment programmes both within institutions and in the community. Within institutions, they concluded, behavioural treatments have had demonstrable effects on the institutional behaviour of the offenders, but there is little evidence that such changes in behaviour have a positive effect on reducing recidivism rates. It may, however, be that positive changes in institutional behaviour are a necessary but not sufficient condition for changes in offending behaviour in the community.

In a review of sex offender recidivism, Furby et al. (1989) conclude that recidivism rates are unusually hard to establish owing to the gross under-reporting of such offences. Their examination of 42 studies, some involving treatment and others not, revealed methodological shortcomongs in almost all the studies, including a dearth of appropriate follow-up periods. However, the qualitative conclusions were that recidivism rates and treatment effects may be quite different between different types of offence and that, in evaluating treatment effectiveness, greater sophistication in offender classification and much longer follow-up periods are required.

In summary, whereas institutional programmes of behavioural treatment for sex offenders may be necessary, they may also be insufficient to bring about reductions in recidivism. Community-based treatment programmes, where these are feasible, show much more promise: this is particularly so where interventions are specifically geared to offence-related problems and needs, are linked to significant others in the offender's natural environment, and are carefully controlled so as to guard against any unforeseen, counter-productive consequences of treatment.

With sexual offenders a balance must be struck between treatment which for the more violent, recidivist or disturbed offender must of necessity begin in a secure setting, and treatment which is carried out post-release in the community. It is suggested that the model of multi-modal historical and behavioural analysis which has been proposed here is a useful scheme for linking institutional and community aspects of therapy in a way which is comprehensive, minimizes risks to the community, and maximizes therapeutic change for the offender.

References

Abel, G. G., Barlow, D. H., and Blanchard, E. B. (1973). Developing heterosexual arousal by altering masturbatory fantasies: A controlled study. Paper presented at the Association for Advancement of Behaviour Therapy, Miami, December 1973.

Abel, G. G., Barlow, D. H., Blanchard, E. B., and Guild, D. (1977). The components of rapists' sexual arousal. *Archives of General Psychiatry*, **34**, 895–903.

Abel, G. G., Becker, J. V., Mittelman, M., Cunningham-Rathner, N., Rouleau, J. L., and Murphy, W. D. (1987). *Self-Reported Sex Crimes of Non-Incarcerated Paraphiliacs* (Final Report No. MH-33678). Washington, DC: Public Health Service.

Abel, G. G., Blanchard, E. B., and Becker, J. V. (1976). Psychological treatment of rapists. In M. J. Walker and S. L. Brodsky (eds), *Sexual Assault*. Lexington, MA: Lexington Books.

Abel, G. G., Mittelman, M. S., and Becker, J. V. (1985). Sexual offenders: Results of assessment and recommendations for treatment. In M. H. Ben-Aron, S. J. Huckle and C. D. Webster (eds), *Clinical Criminology: The Assessment and Treatment of Criminal Behaviour*. Toronto: M & M Graphic, pp. 191–205.

Abel, G. G., Becker, J. V., Mittleman, M., Cunningham-Ruthner, J., Rouleau, J. L., and Murphy, N. L. (1987). Self reported sex crimes of non-incarcerated paraphiliacs. *Journal of Interpersonal Violence*, **2**, 3–25.

Bancroft, J. (1977). *Mongol sexuality. The Practitioner*, **218**, 341.

Bancroft, J. (1979). The nature of the patient–therapist relationship. In Trasler, G. B., Farrington, D. P. (eds). *Behaviour Modification with Offenders: A Criminological Symposium*. Occasional papers No. 5. Cambridge: Institute of Criminology.

Bancroft, J. (1983). *Human Sexuality and its Problems*. London: Churchill Livingstone.

Barlow, D. H. (1973). Increasing heterosexual responsiveness in the treatment of sexual deviation: A review of the clinical and experimental evidence. *Behaviour Therapy*, **4**, 655–71.

Barlow, D. H., Leitenberg, H., and Agras, W. S. (1969). The experimental control of sexual deviation through manipulation of the noxious scene in covert sensitization. *Journal of Abnormal Psychology*, **74**, 596–601.

Baxter, D. J., Barbaree, H. E., and Marshall, W. L. (1986). Sexual responses to consenting and forced sex in a large sample of rapists and nonrapists. *Behaviour Research and Therapy*, **24**, 513–20.

British Association for the Study and Prevention of Child Abuse (BASPCAN) (1980). *Child Sexual Abuse*. London: BASPCAN.

Burchard, J. D., and Wood, T. W. (1982). Crime and delinquency. In A. S. Bellack, M. Hersen and A. E. Kazdin, *International Handbook of Behaviour Modification and Therapy*. New York: Plenum.

Burgess, A. W. (1985). *Rape and Sexual Assault—a Research Handbook*. New York: Garland.

Burgess, A. W., Hartman, C., Ressler, R. K., Douglas, J. E., and McCormack, A. (1986). Sexual homicide: A motivational model. *J. of Interpersonal Violence*, **1**, 251–72.

Burgess, R., Jewitt, R., Sandham, J., and Hudson, B. L. (1980). Working with sex offenders: A social skills training group. *Brit. J. Social Wk.*, **10**, 133–42.

Callahan, E. J., and Leitenberg, H. (1973). Aversion therapy for sexual deviation: Contingent shock and covert sensitization. *Journal of Abnormal Psychology*, **81**, 60–73.

Cautela, J. (1967). Covert sensitization. *Psychological Reports*, **20**, 459–68.

Christie, M. M., Marshall, W. L., and Lanthier, R. D. (1978). A descriptive study of incarcerated rapists and pedophiles. Unpublished monograph, Dept. of Psychology, Queen University, Kingston, Ontario, Canada.

Cohen, M. L., Garofalo, R. F., Boucher, R., and Seghorn, T. (1971). The psychology of rapists. *Seminars in Psychiatry*, **3**, 307–27.

Cole, M. (1982). The use of surrogate sex partners in the treatment of sex dysfunctions and allied conditions. *British Journal of Sexual Medicine*, **9**, 13–20.

Costell, R., and Yalom, L. (1972). Institutional group therapy. In H. L. Resnick and M. E. Wolfgang (eds), *Sexual Behaviour: Social, Clinical and Legal Aspects*. Boston: Little, Brown.

Crawford, D. A., and Allen, J. V. (1979). A social skills training programme with sex offenders. In M. Cook and G. Wilson (eds), *Love and Attraction: Proceedings of an International Conference*, Oxford: Pergamon.

Feldman, M. P. (1977). *Criminal Behaviour: A Psychological Analysis*. Chichester: Wiley.

Festinger, L. (1957). *A Theory of Cognitive Dissonance*. New York: Harper & Row.

Field, H., and Williams, M. (1970). The hormonal treatment of sex offenders. *Medicine, Science and the Law*, **10**, 27–34.

Finkelhor, D. (1979). *Sexually Victimized Children*. New York: Free Press.

Finkelhor, D. (1984). *Child Sexual Abuse: New Theory and Research*. New York: Free Press.

Finkelhor, D. (1986). *A Sourcebook on Child Sexual Abuse*. Beverly Hills, CA: Sage.

Furby, L., Weinrott, M. R., and Blackshaw, L. (1989). Sex offender recidivision: A review. *Psychological Bulletin*, **155** (1), 3–30.

Groth, A. N. (1979). *Men who Rape: The Psychology of the Offender*. New York: Plenum.

Grounds, A. T., Quayle, M. T., France, J., Brett, T., Cox, M., and Hamilton, J. R. (1987). A unit for 'psychopathic disorder' patients in Broadmoor Hospital. *Medicine, Science, and the Law*, **27**, 21–31.

Hallam, R. S., and Rachman, S. (1976). Current status of aversion therapy. In M. Hersen, R. M. Eisler and P. M. Miller (eds), *Progress in Behaviour Modification*, vol. 2. London: Academic Press.

Hartman, V. (1965a). Notes on group psychotherapy with pedophiles. *Canadian Psychiatric Association Journal*, **10**, 283–8.

Hartman, V. (1965b). Group psychotherapy with sexually deviant offenders (pedophiles)—the peer group as an instrument of mutual control. *Criminal Law Quarterly*, **7**, 464–79.

Howard League Working Party (1985). *Unlawful Sex*. Oxford: Pergamon.

Howells, K. (1986). Social skills training and criminal and antisocial behaviour in adults. In C. R. Hollin and P. Trower (eds), *Handbook of Social Skills Training, vol. 1: Applications across the Life Span*. Oxford: Pergamon.

Knight, R. A., and Prentky, R. A. (1987). *Motivational Components in Taxonomy for Rapists: A Validation Analysis*. Unpublished manuscript.

Lazarus, A. A. (1976). *Multimodal Behaviour Therapy*. New York: Springer.

Lipton, D. N., McDonel, E. C., and McFall, R. M. (1987). Heterosocial perception in rapists. *Journal of Consulting and Clinical Psychology*, **55**, 17–21.

MacCulloch, M. J., Snowden, P. R., Wood, P. J. W., and Mills, H. E. (1983). Sadistic fantasy, sadistic behaviour and offending. *British Journal of Psychiatry*, **143**, 20–9.

McGuire, R. J., Carlisle, J. M., and Young, B. G. (1965). Sexual deviations as conditioned behaviour. *Behaviour Research and Therapy*, **2**, 185–90.

Marquis, J. (1970). Orgasmic reconditioning: Changing sexual object choice through controlling masturbation fantasies. *Journal of Behaviour Therapy and Experimental Psychiatry*, **1**, 263–71.

Marshall, W. L. (1973). The modification of sexual fantasies: A combined treatment approach to the reduction of deviant sexual behaviour. *Behaviour Research and Therapy*, **11**, 557–64.

Marshall, W. L., and Barbaree, H. E. (1984). A behavioural view of rape. *International Journal of Law and Psychiatry*, **7**, 51–77.

Marshall, W. L., Williams, S. M., and Christie, M. M. (1977). The treatment of rapists. In C. B. Qualls (ed.), *Perspectives on Rape*. New York: Pergamon.

Mathis, J. L., and Collins, M. (1970). Mandatory group therapy for exhibitionists. *American Journal of Psychiatry*, **126**, 1162–67.

Ortmann, J. (1980). The treatment of sexual offenders: Castration and antihormone therapy. *International Journal of Law and Psychiatry*, **3**, 443–51.

Overholser, J. C., and Beck, S. (1986). Multimethod assessment of rapists, child molesters and three control groups on behavioural and psychological measures. *Journal of Consulting and Clinical Psychology*, **54**, 682–7.

Pacht, A. R. (1976). The rapist in treatment: Professional myths. In M. J. Walker and S. L. Brodsky (eds), *Sexual Assault*. Lexington, MA: Lexington Books, pp. 91–8.

Perkins, D. E. (1983). *The Psychological Treatment of Offenders in Prison and the Community*. Paper presented at a conference on Options for the Mentally Abnormal Offender, Wolfson College, Oxford.

Perkins, D. E. (1984). Psychological Treatment of Offenders in Prison and the Community. In Williams, T., Alves, E., and Shapland, J. (eds), *Options for the Mentally Abnormal Offender*. Issues in Criminological and Legal Psychology, Number 6. Leicester: The British Psychological Society.

Perkins, D. E. (1986). Sex offending: A psychological approach. In C. Hollin, and K. Howells (eds), *Clinical Approaches to Criminal Behaviour*. Issues in Criminological and Legal Psychology No. 9. Leicester: The British Psychological Society.

Perkins, D. E. (1987). A psychological treatment programme for sex offenders. In B. J. McGurk, D. M. Thornton and M. Williams (eds), *Applying Psychology to Imprisonment: Theory & Practice*. London: HMSO.

Perkins, D. E. (1988). Sex therapy with male sex offenders. In M. Cole, and W. Dryden, (eds), *Sex Therapy in Britain*. Buckingham: Open University Press.

Peterson, D. R. (1968). *The Clinical Study of Social Behaviour*. New York: Appleton-Century-Crofts.

Prentky, R., Cohen, M., and Seghorn, T. (1985). Development of a rational taxonomy for the classification of rapists: The Massachusetts treatment center system. *Bulletin of the American Academy of Psychiatry and Law*, **13**, 39–70.

Prentky, R. A., Knight, R. A., and Rosenberg, R. (1987). Validation analyses of the MTC taxonomy for rapists. Paper presented at the New York Academy of Sciences Conference on Human Sexual Aggression: Current Perspectives.

Quayle, M. T. (1989). Group therapy for personality disordered offenders. Paper presented at Annual Conference of Special Hospital Psychologists, Scarborough, UK.

Raboch, J., Cerna, H., and Zemek, P. (1987). Sexual aggressivity and androgens. *British Journal of Psychiatry*, **151**, 398–400.

Resnick, H. L., and Peters, J. J. (1967). Outpatient group therapy with convicted pedophiles. *International Journal of Group Psychotherapy*, **17**, 151–8.

Rutter, M., and Giller, H. (1983). *Juvenile Delinquency: Trends and Perspectives*. Harmondsworth: Penguin.

Salter, A. C. (1988). *Treating Child Sexual Offenders and Victims. A Practical Guide*. Beverly Hills, CA: Sage.

Scully, D., and Marolla, J. (1985). 'Riding the bull at Gilley's': Convicted rapists describe the rewards of rape. *Social Problems*, **32**, 251–63.

Seghorn, T., and Cohen, M. (1980). The psychology of the rape assailant. In W. Cerran, A. L. McGarry, and C. Petty (eds), *Modern Legal Medicine, Psychiatry and Forensic Science*, Philadelphia: F. A. Davis, pp. 533–51.

Serber, M. (1970). Shame aversion therapy. *Journal of Behaviour Therapy and Experimental Psychiatry*, **1**, 217–26.

Serber, M., and Keith, C. G. (1974). The Atascadero project: Model of a sexual re-training program for incarcerated homosexual paedophiles. *Journal of Homosexuality*, **1**, 87–97.

Serber, M., and Wolpe, J. (1972). Behaviour therapy techniques. In H. L. P. Resnick and M. E. Wolfgang (eds), *Sexual Behaviours*. Boston: Little Brown, pp. 239–54.

Sturup, G. (1968). *Treatment of Sexual Offenders in Herstedvester, Denmark: The Rapists*. Copenhagen: Munksgaard.

Sturup, G. (1972). Castration: The total treatment. In H. L. P. Resnick and M. F. Wolf-gang (eds), *Sexual Behaviour*. Boston: Little Brown.

West, D. J., Roy, C., and Nichols, F. (1978). *Understanding Sexual Attacks*. London: Heinemann.

Woodward, R. (1980). Brief report on the effects of a sex education course on borstal trainees. *Home Office Prison Department Psychological Services DPS Reports*, Series II, No. 78.

Wyre, R. (1989). Protecting children: Treatments for offenders. Paper presented at NACRO Conference Preventing child sexual abuse—problems and prospects in dealing with offenders: London.

Yates, E., Barbaree, H. E., and Marshall, W.L. (1984). Anger and deviant sexual arousal. *Behaviour Therapy*, **15**, 187–294.

8

Clinical Work With Families in Which Sexual Abuse Has Occurred

ARNON BENTOVIM
Hospital for Sick Children, Great Ormond Street, London, UK

There is a great deal of current controversy about the place of work with the family when sexual abuse has occurred. Views range from the necessity of working with a family together from the earliest point of diagnosis (Lustig *et al.*, 1966), to the view that work has to be focused on members of the family separately—victim, non-abusing parent and offending parent—with conjoint family work being seen as a final step, in suitable families (Berliner and Wheeler, 1987). There is a growing body of therapeutic experience, practice, and conceptual models to help the clinician, but little empirical data.

CONCEPTUAL MODELS WHICH BRING TOGETHER THE FAMILY, THE INDIVIDUAL AND THE SOCIETAL CONTEXT

It seems that many of the factors which make the family a social organisation which nurtures, supports and socialises individuals, can also make it prone to violence (Gelles and Cornel, 1985). The time family members spend together can make for good parenting, and the opportunity for stimulation and affection, but togetherness can also produce conflict, resentment, and chaos. The family's range of activities and interests has a wide spectrum, which can introduce variety and richness, but this range can also be the source of major difficulties and arguments. The intensity of involvement of family members can lead to closeness, warmth, appropriate intimacy and sexuality between adults; but it can also be a context for anger, grievance, and perverse feelings. Children have involuntary membership of families, and in the privacy of family

Clinical Approaches to Sex Offenders and Their Victims
Edited by C. R. Hollin and K. Howells © 1991 John Wiley & Sons Ltd

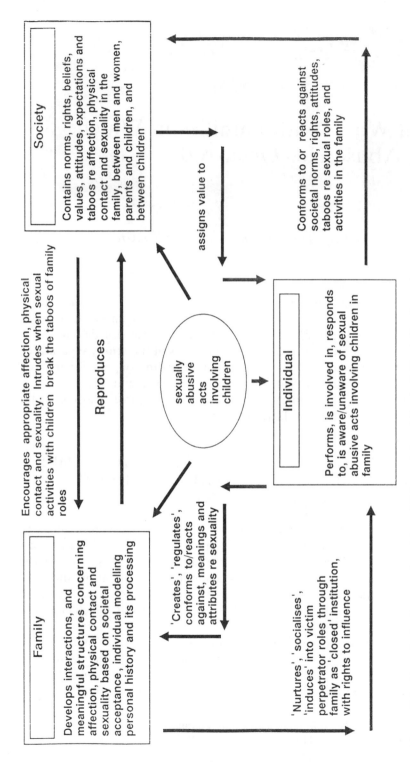

Figure 8.1 Sexual abusive acts involving children—role of the individual, family and society

life there is the possibility of acting out negative feelings, with a belief that actions can be hidden from outside scrutiny.

Parents coming together bring a shared set of meanings and views of the world which impact on their children. Belonging to a family carries rights to influence children and society expects parents to induct individual children into roles which will eventually be helpful to society. However, parents can also develop a view of how children should be treated which is the converse of societal expectation, and may be profoundly handicapping to the future functioning of children within society. Sexual attitudes and behaviour with children have some of the most profoundly traumatic effects on the development of children. Figure 8.1 indicates the way the individual, the family, and society interact around the issues of sexually abusive acts involving children. This diagram is based on the approach of Kinston (1987), Bentovim and Kinston (1990), and Bentovim (1990): it attempts to show that the sexual abuse of children has a relationship with societal attitudes, family relationships, and individual functioning.

Sexual Abuse, Society, the Family and the Individual

Within any society there exists a set of norms, rights, beliefs, values, attitudes, expectations, and taboos about physical affection and sexuality between individuals within the family. There is a major taboo in every society which requires that children should be sheltered and protected from inappropriate sexual knowledge and experiences. It is now clear that the real taboo lies in not speaking about such acts, rather than refraining from carrying them out. This is demonstrated by the high prevalence of sexually abusive acts against children as reported in retrospective studies by adults (Baker and Duncan, 1985; Russell, 1984). Such research indicates that there are extensive numbers of children and women treated as appropriate objects for violent and sexual acts.

Within society there is both a covert and an overt preoccupation with children as sexual objects. Observations of the style of dressing imposed on children, their use in advertising, and near pornographic photographs, indicate that children's natural growing sexuality is seen not as a phenomenon to be protected, but as one to be encouraged and treated as if it were adult sexuality. Thus, society on the one hand gives the message that individual children need to be protected, but also indicates that a sexual interest in children is not excluded. Society assigns values to the individual, and individuals conform to or react against societal norms, rights, attitudes, and taboos re sexual roles in general terms, and also in terms of sexual interest in children. Society operates, therefore, with double standards and double messages.

The family reproduces societal values within itself. Individuals create and regulate family patterns, and they conform or react against societal norms concerning sexuality within the family. Patterns of physical contact and sexuality emerge, based on the individual's history and experiences in their own families of origin, as well as in peer relationships and their newly created family. Thus individual children are nurtured and socialised into a variety of roles which can include that of victim or perpetrator.

Therapeutic emphasis can be placed on society, the individual, or the family. Thus, for example, feminist theoreticians emphasise the necessity to make society the focus, to change basic views if there is to be any change in the prevalence of sexual abuse. Dynamic therapists may focus on the individual, and family systems therapists on the family as a group.

It is likely that any approach which ignores the total systemic pattern in relation to sexual abuse will not be successful. The model supported in this chapter puts forward the view that it is possible to integrate work with individuals, the family as a group, and society as represented by statutory care and criminal justice agencies. Keeping all three domains in mind creates the most favourable context to assist victims, to work with offenders and other family members, and to prevent re-abuse.

A Conceptual Model as a Basis for Clinical Work with Families Where Sexual Abuse has Occurred

There is a bewildering range of sexually abusive activities which can occur within the family context. Many adults can initiate and maintain inappropriate sexual contacts by abusing their authority, and the dependency relationship which children have with them. Although there is major concern about biological parents who sexually abuse their own children, there are other adults who can also sexually abuse within the family context. These include step-parents, extended members of the family, grandparents, uncles, individuals standing in for family members, such as baby sitters, foster parents, and people in trusted relationships in the educational or care context. In addition, children and young people are sexualised in turn and older children may abuse younger children. (Johnson, 1988; Johnson and Berry, 1989).

To understand the extensive nature of sexual abusive patterns requires a systemic view, as expressed in the previous section, to explain the widespread but covert views about children being appropriate objects for sexual interest. The majority of abusers (85–95%) are men, and it may be that children (in a similar way to women) conform to the sort of models that trigger sexual responses in men. Finkelhor (1984) has argued that being smaller than men, having an attractive body shape, and creating an atmosphere of vulnerability, could trigger such responses. Finkelhor (1984) also argues that if such responses are extensive, the question then has to be asked about the factors in a potential abuser which lead to abusive action. He has pointed out that powerful internal and external inhibitors have to be overcome to transform emotional congruence with children to sexually abusive behaviour. Such factors include abuse in childhood of the boy who is destined to become an abuser; and disinhibiting factors such as alcohol and drug misuse, the absence of a protective parent, and a particularly vulnerable child. There is increasing evidence that the abuse of boys is far more extensive than was thought at first (Abel *et al.*, 1984), and that at least 50% of those individuals who do abuse children have been abused themselves.

The question is, what is the mechanism by which this repeating pattern of sexual arousal to children comes into operation? It may be a consequence of

Dynamic/systemic model

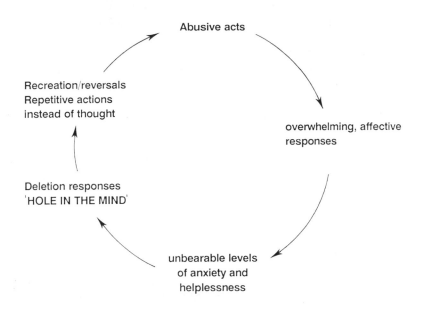

Figure 8.2   Sexual abusive acts involving children—role of the individual, family and society

some modelling effects. However, there is often so much anxiety, fear and secrecy associated with sexual experiences in childhood, that it may be better to apply the notion that sexual abuse in childhood is a traumatic event which is responded to by a wide variety of traumatic responses, including a sexualising effect.

The characteristics of traumatic events and their responses have been described by Pynoos and Eth (1985). The common response to a traumatic event as described in Figure 8.2 is an immediate overwhelming affective response, often linked with unbearable levels of anxiety and helplessness. Such events are frequently not talked about or dealt with, so that 80 or 90% of adults who describe sexually abusive experiences have never spoken about them (Russell, 1984). Thus instead of a memory, a 'hole' is created in the mind, and the memory is deleted. What occurs instead is a response in action—not in thought. The original overwhelming affective response, and associated levels of anxiety and helplessness, have to be dealt with in some way. What seems to be common in children who have been abused, is the enactment of the activities to which they have been subjected. Thus sexual activities are repeated by the child in the form of sexualisation, or there is an increased vulnerability to sexual activities by others—that is victim responses.

We are now aware that such sexualisation responses are part of a post-traumatic stress response to sexual abuse which will be described in more detail in the next section. However, as this phenomenon has only been recognised recently, it is likely that for many years children who have been subjected to abuse have continued with sexualised behaviour through their childhood, to adolescence and adulthood. Once initiated, such patterns become self-maintaining, and may well be triggered towards children born within the family and to children met within a social context. Although such ideas may seem to be far fetched, the extensive observations and reporting of sexual events during childhood and adolescence testify to the significance of the phenomenon.

Looking at the way in which such traumatic patterns occur at individual and family levels will be the focus for work described in this chapter.

Sexual Abuse and the Post-traumatic Stress Response

There are three basic responses which are part of the post-traumatic response to sexual abuse. These take the forms of: (i) the repetition of the ideational, affective and somatic aspects of trauma; (ii) avoidant, depressive phenomena; and (iii) automatic hyper-arousal and attempts to overcome traumatic experiences.

The repetition of the ideational, affective and somatic aspects of trauma

Post-traumatic stress phenomena have been described in response to many major events such as a physical trauma and to sexually abusive acts (Pynoos and Eth, 1985). Terr (1987) has recently attempted to differentiate between the single abusive act as a 'Type 1' form of abuse, and multiple 'Type 2' forms of abuse, which are longstanding traumatic acts accompanied by extreme stress.

Sexually abusive acts are re-experienced in ideational, affective and somatic forms. A variety of phenomena are described by the abused including flashbacks and nightmares, talking about abuse, playing out abuse through inappropriate sexual activities, the visualisation of sexual abusive experiences through drawings, day dreaming and dissociative states. Such re-experiencing is triggered by places, people, or things, viewed as symbolic of the act itself, or triggered by seeing or meeting the individual who carried out the abusive act.

In a typical case, a 14 year old girl who had been abused from the age of 7 to 14 years by a parent was preoccupied by memories of the last abusive act she had experienced before disclosing the abuse. She had flashbacks of being locked in her room, threatened and hit and forced into repeating the same act. She had been made to wear her mother's knickers and bend over, while her father rubbed his erect penis around her anal and perineal areas. A particularly traumatic aspect was that he forced her to turn over and wanted to penetrate her. Even two years after the event she spent many hours in a preoccupied, dissociated state, struggling to deal with the ideas, feelings and responses forced into her by her father's acts.

Avoidant, depressive phenomena

This aspect of post-traumatic stress disorder consists of a numbing of feelings and a withdrawal, an unwillingness to talk about abuse, and an apparently limited memory which can extend to many aspects of the individual's life. This may be described as 'the hole in the mind' associated with avoidance of people, places and things which remind the individual of the abusive context. This denial and deletion can also be seen as a defensive way of dealing with re-experiencing. Families can refuse to talk about events everyone is preoccupied by but which demand a rule of silence.

Autonomic hyper-arousal and attempts to overcome experiences

Common accompaniments of the previously described phenomena are irritability, anger, aggressiveness, and sleep problems which may be associated with distractibility and hyper-alertness, and a sense of anxiety or being easily startled. For example, the 14 year old described earlier continued to have major sleeping difficulties, was often described as irritable with her peers in the foster home, and complained of considerable difficulties in getting down to work. Such hyper-arousal responses can, as described in a later section, develop into a personality style of aggressive, counter-phobic responding; a style that identifies with the aggressor.

These responses may have systemic effects such that, if traumatic events have not been worked through or dealt with, then re-experiencing, avoidance, arousal and reversal can feedback on one another to create a self-maintaining system. This system is reinforced by responses both within the family and within society which mirror and maintain the original traumatic patterns. Finkelhor and Browne (1986) have described such traumatic patterns, using the notion of 'Traumagenic Dynamics'.

Traumagenic Dynamics

The four basic traumagenic dynamics described by Finkelhor and Browne, based on extensive clinical and research review, are as follows: (i) traumatic sexualisation; (ii) stigmatisation; (iii) betrayal; and (iv) powerlessness.

Traumatic sexualisation

The notion of traumatic sexualisation includes the behavioural responses of re-experiencing as described earlier, together with the shaping of sexual response by the adult. The adult may find a way of persuading the child that what is happening is 'normal'. The child may be informed that all children experience sexual activities with their parents, but that nobody speaks about it. There may well be a conditioning effect, and identification with the role of victim through a variety of responses, including the sexual arousal induced in the child. Longer term responses can include intense sexual preoccupations including promiscuity, thereby re-enacting the role. In identifying with the aggressor, a basic pattern of sexual orientation towards children may be activated. This provides the emotional congruence with such activities which Finkelhor (1984) has indicated is the basic precondition for later sexual abuse. There may be an avoidance of sexuality which can have profound effect on later sexual relationships and sexual orientation.

> Mr B described a childhood in which his parents were totally preoccupied with mutual recrimination and battling. He felt ignored and rejected by them. He became interested in solitary pursuits, and when aged 12 to 13, through his fishing interests he met a man who 'slowly and skilfully' initiated a sexal relationship. This man became his sole source of affection but then suddenly disappeared from his life. Mr B's first marriage was a failure and he 'lost' a son to whom he was devoted. He had attempted to reverse his own rejection by focusing on him in an over-caring way, to the detriment of his own marriage. He then met another partner with a daughter aged 12 years who was in a similar situation, having been abandoned by her husband—the girl's father. She was not interested in Mr B at first as she was grieving for her father. Mr B, in trying to get close to the daughter, became involved with her tomboyish pursuits and through play fights and sports activities achieved the desired closeness. However, as in his own childhood, as he became aroused, the fun fights became sexualised. He then continued to intiate sexually abusive activities in a context of silence and secrecy. Thus his own abuse, which became so inextricably linked with affection and closeness, was re-enacted when he attempted to 'replace' the loss of his own son.

Stigmatisation, Betrayal, and Powerlessness

These three dynamics describe an extensive set of responses to being involved in a chronic long-term sexually abusive relationship. *Stigmatisation* arises through the child coming to be blamed and denigrated by the abuser and thus becoming the object of contempt, shame and secrecy, and eventually being treated as 'damaged goods' both within the family and within society. *Betrayal* arises as a result of the child feeling that his trust in the adult has been manipulated, his or her care has been violated, and deserved protection not afforded. Sexual abuse can only occur within a context of a basic disregard of the child's sense of well-being. Thus, *powerlessness* arises out of the child's sense of bodily invasion, vulnerability, and a lack of feeling of protection, and also through a sense of repeated fear and helplessness. A variety of longstanding responses can arise through these three dynamics.

> Such responses are illustrated by Miss P, a 23 year old woman who when seen had given up the care of her 4 year old for the second time. In her own family history her mother had suffered a manic-depressive illness, mostly of the depressive variety, and had given up her care. Her father was extremely strict and punitive, and had sexually abused her, including intercourse, from the age of 7 to 13 years. After being taken into care she had a number of placements in a variety of children's homes and adolescent units; she had emerged from care feeling a deep sense of shame, desperately seeking redeeming relationships, and clinging in a dependent way to relationships with older men who had families themselves. She was quite prepared to see herself as a second wife to the Moslem father of her son.
> At the same time she was involved promiscuously in superficial relations, used drugs and drink to deal with her sense of shame, embarrassment, and stigma, and was frequently depressed, helpless, and hopeless. The care of her son was deeply affected by a lack of energy and depression when she felt overwhelmed and unable to cope—particularly with family members who continued to abuse, control, and

criticise her. She would become suicidal, overdose, and feel like cutting and mutilating herself. Out of her sense of powerlessness and not being in control of events, she was at times able to muster an intense surge of energy which led to a variety of schemes and projects into which she threw herself.

At other times she found herself recreating strictness and punitiveness with her son in identification with her father. At her son's birth she felt an intense sense of antagonism, anger and rage which she found hard to locate and understand. Through Miss P's pattern of behaviour one can see the dynamics of stigmatisation, betrayal, and powerlessness asserting themselves, together with the victim behaviour associated with her traumatic sexualisation. Family scripts are thus 're-established' or 'replicated' as attempts to 'correct' them fail (Byng-Hall, 1989).

TRAUMA AND FAMILY SYSTEMS

The case examples of Mr B and Miss P indicate how traumatic events and relationships come to be replayed and reacted against throughout the life cycle. Figure 8.3 illustrates how traumatic events can influence choice of partners, the childhood and later development of children in the family, their adult life, and finally their own marital choice. Mr B's stepdaughter Amanda was already playing a recluse role within her peer group; Miss P's son was sexualised and extremely aggressive. Although there is controversy about the intergenerational mechanisms by which violent and abusive relationships are created, Strauss and Gelles' (1979) survey of the prevalence of violent behaviour in the family indicates how powerful such intergenerational continuities can be.

To develop a satisfactory family system based approach to clinical work in general, and to family violence in particular, requires a model which takes such

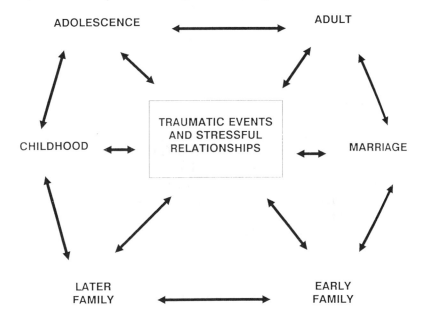

Figure 8.3   Trauma and the life style

traumatic events and stressful relationships into consideration. Bentovim and Kinston (1990) have described a 'focal' model of family assessment and therapy, which defines a focus for work with the family. To create a satisfactory approach, the following is required:

(1) To regard traumatic events as the prime origin of 'disturbance'. Such traumatic events can be represented at an individual, family, or even a societal level. They occur in the childhood of the parents and therefore influence what each parent brings to the family. They lead to the creation of specific meaning and interactional structures which include the 'appropriateness' of the abuse of children.
(2) There must be a concern about 'pathology' of the family and a necessary focus on strengths and potentials, as well as dysfunctions. It is essential to use a developmental perspective and to be concerned about the health of the family in the context of its particular place in the life cycle.
(3) In working with the family it is essential to change both interactions to prevent or ameliorate abuse, and also to understand the specific meanings, beliefs, and realities of the family which connect with the abusive behaviour. Each member carries such realities, whether the family continues together or not, and these also require change.

THE STAGES OF CLINICAL WORK

There are four basic stages of treatment with families when sexual abuse has occurred. These are: (i) the stage of disclosure—the period of crisis around the discovery of abuse; (ii) the stage of separation; (iii) the stage of family rehabilitation; and (iv) a new family stage—when rehabilitation has failed and it is not possible for the child to live with either the non-abusive parent or the aggressor.

FAMILY WORK DURING THE PERIOD OF DISCLOSURE

The disclosure process is a complex one involving recognition of abuse and the assessment of the child and family (Vizard and Tranter, 1988). The professional network has to manage the complex procedures of joint investigation by social work and police, detailed interviewing of alleged perpetrators and non-abusive parents, and assessment of the family. There has to be extensive consultation and case conference work to bring together information from the professional network and to make decisions, within both the child care legal context and the criminal context, about the need for statutory action to protect, prosecute, and make longer term plans.

As well as understanding the extent of abuse perpetrated by the offender, and the effect on the victim, there are two basic processes which involve the family that need to be considered at this stage. These are: (i) breaking the taboo of secrecy around discussion of the sexual abusive relationship within the family;

and (ii) assessing the individual and the family context as a whole, so that appropriate plans can be made and a prognosis for work arrived at.

It is important to carry out such work at an early stage so that a plan for appropriate work can be made in a child care context, decisions made about where and with whom the child should live, and what the longer term prospects will be. Also recommendations need to be made to the criminal court, if an offender is to be tried, so that the possibilities of work with the victim and the family can be put forward to help the court in its decision making about the individual perpetrator.

Breaking the Taboo of Secrecy around Sexual Matters

Breaking the taboo is a primary aim, and one which has to be actively dealt with at various points during the treatment, not just at the disclosure stage itself. The taboo of secrecy is profound and persevering and is a basic constituent of the avoidant response to sexually abusive trauma. Very frequently a child will not be able to talk about his or her abusive experiences until there has been a period of separation from the family. Within the family itself, members may be involved to a considerable extent in a secrecy system. As children become increasingly aware of the inappropriateness of their responses and the activities they are involved in, they begin to show disturbance and desire to draw attention to their abuse or to leave the family.

The secrecy system extends to the abuser himself, who may describe the phenomenon of never thinking about his activities. He may describe abusive activities as being triggered in a particular context, such as when the mother goes out to work. Secrecy may be induced by threats about what will happen if the abuse is spoken about, the possibilities of imprisonment, or the destruction or breakdown of the family. Secrecy, denial, and deletion can have powerful and long-reaching effects on the individual, and have to be considered throughout treatment.

For example, one father was allowed to spend the evenings at home on bail with his family. The 14 year old daughter whom he sadistically abused when he was drunk appeared to be untroubled by his presence in the family. When asked what happened to the 'ordinary' traumatic effects which so many young people experience, she responded that she had constructed a counter fantasy to combat this. She told herself that she had not been abused by her stepfather, although she knew she had, but that she had been abused by somebody else who had got into the house.

Members of the family may be able to speak quite extensively about abusive actions and traumatic experiences on an individual basis, but cannot speak in a family context. It is as if the secrecy processes are evoked by contact with family members. Parents and professionals are often fearful that children or siblings will be hurt by learning details they already know. They are concerned that the victim will be caused unnecessary pain by having to repeat details which have already been disclosed. Families may well want to forget, not remind themselves of the abuse, and rapidly to get back to what they saw as their normal ways of relating to each other. It is very important to explain to families at this point that secrecy within the family has been a central factor in perpetuating the abuse, and that this 'deletion' may be perpetuated throughout the life of the victim if the pattern is not confronted.

In the initial stage, the family is often in a state of crisis, and emotional energy is not focused on long-term effects, only on the wish to return to some sort of normality. There is a need to resolve the trauma of disclosure and professional intrusion by closing ranks and developing a family 'avoidance' response, leaving the child both silenced and remembering in silence.

Techniques to Assist Breaking the Taboo of Secrecy

This task can be made very much easier by dealing with the whole issue in a low-key, matter of fact way, and maintaining an unemotional stance as therapist, particularly if the perpetrator is present at a meeting as well as the victim. Given the distressing nature of abuse this can be extremely difficult to achieve. Empathy is important but it is often better just to say 'That would probably hurt someone your size', rather than asking the victim to describe the physical pain at this point (Bentovim et al., 1988).

If family members protest that younger children do not know why a father is absent, when for example he may be in prison, or living with a family member on bail, we ask parents to find out from the children why they think father is not there. They should find out whether they are the sort of children who can listen to telephone conversations, or even hear conversations when they are supposed to be asleep, without letting their family members know. Very often younger children need permission to say what they actually know as part of breaking the taboo of secrecy within the family.

One of the best ways of talking about the untalkable, is to find out and track the process by which the untalkable was talked about, and therefore the disclosure occurred. To ask the questions 'What made you go to your teacher'? 'What were the exact words you said to your teacher'? 'What did the social worker ask you'? 'What would the police have in their notebooks of your statement'? 'What are the words used in your family for penis, vagina'? 'What did your mother say to you when you said that'? 'What did your teacher say to you'? all help to reconstruct the disclosure process, and in the process it becomes possible to talk about the sexual acts, maintaining a neutral, unemotional, matter of fact response.

Using a circular questioning approach (Tomm, 1987) maintains a low-key approach and brings experiences into the conversational domain. 'Do you know whether your daughter in her flashbacks has mainly memories of touching, mutual masturbation, anal sex, or oral sex'? is a way of speaking about the unspeakable, but doing it in such a way that one appears to be carrying out a low-key exercise.

The essence of breaking the taboo of secrecy is to name sexual activities explicitly, and to share factual information, which includes the feelings of the victim and his or her family about the facts. It is essential at the same time as speaking about the shame, pain and embarrassment shared by many children, to be able to speak about the possibility of a physically pleasurable response, which so many children find it hard to admit to. Such responses can have a profound effect on making children feel that *they* are responsible for the adults. It is extremely important to state that all children do have strong sexual responses, and that sexualisation and provocative behaviour can represent an active learning of sexualised responses: children need to know that masturbation is a normal way of dealing with such feelings. An educational approach is essential as part of the breaking of the taboo.

Within the family, it may only be possible to share a limited amount of sexual information, since it is not appropriate to discuss the parent's own sexual problems or practices in detail in front of the children. It is probably not possible in a mixed group of men and women easily to describe the intensive cycle of arousal, masturbation, and inappropriate sexual aims and impulses that can be explored in very considerable detail in men's groups. It is, however, essential openly to acknowledge within the family context the abusive acts that the children have experienced. The responsibility for such acts needs to be extensively attributed to the adult, freeing the child from the crippling guilt for prosecution of a perpetrator and family separation.

Family Assessment Process

It seems important to have all members of the family present to assess the family aspects of the total picture. The meeting needs to include involved professionals as well as family members: as Kempe (1979) said, once abuse is diagnosed there is no longer an independent family, but a family/professional network. The issue is to determine the extent of the 'problem-determined' system (Goolishian and Winderman, 1988). The family needs assessing, as does the relationship of family and professionals, since this relationship can have a profound effect on the outcome of work. A Great Ormond Street Hospital follow-up of treatment (Bentovim *et al.*, 1988) indicated that the final placement of children was affected more by the quality of work of care professionals and the attitude and family responsibility for the abuse, than by the extent of the abuse itself. It would seem counterproductive, however, to have family meetings with a perpetrator who totally denied any responsibility for the abuse. The victim would be put in a position of intolerable conflict if placed with an adult who denied the allegations, or refused to take any responsibility for his behaviour. It could also be highly misleading to a family to have a joint meeting under these circumstances, since this could be perceived as meaning that rehabilitation would be considered as an active possibility and that the abuse was seen as unimportant. It might then be necessary to have a series of meetings with subsystems of the family, for example with a perpetrator alone with his key professional, and later with the non-abusive parent (if there is contact). It might be appropriate in this context to discover what acknowledgement of responsibility could lead to, whether there are fears of family break-up, rejection, or suicide if the perpetrator accepts the reality of the child's allegations. It is important to find out whether he considers the child to be a liar by nature and to challenge this belief. Similarly, a non-abusive parent who does not believe the child may need to be seen alone with key professionals to assess issues such as fear of marital breakdown, whether she believes the child, or fear of depression if any responsibility were taken for not being available.

Where the perpetrator accepts full responsibility, it seems helpful that all family members, except perhaps some very young children, should be present. Acknowledgement of responsibility is essential to the victims, because it frees them from an overwhelming sense of guilt and confusion. This is particularly necessary when a child has been inducted into abusive acts through the development of beliefs and realities sufficient to convince him or her that abuse is normal but which are at variance with social realities. Our own experience is that a *formal* acknowledgement of responsibility may be all that is possible at this stage, since the perpetrator may be facing prosecution, losses and separation, and may feel too victimised himself to empathise with the child he has hurt.

It is essential to assess the stance of the mother and to find how deeply, genuinely sympathetic she is to the victim, as opposed to how much she is scapegoating and blaming the child. There is also a need for an initial assessment of the likelihood of her taking the father back and rejecting the child. The key event in the stage of disclosure and later separation, is to determine whether the child can live with the non-abusing parent, or if he or she needs to be fostered. It is also essential to make an initial assessment of the mother-victim relationship which may have led to abuse being concealed. We may well see families where there has been a longstanding problematic relationship between a mother and daughter.

> In the 'A' family, Jean, the oldest of two daughters, was conceived when the mother was 16; Mrs A's own mother brought Jean up for the first three years of her life whilst Mrs A continued working. Jean returned to live with her mother and her next sister when Mrs A married the father of both Jean and her sister. Jean inevitably had become attached to her grandmother and a negative, aversive attachment was created with her mother. When Mrs A remarried after the breakdown of her first marriage, there was a space between mother and daughter of which her new partner, a younger man who himself had been abused, took advantage. Whilst comforting Jean he enacted a sexually abusive relationship between them. In this case, therefore, not only was it going to be necessary to help deal with Jean's response to the abuse, but it was also essential to build up a sympathetic relationship between mother and daughter, since the mother blamed the daughter rather than empathised with her.

To complete the picture it is necessary to explore areas such as problems from the family of origin, the history of abuse of either parent, patterns of sexuality and violence, marital relationships, and the development of and relationships with children in the family. Observation of the family whilst sharing such information can help to define characteristic patterns of interaction, as well as the meanings and beliefs held within the family. It should also be possible to think about possible aims for treatment of a family in terms of what needs to change, and to assess the hopefulness of the outcome. In addition, it is helpful to classify families in terms of their prognosis for clinical work (Bentovim *et al.*, 1987).

Classification of the Prognosis for Work with Families (on Clinical Grounds)

There are three basic categories: (i) the families where there is a hopeful prognosis for rehabilitation; (ii) families where there is doubt about the potential for rehabilitation; and (iii) families who are hopeless about the possibility of rehabilitation.

Families who are hopeful

In the following circumstances there is a hopeful prognosis for rehabilitation: initially child and mother together, and subsequently the father after appropriate treatment; when the father fully and unequivocally takes responsibility for the abuse; when the mother believes the child; and when both parents are able to appreciate that child care considerations come first. This latter point implies that the mother has sufficient sense of autonomy and support, both from her own social network and professionally, to be able to manage the care of the children without the presence of the father to sustain her in the marriage. Family assessment needs to reveal the requisite degree of flexibility and potential for change; that family members are not ranged together to scapegoat the child; and that there is a caring atmosphere rather than one of rejection and blame.

There needs also to be a reasonable potential for cooperativeness both in the present and demonstrated in the past between family members and the appropriate professionals. There may well be an understandable sense of anger and indignation at the intervention of professionals into the life of the family, but not such a degree of bitterness that any negotiations lead to rejection. There also needs to be an appropriate availability of treatment resources, and a potential for collaboration between child care, criminal justice agencies, and therapeutic agencies. It is too easy for professionals to reflect the splits and antagonisms within the family, which may also be endemic within the community (Furness, 1983).

The 'B' family mentioned previously provides an example of a family of hopeful prognosis. Mr B was able to describe not only his current abuse of Amanda and take responsibility for it, but he could also begin to construct a coherent explanation and understanding of the origins of his abuse, the dynamics of the family which led to his partner choice and the triggering of his abusive behaviour. Mr B accepted the necessity of having to live separately from his family after coming out of prison, so he could do some far more extensive work in understanding the origin and triggering of his abusive cycles. He was also appropriately sad and aware of his hurtful behaviour. Mrs B was basically protective and supportive to Amanda, did not in any way blame her, and yet wanted to maintain the marital relationship if possible. She was able to manage without her husband. Although Amanda suffered a longstanding post-traumatic effect which had a profound effect on her schooling and her emotional life, she had some positive feelings towards Mr B despite visualisations which indicated angry retaliative wishes towards him. Although there was antagonism towards the professional intrusions in the family's life, they were able to make and follow contracts and were receptive to the offer of therapeutic work.

Families who are doubtful for rehabilitation

In this category we see cases where we are more doubtful about the potential for rehabilitation. There may be insufficient information to be either hopeful or hopeless. In such families the father may be far more doubtful about the amount of responsibility that he is willing to take for the abusive behaviours described by the child. The mother, although accepting that the abuse has happened, cannot see that she had any role in terms of not being available to her child. Rather like the 'A' family mentioned previously, the mother may blame the girl for being involved with the stepfather, rather than totally attributing the problems to the stepfather. The child may be described as promiscuous or provocative, and when trying to address these issues in order to create a change of attitude, the family may be extremely resistant to any changes of their perceptions. The children's needs are thus not seen to be primary. There may be a concern that the parent's needs are such that their dependency for each other predominates. The mother may not be able to manage alone: she may not have the resources to deny the father's needs for her and so the children's needs are lost. The family may be chaotic in its functioning, and there may be a long-term problem between mother and daughter, as in the 'A' family, which means that there is a poor prospect for protective action under stress.

There may be resentment, anger, and difficulties in cooperativeness with professionals, the family turning from one agency to the other with the hope of finding rescue. With such families it is essential to have either a contract of work which includes failure clauses (White, 1984), or a care order. If the required work is not achieved in terms of the protectiveness of mother to children, and a full taking of responsibility by the abuser, then rehabilitation may need to be opposed. Longer term placement of the child may then be essential. The 'A' family would be an example of a doubtful family because of the poor relationships between mother and daughter and the blaming that occurred. The step-father took only a limited degree of responsibility, and the dependency needs of both himself and the mother were considerable. There were doubts about her ability to manage autonomously, and his own traumas were unresolved after a long history of violence which he had experienced from his own family. There was an embattled relationship with professionals which meant that there had to be considerable caution in the contracts made with the family.

Families who are hopeless

These are families where there may be an absolute rejection of responsibility for the abuse and in which the mother blames the child. There is a definite choice of opting for the marriage and rejecting the child, other children may be inducted into the scenario that the abused child is the bad one, and professionals are seen as misapplying physical and psychological assessments or having discovered abuse where there is none. Obviously there are major problems when such situations are brought into the legal arena and differences between professional and family attitudes can be amplified through the adversarial process built into court proceedings.

There may be an avowed concern about the interests of the child, but failure on the part of both the family and the professionals to accept the need for help for what may be longstanding problems of psychiatric illness, addiction, or major marital disputes in the family. In themselves such problems do not make treatment a hopeless process, but unless there is some acceptance of their relevance and importance, and a demonstration of commitment to help, then the outlook for satisfactory treatment would be hopeless.

Where an individual abuser, as evidenced by the number of children abused, has a paedophilic orientation and yet cannot acknowledge it, again this is a matter of major concern for prognosis. The family of the 14 year old girl with severe post-traumatic dissociative syndromes illustrates the hopelessness prognosis. Although the father was prosecuted for abuse of his daughter and imprisoned, the mother refused to believe that he had abused her, and blamed the child for imagining it and convincing others of the truth of her statements. She created a belief that the physical evidence of penetration had been seen by an over-zealous paediatrician, and her beliefs were reinforced in the court where the defending counsel accused the girl of being provocative.

When the social worker asked the mother how she explained the fact that the girl had spoken to her during her primary school years about the abuse, the mother told the social worker to leave and never to return. The other siblings in the family were inducted into a similar belief about the child's description of abuse. The sister who had first informed the police about her sister's abuse also joined in the family belief system. They sustained their own relationships by denial and seeing the abused child as the source of all their problems. This is one of the basic family mechanisms so frequently seen in child sexual abuse where one person is seen as the source of all problems (Bentovim and Kinston, 1990).

Prognosis in Clinical Practice

The rates of hopeful, doubtful, and hopeless prognosis in families seen in clinical practice are reflected in the follow-up of treatment (e.g. Bentovim *et al.*, 1988). The Great Ormond Street Hospital treatment project offers therapeutic facilities to a wide range of families. About 15% of 120 families were able to work fully with the treatment process and achieve rehabilitation of children with both parents (Hopeful Category). Another 30% of children now live with their mothers alone (Doubtful Category). A further 25% of children now live in new families or therapeutic communities without either parent because of joint rejection (Hopeless). Other children (30%) were living independently at follow-up.

Thus, examining the phenomenon of sexual abuse as a whole, the number of families who present with a hopeful prognosis for treatability is limited. Follow-up of the children's mental health (Bentovim *et al.*, 1988) indicated that the children did respond well to treatment, for example the children's sexualisation dropped considerably, and their emotional state improved. But they may well need new family placements, or to live with one parent, rather than rehabilitation to the family as a whole.

This may be a reflection of the limitation of treatment placements available, and its effectiveness; but it may also reflect the tremendous resistance to acknowledging a sexual orientation to children, and the difficulties of putting children's needs before those of adult. Children are often rejected to avoid punishment by society, the family, or the self.

CREATING HYPOTHESES FOR LONGER TERM WORK WITH FAMILIES

To work effectively with families it is essential to formulate the case in a way which defines both the basic family dynamics and the aims to be achieved. A focal approach to family therapeutic work (Bentovim and Kinston, 1990), describes a way of gathering family information and observations. There are four steps in the process.

Step 1: How is the Symptomatic Behaviour Connected to Family Functioning and Vice Versa?

At the most superficial level this describes the particular pattern of abuse and the secrecy system which prevents disclosure, maintains silence, and forms the context which allows the abuser to continue. The severely traumatised girl described earlier (p. 184) spoke to her mother, who said that she would speak to the father, but did not do so. The abuse continued in secrecy, until the child spoke outside the family. Despite prosecution, the silencing, minimising secrecy is still maintained, the couple and family members support each other and attack, denigrate, and disbelieve the child; they reject professional help and maintain abuse of the child.

Second Step: What Would Happen if the Secrecy System, Scapegoating System were not Maintained?

The questions to be asked are: why is this system of denial and blaming maintained? What would happen if the child were believed? The mother would have to confront and to blame the father and exclude him from the home. Other agencies would be asked to come into the family. The father would have to face up to his abusive actions and endure real self-punishment, self-hatred, suicidal feelings, and rejection. There may be fear of marital disruption.

The Third Step: What is the Feared Disaster, What is the Breakdown that is Avoided?

Clearly what needs to be avoided, apart from legal punishment, is marital breakdown, the loss of a relationship between the parents. The loss of the child seems to be far less of a disaster, indeed children seem to be expendable. As the mother wrote to her social worker: 'I no longer have her as a daughter, I only have two children not three, as far as I am concerned she can drop dead, I never want to see her again, she is no longer a daughter of mine.'

Step 4: What are the Origins of the Feared Disaster and Response to it?

One has to ask, what are the major traumas in the history and family background of the parents that make a child expendable, and mean the marriage must be preserved at all costs? One often has to explore the childhood of the parents to discover the stressful relationships and traumatic events which shaped their lives.

What 'holes' do they have in their minds which they must preserve at all costs? Contact with a stressful event automatically evokes a defensive action. The mother in the case above had had a previous traumatic breakdown of her own marriage and her response to a threat of another breakdown was to cling on to her husband at all costs. The father had spent most of his life in care, and had been abused by a care staff member. His defence was to identify with the aggressor, to enact sexually abusive acts of a perverse nature, and then to delete them from his memory. The mother had experienced a number of breakdowns, losses and rejections: perhaps she felt that children could be cared for but she would never find another man like her husband.

Summary of Hypothesis

The parents' need for preservation of their adult relationship can be far greater than their need to preserve their parenting relationships to the abused child, who therefore has to be rejected and scapegoated. Thus such a family as described above (p. 189) comes into the 'hopeless' category as far as regards the possibility of rehabilitation of the child into the family. One would also, of course, be very concerned indeed about the welfare of other children in the family, and the possibility that the father might have a deeply paedophilic orientation. That he was unable to acknowledge the abuse, despite having been imprisoned, is of major concern regarding the possibility of treatment for him, and the protection of other children who might be in his care. The fact that the mother could not put her children's needs before her own or before the marriage would also require considerable exploration.

Assessing the Individuals in the Family

Making a prognosis for rehabilitation of the family, and hypothesising about factors which may make this possible, is a separate process from the evaluation of, and making a prognosis for treatment of each of the individuals.

When there has been a major family breakdown through abuse that requires a child to be taken into care, then there has to be work in a context of a separation before rehabilitation is possible. Thus individual assessment of the offender is required to explore the issues Finkelhor (1984) has described, and to assist a therapist in understanding the basis for abusive behaviour. The individual offender needs to be evaluated in terms of: (i) what factors led to an emotional congruence with a child as sexual object? (ii) what are the internal and external factors which have led to a disinhibition of protective action towards children? (iii) what are the specific factors within the child and family context which have facilitated abusive action? (iv) what are the sexual fantasies and triggering factors?

In addition, it is essential both to assess the degree of the child's traumatic behavioural responses, and to assess the non-abusive parent in terms of personal experiences which may have led to a vulnerability to an abusive partner or to becoming less able to be protective.

Hypothesis in More Hopeful Families

In the 'B' family reported earlier, the parents seemed far more able to be supportive to the child, and to face the feared disaster of the loss of the marital relationship. The traumatic experiences of the parents were thus not of such a nature as to create the size of hole in their minds that triggered both abusive and rejecting attitudes to the abused child. The hypothesis in the 'B' family's case was far more to do with the confusion of emotional closeness and sexuality which originated in Mr B's confusion of emotional and sexual relationships. The marital loss and mourning had created a distance between the mother and daughter and Mr B, coming in as a stepfather, attempted to get close emotionally, which triggered a sexualised response.

Mr B was able to take responsibility for his abusive action, and the mother was protective to the child. This allowed for treatment in which a variety of therapeutic aims could be reached. These included resolving the individual traumatic experiences for the stepfather and the daughter, building up relationships between mother and daughter, dealing with marital differences, and finally considering the possibility of family rehabilitation. These aims are to be achieved during the next period of treatment, the period of family break-up.

FAMILY WORK DURING THE PERIOD OF BREAK-UP

Although there are some who advocate attempts to treat the family together, this has not been demonstrated in an effective manner in clinical practice. In my view it is essential that there be a period of family break-up so that the individual treatment goals can be worked towards, and child care agencies assured that the child will be absolutely protected in the future. This protection can only occur with a major change in the behaviour of the individual perpetrator, and the development of an absolutely protective capacity in the non-abusive parent.

Thus family break-up is most likely to occur through the perpetrator being away from home, and indeed this is the best arrangement from the child care point of view. The length of a family break-up is very much influenced by criminal proceedings, a prison sentence or the imposition of a probation order with treatment, and conditions of separate residence in the community. A probation order with treatment would seem the best option by far for treatable individuals taking reasonable responsibility for the degree of abuse. It may well be that an individual with a deeply paedophilic orientation will require a period in a residential setting, such as a prison with psychiatric treatment available, or a residential clinical treatment programme. Before release to the community it would be essential to demonstrate improvement following treatment, particularly if return to a family is contemplated.

In the case of doubtful families where the child is not supported by the mother, the child will need to be separated from both parents and placed in a residential setting such as a foster home. Some children become so disturbed by their traumatic experiences that they require specialist residential settings for children who have been severely traumatised. If there is a hopeless family then consideration of the placement of a child in a family finding unit may be necessary to work through traumatic experiences and so prepare the child for a new family.

Very often it is not until there is a degree of separation, that the secrecy/denial system can be broken, and the child can begin to relate the degree of abuse experienced. The most difficult form of abuse for children to share, is abuse by a mother. The professional network finds it particularly difficult to hear such allegations, but various studies have described between 5 and 15% of mothers abusing (Bentovim et al., 1988; Faller, 1988; Finkelhor, 1984). During the investigation period there may be a very high suspicion of abuse having occurred, with medical findings and highly sexualised behaviour but with no disclosure. In this situation a separation is often necessary therapeutically to enable the child to share his or her experience without fear of punishment or retaliation.

SPECIFIC AREAS OF WORK DURING THE SEPARATION PHASE

Mother–Child Work

Before attention is paid to the abusive relationship between fathers and children, it is important to consider the basic care of the child. Thus as Furness (1983) has described, the first focus needs to be on improving mother-child relationships: this involves improving communication, building up trust, and repairing or re-building relationships.

The 'A' family were characterised by a longstanding deficit between mother and daughter, and an experiental piece of work was carried out between mother and children. The sculpting method (Byng-Hall, 1979) was used to track the development of their relationship. Major differences were described between the mother and each of her two daughters, in terms of closeness and distance. By using an associated psycho-drama approach, the mother was helped to understand and connect the origins of her distance from her first daughter. After demonstrating the distance with herself, she was asked to show the therapist how she perceived the relationship of her daughter with her own mother, who had provided primary care. She held her daughter closely—for the first time. She reported at the next session that she felt a sudden surge of closeness and a potential in their relationship she had not felt before. This new experience, and the creation of a new reality by this means of changing contact, had a powerful effect in giving a glimpse of new possibilities for relating.

Structural ways of working are helpful (Minuchin and Fishman, 1981) in getting a parent to turn to a child who is distressed and needs comforting. Encouraging parents and children to share their own traumatic experiences of abuse, helps reinstate responsive mother—child relationships.

It is helpful to use contexts such as family centres or day centres for parents and children so that other aspects of parenting can be attended to, for example countering sexualised responses by redeveloping more appropriate modesty skills. The mother–child context is one of the situations where *talking* about abusive experiences without reinforcement can begin to neutralise the abusive responses and reduce anxiety.

Dealing with the anxiety, tension, and the restrictiveness of post-traumatic responses is an important task in work with mothers and children together. Teaching communication skills is particularly important so that in the cycle of victim responses, silencing can be broken and substituted by assertion and communication. Grievances and misunderstandings about communication failures need to be expressed, and all failures to act need to be explored if the mother-child relationship is to be repaired or restored. Resentments on the mother's part concerned with the feeling that the child had displaced or replaced her need expression, and the possibility of sharing both the traumatic and the pleasurable aspects of sexualised contracts needs to be explored. There is also the possibility of mothers helping children through corrective sexual education.

Group Work for Mothers and Victims

Bentovim et al. (1988) described the development of the group component of work with mothers and victims of different ages. Groups can help the individual in his or her development, through sharing traumatic experiences in a safe context and by finding and testing new ways of relating. To be helpful, group work needs to be structured, and must have specific treatment aims and methods. The younger the child the more structured the groups need to be; groups for mothers or parents of abused children also need to be structured and to follow a programme (Bentovim et al., 1988). The important components of group programmes are work on breaking the taboo of secrecy, talking extensively about abusive experiences, delineating traumatic responses and ways of dealing with them, including the use of communication skills, cognitive restructuring, and assertion training (Berliner and Wheeler, 1987; Jehu, 1988).

Such work needs to be adapted to the needs of children of different ages and extended to the mothers and caretakers of abused children. There are a variety of approaches which can be used in groups including examination of genograms, and looking at each individual's perspective (Lieberman, 1980); role-play to increase assertive skills and build up self-esteem (Vizard, 1986); future-orientated scripts to correct old ones (Byng-Hall, 1979); and the use of trigger videos and drawings to help facilitate enactment of problems and new solutions (Berliner and Wheeler, 1987). The group supports members going through particular crises, such as preparation for going to court, or major changes of family context.

There are major differences in specific content depending on developmental stage, such as children who are pre-pubertal, children in early puberty, or those aged around 15–17 who are preparing for actual peer sexual relations. Similarly, parents of children who are abusing younger children in the family have different needs from those where a father has abused.

In principle the more homogeneous the group, and the more individuals share with each other and face similar dilemmas, the more helpful groups seem to be. Ordinarily group practice attempts to bring together individuals with different experiences who can complement each other; however, in the programme approach advocated in this chapter, work during the period of separation attempts to strengthen the individual's capacity to deal with specific family contexts.

There is a considerable dearth of research into the effectiveness of such group programmes, but they have been adopted widely as making good clinical sense. The limited information from follow-up research (Bentovim *et al.*, 1988) supports the progress of children following such a treatment approach. The results of a random assignment research which lists the effect of adding group work are awaited.

Work with Siblings

During the period of separation the experience of non-abused siblings will be very different from that of those children in the family who have been abused. They experience a disruption of their family and may feel pulled between sympathy and concern for the siblings who has been abused, and their own needs in relationship to a father who may have been supportive and loving towards them. Families may wish to maintain secrecy and insist that siblings not be informed of a father's abusive activities, in order to preserve some respect for him. Maintaining a fictitious story that a father is away working or ill is impossible, and is a form of abuse for a sibling not dissimilar to the family friction which hides the sexual abuse. Meeting with a non-abusive parent and children can be helpful in exploring what exactly the siblings know, what have they heard, what have they learnt from conversations that they were not supposed to be listening to. Usually children have a very clear idea of what has happened to their abused siblings and their parents but need permission to share it.

It is of course essential to do such work because it may well be that a sibling has not shared the fact that he or she has also been abused, because of a fear that what happened to the known abused child might happen to them. It is essential to have regular family reviews so that siblings have an opportunity to be heard over a period of therapy. Where resources are available, sibling groups may well be an effective way of helping children deal with experiences and behaviour they have watched or have heard about without having been able to speak.

Work with Perpetrators and Partners—Fathers and Mothers

To work successfully with perpetrators demands clarification of the depth and extent of abusive behaviour, how it originates from early experiences, and what triggers and maintains abusive attitudes. The cyclical nature of abusive patterns and the specific choice of victims also need exploring. Such work can be done individually or, with considerable advantage, in groups (Salter, 1988). It is also likely that such work needs to be longer term than that with the traumatised child or non-abusive parents.

Wheldon (1988) has described long-term groups for adults, perpetrators, and women who have been victimised in early childhood. Such groups need to be long term so that extensive work can be completed. In the Great Ormond Street Hospital project, in addition to work with fathers in groups, work was also carried out with couples that included the perpetrator and the non-abusive parent. If such joint work is done early in the phase of separation it may well have too great an influence on the final outcome, perhaps orientating couples towards possible rehabilitation when longer term separation would have been a preferable outcome.

Our current view is that specific work needs to be done with mothers to help them develop a sense of assertiveness and protectiveness of their child, to help with self-esteem after having to come to terms with a partner's sexual interest in their child, and with the resulting disruption of family life. It is likely that only through women working together will they be able to reverse the inherent structural power relationship within their family. This may well have been one of the factors which enabled the father to overcome the ordinary internal and external inhibitions to abusing a child in his care. There may well be a role for couples' groups during the next phase of rehabilitation when both partners have been able to do sufficient work on abusive behaviour and traumatic responses to be able to work together as a couple with a more equal relationship. Perpetrators, in addition to working with the origins of their abusive behaviour, also need to look at issues of power within male and female relationships, and to begin the most painful and difficult process of empathising the traumatic nature of their activities and its effect on children. A similar process needs to be followed whether the abusers are adults or adolescents (Abel et al., 1984). There is a dearth of controlled research assessing the effectiveness of treatment using group work, specific behavioural approaches, and the role of residential or out-patient work.

Conjoint Family Work During the Period of Separation

For those families where there is a hopeful prognosis, that is with responsibility being taken and support of the abused child, there may be some family work, which includes the perpetrator, during the phase of separation. It should be remembered, however, that changes in family structure observed during this phase cannot be thought of as permanent, since the family has no opportunity to work on problems and therefore change between sessions. The children and young people's therapist and the parents' therapist can come together to share progress with representatives of statutory agencies. Such network meetings can review progress, assign work tasks, and make recommendations to those who make decisions such as courts, senior social work (child care) managers, and case conferences.

Family Professional Work

As Furness (1983) has commented, it is very easy for the conflicts within the family—for example, rejection and scapegoating of a child, rejection of a mother or father—to be reflected within the relationships of the professional agencies themelves. A social worker who is concerned and has a basic responsibility for a child may find it very difficult to believe that any change can occur in the perpetrating parent's attitudes. The probation officer with a major identification with the father as his client, may be concerned that other professionals exclude him and his client, and concentrate too much on the child. It is often important to sort out which agencies are doing which piece of work since there are so many issues that need to be considered. Confusion can reign instead of clarity, and professionals can pull family members in opposite directions. One of the essential areas is the need to define closely: (i) where work with the child is going to occur to help with his or her traumatic responses and the effect of traumagenic dynamics; (ii) where work on mother-child relationships is going to occur; (iii) where work with the mother to help her deal with her own stress is going to be offered; (iv) where work with the father's abusive behaviour is going to be dealt with; (v) where later marital work is going to take place, looking at the issues between them as a couple; (vi) where decisions are going to be taken in terms of placement of children, timing of rehabilitation, and assessment of change.

REHABILITATION PHASE

The timing for rehabilitation, for example the return of a perpetrating father to a home, is extremely difficult to plan. It depends on many issues such as whether there has been a prison sentence, whether work has been done, the motivation of the family and professionals and the family to achieve goals. The offender needs to demonstrate his capacity to act responsibly by working with his probation officer or care authorities. He needs to live separately in the community and to maintain an appropriate degree of separation but without undermining this or trying to recreate a secrecy system with his own family by getting them to ignore transgressions.

It is asking a great deal of a family to live in a community but separately, and there is great temptation to break rules, to flaunt authority, and maintain secrecy. Conversely, sometimes when family members are able to work with therapeutic and statutory agencies, at the moment when rehabilitation becomes possible the family may indicate that they do not wish to live together. Return home has to be worked towards during a period of separation, with plans carefully made, and a graded series of access visits in neutral contexts, followed by later unsupervised periods of access, and weekend staying access.

There are a number of areas to be worked at during the period of rehabilitation. This is the period of maximum work with the family conjointly. Specific tasks during this period include: increasing authority for the mother; marital and sexual counselling; emotional changes to be achieved.

Increasing Authority for the Mother

To create a protective context for a child and facilitate development requires a major shift in the family's way of functioning. The basic change has to be for the mother to have a permanently 'one up' position, a greater authority over the children and the father. This may well represent a rebalancing in a family which has followed a patriarchal pattern in which father holds authority over both women and children.

These changes may be made through groups for women and men separately, which help deal with specific issues and help them to grow as people. Coming together to work as a couple in groups helps deal with shared issues. Learning from the example of other couples' ways of working and relating can help new ways of being for couples. Using a task-based focus with family therapy elements, such as role-play, sculpting, and practising different forms of relating, can have a profound effect on the couple's functioning.

They need to share what each knows of the abuse, to appreciate and understand the views and feelings of the other, to look at issues of sexuality between the couple, and to understand trauma by looking at the effect of the abuse on the other parent. Couples need to help each other to negotiate with statutory agencies, and to sort out rules which enable mothers to be in charge of their children's protection and so boost their self-esteem.

It is often necessary to create quite a strong rule structure for who stays with whom in various rooms during access, visits home, and finally living at home. Children should not stay in the same room as their father without somebody else being present as a matter of course, to protect both child and parent. Establishing different rules establishes different structures in the family. Such patterns need to become habitual, and although they may be artificial and uncomfortable at first, they can become part of the family's rule structure as time goes on. It is as if the therapeutic context becomes a part of the family and a new rule base is created.

Although families often wish to distance themselves from professionals, 'to be left alone', this has to be seen as an attempt to move back into a familiar secrecy system which the family knows how to work only too well. That presents a good outside face to the world, whilst inside maintaining the abusive pattern of control, threat, and secrecy. Abuse occurs within a context of secrecy and rigid boundaries between the family and the outside world. The boundary has to be flexible and the family has to be open. Painful and stressful as it may be to have professionals as part of the family, it is essential to do so, and to work in such a way that the family subsequently develops its own models without the professionals being present.

Boundaries which are often confused in terms of who is parent, who is child, who is sexual partner, who is parental partner, have to be clear. Adults create a parental subsystem and the children a sibship and peer system. In many families there is role confusion, with the mother at some point being the parent for a husband who behaves like one of the older adolescent siblings. At other times she acts as the child responding to the father's needs. The child may take the parental role or be partner in relationship to one or both parents. Parents are seen as children to be protected or sacrificed for. These issues need to be addressed in family therapy sessions, using a variety of structural or strategic approaches. Permanent changes need to be created to ensure that therapy is satisfactorily completed and rehabilitation a real possibility. It must be stressed that the number of families reaching this rehabilitation point are limited.

Marital and Sexual Counselling

Although the abuser's sexual orientation towards the children needs extensive and detailed consideration and is often the prime issue, there are often other sexual problems associated with it. Through unconscious patterns of interlocking pathology between parents, the mother in her own right may have to deal with effects of longstanding abusive experiences. It may take a long period of trust before the mother can confide and share with a worker her own abusive experiences, her sexual frigidity, and her anger and rejection of the father's sexual contact with her, both past and present. Joint counselling is then needed to help develop new patterns of relating, and such work often needs to take place both in the group context of working with couples and in a specific way through couples' counselling.

Emotional Changes to be Achieved

In the longer term, the offender needs to understand the origins of his abusive behaviour, and to be put in touch with his own traumatic experience which may have triggered abuser roles. He should be able to demonstrate real penitence and awareness of the painful effects of his abusive action, rather than acknowledging responsibility in a restricted way. Early on there may be risks of suicidal behaviour as the offender tries to escape the consequences of his acts, the feared disaster of loss of liberty, or condemnation by others. There is a later danger that the offender may come to realise the true extent of his abusive behaviour and suicidal behaviour may then occur.

It is important that the victim should have confidence both in him or herself and in protectors available within and outside the family without feeling inappropriately in control of the whole network. It is also essential to clarify the views of the extended family, and to restore relationships which may have been deeply affected by publicity, periods of imprisonment, and the necessary action of statutory agencies. The family also needs to face and consider possible future crisis points, particular risk points for the recurrence of sexual abuse, either for the victim or for other children within the family. It is not surprising, considering the extensive work that needs to be achieved to bring about change in major sexually abusive cases, that the rate of rehabilitation in an unselected group of cases is so limited (Bentovim *et al.*, 1988), compared to a self-selected group (Giaretto, 1981).

There needs to be a basic change in societal attitudes, towards offering help to abusers rather than punishing them alone. This means the development of offender as well as victim treatment programmes, and appropriate help for other family members. It may then be far easier for victims to speak about abuse, for non-abusive parents to hear what is being said, and for offenders to take responsibility. If it were known that there would be a compassionate response rather than scapegoating, rejection, and total loss of liberty, then it may be easier for the many who cannot speak to be able to do so, and to become more open. However well organised treatment programmes become, there will always be children who require alternative family care for shorter periods in early phases of treatment, or longer periods if treatment fails.

TOWARDS A NEW FAMILY

New families are required for abused children when they have been extruded by their parents, or where their parents are manifestly unable to take on responsibility and to change appropriately. In these situations long-term alternative care is needed, with adoption if necessary, particularly for younger children. In addition to all the ordinary work done in preparing a *child* for fostering or adoption, including handling feelings of loss, guilt, failure, anger and let down, foster and adoptive parents need to be offered specific counselling.

The new family have to feel confident in their own sexuality, and to be prepared to alter their own expectations of the pace at which their children learn about sexual matters. There is also the necessity to meet overtly sexual acting out, to recognise the covert and unconsciously inappropriate sexualised behaviour of the children, and to develop rules to prevent confusion. The child needs to be helped to relearn a safer and modest demeanour.

Such work can be achieved in groups for foster or adoptive parents in parallel with work with children. These groups can explore the short- and long-term effects of sexual abuse, and can share information about what to expect, and how to deal with worrying patterns of behaviour. It is necessary to deal with their extremely strong feelings about natural family members, particularly the perpetrator or the mother who may have rejected the child and denied the abusive behaviour. Such feelings make it extremely difficult to help the victim with their feelings towards the natural family. Despite anger and distress the child may persist in a longing and a wish to be with them. Members of the foster family may not be able to hear and deal with such ambivalent feelings.

CONCLUSIONS

In working with families where sexual abuse occurs, it is clear that there is a broad set of aims for the individual, for the couple, and for the family as a whole.

There is no one particular way of working with families which is going to meet all these needs. It is essential to have a set of concepts which can helpfully focus on the effect of traumatic and stressful relationships, and to help understand and formulate ways of helping all members of the family, and those professionals who are trying to help.

There is currently a wide variety of techniques available to work with families, in individuals, dyads or larger family groups, for example sibling groups, couples, and also families together with their networks. Such approaches are derived from various family therapy schools, including Structural, Milan Systemic, and Dynamic. All have techniques and ways of working which are powerful and can achieve considerable change.

Kinston and Bentovim (1990) have advanced a view which challenges the theories put forward by various family therapy approaches which are held to account for the action and effectiveness of techniques. They see such theories as rationalisations for what are themselves effective ways of practising clinically. What is needed is to harness such ways of working with family members to create specific changes. These include preventing further abuse, reversing traumatic reactions, and providing a supportive family context for the child and family members.

The choice of approach used obviously depends on the training and view of the professional carrying out the work. There is no substitute for experience, training, good supervision, and consultation to broaden the thinking which needs to be brought to bear on the extremely complex issues which arise when sexual abuse occurs.

References

Abel, G. G., Becker, J. V., Cunningham-Rathner, J., Rouleau, J., Kaplan, M., and Reich, J. (1984). The treatment of child molesters. SBC-TM, 722 W. 16th Street, Box 17, New York.

Baker, T., and Duncan, S. (1985). Child sexual abuse: A study of prevalence in Great Britain. *Child Abuse and Neglect*, **9**, 457–67.

Bentovim, A. (1990). Physical violence in the family. In P. Bowden and R. Bluglass (eds), *Principles and Practice of Forensic Psychiatry*. London: Livingston.

Bentovim, A., Elton, A., Hildebrand, J., Tranter, M., and Vizard, E. (1988). *Sexual Abuse in the Family*. Bristol: John Wright.

Bentovim, A., Elton, A., and Tranter, M. (1987). Prognosis for rehabilitation after abuse. *Adoption and Fostering*, **11**, 28–31.

Bentovim, A., Van Elburg, A., and Boston, P. (1988). The results of treatment. In A. Bentovim, A. Elton, J. Hildebrand, M. Tranter and E. Vizard (eds), *Child Sexual Abuse in the Family*. Bristol: John Wright.

Bentovim, A., and Kinston, W. (1990). Focal family therapy—Joining systems theory with psychodynamic understanding. In A. Gurman and D. Kniskern (eds), *A Handbook of Family Therapy*. New York: Basic Books.

Berliner, L., and Wheeler, J.R. (1987). Treating the effects of sexual abuse on children. *Journal of Interpersonal Violence*, **2**, 415–34.

Byng-Hall, J. (1979). Re-editing family mythology during family therapy. *Journal of Family Therapy*, **1**, 103–16.

Byng-Hall, J. (1989). Replicative and corrective scripts. Presentation to the Institute for Family Therapy (London).

Faller, K. (1988). *Child Sexual Abuse: An Interdisciplinary Manual for Diagnosis, Case Management and Treatment*. New York: Columbia University Press.

Finkelhor, D. (1984). *Child Sexual Abuse: New Theory and Research*. New York: Free Press.

Finkelhor, D., and Browne, A. (1986). Sexual abuse: Initial and long-term effects: A conceptual framework. In D. Finkelhor (ed.), *A Sourcebook on Child Sexual Abuse*. Beverly Hills, CA: Sage.

Furness, T. (1983). Mutual influence and interlocking professional-family process in the treatment of child sexual abuse and incest. *Child Abuse and Neglect*, **7**, 207–23.

Gelles, R. J., and Cornell, C. P. (1985). *Intimate Violence in Families*. Beverly Hills, CA: Sage.

Giaretto, H. (1981). A comprehensive child sexual abuse treatment programme. In P. B. Mrazek and C. H. Kempe (eds), *Sexually Abused Children and Their Families*. Oxford: Pergamon Press.

Goolishian, H. A., and Winderman, L. (1988). Constructivism, autopoiesis and problem determining systems. *Irish Journal of Psychology*, **9**, 130–43.

Jehu, D. (1988). *Beyond Sexual Abuse*. Chichester: John Wiley.

Johnson, T. C. (1988). Child perpetrators: Children who molest other children. *Child Abuse and Neglect*, **12**, 219–29.

Johnson, T. C., and Berry, C. (1989). Children who molest—a treatment program. *Journal of Interpersonal Violence*, **4**, 185–203.

Kempe, C. H. (1979). Recent developments in the field of child abuse. *Child Abuse and Neglect*, **3**, ix–xv.

Kinston, W. (1987). A general theory of symptom formation (discussion paper).

Lieberman, S. (1980). *Intergenerational Family Therapy*. London: Croom-Helm.

Lustig, N., Dresser, J. W., Spellman, S. W., and Murray, T. B. (1966). Incest: A family group survival pattern. *Archives of General Psychiatry*, **14**, 31–40.

Minuchin, S., and Fishman, C. (1981). *Family Therapy Techniques*. Cambridge, MA: Harvard University Press.

Pynoos, R. S., and Eth, S. (1985). *Post-traumatic Stress Disorder in Children*. Los Angeles, CA: American Psychiatric Association.

Russell, D. E. H. (1984). *Sexual Exploitation*. Beverly Hills, CA: Sage.

Salter, A. C. (1988). *Treating Child Sex Offenders and Victims*. Beverly Hills, CA: Sage.

Strauss, M., and Gelles, R. (1979). *Behind Closed Doors: Violence in the American Family*. Garden City, NY: Anchor Press.

Terr, L. (1987). Post traumatic states—Types I & II. Severe trauma and sudden shock. Sam Hibbs Lecture. Chicago: American Psychiatric Association.

Tomm, K. (1987). Circular interviewing—a multifaced clinical tool. In D. Cambell and R. Draper (eds), *Application of Systemic Therapy*. London: Grune & Stratton.

Vizard, E. (1986). *Self-Esteem and Personal Safety*. (Video) London: Tavistock.

Vizard, E., and Tranter, M. (1988). Interviewing sexually abused children. In A. Bentovim, A. Elton, J. Hildebrand, M. Tranter and E. Vizard (eds), *Treatment of Sexual Abuse in the Family*. Bristol: John Wright.

Wheldon, E. (1988). Therapeutic work with male perpetrators and female victims in groups. Paper given to Tavistock Clinic, London.

White, R. (1984). Written agreements with families. In R. Adcock and R. White (eds), *Good-Enough Parenting*. London: British Agencies Adoption and Fostering.

9

Clinical Work With Sexually Abused Children

Lucy Berliner
Harborview Medical Center, Seattle, USA

Clinical intervention with sexually abused children attempts to treat the effects of abuse experiences. Although it is widely assumed that abuse experiences may have a negative psychological impact, only recently has there been recognition among mental health professionals that sexual abuse may have far deeper and long lasting effects and be an important correlate for a variety of mental health conditions in children and adults. Understanding the nature and scope of these effects is critical to the development of effective intervention strategies.

Over the last decade there has been a tremendous accumulation of knowledge about the long-term effects of abuse. The earliest systematic reports focussed on incest victims in therapy and found them to have more severe symptoms than non-abuse survivors (Herman, 1981; Meiselman, 1978; Tsai *et al.*, 1978). Since then a number of studies of women in the general population have confirmed that abuse survivors experience higher levels of symptomatic distress (Briere and Runtz, 1988; Gold, 1986; Murphy *et al.*, 1988). They are more depressed, more anxious, have more dissociative and somatic symptoms and have lower self-esteem. They are also at significantly higher risk of developing psychiatric disorders including depression, various anxiety disorders including Post-Traumatic Stress Disorder, substance abuse disorders, and sexual dysfunction (Bagley and Ramsey, 1985; Saunders *et al.*, 1987; Stein *et al.*, 1988).

Until recently the clinical literature on children consisted primarily of descriptions of typical emotional and behavioral reactions found in daughters abused by fathers (see e.g. James and Nasjleti, 1983; Porter *et al.*, 1982). These reactions usually were described as fears and anxieties, feelings of guilt, shame and anger, self-destructiveness, low self-esteem and acting out. Systematic clinical studies

Clinical Approaches to Sex Offenders and Their Victims
Edited by C. R. Hollin and K. Howells © 1991 John Wiley & Sons Ltd

tended to confirm the presence of the symptoms (see e.g. Adams-Tucker, 1982; Anderson *et al.*, 1981; Browning and Boatman, 1977; Mian *et al.*, 1986; Peters, 1976; Rogers and Terry, 1984).

Two reviews of empirical research on the impact of abuse (Browne and Finkelhor, 1986; Haugaard and Repucci, 1988) currently are available. They confirm that there are symptoms present to varying degrees among samples of abused children; but both sets of authors point out that there is great variability in the type and severity of the children's disturbance. They have also noted a number of weaknesses in methodology and design in much of the available literature on the effects of abuse. Many of the studies did not use standardized measures of psychological disturbance or did not employ comparison groups. Without comparison data it is not possible to conclude that the observed effects significantly discriminate abused children from other groups of children.

Recent empirical investigations are beginning to provide a more complete picture of the effects. In these studies the researchers attempt to overcome the methodological weaknesses of clinical reports by using standardized measures which have normal and clinical values established and/or by having comparison groups. There is direct assessment of the children either by parent or teacher report or by self-report. Currently there are data available from almost a dozen major investigations; (Cohen and Mannarino, 1988; Conte and Berliner, 1988; Conte *et al.*, 1986; Conte and Schuerman, 1987; Einbender and Friedrich, 1989; Friedrich *et al.*, 1986, 1987; Gomes-Schwartz *et al.*, 1990; Runyon *et al.*, 1987; Saunders *et al.*, 1987; Tong *et al.*, 1987; White *et al.*, 1988; Wolfe *et al.*, 1989). Across studies there were similar results. Using parent report, abused children are consistently found to be more behaviorally distressed than non-abused children. However, the levels of behavioral disturbance are not as significant as in psychiatric populations of children. Depending on the study and the subscale used, different proportions of children scored in the clinically significant range.

Those studies which used self-report measures with the children generally did not find differences from comparison groups or did not show clinically significant elevations in the scores. Depending on the study, children were administered instruments to measure self-concept, depression and anxiety. Several studies used projective psychological tests designed to measure emotional adjustment with standardized scoring schemes and did not find significant differences. In only one study which used a standardized structured interview of the children (Runyon *et al.*, 1987) containing items related to behavior and other functioning did the children seem as disturbed as a psychiatric population. Wolfe *et al.* (1989) have some early evidence that abuse specific measures do discriminate abused and non-abused children. On general mental health and behavioral measures the children were not different. However, using abuse specific self-report measures the children demonstrated significant differences; specifically, they had elevations in intrusive thoughts related to the event and abuse specific fears (e.g. revictimization).

There are a number of conclusions which can be drawn from these investigations. Abused children as a group differ behaviorally from non-abused children but overall have less pathology than a psychiatrically disturbed population.

Within the group of abused children there is a broad range of level of disturbance. Some children do not appear to be behaviorally distressed. In one study
on a therapist completed symptom checklist, 21% of the children were asymptomatic (Conte and Berliner, 1988). However, depending on the study, upwards to
60% of the children scored in the clinically significant range on some measures,
indicating a level of acute distress requiring immediate clinical intervention.

Investigators have attempted to identify variables which are associated with
more serious impact. Most studies find that there are some abuse variables which
are related to a worse outcome. Closer relationship to offender, more intrusive
sexual behavior (e.g. intercourse), longer duration or more frequent contact, and
the use of violence appear related in most studies but not in all. In some cases
even relationship to offender is not significantly related to negative outcome
(Cohen and Mannarino, 1988; Einbender and Friedrich, 1989). The relationship
is sometimes a more complex one: for example, one study found that children
abused by stepfathers were worse off than those abused by biological parents
(Gomes-Schwartz et al., 1990). Sometimes different abuse variables predicted
differences in different kinds of outcomes. For example, in the Friedrich et al.
(1987) study different variables were correlated with internalizing and externalizing responses in boys and girls. However, characteristics of the abuse, even
when correlated, only explain a relatively small amount of the differences in
functioning. No consistent relationship to age at the time of the offense has been
found.

Several studies have found that there is a relationship between the amount of
support available to the children and post-abuse functioning. Conte and Schuerman (1987) found that a supportive relationship with a non-offending parent and
with a sibling was important. The support available may be associated with other
variables as well. Mothers tend to be less supportive in certain relationships with
offenders and the children more distressed (Everson et al., 1989; Gomes-
Schwartz et al., 1990). Characteristics of family functioning also seem to be
related. When there are more negative qualities to family relations or where
families are rated to have more conflict and less cohesion the children are in a
worse condition (Conte and Schuerman, 1987; Friedrich et al., 1987).

The type of intervention may also be relevant to impact. In one study,
however, none of the official interventions including interviews with authorities,
placement out of the home, attending a legal hearing or testifying was related to
impact one year later (Conte et al., 1986). Children placed out of the home are
worse off initially but seem to improve comparably with non-placed children
(Runyon et al., 1988), suggesting that it is not the placement which causes the
more serious dysfunction. It may be that situations which require placement (e.g.
non-supporting parent) produce the negative effects, or that it is the disturbed
behavior in the child which leads to placement.

Runyon et al. (1988) found that children not involved in the legal system and
those whose involvement was completed were similarly distressed while children
whose cases were still pending showed significantly more distress. This may
mean that it is not participation per se which is disturbing but the effects of the
lack of resolution. They also found that children who testified in juvenile court,

while starting off more distressed actually improved. Again, it may be the characteristics of a case where testimony is required (e.g. denying offender) which is the cause of harm, not the testifying. This also lends weight to the clinical observation that some children seem to be better off following the opportunity to testify (Berliner and Barbieri, 1984).

The effects which most consistently appear and differentiate abuse victims are related to the abuse experience itself. Sexualized responses might be expected to sexual involvement with adult or significantly older youth because it is developmentally abnormal and usually coercive in some way. It may produce unusual or age inappropriate behaviors through learning or emotional adjustment to the experience. The literature has commented that children might react sexually to the experience and that this might produce sexualized responses (Yates, 1982). Differences between victims and other children in sexual behavior have been consistently found on assessment using standardized behavior checklists (e.g. Friedrich et al., 1986), a specially constructed checklist (White et al., 1988), or chart review (Gale et al., 1988; Mian et al., 1986). A specific standardized measure of sexual behavior in children has been developed and is currently being tested (Friedrich, 1988). Preliminary findings on data comparing five geographically different abuse samples with normal values established from a large non-abused sample confirm that sexually abused children are significantly different in sexual behavior from non-abused children. These differences appear to be most pronounced in younger children.

Similar emphasis on sexual responses has been noted in the clinical literature on adolescent victims. Abused girls are frequently described as engaging in sexual acting out. Prostitution is itself a form of sexual acting out and a very large proportion of youth involved in prostitution have been sexually victimized (James and Meyerding, 1977; Silbert and Pines, 1981).

Anxiety symptoms are the other most commonly reported symptom clusters. All clinical studies describe various reactions which are classified as fear and anxiety, including sleep disturbances and nightmares, flashbacks, startle reactions and hypervigilance, regression, phobic behavior, withdrawal from usual activities, nervousness, and clingyness. These symptoms are consistent with symptoms noted in children who have suffered other traumas such as witnessing violent acts (Pynoos and Eth, 1985) and other dramatic experiences such as kidnapping or natural disasters (Terr, 1985). Children who have experienced other disruptive events such as divorce also have elevations in anxiety symptoms (see e.g. Wallerstein and Kelly, 1976). This group of responses is thought to be related to the anxiety associated with sudden, unusual, or personally disturbing events.

It is quite clear that while many children evaluated shortly after disclosure of abuse do not exhibit severe symptoms, an abuse history is highly correlated with a number of very serious disturbances, that abuse survivors continue to experience elevated levels of symptomatic distress many years later, and that they are at significantly increased risk for developing a range of psychiatric disorders. The full impact on a particular child could not really be known unless the child was followed longitudinally until adulthood.

It is possible that some children are asymptomatic because they are especially resilient to unpleasant experiences or that the aversiveness of the experience does not achieve dramatic levels. The children may have well-developed coping skills and come from supportive environments thereby making them able to handle abuse experiences with a minimum of distress.

Another reason why children might not exhibit effects relates to coping strategies employed in response to abuse experiences which involve avoiding or blocking out memories or feelings about the experience. Post-Traumatic Stress Disorder (PTSD) is an anxiety disorder which is caused by the memories of a traumatic experience which either intrude unwanted into the consciousness of the individual through flashbacks or nightmares or which the person attempts to repress or avoid through withdrawal or amnesia (American Psychiatric Association, 1987). The literature on the effects of traumatic events frequently refers to various psychological defenses which permit a person to reduce or avoid the anxiety attendant with remembering including repression, denial, splitting, dissociation, somatization, and amnesia. PTSD has been specifically documented in child sexual abuse victims (Goodwin, 1985; Kiser et al., 1988; McLeer et al., 1988; Wolfe et al., 1989).

The goal of this type of coping response is the reduction in internal discomfort and symptoms. Therefore children who appear to lack emotional responses or to exhibit no distress, might simply be coping with abuse experiences through strategies designed to allow escape from memories which are unpleasant. Not only does the memory of the actual abuse produce discomfort but explaining why it happened and what it means may cause psychological distress (Berliner and Wheeler, 1987). The need cognitively to adapt to traumatic experiences has been documented among many populations (Taylor, 1983). It has also been noted that victimization shatters beliefs about oneself, others, and the world (Janoff-Bulman, 1985). The conflict between needing an explanation and accepting an explanation may lead to denial and repression.

Ultimately, the cumulative negative effects of an internalized negative attributional style or avoidance coping responses may lead to other serious psychological consequences such as low self-esteem or depression. The absence of findings of impaired self-esteem in children but the consistent finding in adults may be explained by this mechanism. Abuse experiences alter beliefs or assumptions, and the way in which a person explains and makes sense out of what has happened to them could have an effect on many aspects of functioning. There is empirical evidence that the search for meaning in abuse experiences is correlated with outcome in adults (Silver et al., 1983). Adult survivors who have found a satisfactory explanation for the incest are better adjusted. There is also evidence that cognitive style and attributional approach is related to adult adjustment (Gold, 1986). Victims who have an internal, stable and global attributional style are less well adjusted.

The interaction with developmental process may explain delayed effects; some effects may not surface until certain stages of development or critical life events (Gelinas, 1983). It may not be possible to know the effects on ability to relate to others, sexual self-esteem, or sense of personal efficacy until adolescence or adulthood when these become salient developmental issues. If children are expending a significant amount of psychological energy on either dealing with or avoiding abuse, resources for completing normal developmental tasks may be diminished. Maladaptive coping responses may work to influence children's personality development in such a way as to become incorporated into their personality structure and functioning. This may explain why abuse survivors seem to have significantly higher rates of certain kinds of personality disorders (Briere and Runtz, 1988). In other words, psychopathology may be the end result of certain learned responses to abuse (Briere and Runtz, 1987).

EFFECTS OF ABUSE—INTERVENTION

The most important implication of current knowledge is that the victimization experience itself produces traumatic effects and should be the focus of therapeutic intervention. Abuse focussed therapy may not resolve all of a child's or a family's problems, but failure to address the abuse directly will miss issues of significance for the child's psychological development. Individual or group modalities seem most likely to promote an abuse focus for the children. Although families are also affected by the victimization of a child, the experience of being abused is quite different from living in a family where a member is abused. Especially considering that many children do not report abuse because they fear the consequences or seek to protect other family members, the abuse environment may be recapitulated in the family therapy context. Family or dyadic approaches should be considered as adjunctive to victimization therapy.

The possibility that minimal symptomatology represents avoidance and denial implies that directive therapeutic approaches would be more effective. In a nondirective or client determined therapy context children may not make genuine progress toward resolution or integration. While avoidance and denial can be appropriate in situations where more direct control is not possible eventually approach strategies designed to achieve mastery are desirable (Roth and Cohen, 1986). However, care must be taken not to be so confrontive that aversive associations to therapy are created. A persistent but gentle emphasis on abuse related material is recommended. This also suggests that very brief intervention may not provide enough opportunity to explore the extent of internalized impact.

The evidence of potential long-term effects dictates that even in the absence of acute or severe symptoms, children may benefit from treatment. From this perspective it has a preventive as well as an ameliorative purpose. Parents as well as children may not recognize the importance of intervention when there are few overt signs of disturbance. A natural desire to believe the experience has had minimal impact as well as the emotional, financial or logistical complications of involvement in therapy may serve as barriers to compliance. Therapists should be prepared to explain how therapy can help avoid subsequent dysfunction.

THERAPY TARGETS

Two basic therapeutic targets emerge from the extant knowledge; *emotional and cognitive processing of the experience*. Successful emotional processing involves decreasing the affective response to the memories of the abuse and 'can be gauged from the person's ability to talk about, see, listen to or be reminded of the emotional events without experiencing distress or disruptions' (Rachman, 1980, p. 52). Successful cognitive processing involves assisting the child in arriving at an internalized understanding of the experience which is accurate and which does not include unwarranted self-blame. In other words the child should be able to remember the abuse without experiencing significant distress and understand it as primarily the result of the adult offender's disordered behavior.

Further, the child should not have developed ways of thinking and behaving which reflect an avoidance of the experience or a generalized maladaptive response to other significant dimensions of life (e.g. distrust of all men). A useful heuristic device for organizing the potential areas of generalized impact is the notion of traumogenic dynamics as explicated by Finkelhor and Browne (1985). The four dynamics are traumatic sexualization, betrayal, powerlessness and stigmatization (see also Chapter 8).

ASSESSMENT

The importance of a thorough assessment prior to initiating abuse-focussed intervention is underscored by the fact that much of the impact of abuse may be internalized in the form of either avoidance responses or distorted beliefs. Unless the therapist has specifically evaluated these areas it may appear that there is no psychological impact requiring intervention. Unfortunately most standardized measures of child distress either focus on overt behavior (e.g. behavior checklists) or are not specific to abuse experiences (e.g. depression or anxiety measures). It is recommended that therapists use or develop assessment measures which will systematically elicit responses in the desired areas.

For example, in evaluating the extent to which a child is still distressed about the abuse memory, it is crucial to determine both the level of intrusiveness and the level of psychological effort expended on avoidance. The Children's Impact of Traumatic Events Scale (Wolfe *et al.*, 1986) seeks to elicit responses about intrusion and avoidance. An Impact Checklist which covers a range of thoughts, feelings and behaviors which could be abuse related is being used for clinical and research purposes in one program (Sexual Assault Center, 1986).

The capacity of the family to support the child victim should also be evaluated to identify areas for intervention. The degree of belief and support can be determined both by directed questioning and by assessment and observation of general family functioning. Such areas as the extent to which family members believe that the child was abused, have demonstrated this to the child and other family members, have taken appropriate actions to protect and assist the child as well as attitudes and behavior toward the offender can be specifically elicited.

A factor which often hinders a thorough assessment process is that many families are in a state of crisis at the point they first present for intervention. This crisis is primarily related to the disclosure of the abuse and both the child's and the family's acute response to the revelation. Children who have feared the consequences of reporting may be focussed on parental and system responses more than the abuse effects. Parents may vacillate between belief and denial or be overcome by the implications of this information. They may be preoccupied with the meaning of their child's victimization in terms of their own failures to protect or to be available. There may also be concrete actions which involve significant disruptions such as placement of a child or removal of an offender, moving, and changes in financial status. These concerns and reactions are legitimate and expected initial issues which deserve therapeutic attention. However, crisis intervention cannot substitute for victimization therapy.

INITIAL INTERVENTION

It is appropriate to begin therapy with a focus on the crisis responses to disclosure. The goal is to stabilize the family and insure an adequate level of support for the child. Obviously safety, both physical and psychological, is the most fundamental issue, and therapists may be required to initiate legal interventions by reporting to authorities. In virtually every case this means separation from the accused offender. Even when a parent agrees to supervise all contact there are adverse psychological impacts for children to continue contact with untreated or denying offenders. When the offender denies the abuse, the child's sense of reality is challenged and anxiety is generated about whether others will believe him/her. Even an admitting offender poses a threat to the child. Without extensive treatment offenders will invariably minimize the seriousness or extent of abuse or project blame onto others. They will likely employ various strategies to engender guilt in the child or other family members, or to control the extent of negative consequences to themselves.

Information and assistance with negotiating the initial tasks is part of the therapist responsibility. The therapist who seeks to treat abused children must be knowledgeable about the requirements related to system intervention. Laws and practices vary depending on the particular community. Familiarity with local agencies and typical procedures is essential to enable the therapist to prepare the family. Reducing anxiety associated with anticipated system interventions is a part of the therapist's responsibility. Information and preparation will enhance the victim's and the family's ability to manage the external expectations.

Creating a climate of belief and support is crucial to enable the child victim to shift focus onto the actual abuse effects. Depending on the family's stance this will involve different sorts of interventions. In the majority of cases there will be a parent or parents who believe that the abuse occurred. However, even in this case they may not realize the actual nature or extent of abuse or may not want to know. The most effective means of overcoming this resistance is for the child victim directly to tell the parent(s). However, this may be quite difficult for the child to do and may take some period of time to accomplish. Indirect methods may be helpful, such as a written description or drawings done by the child, observation of therapy sessions by one-way mirror, or video with the child's consent. Eventually the therapist should facilitate some direct exposure of the parent to the child's experience.

When the parent does not believe the child the difficulties are clearly magnified. It is useful under these circumstances to make sure that the nonbelieving parent is in therapy. It may be preferable to select a different therapist than the child's to reduce the defensiveness of the parent. Instead of confronting or berating the parent, clinical experience suggests that it is more effective to explore the basis for the parent's lack of belief. It is almost always possible to discover why the parent is having trouble acknowledging the abuse of the child. The parent may take the position that the accused offender could not possibly have done it. Sometimes this is because of inadequate information about the characteristics of offenders. More often it is because the parent has trusted the offender or depends on the offender and there are significant implications for believing the child. It may mean facing her own inadequacies or a substantial change in circumstances.

Another possibility is that the parent—child relationship has been characterized by conflict, competitiveness and lack of closeness. The parent may think that the accusation of abuse is simply a means of getting attention or hurting the other parent. There may be deficits in attachment to the child or an accumulation of negative interactions which hampers the parent's ability to respond positively to the child.

VICTIMIZATION INTERVENTION

Emotional Processing

Emotional processing of a fear-producing experience requires exposure to the memories (Foa and Kozak, 1986). This means that the child victim will be expected to talk about the abuse in therapy. Repeated exposure to the memories in the safe and supportive therapy environment is designed to decondition the affective associations. Initially, some distress is inevitable and if not observed should raise the possibility that the child is continuing to dissociate from the emotional content, rather than being evidence for integration (Blake-White and Kline, 1985).

Children should be prepared for the likelihood that there will be discomfort and ways of managing this should be discussed. With the child who has the cognitive capacity to comprehend an explanation of the reasons and goals of the procedure is helpful. For example, a therapist might tell the child something like:

> When you think about or talk about what happened you might get back the feelings you had when it happened. Nobody likes to have those kind of feelings and do different things to try not to have them. I want you to be able to remember it without feeling bad so you don't have to worry about the memories hurting you.

The best way to do that is to talk about it until it doesn't feel so bad. In the beginning it will probably feel bad so I will help you and we will go slowly until you are ready.

Recollection of all aspects of the experience is necessary to identify the stimuli which evoke abuse associations. This is particularly complicated where the abuse has involved multiple events over an extended period. Some episodes may be forgotten or repressed, or elements of different experiences mixed up. One method for addressing this is to have the children list everything which reminds them of abuse or which causes anxiety. The list will include places, sounds, smells, and things: by relating the emotions to specific triggers the child can anticipate or understand reactions and mobilize coping responses.

Teaching strategies for managing fear and anxiety increase the child's sense of self-efficacy and control. These strategies can include learning to reduce the physical sensations such as tension, difficulty in breathing, or rapid heart rate, by employing systematic relaxation and controlled breathing. Cognitive approaches like thought stopping, reassuring self-statements, covert rehearsal, and cognitive restructuring are useful. Environmental alterations can be used to inhibit anxiety responses, such as rearranging or moving from the bedroom where the abuse occurred, or changing routines to insure that the physical environment is secure. Especially in the beginning, accommodating the child's fears through increased supervision or exceptional sleeping arrangements (e.g. child temporarily sleeps with parent) is acceptable.

An example of how this might work is with the child who reports awaking at night and being afraid. At first she might be instructed that it is OK to get up and go into the parent's room for reassurance in order to decrease initial levels of fear. Then she will be taught how to breath in a controlled way to calm herself as soon as she awakes. Next she will tell herself that she is feeling afraid because of abuse memories, that the house is secure, that her mother is nearby, that the offender can't hurt her. These statements would be generated in counseling sessions and perhaps written down and carried on a paper. She will design a room arrangement which feels safe (e.g. move bed away from window), identify symbols or objects which evoke a sense of safety or power (e.g. a certain poster of a powerful figure, placement of toys or stuffed animals), establish a pre-bedtime ritual (e.g. checking closets, special story).

Cognitive Processing

Cognitive processing addresses the way in which the child understands the abuse experience. There are a number of ways in which children may come to adopt inaccurate or harmful beliefs about the abuse. Youth and inexperience with sexuality may cause them to be confused or misunderstand the sexual activity. However, of greater concern is the often observed tendency of children to misattribute responsibility for the abuse. In many cases these ideas come from offenders who tell children during abuse situations that it is their fault, that they want it, or that it is normal. Especially where abuse has occurred over an extended period, it is natural for victims to come to accept such false explanations.

Children may make these attributions even in the absence of direct statements from offenders. Because of limited experience with such relationships they may logically construe their own behavior to be complicit. Not saying no or not telling may seem like consent. Commonly observed abuse dynamics such as initiating contact, being sexually responsive, or accepting favors are likely to produce a sense of active participation. Self-blame may also have an adaptive quality: it may be preferable for children to believe there is something about them which caused the abuse, than to accept the more frightening possibility that adults on whom they depend or love would use and take advantage of them.

In addition children may make attributions to diminish the intentionality of the abuse. They may think of it as accidental, caused by intoxication, or because of difficulties in the marital relationship. It is quite logical that children might assume that the wives of offenders are denying them sex. This kind of attribution might lead a child mistakenly to blame the mother for the offender's behavior or to not appreciate the risks posed by the offender. Unfortunately, many professionals unfamiliar with offender characteristics share the inaccurate view that sex offending is not an intentional activity and thereby they reinforce the child's misunderstanding.

The most effective way therapeutically to address misattributions about sexual abuse experiences is to encourage exploration of the basis for these beliefs instead of simply telling children it is not their fault. What the children believe, the source of the belief, and the purpose it serves must be determined. The reasons both for the offender's conduct and for their own are important to understand. The perceived consequences for adopting a new perspective also need to be uncovered.

Children should be provided a simple but honest explanation for sexually deviant behavior which might go something like: 'Some adults have sexual feelings for children and then they convince themselves it's OK to act on the feelings even though they know it's wrong. It's a little bit like when you want to steal something from a store and you tell yourself it's not that bad or it's not really hurting anyone. A big difference in sexual abuse is someone really does get hurt.' Since it is not entirely clear how adults develop a sexual attraction to children or to a particular child, it is sufficient to tell children that this process is not totally understood.

In order for children to make sense out of their own behavior it is necessary to have them recall their emotional and knowledge status at the time. What they feel and know in retrospect are rarely the same as during the abuse situation. In this way they can be helped to understand that their behavior was logical and legitimate at the time. Whether they were unaware, afraid or meeting other needs can be explicated. In some cases acquiescence to long-term abuse can be reinterpreted for the child as an act of love which protected a family member or preserved family intactness.

Education about the process of victimization and offender characteristics is provided. The ways in which the offender groomed the child to accept sexual behavior and then remain silent are specifically identified. For example, the child may describe a gradual process of so-called accidental contact, inappropriate intimacy or lack of respect for privacy which eventually culminated in overt sexual behavior. Offender qualities of self-centeredness and exploitiveness in other areas are also uncovered so that the child understands the deviance as a part of a broader characterological disturbance.

It is helpful whenever possible for offenders to communicate this directly to their victims. Whenever offenders are in treatment, efforts should be made to have them write letters of clarification or to have in person sessions where they accept full responsibility and explain why they behaved the way they did. If the therapist has access to information about the offender it should be communicated to the child. For example, if it is known that there were previous offenses the burden of causing the deviance is removed from the child.

Eventually, the child should be able to give, at an age appropriate level of comprehension, an explanation for both the offender and the child's behavior which is accurate and meaningful. In addition, the victim should be able to identify what is different now in terms of knowledge and resources which would enable them to avoid victimization in the future.

TRAUMATIC SEXUALIZATION

Sexual abuse experiences are likely to produce distorted ideas about sexuality especially since it is usually these children's first sexual experience. They may have sexual feelings which are confusing or difficult to manage, an intense curiosity or preoccupation with sex, or have learned to behave in inappropriate sexual ways. Therapy includes providing children with accurate information, correcting distorted beliefs, clarifying and establishing sexual values, and assistance in managing feelings and behavior. This must be done in the context of family and community values in order to be useful. For example, in some families it is acceptable for children to masturbate as long as it is done in private. In this case the child would identify situations when sexual feelings arise (e.g. watching scene on TV, at night in bed) and make a plan for how to handle the desire appropriately. In many families self-stimulation is prohibited for personal or religious reasons. The child would be helped to identify alternatives to masturbation (e.g. make contact with an adult) or to explore the consequences of violating family norms so that guilt is reduced.

Whenever children are behaving in inappropriate sexual ways the behavior needs to be directly confronted. Usually parents or others have clearly communicated that the activity is unacceptable and the child has persisted. This is an indication that the child is unable simply to stop the behavior. With younger children increased supervision is often necessary to protect the child from continuing to misbehave and to protect other children. The child learns to identify the feelings and situations which precede the behavior and strategies for avoiding acting out. Both behavioral and cognitive approaches are developed. For example, the child has a plan to remove him or herself from the situation and a series of self-statements to invoke (e.g. I will get into trouble; other kids won't like me).

With teenagers the emphasis would be primarily on understanding what needs the adolescent is seeking to meet through the sexual behavior. The negative consequences in terms of diminished self-esteem, labeling by others and risks of emotional harm, disease, pregnancy and rape are identified. Alternative methods of obtaining approval, love or power are explored and practiced. Where the child is sexually active the therapist should encourage or facilitate use of birth control and safe sex practices.

One of the greatest concerns relates to the increased risk of becoming an offender (Ryan, 1989). Many children or their parents harbor such fears and popular media reinforce this as a likely outcome. One potentially dangerous context is where a teenager is acting in a supervisory role with a younger child (e.g. babysitting). While changing a diaper, thoughts about what it might have been like from the offender's perspective may lead to actual sexual contact with the child. Another possibility is that when a child begins to have sexual feelings, fantasies may involve children instead of adults, thus beginning a conditioning process of associating arousal with children. These kinds of thoughts or fantasies will rarely be volunteered by children: therapists must be prepared to elicit them and then provide the childen with acceptable alternatives.

BETRAYAL

Sexual abuse by a teenager or adult is inherently a betrayal of a relationship. The older person has taken advantage of superior knowledge, size, resources and power to engage the child in illegal activity. The concern here is that children do not generalize this particular betrayal to an unwarranted mistrust of others. One way to contain the experience is by having the child identify adults or friends who have been reliable and trustworthy. Generating a list of adults in helping roles, such as teachers, pastors, and youth leaders, as well as police officers and counselors who are potential resources helps reduce the perception that all adults are a source of exploitation.

It is also important to explore the status of their relationships with others to insure that they are not in situations which reinforce negative beliefs. For example, the teenager who gets involved with a series of boys who take advantage is more likely to develop the idea that all men are untrustworthy. Helping them set standards for recognizing exploitative relationships and expectations for respect from others will go towards a more realistic view that some people cannot be trusted but most can.

The therapeutic relationship offers an opportunity to model a caring and responsible relationship with an adult. The therapist can assist the child by maintaining appropriate emotional and physical boundaries, challenging and correcting intrusive or inappropriate behavior and being dependable and honest. For example, many abused children are noted to engage in excessive physical contact, or to ask invasive personal questions, or to rummage in desks and drawers. The therapist can gently instruct the child about proper behavior and expectations as well as setting limits.

POWERLESSNESS

Abuse experiences can cause a child to feel powerless over external events and ultimately lead to a kind of learned helplessness. One very specific way to address this is by incorporating prevention education into the therapy process. Not only do children fear revictimization, there is substantial evidence that there is an increased risk for subsequent abuse or rape (Russell, 1986). There are numerous prevention materials currently available which can be used as part of therapy sessions with children and/or their parents.

The child's accumulated knowledge about victimization derived from their own experience can be converted into protective information. The victimized child may be better able to recognize the warning signs of potentially dangerous situations than the inexperienced child. The grooming process or the feeling that something is not right about the offender's behavior is already familiar to victims (Berliner and Conte, 1990). Reframing their experiences as enabling them to protect themselves in the future may produce an increased sense of self-efficacy as well as actually reducing the risk.

Another means of combatting a feeling of powerlessness is to reinterpret aspects of the victimization experience as evidence for the victim's powerfulness. They may be helped to understand that not telling about abuse gave them significant influence over the lives of others. The capacity to endure victimization is further evidence of personal power. The child may come to consider having been abused, surviving the experience and working toward recovery as a sign of strength.

Participation in legal actions may be used to engender a sense of empowerment. Making a report and possibly testifying allows the system to invoke its authority to sanction and control a dangerous person. Without victim cooperation the criminal justice system cannot proceed. Their actions help and protect other vulnerable children. Personal discomfort, public exposure and financial hardship for offenders come about as the result of victim's actions. A civil damage suit is another potential avenue for child victims to attain influence and obtain a sense of justice by literally making offenders pay.

STIGMATIZATION

It has often been noted that victims feel different and damaged. They express fears about others knowing and ostracizing them. They suspect that people can tell what happened. They may have negative feelings about their bodies that can lead to alienation from others or lowered self-esteem. The most specific method of addressing stigmatization is to create a community of individuals who know about the abuse and who demonstrate continued acceptance for the victim. In the past children were advised not to tell other people because of the possibility of rejection. This admonition simply reinforces the idea that sharing the abuse experience will have negative outcomes. Instead, therapists should assist children in expanding the number of people who know. An obvious initial mechanism is through involvement in group therapy where there is immediate acceptance by virtue of victimization status. The experience of group therapy allows children to share in a highly structured and supportive environment.

It is important, however, to help children identify others outside the therapy who can be told. A recommended strategy is to have the victim select people whom they believe will be likely to be supportive and rehearse the telling. Many children have discovered that by broaching the subject they encounter other children with similar experiences or receive complete support. The biggest risk is that children will gossip and that people who do not really know the victim will talk or make remarks. Anticipating and devising responses in therapy can minimize the hurt of such an eventuality.

Promoting a positive body image is an important way of enhancing self-esteem. Abused children may feel dirty or unattractive, or may attempt to appear unappealing in order to avoid sexual interest from others. Encouraging self-care and efforts to dress and look well have the effect of reducing ostracization by others. Participation in physical activities such as exercising, dance or sports increases comfort with the physical self.

Children who are part of a peer group are less likely to feel like outsiders therefore part of therapy is to teach children how to make and keep friends. The qualities and skills which are required can be identified and plans for acquiring them developed. Therapists should also encourage parents to have their children belong to an organized youth activity, such as a church youth group, Scouts, a team or a club. These experiences offer the children an opportunity to develop relationships and skills in a natural environment. Situations which arise can then become the basis for therapy discussions.

AFFECTIVE VENTILATION

Abuse experiences and the aftermath produce strong feelings for childen. One coping response is to constrict the range of emotions altogether. Another possibility is the inappropriate or displaced expression of these feelings. It is an appropriate, legitimate reaction to be angry at the violation, to be sad at the loss, to feel guilty about personal actions. A host of other emotions may be evoked as well.

An important objective of therapeutic intervention is to enable children to feel the feelings, to be provided with safe opportunities for ventilation, and to learn appropriate expression. Teaching children to recognize and allow their feelings and to associate them with events or thoughts should be a routine aspect of therapy sessions. As a regular component of therapy children can be asked to identify situations which have evoked strong feelings and describe the ways they handled them.

Anger about abuse can be expressed through a variety of modalities; writing or drawings are particularly useful. Children can write letters to offenders and others with whom they are angry: these letters may or may not actually be sent but the process of doing it can dissipate the intensity. There are physical activities such as wadding up paper and throwing it while verbalizing a feeling like 'I hate you' or 'you are a creep.' Describing what should happen to the offender or engaging in a mock sentencing often produces such drastic suggestions as electrocution or rape in prison. When a case is in the criminal justice system a letter can be written to the judge. If the offender is in treatment the child may want to have a joint session where feelings can be directly expressed.

Children frequently express anger toward others who they believe should have known and protected them. Even though these feelings may not be consistent with what the parent actually knew it is appropriate to encourage the victim to express them directly. For example, the child who believes that his mother left him with an abusing babysitter on purpose will benefit by an opportunity to say how he feels and see the parent tolerate and accept the anger as legitimate.

TREATING THE FAMILY

One objective of family intervention is to increase the capacity of the family to be supportive to the child victim. One component involves educating the parent(s) about victimization and its impact. They learn how to be helpful to their child. The most important aspect is the willingness to acknowledge and talk with the child about what happened. This means not pressing the child for details but communicating a clear message of receptiveness to hearing about the child's experience and feelings. Parents should be actively discouraged from giving children the message to forget or 'get over it.' This only conveys that the parent is not interested or available to the child.

A second important factor is providing the parent with direction in supporting and assisting the child in the family environment. This can include parental involvement in specific therapeutic strategies to make the home safer, increase supervision, provide positive reinforcement, set limits, and access resources. The extent to which the therapist can engage the parent as a partner in the therapeutic process, especially with younger children, will result in out-of-therapy benefits for the child.

It is common for parents to find themselves experiencing significant distress following disclosure of their child's abuse. They may feel they have failed to protect or have been unavailable because they were not told sooner. Their issues should be addressed separately from the child's victimization therapy so that the parent's needs do not overshadow the victim's. Where major issues for the parent arise, therapeutic outlets should be provided. For example, the parent who was abused as a child may find their own issues surfacing, or the mother may be in conflict about her own relationship with the offender. Individual or supportive group therapy may be indicated.

When there is evidence of family dysfunction independent of the abuse experience, which is always the case in incest situations and sometimes true in other families, family therapy is recommended. However, it is not always possible to engage families in a process which requires a substantial effort. There may be justification for insisting on participation in family therapy such as when reunification is contemplated. On the other hand, in every case where families are in trouble, not to provide individual intervention to victimized children unless the entire family cooperates would mean many abused children would not receive therapy. Good clinical judgement may result in a decision to treat the child's victimization experience and refer for family therapy.

Even when therapy goals are achieved with children it is very possible that at subsequent developmental stages abuse related concerns will arise. Many of the potentially affected aspects of functioning do not become relevant until adolescence and young adulthood. Forming healthy sexual relationships, developing significant personal and community support systems, being competent and effective outside the family are important development tasks which become salient at this point. This means treatment might best be characterized as a process which may require later tune-ups or refresher sessions.

References

Adams-Tucker, C. (1982). Proximate effects of sexual abuse in childhood: A report on 28 children. *American Journal of Psychiatry*, **139**, 1252–6.

American Psychiatric Association (1987). *Diagnostic and Statistical Manual of Mental Disorders* (3rd edition, revised). Washington, DC: American Psychiatric Association.

Anderson, S., Bach, C., and Griffiths, S. (1981). Psychosocial sequelae in intrafamilial victims of sexual assault and abuse. Paper presented at the Third International Conference on Child Abuse and Neglect, Amsterdam, The Netherlands.

Bagley, C., and Ramsay, R. (1985). Sexual abuse in childhood: Psychosocial outcomes and implications for social work practice. *Journal of Social Work and Human Sexuality*, **4**, 33–47.

Berliner, L., and Barbieri, M. (1984). The testimony of the child victim of sexual assault. *Journal of Social Issues*, **40**, 125–30.

Berliner, L., and Conte, J. (1990). The process of victimization: The victims' perspective, *Child Abuse and Neglect*, **14**, 29–40.

Berliner, L., and Wheeler, R. (1987). Treating the effects of sexual abuse on children. *Journal of Interpersonal Violence*, **2**, 415–34.

Blake-White, J., and Kline, C. (1985). Treating the dissociative process in adult victims of childhood incest. *Social Casework*, September, 394–402.

Briere, J., and Runtz, M. (1987). Post sexual abuse trauma: Data and implications for clinical practice. *Journal of Interpersonal Violence*, **2**, 67–79.

Briere, J., and Runtz, M. (1988). Symptomatology associated with childhood sexual victimization in a non-clinical sample. *Child Abuse and Neglect*, **12**, 51–60.

Browne, A., and Finkelhor, D. (1986). Impact of child sexual abuse: A review of the literature. *Psychological Bulletin*, **99**, 66–77.

Browning, D., and Boatman, B. (1977). Incest: Children at risk. *American Journal of Psychiatry*, **134**, 69–72.

Cohen, J., and Mannarino, A. (1988). Psychological symptoms in sexually abused girls. *Child Abuse and Neglect*, **12**, 571–8.

Conte, J., and Berliner, L. (1988). The impact of sexual abuse on children: The empirical findings. In L. Walker (ed.), *Handbook on Sexual Abuse of Children: Assessment and Treatment Issues*. New York: Springer Publishing, pp. 72–93.

Conte, J., Berliner, L., and Schuerman, J. (1986). The impact of sexual abuse on children. Final Technical Report NIMH grant No. MH37133, Department of HHS, Washington, DC.

Conte, J., and Schuerman, J. (1987). Factors associated with an increased impact of child sexual abuse. *Child Abuse and Neglect*, **11**, 201–11.

Einbender, A., and Friedrich, W. (1989). The psychological functioning and behavior of sexually abused girls. *Journal of Clinical and Consulting Psychology*, **57**, 155–7.

Everson, M., Hunter, W., Runyon, D., Edelsohn and Coulter, M. (1989). Maternal support following disclosure of incest. *American Journal of Orthopsychiatry*, **59**, 197–207.

Finkelhor, D., and Browne, A. (1985). The traumatic impact of child sexual abuse: A conceptualization. *American Journal of Orthopsychiatry*, **55**, 530–40.

Foa, E., and Kozak, M. (1986). Emotional processing of fear: Exposure to corrective information. *Psychological Bulletin*, **99**, 20–35.

Friedrich, W. (1988). Personal communication regarding the Child Sexual Behavior Inventory. William Friedrich, PhD, Department of Psychology, Mayo Clinic, Rochester, MN.

Friedrich, W., Beilke, R., and Urquiza, A. (1987). Children from sexually abusive families: A behavioral comparison. *Journal of Interpersonal Violence*, **2**, 391–402.

Friedrich, W., Urquiza, A., and Beilke, R. (1986). Behavior problems in young sexually abused children. *Journal of Pediatric Psychology*, **11**, 47–57.

Gale, S., Thompson, R., Moran, T., and Sack, W. (1988). Sexual abuse in young children: Its clinical presentation and characteristic patterns. *Child Abuse and Neglect*, **12**, 163–70.

Gelinas, D. (1983). The persisting negative effects of incest. *Psychiatry*, **46**, 312–32.

Gold, E. (1986). Long term effects of sexual victimization in childhood: An attributional approach. *Journal of Clinical and Consulting Psychology*, **54**, 471–5.

Goodwin, J. (1985). Post traumatic stress symptoms in incest victims. In R. Pynoos and S. Eth (eds), *Post Traumatic Stress Disorders in Children*. Washington, DC: American Psychiatric Press, pp. 157–86.

Gomes-Schwartz, B., Horowitz, J., and Cardarelli, A. (1990). *Child Sexual Abuse: The Initial Effects*. Beverly Hills, CA: Sage.

Haugaard, J., and Repucci, D. (1988). *The Sexual Abuse of Children*. San Francisco, CA: Jossey-Bass.

Herman, J. (1981). *Father-daughter Incest*. Cambridge, MA: Harvard University Press.

Janoff-Bulman, R. (1985). The aftermath of victimization: Rebuilding shattered assumptions. In C. Figley (ed.), *Trauma and Its Wake: Study and Treatment of Post-traumatic Stress Disorder*. New York: Brunner-Mazel, pp. 15–36.

James, B., and Nasjleti, M. (1983). *Treating Sexually Abused Children and their Families*. Palo Alto: Consulting Psychologists Press.

James, J., and Meyerding, (1977). Early sexual experience and prostitution. *American Journal of Psychiatry*, **134**, 1381–5.

Kiser, L., Ackerman, B., Brown, E., Edwards, N., McColgan, E., Pugh, R., and Pruitt, D. (1988). Post-traumatic stress disorder in young children; A reaction to purported sexual abuse. *Journal American Academy of Child and Adolescent Psychiatry*, **27**, 645–9.

McLeer, S., Deblinger, E., Atkins, M., Foa, E., and Ralphe, D. (1988). Post-traumatic stress disorder in sexually abused children. *Journal American Academy of Child and Adolescent Psychiatry*, **27**, 650–4.

Meiselman, K. (1978). *Incest: A Psychological Study of Causes and Effects with Treatment Recommendations*. San Francisco, CA: Jossey-Bass.

Mian, M., Wehrspann, W., Klajner-Diamond, H., Le Baron, D., and Winder, C. (1986). Review of 125 children 6 years of age and under who were sexually abused. *Child Abuse and Neglect*, **10**, 223–9.

Murphy, S., Kilpatrick, D., Amick-Mullen, A., Paduhovich, J., Best, C., Villeponteux, L., and Saunders, B. (1988). Current psychological functioning of childhood sexual assault survivors. *Journal of Interpersonal Violence*, **3**, 55–79.

Peters, J. (1976). Children who are victims of sexual assault and the psychology of offenders. *American Journal of Psychotherapy*, **30**, 398–421.

Porter, F., Blick, L., and Sgroi, S. (1982). Treatment of the sexually abused child. In S. Sgroi (ed.), *Handbook of Clinical Intervention in Child Sexual Abuse*. Lexington, MA: D. C. Heath, pp. 109–46.

Pynoos, R., and Eth, S. (1985). Children traumatized by witnessing acts of personal violence: Homicide, rape or suicide behavior. In S. Eth and R. Pynoos (eds), *Posttraumatic Stress Disorder in Children*. Washington DC: American Psychiatric Press, pp. 19–43.

Rachman, S. (1980). Emotional processing. *Behaviour Research & Therapy*, **18**, 51–60.

Rogers, C., and Terry, T. (1984). Clinical intervention with boy victims of sexual abuse. In I. Stuart and J. Greer (eds), *Victims of Sexual Aggression*. New York: Van Nostrand & Reinhold, pp. 1–104.

Roth, W., and Cohen, C. (1986). Approaching avoidance and coping with stress. *American Psychologist*, **41**, 813–19.

Runyon, D., Everson, M., Edelsohn, G., Hunter, W., and Coulter, M. (1988). Impact of legal intervention on sexually abused children. *Journal of Pediatrics*, **113**, 647–53.

Russell, D. (1986). *The Secret Trauma: Incest in the Lives of Girls and Women*. New York: Basic Books.

Ryan, G. (1989). Victim to victimized: Rethinking victim treatment. *Journal of Interpersonal Violence*, **4**, 325–41.

Saunders, B., McClure, S., and Murphy, S. (1987). Structure, function and symptoms in father-child sexual abuse families: A multi-level, multi-respondent empirical assessment. Grant from the Family Support Program, Department of the Navy. Crime Victims Center, Medical University of South Carolina, 1972 Ashley St, Charleston, SC.

Saunders, B., Villeponteaux, L., Kilpatrick, D., and Veronen, L. (October 1987). Child sexual assault as a risk factor in mental health. Paper presented at annual meeting of National Association of Social Workers, New Orleans, LA.

Sexual Assault Center (1986). *Impact Checklist*. Harborview Sexual Assault Centre, 325 Ninth Avenue, Seattle, WA 98104.

Silbert, M., and Pines, A. (1981). Sexual abuse as an antecedent to prostitution. *Child Abuse and Neglect*, **5**, 407–11.

Silver, R., Boon, C., and Stones, M. (1983). Search for meaning in misfortune: Making sense of incest. *Journal of Social Issues*, **39**, 81–102.

Stein, J., Golding, J., Seigel, J., Burnam, A., and Sorenson, S. (1988). Long term psychological sequelae of child sexual abuse: The Los Angeles Epidemeology Catchment Area Study. In G. Wyatt and G. Powell (eds), *Lasting Effects of Child Sexual Abuse*. Beverly Hills, CA: Sage, pp. 135–54.

Taylor, S. (1983). Adjustment to life threatening events: A theory of cognitive adaptation. *American Psychologist*, **38**, 1161–73.

Terr, L. (1985). Psychic trauma in children and adolescents. *Symposium on Child Psychiatry*, **8**, 815–35.

Tong, L., Oates, K., and McDowell, M. (1987). Personality development following sexual abuse. *Child Abuse and Neglect*, **11**, 371–83.

Tsai, M., Feldman-Summers, S., and Edgar, M. (1978). Childhood molestation: Variables related to differential impacts of psychosexual functioning in adult women. *Journal of Abnormal Psychology*, **66**, 407–29.

Wallerstein, J., and Kelly, J. (1976). The effects of parental divorce: Experiences of the child in later latency. *American Journal of Orthopsychiatry*, **46**, 256–69.

White, S., Halpin, B., Strom, G., and Santelli, G. (1988). Behavioral comparisons of young sexually abused, neglected and non-referred children. *Journal of Clinical Child Psychology*, **17**, 53–61.

Wolfe, V., Gentile, C., and Wolfe, D. (1989). The impact of sexual abuse on children: A PTSD formulation. *Behavior Therapy*, **20**, 215–28.

Wolfe, V., Wolfe, D., and LaRose, L. (1986). The Children's Impact of Traumatic Events Scale (CITES). Unpublished manuscript available from the authors at the Department of Psychology, University of Western Ontario, London, Canada, N6A 5C2.

Yates, A. (1982). Children eroticized by incest. *American Journal of Psychiatry*, **139**, 482–5.

10

Clinical Work With Adults Who Were Sexually Abused in Childhood

DEREK JEHU
Department of Psychology, University of Leicester, UK

The very sparse literature on males who were sexually abused in childhood is reviewed at the beginning of this chapter and the remaining sections, on the prevalence of such abuse, the problems associated with it in the later lives of some victims, and the interventions that have been deployed with these problems, are all restricted to women clients.

MALE VICTIMS

Male victims of sexual abuse are relatively neglected in the professional literature and the provision of programs. One reason for this oversight may be that a major source of the current attention to child sexual abuse is the women's movement, which has been especially concerned about the plight of female victims. There is also some societal reluctance to recognize abused boys as victims rather than willing participants in sexual encounters. Furthermore, boys may be held responsible for their abuse because they did not resist physically as 'a real boy would have done', or they prostituted themselves by receiving material rewards for sex, or they had identified themselves as homosexual prior to being abused (Rogers and Terry, 1984). Clearly, none of these putative reasons for blaming the victim constitutes an adequate argument for lessening or removing the responsibility from the adult offender.

Clinical Approaches to Sex Offenders and Their Victims
Edited by C. R. Hollin and K. Howells © 1991 John Wiley & Sons Ltd

Prevalence

That the sexual abuse of boys is certainly not a rarity is evident from several studies of general populations. In Lewis's (1985) sample from the entire United States, 16% of 1252 men reported having been sexually abused during childhood. A national population survey in Canada revealed that 12% of 1002 males had undergone an unwanted touching of 'a sex part' of their bodies and 10% had experienced an attempted or actual sexual assault. More than 80% of the male victims were aged under 18 years when they were first sexually abused (*Sexual offenses against children in Canada*, 1984). Among a nationally representative sample of 970 males in Britain, 8% reported that they had been sexually abused before the age of 16 (Baker and Duncan, 1985). Thus, in terms of numbers alone there is ample justification for substantial professional attention to the problems and treatment of male victims.

Offenders

Data from the USA (Finkelhor, 1984) and Canada (*Sexual offenses against children in Canada*, 1984) indicate that sexual offenders against boys are overwhelmingly male rather than female. For example, in the Canadian national population survey only 3% of offenders against boys were female. The fact that most offenders against boys are men does not imply that these men are necessarily homosexual. Many are heterosexual and some are pedophiles with no interest in adult males (Newton, 1978). There is some recent evidence, however, that the sexual abuse of boys by adult women may be more prevalent than most of the current data indicate (Condy *et al.*, 1987; Fritz *et al.*, 1981; Johnson and Shrier, 1987).

Psychosocial Adjustment

What is probably the first empirical study of psychological symptomatology among men who had been sexually abused in childhood was conducted by Briere *et al.* (1988). They administered the Trauma Symptom Checklist (TSC-33; Briere and Runtz, 1989) with an additional Anger subscale to 20 abused men and 20 non-abused men presenting in a crisis counseling program. The abused men were found to have a significantly greater incidence of previous suicide attempts and significantly higher scores on the dissociation, anxiety, anger, sleep disturbance, and hypothesized post sexual abuse trauma subscales on the TSC-33. The last mentioned subscale includes nightmares, 'flashbacks', sexual problems, fear of men, feelings that things are 'unreal', and memory problems. These findings are very consistent with a number of clinical reports (Bruckner and Johnson, 1987; Condy *et al.*, 1987; Courtois, 1988; Dimock, 1988; Janus *et al.*, 1987; Johnson and Shrier, 1987; Rogers and Terry, 1984; Sebold, 1987). Incidently, Briere *et al.* (1988) found also that there were no significant differences between abused males and abused females in their histories of attempted suicide or in the symptoms covered by the TSC-33.

Some evidence on an alleged association between child sexual abuse and later homosexuality in male college students is presented by Finkelhor (1984) who found that those who had been abused by older men were more than four times as likely to be currently engaged in homosexual activity than those who had not been so abused, and almost half of the abused males were currently involved in homosexual activity. The association between homosexual experiences in child-hood held only in respect of such experiences with much older males and not for similar experiences with peers. Several possible reasons for an association be-tween child sexual abuse and adult homosexuality have been suggested (Finkelhor, 1984; Rogers and Terry, 1984). Some boys might experience homosexual interest and curiosity at an early age which may render them vulner-able to exploitation by older predatory males. Boys who have been abused by an older man may label themselves as homosexual inappropriately because: (i) they were attractive partners to him; (ii) they did not physically resist his advances; (iii) they engaged in homosexual acts; and (iv) they experienced erotic pleasure during the encounter. If for any of these or other reasons a boy labels himself as homosexual then he may adopt this role and lifestyle, and such self-labeling may be reinforced by parents or peers who make similar misjudgements of the boy's reactions to the abuse and his sexual orientation.

Although systemic evidence is largely lacking it may be that sexually abused males are prone to engage in violent behavior in later life and in this respect they may differ from most female victims (Carmen *et al.*, 1984). Several possible reasons have been advanced for this alleged tendency towards aggressive be-havior. It may be an attempt to resolve doubts and confusion about their sexual identity through overidentification with a stereotypical machismo image which serves to reassure the male about his masculinity and to convince others of this. It may counter feelings of powerlessness that were evoked during the abuse and be a means of protection against any revictimization. It may reflect a hatred of women derived from the victim's perception of his mother as unprotective and uncaring, which may also contribute to the sexually assaultive behavior that is discussed next.

There is some evidence for an association between such behavior in adulthood and a history of sexual abuse in childhood. As discussed above, the reported prevalence rates for child sexual abuse among men in the general populations of several countries varied from 8% to 16%. The equivalent rate for incarcerated rapists was reported by Seghorn *et al.* (1987) as 23%, and by Groth (1979) as 29%. Among incarcerated child molesters the equivalent rate was reported by Groth (1979) as 32% and by Seghorn *et al.* as 57%. Such results do not of course mean that all male sexual abuse victims become sexual abusers, and at present it is not known what proportion of victims do so or what factors influence whether this happens (Finkelhor, 1986). The offender's need to dominate or control another person may be an important contributory factor to sexually assaultive behavior, perhaps especially to the sexual abuse of children. Such needs may to some extent represent an attempt by the offender to master the helplessness and hurt of his own victimization by reenacting similar encounters with himself in the position of power, although no doubt many other factors also contribute to the sexually assaultive behavior of men who were themselves abused in childhood (Finkelhor, 1984, 1986).

Treatment

To my knowledge the literature contains only one account of a treatment program for men who were sexually abused in childhood. This is a report by Bruckner and Johnson (1987) on two pilot groups for six and five men respectively, all of whom were in their twenties or early thirties. Each group was facilitated by a male and a female therapist, and comprised six sessions of two and a half hours duration at weekly intervals.

The goals of the program were to reduce isolation, improve self-esteem, and to provide an opportunity to reevaluate experiences. The major themes explored included: (i) disclosure of the abuse; (ii) the expression and management of feelings of anger arising from it; (iii) the provision of information and the modification of attitudes concerning sexuality; (iv) the participants' aggressive and sexually exploitive behavior, and their fear of sexually abusing children; and (v) the facilitation of intimacy and trust in relationships. Within the general context of the group process, these themes were addressed by means of the more specific techniques of catharsis-producing exercises, bibliotherapy, and cognitive restructuring. Progress and outcome were not systematically evaluated but the authors report increased scores on the Tennessee Self-Concept Scale for the majority of participants.

The prevalence of earlier sexual abuse experiences among adult males, the range of problems presented by some currently unknown proportion of these men, and the extreme paucity of information about the treatment of these problems in this client group, all indicate a strong need for widely available, comprehensive and adequately evaluated intervention programs. The fact that many of the problems of male victims are similar to those experienced by females (e.g. Briere et al., 1988) suggests that some of the more developed programs for females that are reviewed below may contain a useful basis for the further exploration of therapy for males, although such therapy may also require greater emphasis on issues such as confusion over sexual orientation and violent and sexually assaultive behavior among male clients.

Table 10.1   Prevalence of child sexual abuse among women in general population samples

Source	Country	Size of sample (N)	Proportion abused (%)
Baker and Duncan (1985)	UK	1049	12
Sexual offences against children (1984)	Canada	1006	15
Lewis (1985)	USA	1374	27
Russell (1983)	USA	930	54
Wyatt (1985)	USA	248	55

PREVALENCE

The prevalence of child sexual abuse among women in the general populations of several countries (Table 10.1) and in a variety of clinical groups (Table 10.2) makes it certain that most clinicians will encounter among their clients women who have had such experiences.

It is beyond the scope of this chapter to examine reasons for the wide variation in rates both within and across countries and patient groups, but differences in

Table 10.2   Prevalence of child sexual abuse among women in clinical samples

Description of sample and source	Country	Size of sample (N)	Proportion abused (%)
Psychiatric outpatients			
Herman (1986)	USA	105	13
Zverina *et al.* (1987)	Czechoslovakia	104	13
Psychiatry emergency room patients			
Briere and Zaidi (1988)			
Phase 1	USA	50	6
Phase 2	USA	50	70
Psychiatric inpatients			
Jacobson and Richardson (1987)	USA	50	22
Beck and van der Kolk (1987)	USA	26	46
Craine *et al.* (1988)	USA	105	51
Friedman and Harrison (1984)	USA	20	60
Multiple personality disorder			
Coons and Milstein (1986)	USA	17	82
Bliss (1984)	USA	70	90
Psychotherapy/counseling patients			
Sheldon (1988)	UK	115	21
Briere and Runtz (1987)	Canada	152	44
Hartman *et al.* (1987)	USA	87	70
Sexual dysfunction			
Zverina *et al.* (1987)	Czechoslovakia	102	22
Baisden and Baisden (1979)	USA	240	90
Alcoholism			
Miller *et al.* (1987)	USA	45	67
Drug abuse			
Benward and Densen-Gerbert (1975)	USA	118	44
Anorexia/bulimia			
Oppenheimer *et al.* (1985)	UK	78	51
Bulimia			
Root and Fallon (1988)	USA	172	28
Chronic pelvic pain			
Gross *et al.* (1980)	USA	25	36
Walker *et al.* (1988)	USA	25	64

definition, sampling, and methodology are probable sources (Painter, 1986; Peters *et al.*, 1986; Widom, 1988; Wyatt and Peters, 1986a,b). An interesting example of the influence of the last factor is evident in the study by Briere and Zaidi (1988) which is cited in Table 10.2. Phase 1 consisted of a retrospective review of 50 charts that were compiled when clinicians did not routinely enquire about sexual abuse, and this yielded a prevalence rate of 6%. In phase 2 with another 50 clients the clinicians were requested to ask specifically about such abuse and the prevalence rate was found to be 70%.

PROBLEMS

Although substantial prevalence rates for child sexual abuse are reported in the general populations of several countries, only a proportion of those victimized experience psychosocial problems in adulthood that appear to be related to the abuse and its surrounding circumstances. The size of the proportion affected is not clear at present, but it has been estimated as 13% in Britain (Baker and Duncan, 1985) and 25% in San Francisco (Russell, 1986).

Such adult problems might arise from the sexual abuse *per se* and/or from other surrounding circumstances such as the adverse family situations in which many victims grow up, and at present it is not possible to distinguish the respective causal contributions of these two sources (Alexander and Lupfer, 1987; Briere, 1988a; Jehu, 1988). As far as the abuse is concerned, several features are alleged to be especially traumatic and pathogenic: the list includes: (i) abuse over a lengthy period; (ii) bodily penetration, including intercourse or anal or vaginal insertion of objects; (iii) bizarre sexual activities such as 'black magic' or pseudoreligious rituals, or the involvement of animals; (iv) offenders who were substantially older than their victims; (v) more than one offender, including participation in sex rings or group sex; (vi) abuse by father figures; (vii) coercion or force by offenders; (viii) negative reactions to abuse by victims; and (ix) negative reactions by other individuals or institutions to disclosure or discovery (Briere, 1988b; Browne and Finkelhor, 1986; Courtois, 1988; Jehu, 1988; Russell, 1986; Wyatt and Mickey, 1987).

The problems exhibited by some victims in adulthood can be categorized as mood disturbances, self-damaging behavior, interpersonal problems, stress disorders, and sexual difficulties. These categories are reviewed next.

Mood Disturbances

Frequent reference is made in this chapter to a series of 51 previously sexually abused women who were treated in a clinical research program at the University of Manitoba for a range of problems that appeared to be related to their earlier victimization. Hereafter this is referred to as the U. of M. program and it is described fully elsewhere (Jehu, 1988). In a semi-structured interview during the initial assessments of these clients it was found that 92% reported low self-esteem, 88% feelings of guilt, 70% depressive episodes, and 92% at least one of these mood disturbances. At the same time there was support for these reports in the results from three questionnaires: on the Battle Self-Esteem Inventory (Battle, 1981) 88% of 27 clients scored 26 or less which is deemed to indicate intermediate, low, or very low self-esteem; among 24 different clients, 91% scored 30 or above on the Hudson Index of Self-Esteem (Hudson, 1982) which is indicative of significantly low self-esteem; and on the Beck Depression Inventory (Beck, 1978) 56% or 51 clients scored 21 or more which is indicative of clinically significant depression. Similar disturbances among previously sexually abused women are reported by many other writers (Browne and Finkelhor, 1986). In addition, significantly higher scores on the depression scale of the Trauma Symptom Checklist have been found among abused women compared to those who were not abused, among 195 outpatients in a crisis intervention center (Briere *et al.*, 1988; Briere and Runtz, 1989).

At least to some extent these mood disturbances may arise from certain self-blaming and self-denigratory beliefs associated with the earlier abuse that are commonly held by victims, as exemplified in Table 10.3. These examples are drawn from the Belief Inventory that has developed in the U. of M. program and is described fully elsewhere (Jehu, 1988).

Such distorted beliefs could be acquired through the internalization of certain messages from others that impair the victim's self-image and lead her to regard herself as a bad and worthless person. Examples of these messages include: the offender blaming the victim for seducing him; the offender conveying a sense of guilt by his concealment of the abuse and his pressure for secrecy; the anger,

Table 10.3 Examples of distorted beliefs among previously sexually abused women clients (N = 50) (Jehu, 1988)

Belief	Proportion of clients describing as partly, mostly, or absolutely true (%)
Self-blaming beliefs	
I must have been responsible for sex when I was young because it went on so long	86
I must have permitted sex to happen because I wasn't forced into it	84
I must have been seductive and provocative when I was young	62
Self-denigratory beliefs	
I am inferior to other people because I did not have normal experiences	90
Anyone who knows what happened to me sexually will not want anything to do with me	82
I am worthless and bad	78
I will never be able to lead a normal life, the damage is permanent	76

rejection, and blaming the victim that commonly follow disclosure of the abuse; the victim learning that sex between children and adults is generally regarded as socially deviant and morally reprehensible—this knowledge is likely to be accompanied by feelings of difference from others, a sense of inferiority, and grief over the losses of a normal childhood, good parent-child relationships, and positive experiences; the offender may lead the victim to feel worthless and unlovable by his remorseless exploitation of her for his own gratification, and this may be reinforced and compounded by the failure of significant others to provide effective protection; and the victim's powerlessness in the abuse situation may result in her labelling and disparaging herself as a helpless and inadequate person. Another relevant factor in the acquisition of distorted beliefs is the dependence of children on their parents. Thus, children need to preserve a good image of their parents as caring and loving people, and to feel that they have a secure relationship with them. This image and relationship would be threatened if the victim blamed her parents for the abuse, therefore she is likely to adopt the safer course of accepting responsibility herself.

Self-damaging Behavior

Closely related to mood disturbances among previously sexually abused women are various forms of self-damaging behavior including attempted suicide, self-mutilation, substance abuse, and eating disorders.

Attempted suicide

In the U. of M. program 60% of the clients had attempted suicide (Jehu, 1988), and among 152 clients at a crisis center 51% of previously sexually abused women had a history of attempted suicide compared to 34% of non-abused women (Briere and Runtz, 1987).

Several possible motives for attempting suicide are cited in the abuse literature, including relief from intolerable distress, a cry for help, a means for victims to exercise some control in their lives, self-punishment for being such a bad and unworthy person who does not deserve to live, rage reactions to the abuse being directed inwards, and a way of punishing the abuser.

Self-mutilation

Several writers have alleged an association between child sexual abuse and self-mutilation often involving cutting and burning (e.g. Courtois, 1988; de Young, 1982a; Shapiro, 1987). This behavior on a repeated basis was reported by 58% of 45 incest victims, and in all cases the mutilation started after the commencement of the abuse (de Young, 1982a). Among the suggested motives for self-mutilation among victims are: (i) the victim attempting to prevent further abuse by making her body unattractive; (ii) demonstrating control and ownership over her body; (iii) directing rage evoked by the abuse towards herself rather than the offender; (iv) inflicting pain on one part of her body to distract from the pain experienced in the abused organs; (v) a cry for help; (vi) self-punishment or atonement for her perceived responsibility for the abuse or her pleasure during it; (vii) the relief of tension or the termination of dissociative episodes; and (viii) addictive behavior used to regulate intense affect.

Substance abuse

Among 152 women clients in a crisis counseling center, 21% of those who had been sexually abused had a history of drug addiction compared to 2% of those who had not been abused: the equivalent proportions for a history of alcoholism were 27% of the abused women compared to 10% of the non-abused (Briere and Runtz, 1987). In another study, 67% of 45 alcoholic women were found to have been sexually abused in childhood compared to 28% of 40 non-alcoholic women (Miller *et al.*, 1987). In the literature it is suggested that previously sexually abused women may use alcohol or drugs to numb the pain and distress of the abuse, to escape into a better fantasy world, and to damage themselves for motives similar to those cited in the sections on attempted suicide and self-mutilation.

Eating disorders

There are several early reports of associations between child sexual abuse and anorexia, bulimia, and obesity (Calam and Slade, 1986; Courtois, 1988; Hambridge, 1988; Oppenheimer *et al.*, 1985). In the last cited source 29% of 78 anorexic and/or bulimic women patients reported that they had been sexually abused in childhood. Among the reasons advanced to explain these associations are: (i) the victim's desire to render herself sexually unattractive; (ii) aversion to her own femininity and sexuality, perhaps involving the reversal of her menarche and secondary sexual characteristics; (iii) a need to exercise control and owner-ship over her own body; and (iv) the self-punishment which is common to all the types of self-damaging behavior reviewed here.

Table 10.4 Examples of interpersonal problems among previously sexually abused women clients (Jehu, 1988)

Problem	Victims	
	(N)	(%)
Isolation (N = 51)		
Feelings of difference from others	45	88.2
Isolation/alienation from others	32	62.7
Insecurity (N = 51)		
Insecurity in relationships	42	82.4
Mistrust of others	40	78.4
Fear of men	35	68.6
Discord		
Discord with partner (N = 24)	24	100.0
Anger/hostility towards men (N = 51)	28	54.9
Inadequacy (N = 51)		
Limited social skills	42	82.4

Interpersonal Problems

All the clients in the U. of M. series complained of some difficulty in their interpersonal functioning and, as shown in Table 10.4, these problems appear to reflect the general themes of isolation, insecurity, discord, and inadequacy.

Isolation

Some additional evidence on this type of problem is provided in a study of 152 women clients at a crisis counseling center where 64% of those who had been sexually abused complained of isolation compared to 49% of the non-abused (Briere and Runtz, 1987). There are several possible reasons for the feelings of isolation, difference, alienation, and loneliness experienced by many victims. They may consider their abuse to be highly unusual and beyond the understanding of most people; for instance, the Belief Inventory item, 'I must be an extremely rare woman to have experienced sex with an older person when I was a child', was endorsed as partly, mostly, or absolutely true by 82% of the U. of M. clients. Another reason is that victims may feel stigmatized and vulnerable to rejection by others: thus, the Belief Inventory item, 'Anyone who knows what happened to me sexually will not want anything to do with me', was also endorsed as in some degree true by 82% of the same clients (Jehu, 1988). Additionally, the inability to trust others, the discordant relationships, and the lack of social skills that are reviewed in the next three sections may also contribute to the isolation of victims.

Insecurity

Further evidence on this aspect of victims' interpersonal functioning is provided by Briere and Runtz (1987) who found that among 152 women clients in a crisis counseling center fear of men was reported by 48% of those who were sexually abused in childhood compared to 15% of the non-abused.

The responses of the U. of M. clients to two items on the Belief Inventory may cast some light on the insecurity of victims: 'It is dangerous to get close to anyone because they always betray, exploit, or hurt you' was endorsed as partly, mostly, or absolutely true by 92% of these clients; and 'No man can be trusted' was similarly endorsed by 90% (Jehu, 1988).

The interpersonal insecurity felt by many victims is commonly accompanied by a strong need to retain control in relationships, rather than trusting others to share this without exploiting the victim. The insecurity and need to control experienced by victims may well stem from the betrayal and powerlessness involved in their abuse (Finkelhor, 1987). They were betrayed in that an offender whom the victim trusted and loved exploited her for his own gratification, and/or that someone else on whom she was dependent failed to protect her from distress and harm. A victim experiences powerlessness in the abuse situation in that her own wishes and sense of mastery over what happens to her are persistently overriden by the offender, and any attempts she makes to obtain support from others to counter his control over her are found to be ineffective. In the light of such breaches of trust and lack of control it is understandable that victims grow up feeling insecure and vulnerable in their relationships with others and with a strong need to retain personal control in their social interactions.

Discord

As indicated in Table 10.4, the relationships of many previously sexually abused women with their partner tend to be characterized by discord. This often arises from the exploitation of the victim by the partner, overdependence of the partner on the victim, and the dissatisfaction and distress felt by the partner concerning certain aspects of the relationship (Jehu, 1988). Such problems have been reported by other investigators. For example, Briere and Runtz (1987) found that among 152 women seeking counseling in a crisis center, 49% of those who had been sexually abused complained of battering by a partner, compared to 18% of those who had not been sexually abused. Similarly, in Russell's (1986) random sample of San Francisco women, 27% of the victims of intrafamilial sexual abuse had suffered physical violence from a husband compared to 12% of non-victims. Moreover, Russell found a significant positive correlation between the reported degree of trauma associated with the abuse and later separation or divorce. These marital disruptions occurred in 37% of those who were extremely traumatized, 31% of those who were considerably traumatized, 22% of those who reported some trauma, and 7% of those who reported no trauma.

Victims sometimes express anger, rage, or hostility directly to those who have abused or failed to protect them, as well as to people more generally. Often, however, these emotions are very threatening to victims, perhaps because they believe that: (i) they do not have any right to be angry; (ii) it is wrong to feel angry towards people one is supposed to love; (iii) anger may become overwhelming and out of control; or (iv) it may bring retaliation, harm, and disapproval from others. Victims may attempt to cope with such threats by totally suppressing or denying their angry feelings, which may adversely affect their self-esteem, psychological stability, and lifestyle.

Inadequacy

The limited social skills complained of by many of the U. of M. clients were in areas such as communication, problem-solving, assertiveness, and coping with stressful encounters (Jehu, 1988). While the isolation, insecurity, and discord that pervade the relationships of many victims often originate in their sexual abuse experiences, it is also true that limited social skills can maintain and exacerbate these problems. For example, isolation may be maintained by communication difficulties, insecurity may persist because the victim is unable to handle stress or to be assertive, and discord may continue because the necessary problem-solving skills are lacking. These and other limitations in social skills may be due at least in part to the victim's modeling of her mother's passivity and misuse with a dominant father-figure, a situation that is typical of the families of origin of many victims (Jehu, 1988). An oppressed and demoralized mother is in a poor position to transmit appropriate interpersonal expectations and skills to her daughter.

Stress Disorders

These include post-traumatic stress disorder, dissociative disorders, generalized anxiety/phobic/panic disorders, and psychosomatic disorders. Individual victims commonly suffer from problems in more than one of these diagnostic categories.

Post-traumatic stress disorder (PTSD)

The DSM III-R (American Psychiatric Association, 1987) criteria for this disorder are shown in Table 10.5, together with some ways in which previously sexually abused women commonly meet these criteria.

At present there are only very limited data available on the prevalence of PTSD among previously sexually abused women. In a sample of 126 such women, 10% were found to be suffering from PTSD currently, while it had been present at some time in the lives of 36% (Kilpatrick *et al.*, 1986). A much higher rate of 96% is reported in a series of 26 incest victims who presented with a range of problems in an outpatient family service agency (Donaldson and Gardner, 1985). Finally, the hypothesized post-sexual abuse trauma subscale on the Trauma Symptom Checklist taps symptoms that are similar to those in PTSD, and among 195 female crisis clinic outpatients those who had been abused had higher scores on this subscale compared to those who had not been abused (Briere and Runtz, 1989).

Table 10.5   Post-traumatic stress disorder: criteria and symptoms in victims

(1) The person has experienced an event that is outside the range of usual human experience and that would be markedly distressing to almost anyone, e.g. the abuse and surrounding circumstances

(2) The traumatic event is persistently reexperienced, e.g.:
    (i)   in distressing dreams related to the abuse;
    (ii)   in flashbacks to the abuse;
    (iii) by psychological distress when exposed to events that symbolize or resemble the abuse

(3) Persistent avoidance of stimuli associated with the trauma or numbing of general responsiveness, e.g.:
    (i)   avoidance of thoughts or feelings associated with the abuse;
    (ii)   avoidance of activities or situations that arouse recollections of the abuse;
    (iii) inability to recall an important aspect of the abuse (psychogenic amnesia);
    (iv)   markedly diminished interest in significant activities, e.g. sex;
    (v)   feeling of detachment or estrangement from others;
    (vi)   restricted range of affect, e.g. unable to tolerate intimacy

(4) Persistent symptoms of increased arousal, e.g.:
    (i)   difficulty in falling or staying asleep;
    (ii)   hypervigilance, e.g. in presence of men;
    (iii) physiologic activity (e.g. sweating, nausea, rapid breathing, palpitations) upon exposure to events that symbolize or resemble an aspect of the abuse

There are probably two major theoretical models that contribute to an understanding of how post-traumatic stress reactions are acquired and maintained (Jehu, 1988). One model is Mowrer's two factor learning theory with some modifications (Holmes and St. Lawrence, 1983; Keane *et al.*, 1985; Mowrer, 1960). Being sexually abused is commonly very disturbing to children and they respond to it with a variety of stress reactions. Through classical conditioning processes any features present during the abuse are liable to become cues or triggers that elicit similar reactions on future occasions. By means of avoidance learning, certain ways of avoiding such as stressful stimuli are then acquired: these avoidance reactions are maintained because they enable victims to evade these stimuli and so reduce the distress evoked by them.

A second, cognitive model is derived from Beck and Emery (1985). This is based on the premise that stress reactions are precipitated by distorted thoughts and images that signal some kind of threat: for example, the Belief Inventory items, 'It is dangerous to get close to anyone, because they always betray, exploit, or hurt you'; and, 'No man can be trusted'. Furthermore, victims may be vulnerable to such thoughts and images because they hold certain dysfunctional assumptions or rules according to which they interpret their experiences and regulate their behavior. Thus, the distorted beliefs cited immediately above might arise from the dysfunctional assumption which is very common among victims that they must always retain control over themselves and others if they are to be safe from harm. In summary, in this model it is proposed that post-traumatic stress reactions are mediated by some disturbance in the victim's cognitive processes that precipitates these reactions or renders the victim prone to them. A very similar view is expounded by Janoff-Bulman (1985) who attributes post-traumatic stress following many kinds of victimization to the shattering of certain basic assumptions victims hold about themselves and their world, including the belief in personal invulnerability, the perception of the world as meaningful, and a positive self-concept.

Dissociative disorders

Psychogenic amnesia, depersonalization, and multiple personality disorder are reported among previously sexually abused women (Jehu, 1988). In a series of 53 such women in group therapy, 64% did not have full recall of the abuse, and 28% reported severe memory deficits (Herman and Schatzow, 1987). Some victims either cannot recall or they deny the whole event, but more commonly they are not aware of some particularly disturbing aspects of the abuse such as that it included oral sex as well as fondling, or that the victim experienced sexual pleasure (Jehu, 1988). Such amnesia or denial is generally regarded as a means of escaping from or avoiding stressful material.

Depersonalization is 'manifested by a feeling of detachment from and being an outside observer of one's own mental process or body, or of feeling like an automaton or as if in a dream' (American Psychiatric Association, 1987, p. 275). It is commonly accompanied by derealization involving feelings of unreality or altered perceptions of oneself and the external world. In a series of 152 women clients in a crisis counseling center, 42% of those who had been sexually abused reported 'spacing out' compared to 22% of the non-abused clients. The equivalent proportions for derealization were 33% compared to 11%, and for out of body experiences 21% compared to 8% (Briere and Runtz, 1987). Because children often cannot escape physically from sexual abuse, they commonly detach themselves from the experience through depersonalization, and this means of coping with stress tends to persist into adulthood (Jehu, 1988).

Perhaps the most extreme form of dissociation is multiple personality disorder (MPD). In the U. of M. series only 1 (2%) of 51 clients met the DSM III-R criteria for this disorder, and I am unaware of any other published prevalence rate for previously sexually abused women. There is, however, considerable evidence that sexual and physical abuse are very common in the histories of patients exhibiting multiple personalities (Jehu, 1988). For instance, Coons and Milstein (1984) report that among 20 such patients, 75% had been sexually abused, 59% physically abused, and 85% abused in at least one of these ways. In a later paper (1986) the same authors report that these childhood experiences were significantly more common among MPD patients than in a matched non-dissociative order control group. Several writers have suggested that children develop different personalities in order to cope with specific aspects of the abuse situation such as loving the offender while at the same time hating his abusive acts, or experiencing feelings of disgust accompanied by sexual pleasure. Such incompatible experiences may be coped with by splitting them on to separate personalities (Bowman et al., 1985; Kluft, 1987; Spiegel, 1985).

Generalized anxiety/phobic/panic disorders

The prevalence rate for each of these disorders is not distinguishable in the sexual abuse literature but there are indications of their frequent occurrence among victims. For instance, among 195 female crisis clinic outpatients, those who had been sexually abused in childhood obtained higher scores on the anxiety scale of the Trauma Symptom Checklist than those who had not been abused (Briere and Runtz, 1989). More specifically, among 152 female crisis counseling center clients, anxiety attacks were reported by 54% of the sexually abused clients compared to 28% of the non-abused, and the equivalent percentages for chronic muscle tension were 66% and 44% (Briere and Runtz, 1987).

Psychosomatic disorders

Some of these disorders in victims appear to be related to the sexual acts and organs involved in the abuse. For example, in one study, among 25 women with chronic pelvic pain, 64% had been sexually abused in childhood compared to 23% of a comparison group of women with other gynecological problems (Harrop-Griffiths et al., 1988; Walker et al., 1988). In another study it was found that 82% of 28 previously sexually abused women had sought help for reproductive problems compared to 42% of non-abused women (Cunningham et al., 1988). In the latter study a range of medical complaints in addition to pelvic pain was found also to occur significantly more frequently among abused compared to non-abused women. These complaints included headache (see also Domino and Haber, 1987), stomach pain, hypoglycemia, spastic colitis, heart palpitations, and asthma.

Several posible explanations have been advanced for the alleged association between child sexual abuse and psychosomatic disorders: these disorders may reflect the physiological components of traumatic anxiety; they may be a means of avoiding stressful interpersonal or sexual encounters; they may arise from the victim's disregard and neglect of her own bodily needs, as she was taught to do during the abuse; they may be an expression of self-hatred directed at the body; or psychological distress may be converted into physical complaints, perhaps as a substitute for emotional pain that is too overwhelming for the victim to acknowledge.

Sexual Difficulties

Among 152 female clients at a crisis counseling center, sexual problems were reported by 45% of those who had been sexually abused compared to 15% of the non-abused (Briere and Runtz, 1987). The type of problem is not specified but elsewhere in the literature certain areas of difficulty are identified. These are reviewed below in the general categories of sexual dysfunction, sexual orientation, rape, prostitution, and compulsive sexuality.

Sexual dysfunction

During initial assessment, 78% of the clients in the U. of M. series complained of at least one of the sexual dysfunctions shown in Table 10.6, with negative reactions to sex such as phobias, aversions, and dissatisfaction being the most common problems. A further eight victims were ascertained to be sexually dysfunctional during therapy, making a total prevalence rate of 94% (Jehu, 1988).

The mood disturbances, self-damaging behavior, interpersonal problems, and stress disorders reviewed above may all contribute to sexual dysfunction among previously sexually abused women. Thus, guilt, low self-esteem, and depression

Table 10.6 Previously sexually abused women clients presenting with sexual dysfunctions at initial assessment (N = 51; Jehu, 1988)

Dysfunction	Victims	
	(N)	(%)
Phobia/aversion	30	58.8
Dissatisfaction	30	58.8
Impaired motivation	29	56.9
Impaired arousal	25	49.0
Impaired orgasm	23	45.1
Dyspareunia	14	27.4
Vaginismus	4	7.8
At least one of these dysfunctions	40	78.4

are each likely to affect sexual functioning in adverse ways (Jehu, 1988). Both substance abuse (e.g. Klassen and Wilsnack, 1986; Pinhas, 1987) and eating disorders (e.g. Crisp, 1978; McCrea and Yaffe, 1981) have been shown to be associated with sexual dysfunction. This is also very likely to accompany discord and insecurity in relationships (Jehu, 1988). Finally, sexual functioning may be impaired by stress reactions to sex-related stimuli, including aversion, anxiety, avoidance, flashbacks, and dissociation (Jehu, 1988).

Sexual orientation

The inclusion of this topic does not imply that lesbian relationships are necessarily a problem, they may be just as loving and satisfying as heterosexual relationships, but some previously sexually abused women are confused about their sexual orientation or this appears to have been distorted by their abuse experiences.

The evidence available on the prevalence of homosexuality among victims is inconsistent and indeed contradictory so that it is not possible to reach any reasonable conclusion on whether victims are more likely than non-victims to have a predominantly homosexual orientation in adulthood. Fromuth (1986) did find a significant positive correlation between a history of sexual abuse and having a homosexual experience after the age of 12 years, in her college student sample. In a questionnaire study of 225 homosexual and 223 heterosexual women conducted by Gundlach (1977) there were 18 subjects who had been molested or raped by a male *stranger* when the victim was aged 15 or younger. Of these victims, 55% were homosexual in adulthood. There were also 17 women who had been molested or rapied by a male *relative or close friend* when the victim was aged 15 or under, and in most cases the victimization was strongly coercive. Of these victims, 94% were homosexual in adulthood. Much lower rates are reported by several other investigators. For example, in Meiselman's (1978) psychotherapy patient sample, 30% of 23 victims of father-daughter incest had either adopted a gay life style or they reported significant homosexual experiences or feelings. The equivalent proportion for the control subjects is not cited, but homosexuality is said to be rare amongst them. Among 40 father-daughter incest victims studied by Herman (1981) only 5% were homosexual and 7% bisexual. Thus, no firm conclusions can be drawn on the prevalence of homosexuality among previously sexually abused women.

Some victims express confusion about their sexual orientation although they are not engaging in overt lesbian activity (Jehu, 1988). Such doubts are not surprising in view of the difficulties, and particularly the aversion and dissatisfaction, that victims often experience in their sexual relationships with men. Both women and men who are sexually dysfunctional quite commonly wonder whether this is because they are homosexual and this concern is not restricted to those who have been sexually abused.

Some victims who are involved in lesbian relationships have a basic sexual preference for female partners which is relatively unaffected by their earlier sexual abuse. Other such victims may be basically heterosexual but may choose female partners for several possible reasons. Meiselman (1978) among others have suggested that many homosexually oriented victims appear to be reacting to very negative heterosexual experiences, often involving phobic reactions to sexual activity and frequently culminating in a strong hatred of men. Quite commonly, the homosexual orientation is not manifested until after many years of heterosexual experience. Another suggestion by Meiselman is that some victims may be influenced towards a lesbian identity because difficulties in relationships with their mothers may have led to an unwillingness to assume a traditional female role in life. Similarly, Kaufman *et al.* (1954) speculate that the homosexuality of some victims might be motivated by their wish to be loved by an older woman to make up for the rejection they had experienced from their own mothers.

Rape

An increased vulnerability to rape and sexual assault in adulthood among previously sexually abused women is reported by several investigators. Among 195 crisis counseling center clients, 52% of those who had been sexually abused were sexually assaulted later, compared to 14% of the non-abused (Runtz and Briere, 1988). In a random sample drawn from the San Francisco population, Russell (1986) found that 65% of women who experienced serious incestuous abuse prior to age 14, and 61% of women who had suffered severe extrafamilial sexual abuse before that age, were victimized by rape or attempted rape after that age. The corresponding proportion for women who were never sexually abused before age 14 was 35%. Similarly, in her college student sample, Fromuth (1986) found a significant positive correlation between having been sexually abused before age 13 and having non-consensual sexual experiences involving force or threat after age 12 years.

The increased risk of rape for victims of child sexual abuse may be due to: (i) low self-esteem, so that they do not feel that they have any right to deny or resist unwanted sexual demands; (ii) unassertiveness, so that they lack the capacity to cope effectively with such demands; (iii) poor social judgement, so that they find it difficult to distinguish between safe and risky situations; and (iv) the danger of being on the streets after running away from home because of the abuse (McCormack *et al.*, 1986).

Prostitution

Several investigators have reported high rates of sexual abuse among prostitutes (James and Meyerding, 1977; Silbert, 1984; Vitaliano *et al.*, 1981). For example, among 200 street prostitutes 60% had been sexually abused prior to age 16 by an average of two offenders each over an average period of 20 months. The mean age at commencement of the abuse was 10 years, for 67% of victims the offender was a father figure, and in 82% of cases some sort of force was used; 70% of the women reported that the sexual exploitation affected their entry into prostitution (Silbert and Pines, 1981, 1983).

It is possible that sexual abuse lessens a victim's resistance to viewing herself as a saleable commodity. For example, the prostitutes interviewed in the Silbert and Pines study made remarks such as 'My brother could do it; why not somebody else? Might as well make them pay for it.' and 'My father bought me, so who cares who else does' (1981, p. 410). Making a customer pay for specified sexual acts may also be a way for the victim to exercise some control in sexual situations which she lacked during the abuse. In addition, the factors of running away, low self-esteem, and unassertiveness, that were mentioned above as possible facilitators of rape, may also contribute to the involvement of victims in prostitution.

Compulsive sexuality

This term refers to the related problems of 'promiscuity' and the oversexualization of relationships which have been noted among victims of sexual abuse by several writers (e.g. de Young, 1982b; Gordy, 1983; Herman, 1981; Meiselman, 1978). In this context promiscuity means engagement in a series of transient, casual, and superficial relationships that the victim seems to pursue compulsively and from a sense of obligation rather than desire. Many victims appear to have a promiscuous stage at some time in their lives and 60% of those in the U. of M. series reported having been promiscuous in the past, although this continued to the time of initial assessment for only 17% of these victims (Jehu, 1988). Fromuth (1986) has added a note of caution to findings such as these. In her college student sample she found that previously sexually abused women were more likely to describe themselves as promiscuous than non-abused women, although the two groups did not differ in the actual number of sexual partners. Thus, the reported promiscuity of victims may to some extent reflect their negative self-labeling rather than their actual behavior.

Oversexualization implies that a relationship must include a sexual component however inappropriate it may be, or that the relationship is perceived to have such a component when none exists. Among the U. of M. victims 51% reported that they had oversexualized their relationships with men in the past, while only 29% were doing so at initial assessment. On the Belief Inventory the following items were endorsed as partly, mostly or absolutely true by the proportions of victims shown: (i) 'No man could care for me without a sexual relationship' by 86%; (ii) 'I've already been used so it doesn't matter if other men use me' by 54%; and (iii) 'I don't have the right to deny my body to any man who demands it' by 48% (Jehu, 1988).

There are several possible reasons for the compulsive sexuality reported among previously sexually abused women. They may not be able to distinguish between sex and affection because of the confusion of parental love and sexuality in childhood. They may have a compulsive need for sex as proof of being loved and of being an adequate woman. Their sexual attractiveness and favors may be a means of exercising power over men. They may feel that they do not have any right to deny sex to a man. Finally, compulsive sexuality can serve a self-damaging function for victims in that it may be accompanied by sexually transmitted disease, unwanted pregnancy, abortion, and rape or sexual assault in adulthood.

INTERVENTIONS

The current literature on therapy with previously sexually abused women largely comprises a small number of contributions dealing with limited aspects of their wide-ranging problems and it is only very recently that more extensive coverage has become available (e.g. Courtois, 1988; Jehu, 1988). More particularly, very few of the interventions in the literature include any systematic evaluation of the progress and outcome of the clients. When such evaluative data are provided they are included in the following review, but in order to avoid tedious repetition no mention is made of their absence in other studies of a purely descriptive nature.

The interventions have usually been implemented in an individual, couple, or group format. They can be conceptualized as comprising certain general therapeutic processes, together with some more specific procedures used with particular types of problem. The general processes are outlined next, followed by a review of the treatment of some particular problems, and then by a discussion of the provision of therapy in groups.

General Therapeutic Processes (Courtois, 1988; Jehu, 1988)

At the core of these processes is a *relationship* between client and therapist that is characterized by mutual liking, respect, and trust. *Inter alia*, this is likely to decrease a client's defensiveness and to increase her openness to influence from the therapist toward the achievement of the client's chosen goals. Additionally, her maladaptive interpersonal relationship patterns may be replicated in her interactions with the therapist, whose responses can constitute new learning experiences for the client through which she may acquire more appropriate ways of relating to others. The influence of abuse experiences on the interactions between client and therapist is conceptualized and reviewed as transference and countertransference issues by Courtois (1988). At present there is no empirical evidence available on the influence of the gender of the therapist on the nature of the relationship with client or on the progress and outcome of treatment, but several potential advantages and disadvantages of male and female therapists have been hypothesized (Courtois, 1988; Jehu, 1988).

A second general therapeutic process is the promotion of a positive *prognostic expectancy*. Many previously sexually abused women have feelings of hopelessness when they present for therapy and it is important to communicate to them that while the effects of abuse can be long-term and very distressing, this does not mean necessarily that they are irremediable and permanent. Clients are assured that they can reasonably expect to receive effective help, but at the same time they are warned that treatment is unlikely to follow a completely smooth course or to produce an extremely rapid improvement.

On the bases of a therapeutic relationship and the prospect of effective help clients are likely to enter the painful process of *exploring* and *disclosing* their abuse experiences and associated problems, as well as *expressing* their often intense emotional reactions to these stresses. More specifically, for some victims this is the first time that they have shared the secret of the abuse with anyone, while the attempted revelations of other victims have been met with disbelief, blame, or anger. Consequently, it can be an enormous relief for a client to unburden herself of the secret to a therapist who accepts the truth of the disclosure and responds to it in positive ways.

The client's disclosure of her abuse and associated problems is often accompanied by intense feelings of shame, and perhaps by fear that the therapist will not be willing or able to deal with these issues. It is therefore very important that she is *accepted* and *supported*. Thus, a therapist who is respectful, non-judgemental, and immune to shock or embarrassment offers a non-threatening, safe, and trusting relationship in which the client is free to explore her experiences without restraint or restriction, and that enhances her self-esteem. Associated with such acceptance is the therapist's genuine concern for the client's welfare and a deep commitment to helping her. This can be very supportive to the client, who now has a source of aid and is no longer alone in attempting to cope with her problems. She is, moreover, seeing a therapist who views these problems as not unusual and as potentially amenable to treatment.

The quality of a therapeutic relationship and the outcome of treatment are both strongly influenced by the level of *empathic understanding* exhibited by the therapist and perceived by the client. Such understanding involves the ability to comprehend both the experiences and the feelings of a client, together with their meaning and significance for her. It is essential also that this comprehension is communicated to the client so that she feels deeply understood by the therapist.

A closely related process is the formulation of a *causal explanation* for the client's problems that is shared and negotiated with her. It is based upon an empathic understanding of the individual client, together with the hypotheses and theoretical conceptualizations advanced as possible reasons for the problems reviewed in the previous section. Clients often experience difficulties that seem inexplicable, strange, and bizarre; for example, flashbacks and dissociative reactions. It can be very reassuring for them to have a plausible explanation for such difficulties, and the fact that the therapist appears to understand their problems also tends to reduce anxiety and to engender hope for successful treatment. Finally, a causal explanation for the problems which is shared by client and therapist constitutes a rationale for the more specific procedures to be used in the treatment of particular problems, which are discussed next.

Specific Treatment of Mood Disturbances

In the previous discussion of guilt, low self-esteem, and depression as common problems among victims, it was hypothesized that their distorted beliefs concerning the abuse are an important source of these mood disturbances. It follows that restructuring, reframing, or reattributing the pathogenic beliefs is likely to be accompanied by an alleviation of the disturbances (Courtois, 1988; Donaldson and Gardner, 1985; Jehu, 1988; Reiker and Carmen, 1986).

In the U. of M. program the clients were helped to become aware of their self-blaming and self-denigratory beliefs, to recognize any distortions contained

Table 10.7   Illustration of distorted beliefs and exploring alternatives

Distorted beliefs
I must have been responsible for sex when I was a child because I wasn't forced into it and it went on so long

Alternative beliefs
In a sense I was forced into it and could not stop it because: (i) the offender kept persuading me by saying 'What's the matter, don't you want to help an old man?' I had been indoctrinated with the belief that nice little girls were supposed to help and please people, especially older people, and did not want to hurt him by not continuing to participate; (ii) I desperately wanted attention from someone outside my family; (iii) I could not refuse to take his lunch out to the field where the abuse often happened, because I would have to explain to his wife why I was refusing and I did not want to upset her; (iv) I feared that if I told my mother she would do nothing to protect me; (v) I could not consider telling my father because I hated him, I feared that he would blame me or punish me or not do anything

within them, and to explore and substitute more accurate alternative beliefs by means of information provision, logical analysis, decatastrophizing, distancing, reattribution, and assigned activities. This cognitive restructuring was accompanied by clinically and statistically significant improvements in the belief systems and mood states of a series of 36 clients (Jehu, 1988).

Both the distorted beliefs and the more accurate alternatives are individualized for each victim as illustrated in Table 10.7, but there are some common themes that are often applicable in the exploration of alternative beliefs (Jehu, 1988). For instance, the fact that they complied with the sexual demands of the offender connotes self-blame to many victims. An alternative theme is that the power differential between a child and an adult makes it very difficult indeed for a child to say 'no' to sexual advances by an adult. Furthermore, it is customary for children to be taught to obey their elders, who thereby acquire psychological authority over victims, and this is particularly relevant if the offender is a father figure or close relative.

Specific Treatment of Self-damaging Behavior

I am not aware of any reports on the treatment of such behavior specifically among previously sexually abused women, although some useful pointers for clinicians are offered by Courtois (1988) and the alleviation of mood disturbances such as self-hatred and depression may also reduce propensities for self-damage.

Specific Treatment of Interpersonal Problems

Most writers appear to rely exclusively on the general therapeutic processes discussed above to resolve these problems among victims, although Gestalt techniques are also mentioned (Courtois, 1988; Joy, 1987). There can be little doubt about the importance of these processes: for example, acceptance and support can help to alleviate feelings of rejection and isolation, and a victim's profound mistrust of other people may be replicated in her relationship with a therapist who does not dominate, exploit, or neglect her and thereby increases her capacity to trust others. In the U. of M. program these processes were supplemented by a range of more specific procedures (Jehu, 1988).

Distorted beliefs such as 'It is dangerous to get close to anyone because they always betray, exploit, or hurt you' might be contributing to a victim's interpersonal problems, in which case *cognitive restructuring* procedures were deployed. *Communication training* was provided to improve any deficiencies in listening and speaking skills or in the non-verbal components of effective communication. To enhance *problem solving*, conflict resolution, or decision making capacities, clients were trained to define the problem, to generate possible solutions, to evaluate these solutions, and finally to negotiate an agreed solution. When certain interpersonal situations evoked stress reactions such as anxiety or avoidance then *stress management* procedures were employed, as discussed below. *Anger control* is a particular application of stress management that is used to prevent inappropriate anger responses, to regulate the level of anger, and to manage experiences that may provoke anger. Clients who were inappropriately passive or aggressive in their relationships were given *assertiveness training*. These procedures were implemented either singly or more usually in appropriate combinations according to the individual needs of particular clients. Single subject designs were used to evaluate progress and outcome, but further replication and development are required.

Specific Treatment of Stress Disorders

Two major approaches have been proposed for the treatment of these disorders among victims of child sexual abuse: stress response therapy, which is broadly psychodynamically oriented, and stress management, involving cognitive-behavioral procedures. Additionally, there are case reports with single subject design evaluations on the use of implosive techniques (Rychtarik *et al.*, 1984), and of systematic desensitization with negative practice (Wolff, 1977).

Stress response therapy is based on Horowitz's (1986) model of the stress response syndrome, and its use with victims of sexual abuse is proposed by Courtois (1988) and Donaldson and Gardner (1985). Ideally, stressful events should be correctly perceived, given clear meaning, responded to appropriately, and incorporated into the individual's memories, attitudes, and belief systems. If this psychological processing does not take place then the thoughts, feelings, and memories associated with the events will always push toward release and be experienced as intrusive-repetitious thoughts and images (e.g. flashbacks). This is so distressing that individuals deny and numb their emotional reactions. Typically, the intrusive-repetitious and denial-numbing phases alternate in a cyclical manner. The aim of stress response therapy is to break this cycle by providing a safe environment in which the client can experience her emotional responses without denial or numbing. These defences are reduced by means of abreactive-cathartic techniques which facilitate the recall of the traumatic events, repetition of the accompanying emotional responses, and recapitulation of the individual's understanding of the events when they occurred. To alleviate the intensity of the intrusive-repetitious phase symptoms and to strengthen control over them a wide range of interventions is advocated, including rest, containment, and supportive techniques. Throughout therapy a balance is maintained between emotional expression and defensive denial so that the client is not overwhelmed by the recalled material (Cole and Barney, 1987).

A stress management approach derived from Beck and Emery (1985) and Meichenbaum (1985), and comprising coping skills training and cognitive restructuring was used in the U. of M. program (Jehu, 1988). Training in skills to help clients to cope with stresses included breath control and deep muscle relaxation, thought and image stopping, guided self-dialogue, imagery rehearsal, role-playing, and *in vivo* exposure to stressful situations. Cognitive restructuring was used to correct any distorted beliefs or dysfunctional assumptions that contributed to the stresses experienced by victims; for example, 'No man can be trusted'; or 'To be safe, I must be in absolute control of myself and other people' (see also Janoff-Bulman, 1985; Scurfield, 1985). This stress management approach was most usually used with stress reactions evoked in social or sexual situations, and progress and outcome were evaluated by means of single subject designs. More extensive application and evaluation remain to be undertaken.

Specific Treatment of Sexual Difficulties

Most discussion of the treatment of these difficulties among previously sexually abused women has focused upon sexual dysfunction and is exploratory and descriptive in nature (Becker and Skinner, 1984; Maltz and Holman, 1987; McCarthy, 1986; McGuire and Wagner, 1978; Nadelson, 1982; Sprei and Courtois, 1988).

As outlined above, sexual dysfunctions may arise from mood disturbances, substance abuse or eating disorders, relationship problems, and stress reactions to sex-related stimuli. Consequently, in the U. of M. program sexual dysfunctions were treated by addressing any of these etiological factors operating in the client concerned by means of the interventions described above. For example, if she was depressed then cognitive restructuring was implemented, if her relationship with her partner was discordant then *inter alia* communication training and problem solving were provided for the couple, and if sex was stressful for her then stress management procedures were employed. The effectiveness of these interventions in improving the clients' sexual functioning and satisfaction was evaluated by single subject designs which require further replication (Jehu, 1988).

Group Treatment

Many reported interventions with previously sexually abused women have been implemented in group formats (Bergart, 1986; Blake-White and Kline, 1985;

Table 10.8   Potential therapeutic benefits of group treatment

(1) Feelings of difference, alienation, isolation, loneliness, and boredom are likely to be mitigated

(2) In the understanding and supportive environment of the group the members can extend their sharing of the abuse experience and related problems beyond their individual therapist or other confidants

(3) Through the shared experiences of other participants a victim may gain a better understanding of her own reactions to the abuse and of its subsequent consequences

(4) Effective methods of coping with problems may be disseminated between members

(5) There is an opportunity to develop trust in other participants as a possible basis for trusting people on a wider basis

(6) Respect for other women may be enhanced

(7) Ability to help others in the group may increase self-respect and self-confidence in social relationships

(8) The group may provide a springboard for social action concerning, e.g. public education about sexual abuse or the provision of therapeutic resources for victims

Cole and Barney, 1987; Deighton and McPeek, 1985; Faria and Belohlavek, 1984; Fowler *et al.*, 1983; Goodman and Nowak-Schibelli, 1985; Gordy, 1983; Herman and Schatzow, 1984; Jehu, 1988; Leehan and Wilson, 1985; McCallum, 1987; Schwab, 1986; Tsai and Wagner, 1978; Van Buskirk and Cole, 1983). Some potential therapeutic benefits of such group treatment are listed in Table 10.8.

This form of treatment might be provided either as an alternative or as an adjunct to individual or couple therapy. Some victims are unsuitable or unwilling to participate in a group, and there may not be enough victims available to constitute a group at a particular point in time, therefore it is important to keep open the options of individual or couple therapy for those who need or prefer them. There is also the question of whether some victims can obtain sufficient attention and support to meet their individual needs in a group context, which has led some clinicians to advocate an adjunctive role for group treatment (e.g. Cole and Barney, 1987; Herman and Schatzow, 1984). On the other hand, to the extent that group treatment can replace individual or couple therapy, then this may conserve scarce professional resources. For reasons of space only professionally led groups are reviewed here, although there are many self-help groups conducted by and for victims (e.g. Giaretto, 1982; Wachtel and Lawton-Speert, 1983) and their merits and limitations are discussed elsewhere (Courtois, 1988; Herman, 1981).

Themes/goals

The themes and goals shown in Table 10.9 are typical of the majority of group interventions. Less frequent are groups focused upon more specific problems such as lack of assertiveness (Jehu, 1988; Schwab, 1986) or sexual dysfunction (McCarthy, 1986; Tsai and Wagner, 1978).

Table 10.9   Typical themes/goals for groups (e.g. McCallum, 1987)

---

(1) Building self-esteem by: (i) receiving assurances from group on personal value; (ii) focusing on strengths; (iii) becoming a survivor; (iv) examining automatic negative thoughts that lower self-esteem; and (v) improving body image

(2) Alleviating guilt by: (i) returning responsibility for the abuse to the adult offenders; (ii) granting absolution to self and other group members; and (iii) understanding human sexual response and the psychological, social, and sexual development of the child

(3) Building trust by: (i) making the group a safe place for disclosure; and (ii) learning to take risks and deal with consequences

(4) Dealing with anger by: (i) identifying source and direction of anger; (ii) validation of right to anger; (iii) acceptance and support of intense feelings; (iv) externalizing rather than interalizing anger; and (v) learning constructive methods of expressing anger

(5) Changing interpersonal relationships by: (i) reducing feelings of isolation and alienation; (ii) learning appropriate ways to show affection; (iii) identifying old patterns of fleeing from relationships; and (iv) networking with support systems

(6) Taking control by: (i) changing self-destructive, self-defeating behaviour; (ii) letting go of learned helplessness; (iii) gaining control through assertive behaviour; and (iv developing coping strategies

---

Clients

Many clinicians suggest 6 to 8 members as the ideal size for a group, and there is widespread recognition that this form of treatment is contraindicated for certain victims on grounds which include: (i) acute psychosis; (ii) current suicidal behavior; (iii) recent substance abuse; (iv) paranoid, sociopathic, narcissistic, or borderline personality; (v) current personal crisis (e.g. marital, medical, or occupational); (vi) strong denial of abuse and reactions; (vii) self-disclosure excessively stressful; (viii) lack of motivation to change; (ix) ambivalence or resistance toward joining group; (x) unsuitability for participation in a balanced and reasonably homogeneous group in terms of age, race, socio-economic class, sexual orientation, nature of sexual abuse, and previous or concurrent therapy.

Therapists

Empirical evidence is lacking but useful *a priori* discussions are provided by Courtois (1988) on the desirable features and roles of therapists, the number of therapists (co-leadership being widely advocated), the gender of the therapist(s), females being most commonly employed, and if the client is receiving both group and individual therapy whether this should be with the same or different therapists, the former being considered more advantageous.

Despite the general preference for female therapists some clinicians do advocate male–female co-therapy teams (e.g. Deighton and McPeek, 1985; Fowler *et al.*, 1983; Jehu, 1988; Schwab, 1986; Tsai and Wagner, 1978). For instance, in Schwab's assertiveness training group the presence of a male co-therapist was designed to provide the clients with an opportunity to relate more positively to a man within a protective and supportive environment and to assist them in resolving some of the problems such as oversexualization as well as fear and mistrust of men which are commonly encountered in their heterosocial relations. Among these 5 clients, 4 subsequently rated the presence of a male therapist as *very helpful* and 1 as *slightly helpful*. In their general comments they commonly reported that the availability of a male opinion and perspective was extremely useful, and that a male therapist assisted them in differentiating trustworthy males from those who are abusive and exploitive (Jehu, 1988; Schwab, 1986).

Timing

Most groups reported in the literature have been time-limited, and several possible merits of this format are reviewed by Courtois (1988). The number of sessions ranges from 4 to 20, with 10 to 20 being recommended by many clinicians.

Interventions

Ground rules are very commonly established on issues such as confidentiality, attendance, expression of feelings, group process, contact outside sessions, and withdrawal from the group (Cole and Barney, 1987; Courtois, 1988). Many clinicians appear to rely on the general therapeutic processes reviewed above to achieve change in group members, although in this format these members as well as the therapist(s) are sources of corrective relationships, positive prognostic expectancies, acceptance, support, and understanding for each other (e.g. Blake-White and Kline, 1985; Goodman and Nowak-Scibelli, 1985; Gordy, 1983; Herman and Schatzow, 1984). Other clinicians supplement these general processes with a selection of more specific procedures from the very wide range mentioned in the literature (e.g. Bergart, 1986; Cole and Barney, 1987; Courtois, 1988; Jehu, 1988). These procedures may be implemented during group sessions or as homework assignments. They include: (i) information provision by means of bibliotherapy and audio-visual material; (ii) expressive methods such as gestalt techniques, psychodrama, creative arts, guided imagery, journal keeping, letter writing, and compiling an autobiography; (iii) cognitive restructuring; (iv) assertiveness training; (v) anger control; and (vi) stress management procedures.

Evaluation

Evidence on the outcome of group treatment with previously sexually abused women is currently very meager and inadequate. Anecdotal reports by therapists indicate positive feedback from participants, decreases in suicidal ideation, suicide attempts, and depressive episodes, and increased contact and improved relationships with family of origin (Deighton and McPeek, 1985; Goodman and Nowak-Scibelli, 1985). Several clinicians have asked clients to complete evaluation questionnaires about their experiences in and reactions to group treatment. This was considered to have been very helpful by almost all participants, in particular because it enabled them to meet other women who had been sexually abused in childhood. Also mentioned are lessening of guilt and isolation, and improvement in self-esteem, self-protection, and relationships with partners (Herman and Schatzow, 1984; Jehu, 1988; McCallum, 1987; Schwab, 1986; Tsai and Wagner, 1978).

More systematic studies of outcome using standardized and individualized measures in single subject and one-group pre-test and post-test designs have been conducted by McCallum (1987) and by Schwab (1986), although in each case with only five subjects. McCallum found some degree of improvement in the clients' belief systems concerning the abuse, levels of depression, and self-esteem. Schwab's group focused upon assertiveness training and it was accompanied by the facilitation of assertive responding, increased understanding and acceptance of personal rights, and the mitigation of difficulties in heterosocial relationships.

CONCLUSION

With few exceptions, the current knowledge base for the provision of therapy to previously sexually abused men and women contains little information on feasible, acceptable, and effective treatment packages for the wide range of problems presenting in these client groups. The effectiveness of such interventions needs to be demonstrated in well designed and rigorous studies of the progress and outcome of clients, which are almost entirely lacking in the available literature.

Once a package is shown to be an effective treatment for specific problems in particular clients then several other clinical research issues arise, including:

(1) What are the necessary and sufficient components in the package that contribute to the efficacy? Once these crucial ingredients are identified then the package can be refined by optimizing these ingredients and eliminating those that are unnecessary.

(2) What is the effect on the efficacy of the package of varying certain parameters such as its duration or the spacing of sessions? This information can be used to increase the efficiency of delivery.

(3) What is the effect on the efficacy of the package of varying the clients or therapists? The extensions to male victims or to groups of victims, and the inclusion of male therapists, which are discussed above, are examples of research topics in this category.

(4) How effective is the package compared to other treatment approaches? Only when a package has been shown to be effective is it worth while mounting comparative studies that usually require considerable resources.

Such a cumulative process of inquiry will improve progressively the quality of help that can be offered to the many troubled victims of child sexual abuse.

References

Alexander, P. C., and Lupfer, S. L. (1987). Family characteristics and long-term consequences associated with sexual abuse. *Archives of Sexual Behavior*, **16**, 235–45.

American Psychiatric Association (1987). *Diagnostic and Statistical Manual of Mental Disorders*. (3rd edn rev.). Washington, DC: American Psychiatric Association Press.

Baisden, M. J., and Baisden, J. R. (1979). A profile of women who seek counseling for sexual dysfunctions. *American Journal of Family Therapy*, **7**, 68–76.

Baker, A. W., and Duncan, S. P. (1985). Child sexual abuse: A study of prevalence in Great Britain. *Child Abuse and Neglect*, **9**, 457–67.

Battle, J. (1981). *Culture-free Self-esteem Inventories for Children and Adults*. Seattle: Special Child Publications.

Beck, A. T. (1978). *Depression Inventory*. Philadelphia: Center for Cognitive Therapy.

Beck, A. T., and Emery, G. (1985). *Anxiety Disorders and Phobias: a Cognitive Perspective*. New York: Basic Books.

Beck, J. C., and van der Kolk, B. (1987). Reports of childhood incest and current behavior of chronically hospitalized psychotic women. *American Journal of Psychiatry*, **144**, 1474–6.

Becker, J. V., and Skinner, L. J. (1984). Behavioral treatment of sexual dysfunctions in sexual assault survivors. In I. R. Stuart and J. G. Greer (eds), *Victims of Sexual Aggression: Treatment of Children, Women, and Men*. New York: Van Nostrand Reinhold, pp. 211–33.

Benward, J., and Densen-Gerbert, J. (1975). Incest as a causative factor in antisocial behaviour: An exploratory study. *Contemporary Drug Problems*, **4**, 323–40.

Bergart, A. M. (1986). Isolation to intimacy: Incest survivors in group therapy. *Social Casework*, **67**, 266–75.

Blake-White, J., and Kline, C. (1985). Treating the dissociative process in adult victims of childhood incest. *Social Casework*, **66**, 394–402.

Bliss, E. L. (1984). A symptom profile of patients with multiple personalities including MMPI results. *Journal of Nervous and Mental Disease*, **172**, 197–202.

Bowman, E. S., Blix, S., and Coons, P. M. (1985). Multiple personality in adolescence: Relationship to incestual experiences. *Journal of the American Academy of Child Psychiatry*, **24**, 109–14.

Briere, J. (1988a). Controlling for family variables in abuse effects research: A critique of the 'partialling' approach. *Journal of Interpersonal Violence*, **3**, 80–9.

Briere, J. (1988b). The long-term clinical correlates of childhood sexual victimization. In R. A. Prentky and V. L. Quinsey (eds), *Human Sexual Aggression: Current Perspectives*. New York: New York Academy of Sciences, pp. 327–34.

Briere, J., Evans, D., Runtz, M., and Wall, T. (1988). Symptomatology in men who were molested as children: A comparison study. *American Journal of Orthopsychiatry*, **58**, 457–61.

Briere, J., and Runtz, M. (1987). Post sexual abuse trauma: Data and implications for clinical practice. *Journal of Interpersonal Violence*, **2**, 367–79.

Briere, J., and Runtz, M. (1989). The Trauma Symptom Checklist (TSC-33): Early data on a new scale. *Journal of Interpersonal Violence*, **4**, 151–63.

Briere, J., and Zaidi, L. Y. (1988, August). Sexual abuse histories and sequelae in psychiatric emergency room patients. Paper presented at the annual meeting of the American Psychological Association, Atlanta, Georgia.

Browne, A., and Finkelhor, D. (1986). Initial and long-term effects: A review of research. In D. Finkelhor, *A Sourcebook of Child Sexual Abuse*. Beverly Hills, CA: Sage, pp. 143–79.

Bruckner, D. F., and Johnson, P. E. (1987). Treatment of male victims of childhood sexual abuse. *Social Casework: The Journal of Contemporary Social Work*, **68**, 81–7.

Calam, R. M., and Slade, P. D. (1986, December). Relationships between sexual abuse and eating disorders. Paper presented at the meeting of the British Psychological Society, London.

Carmen, E., Rieker, P. P., and Mills, T. (1984). Victims of violence and psychiatric illness. *American Journal of Psychiatry*, **141**, 378–83.

Cole, C. H., and Barney, E. E. (1987). Safeguards and the therapeutic window: A group treatment strategy for adult incest survivors. *The American Journal of Orthopsychiatry*, **57**, 601–9.

Condy, S. R., Templer, D. I., Brown, R., and Veaco, L. (1987). Parameters of sexual contact of boys with women. *Archives of Sexual Behavior*, **16**, 379–93.

Coons, P. M., and Milstein, V. (1984). Rape and post-traumatic stress in multiple personality. *Psychological Reports*, **55**, 839–45.

Coons, P. M., and Milstein, V. (1986). Psychosexual disturbances in multiple personality: Characteristic etiology and treatment. *Journal of Clinical Psychiatry*, **47**, 106–10.

Courtois, C. A. (1988). *Healing the Incest Wound: Adult Survivors in Therapy*. New York: Norton.

Craine, L. S., Henson, C. E., Colliver, J. A., and MacLean, D. G. (1988). Prevalence of a history of sexual abuse among female psychiatric patients in a state hospital system. *Hospital and Community Psychiatry*, **39**, 300–4.

Crisp, A. H. (1978). Some aspects of the relationship between body weight and sexual behaviour with particular reference to massive obesity and anorexia nervosa. *International Journal of Obesity*, **2**, 17–32.

Cunningham, J., Pearce, T., and Pearce, P. (1988). Childhood sexual abuse and medical complaints in adult women. *Journal of Interpersonal Violence*, **3**, 131–44.

Deighton, J., and McPeek, P. (1985). Group treatment: Adult victims of childhood sexual abuse. *Social Casework*, **66**, 403–10.

de Young, M. (1982a). Self-injurious behavior in incest victims: A research note. *Child Welfare*, **LXI**, 577–84.

de Young, M. (1982b). Innocent seducer or innocently seduced? The role of the child incest victim. *Journal of Clinical Child Psychology*, **11**, 56–60.

Dimock, P. T. (1988). Adult males sexually abused as children: Characteristics and implications for treatment. *Journal of Interpersonal Violence*, **3**, 203–21.

Domino, J. V., and Haber, J. D. (1987). Prior physical and sexual abuse in women with chronic headache: Clinical correlates. *Headache*, **27**, 310–14.

Donaldson, M. A., and Gardner, R. Jr (1985). Diagnosis and treatment of traumatic stress among women after childhood incest. In C. R. Figley (eds), *Trauma and its Wake: the Study and Treatment of Post-traumatic Stress Disorder*. New York: Brunner/Mazel, pp. 356–77.

Faria, G., and Belohlavek, N. (1984). Treating female adult survivors of childhood incest. *Social Casework*, **65**, 465–71.

Finkelhor, D. (1984). *Child Sexual Abuse: New Theory and Research*. New York: Free Press.

Finkelhor, D. (1986). *A Sourcebook on Child Sexual Abuse*. Beverly Hills, CA: Sage.

Finkelhor, D. (1987). The trauma of child sexual abuse: Two models. *Journal of Interpersonal Violence*, **2**, 348–66.

Fowler, C., Burns, S. R., and Roehl, J. E. (1983). The role of group therapy in incest counseling. *International Journal of Family Therapy*, **5**, 127–35.

Friedman, S., and Harrison, G. (1984). Sexual histories, attitudes and behavior of schizophrenic and 'normal' women. *Archives of Sexual Behavior*, **13**, 555–67.

Fritz, G. T., Stoller, K., and Wagner, N. (1981). A comparison of males and females who were sexually molested as children. *Journal of Sex and Marital Therapy*, **7**, 54–9.

Fromuth, M. E. (1986). The relationship of childhood sexual abuse with later psychological and sexual adjustment in a sample of college women. *Child Abuse and Neglect*, **10**, 5–15.

Giaretto, H. A. (1982). *Integrated Treatment of Child Sexual Abuse*. Palo Alto, CA: Science and Behavior Books.

Goodman, B., and Nowak-Scibelli, D. (1985). Group treatment for women incestuously abused as children. *International Journal of Group Psychotherapy*, **35**, 531–44.

Gordy, P. L. (1983). Group work that supports adult victims of childhood incest. *Social Casework*, **64**, 300–7.

Gross, R. J., Doerr, H., Caldirola, D., Guzinski, G. M., and Ripley, H. S. (1980). Borderline syndrome and incest in chronic pelvic pain patients. *International Journal of Psychiatry in Medicine*, **10**, 79–96.

Groth, A. M. (1979). Sexual trauma in the life histories of rapists and child molesters. *Victimology*, **4**, 10–16.

Gundlach, R. H. (1977). Sexual molestation and rape reported by homosexual and hetero-sexual women. *Journal of Homosexuality*, **2**, 367–84.

Hambridge, D. M. (1988). Incest and anorexia nervosa: What is the link? *British Journal of Psychiatry*, **152**, 145–6.

Harrop-Griffiths, J., Katon, W., Walker, E., Holm, L., Russo, J., and Hickok, L. (1988). The association between chronic pelvic pain, psychiatric diagnosis, and childhood sex-ual abuse. *Obstetrics & Gynecology*, **71**, 589–94.

Hartman, M., Finn, S. A., and Leon, G. R. (1987). Sexual abuse experiences in a clinical population: Comparisons of familial and nonfamilial abuse. *Psychotherapy*, **24**, 154–9.

Herman, J. L. (1981). *Father-daughter incest*. Cambridge, MA: Harvard University Press.

Herman, J. L. (1986). Histories of violence in an outpatient population: An exploratory study. *American Journal of Orthopsychiatry*, **56**, 137–41.

Herman, J., and Schatzow, E. (1984). Time-limited group therapy for women with a history of incest. *International Journal of Group Psychotherapy*, **34**, 605–16.

Herman, J., and Schatzow, E. (1987). Recovery and verification of memories of childhood sexual trauma. *Psychoanalytic Psychology*, **4**, 1–14.

Holmes, M. R., and St. Lawrence, J. S. (1983). Treatment of rape-induced trauma: Pro-posed behavioural conceptualization and review of the literature. *Clinical Psychology Review*, **3**, 417–33.

Horowitz, M. J. (1986). *Stress Response Syndromes*. (2nd edn). Northvale NJ: Jason Aronson.

Hudson, W. W. (1982). *The Clinical Measurement Package: a Field Manual*. Homewood, IL: Dorsey.

Jacobson, A., and Richardson, B. (1987). Assault experiences of 100 psychiatric inpatients: Evidence of the need for routine inquiry. *American Journal of Psychiatry*, **144**, 908–13.

James, J., and Meyerding, J. (1977). Early sexual experience as a factory in prostitution. *Archives of Sexual Behavior*, **1**, 31–42.

Janoff-Bulman, R. (1985). The aftermath of victimization: rebuilding shattered assump-tions. In C. R. Figley (ed.), *Trauma and its Wake: the Study and Treatment of Post-traumatic Stress Disorder*. New York: Brunner/Mazel, pp. 15–35.

Janus, M. D., Burgess, A. W., and McCormack, A. (1987). Histories of sexual abuse in adolescent male runaways. *Adolescence*, **22**, 405–17.

Jehu, D. (1988). *Beyond Sexual Abuse: Therapy with Women who were Childhood Vic-tims*. Chichester: Wiley.

Johnson, R. L., and Shrier, D. (1987). Past sexual victimization by females of male patients in an adolescent medicine clinic population. *American Journal of Psychiatry*, **144**, 650–2.

Joy, S. (1987). Retrospective presentations of incest: Treatment strategies for use with adult women. *Journal of Counseling and Development*, **65**, 317–19.

Kaufman, L., Peck, A. L., and Tagiuri, C. K. (1954). The family constellation and overt incestuous relations between father and daughter. *American Journal of Orthopsychia-try*, **24**, 266–77.

Keane, T. M., Zimering, R. T., and Cadell, J. M. (1985). A behavioral formulation of post-traumatic stress disorder in Vietnam veterans. *The Behavior Therapist*, **8**, 9–12.

Kilpatrick, D. G., Amick-McMullan, A., Best, C. L., Burke, M. M., and Saunders, B. E. (1986, May). Impact of child sexual abuse: recent research findings. Paper presented to the Fourth National Conference on the Sexual Victimization of Children, New Orleans, LA.

Klassen, A. D., and Wilsnack, S. C. (1986). Sexual experience and drinking among women in a U.S. national survey. *Archives of Sexual Behavior*, **15**, 363–92.

Kluft, R. P. (1987). An update on multiple personality disorder. *Hospital and Community Psychiatry*, **38**, 363–73.

Leehan, J., and Wilson, L. P. (1985). *Grown-up Abused Children*. Springfield, IL: Charles C. Thomas.

Lewis, I. A. (1985). [*Los Angeles Times* Poll Nol 98]. Unpublished raw data.

Maltz, W., and Holman, B. (1987). *Incest and Sexuality*. Lexington, MA: Lexington Books.

McCallum, J. (1987). Group treatment of adult women who were sexually victimized in childhood. Unpublished master's practicum report, University of Manitoba, Winnipeg.

McCarthy, B. W. (1986). A cognitive behavioral approach to understanding and treating sexual trauma. *Journal of Sex and Marital Therapy*, **12**, 322–9.

McCormack, A., Janus, M.–D., and Burgess, A. W. (1986). Runaway youths and sexual victimization: Gender differences in an adolescent runaway population. *Child Abuse and Neglect*, **10**, 387–95.

McCrea, C., and Yaffe, M. (1981). Sexuality in the obese. *British Journal of Sexual Medicine*, **8**, 24–37.

McGuire, L. A., and Wagner, N. N. (1978). Sexual dysfunction in women who were molested as children: One response pattern and suggestions for treatment. *Journal of Sex and Marital Therapy*, **4**, 11–15.

Meichenbaum, D. (1985). *Stress Inoculation Training*. New York: Pergamon.

Meiselman, K. C. (1978). *Incest: A Psychological Study of Causes and Effects with Treatment Recommendations*. San Francisco, CA: Jossey-Bass.

Miller, B. A., Downs, W. R., Gondoli, D. M., and Keil, A. (1987). The role of childhood sexual abuse in the development of alcoholism in women. *Violence and Victims*, **2**, 157–72.

Mowrer, O. H. (1960). *Learning Theory and Behavior*. New York: Wiley.

Nadelson, C. C. (1982). Incest and rape: Repercussions in sexual behavior. In L. Greenspoon (ed.), *The Annual Review of Psychiatry*. Washington DC: American Psychiatric Association Press.

Newton, D. (1978). Homosexual behavior and child molestation: a review of the evidence. *Adolescence*, **13**, 29–43.

Oppenheimer, R., Howells, K., Palmer, R.L., and Chaloner, D. A. (1985). Adverse sexual experience in childhood and clinical eating disorders: A preliminary description. *Journal of Psychosomatic Research*, **19**, 357–61.

Painter, S. L. (1986). Research on the prevalence of child sexual abuse: New directions. *Canadian Journal of Behavioural Science*, **18**, 323–39.

Peters, S. D., Wyatt, G. E., and Finkelhor, D. (1986). Prevalence. In D. Finkelhor, *A Sourcebook on Child Sexual Abuse*. Beverly Hills, CA: Sage, pp. 15–59.

Pinhas, V. (1987). Sexual dysfunction in women alcoholics. *Medical Aspects of Human Sexuality*, **21**, 97–101.

Reiker, P., and Carmen, E. (1986). The victim-to-patient process: The disconfirmation and transformation of abuse. *American Journal of Orthopsychiatry*, **56**, 360–70.

Rogers, C. M., and Terry, T. (1984). Clinical intervention with boy victims of sexual abuse. In I. R. Stuart and J. G. Greer (eds), *Victims of Sexual Aggression: Treatment of Children, Women and Men*. New York: Van Nostrand Reinhold, pp. 91–104.

Root, M. P. P., and Fallon, P. (1988). The incidence of victimization experiences in a bulimia sample. *Journal of Interpersonal Violence*, **3**, 161–73.

Runtz, M. G., and Briere, J. (1988, April). Childhood sexual abuse, revictimization as an adult, and current symptomatology. Paper presented at the National Symposium on Child Victimization, Anaheim, California.

Russell, D. E. H. (1983). The incidence and prevalence of intrafamilial and extrafamilial sexual abuse of female children. *Child Abuse and Neglect*, **7**, 133–46.

Russell, D. E. H. (1986). *The Secret Trauma: Incest in the Lives of Girls and Women*. New York: Basic Books.

Rychtarik, R. G., Silverman, W. K., Van Landringham, W. P., and Prue, D. M. (1984). Treatment of an incest victim with implosive therapy: A case study. *Behavior Therapy*, **15**, 410–20.

Schwab, D. (1986). An assertiveness training therapy group for women who have been sexually victimized in childhood or adolescence. Unpublished master's practicum report, University of Manitoba, Winnipeg.

Scurfield, R. M. (1985). Post-trauma stress assessment and treatment. In C. R. Figley (ed.), *Trauma and its Wake: the Study and Treatment of Post-traumatic Stress Disorder.* New York: Brunner/Mazel, pp. 219–55.

Sebold, J. (1987). Indicators of child sexual abuse in males. *Social Casework: The Journal of Contemporary Social Work*, **68**, 75–80.

Seghorn, T. K., Prentky, R. A., and Boucher, R. J. (1987). Childhood sexual abuse in the lives of sexually aggressive offenders. *Journal of the American Academy of Child and Adolescent Psychiatry*, **26**, 262–7.

Sexual offences against children in Canada (1984). Two volumes. Ottawa: Supply and Services, Canada.

Shapiro, S. (1987). Self-mutilation and self-blame in incest victims. *American Journal of Psychotherapy*, **XLI**, 46–54.

Sheldon, H. (1988). Childhood sexual abuse in adult female psychotherapy referrals. *British Journal of Psychiatry*, **152**, 107–11.

Silbert, M. H. (1984). Treatment of prostitute victims of sexual assault. In I. R. Stuart and J. G. Greer (eds), *Victims of Sexual Aggression: Treatment of Children, Women, And Men.* New York: Van Nostrand Reinhold, pp. 251–82.

Silbert, M. H., and Pines, A. M. (1981). Sexual child abuse as an antecedent to prostitution. *Child Abuse and Neglect*, **5**, 407–11.

Silbert, M. H., and Pines, A. M. (1983). Early sexual exploitation as an influence in prostitution. *Social Work*, **28**, 285–9.

Spiegel, D. (1985). Multiple personality as a post-traumatic stress disorders. *Psychiatric Clinics of North America*, **7**, 101–10.

Sprei, J., and Courtois, C. (1988). The treatment of women's sexual dysfunctions arising from sexual assault. In J. R. Field and R. A. Brown (eds), *Advances in the Understanding and Treatment of Sexual Problems: Compendium for the Individual and Marital Therapist.* New York: Spectrum.

Tsai, M., and Wagner, N. N. (1978). Therapy groups for women sexually molested as children. *Archives of Sexual Behavior*, **7**, 417–28.

Van Buskirk, S. S., and Cole, C. F. (1983). Characteristics of eight women seeking therapy for the effects of incest. *Psychotherapy*, **20**, 503–14.

Vitaliano, P. P., James, J., and Boyer, D. (1981). Sexuality of deviant females: Adolescent and adult correlates. *Social Work*, **26**, 468–72.

Wachtel, A., and Lawton-Speert, S. (1983). *Child Sexual Abuse: Descriptions of Nine Program Approaches to Treatment.* Vancouver: United Way of Lower Mainland.

Walker, E., Katon, W., Harrop-Griffiths, J., Holm, L., Russo, J., and Hickok, L. R. (1988). Relationship of chronic pelvic pain to psychiatric diagnosis and childhood sexual abuse. *American Journal of Psychiatry*, **145**, 75–80.

Widom, C. S. (1988). Sampling biases and implications for child abuse research. *American Journal of Orthopsychiatry*, **58**, 260–70.

Wolff, R. (1977). Systemic desensitization and negative practice to alter the after effects of a rape attempts. *Journal of Behavior Therapy and Experimental Psychiatry*, **8**, 423–5.

Wyatt, G. E., and Mickey, M. R. (1987). Ameliorating the effects of child sexual abuse: An exploratory study of support by parents and others. *Journal of Interpersonal Violence*, **2**, 403–14.

Wyatt, G. E., and Peters, S. D. (1986a). Issues in the definition of child sexual abuse in prevalence research. *Child Abuse and Neglect*, **10**, 231–40.

Wyatt, G. E., and Peters, S. D. (1986b). Methodological considerations in research on the prevalence of child sexual abuse. *Child Abuse and Neglect*, **10**, 241–51.

Zverina, J., Lachman, M., Pondelickova, J., and Vanek, J. (1987). The occurrence of atypical sexual experience among various female patient groups. *Archives of Sexual Behavior*, **16**, 321–6.

11

Clinical Treatment of Adult Female Victims of Sexual Assault

PATRICIA A. RESICK

and

BARBARA E. GERTH MARKAWAY
Department of Psychology, University of Missouri-St Louis, USA

> There is no difference between being raped and being bit on the ankle by a rattle-snake except that people ask if your skirt was short and why you were out alone anyhow.
>
> (Marge Piercy,
> excerpt from 'Rape Poem')

Although there has been increased attention paid in both the popular and the scholarly press to the growing problem of sexual assault, tenacious social stigmas remain. Traditional views led women to believe they were 'damaged goods' following sexual assault. Even today, victims are frequently viewed as at least partially precipitating, or even participating, in the crime. This may be especially true in sexual assault cases in which the woman knows her assailant (Koss, 1987). These lingering social forces make it particularly difficult for a woman to acknowledge and share her trauma. Despite known underreporting, statistics indicate an alarming number of reported rapes. There were 87 340 reported crimes that qualified as sexual assault in 1985 (FBI, 1986). Estimated figures double when unreported rapes are included (Dormanen, 1980). Since 1977, reported rapes have increased 21% (FBI, 1986). Lifetime prevalence rates vary from 4.86% (George and Winfield-Laird, 1986) to 44% (Russell, 1982). Lack of reporting not only hinders attempts to gain an accurate profile of the frequency of sexual assault, but also diminishes the chance that victims will receive appropriate clinical treatment.

This chapter will begin with a brief overview of psychological reactions rape victims typically experience. For a more complete review of the impact of sexual

Clinical Approaches to Sex Offenders and Their Victims
Edited by C. R. Hollin and K. Howells © 1991 John Wiley & Sons Ltd

assault on psychological functioning, including information on pre-assault, assault, and post-assault variables, the interested reader is referred to Resick's (1987) review of the literature. Following the overview of victim reactions, theoretical perspectives related to sexual assault will be described. Next, treatment strategies and outcome information will be reviewed. A case example from our clinical work will then be presented to illustrate some of these strategies. Lastly, issues requiring further consideration will be discussed.

PSYCHOLOGICAL REACTIONS TO SEXUAL ASSAULT

Cognitive, behavioral, and emotional reactions subsequent to sexual assault typically follow a predictable pattern, with strong reactions likely immediately after the assault. In a longitudinal study of sexual assault victims' reactions, participants were asked to describe their reactions during the assault and a few hours post-assault (Veronen et al., 1979). Feelings of being scared and worried, and physical manifestations of shaking and trembling, were reported by 96% of the women. In addition, 92% of the women reported being terrified and confused. These reactions decreased only minimally in the few hours following the assault, while depression (84%), exhaustion (96%), and restlessness (88%) increased. Results from a landmark study conducted in a hospital emergency room showed similar distress reactions in sexual assault victims (Burgess and Holmstrom, 1974, 1979). Early reactions to sexual assault have been found to follow a pattern of high distress in the first week post-assault, followed by a small decrease at week two, and then an increase at week three to a peak distress level (Peterson et al., 1987). Other studies of early victim reactions also point to self-esteem, social adjustment, and sexual dysfunction difficulties during the two weeks following the sexual assault (Atkeson et al., 1982; Murphy et al., 1988; Resick et al., 1981).

Following the period of intense distress immediately after the assault, most victims show improvement on some symptom scales to a normal level approximately two to three months later (Atkeson et al., 1982; Kilpatrick et al., 1981). However, scales measuring fear, anxiety, self-esteem, and sexual dysfunctions remain higher in assault victims than in non-victim comparison groups. Such differences are evidenced even one or more years after the assault (Calhoun et al., 1982; Kilpatrick and Veronen, 1983). Other studies concerned with the long-term effects of sexual assault have found clinically significant problems with fear, social adjustment, depression, and sexual dysfunction in women who had experienced a sexual assault an average of six years ago (Kilpatrick et al., 1985; Kilpatrick et al., 1987b).

Many of the reactions described above, especially fear and anxiety, are consistent with the DSM-III-R (APA, 1987) category of Post-Traumatic Stress Disorder (PTSD). However, in order to diagnose PTSD three other criteria in addition to fear and anxiety must be met. First, victims much suffer from a reexperiencing of the trauma, which typically takes the form of intrusive recollections, nightmares or 'flashbacks.' Second, victims must demonstrate numbing of responsiveness or reduced involvement in usual activities. Third, an increased arousal level, as evidenced by hyperalertness or exaggerated startle responses, must be evidenced. Sexual assault victims constitute the largest single group of PTSD sufferers (Foa *et al.*, 1987). In addition, in a community-based survey, nearly 60% of sexual assault victims met criteria for PTSD at some point in their lives (Kilpatrick *et al.*, 1987a).

Other severe reactions have been described in the literature. Suicidal ideation and suicide attempts are not uncommonly reported in victims. In a random survey, Kilpatrick and Veronen (1983) found that 44% of sexual assault victims experienced suicidal ideation and 14% of the sample had made an actual attempt. Similarly, in a study of sexual assault victims seeking treatment, 43% had thought about suicide and 17% had attempted (Resick *et al.*, 1988). In addition to suicidal ideation and attempts, sexual assault victims have been found to score higher than non-victims on the psychoticism and paranoid ideation subscales of the SCL-90 (Kilpatrick and Veronen, 1984; Kilpatrick *et al.*, 1987b; Resick, 1988). Elevations are probably reflective of feelings of fear, alienation, and confusion.

Given the increasing number of sexual assaults and the high percentage of victims who experience chronic and disabling psychological difficulties, detecting effective treatment strategies for these women is crucial. Before turning our attention to a review of treatment strategies, theoretical perspectives upon which such strategies are based will be presented.

THEORETICAL PERSPECTIVES

Although the study of sexual assault and the treatment of its victims is gaining increased political and scientific prominence, the area is still in its genesis. As such, there is little consensus with regard to the conceptualization of sexual assault or the most effective way to treat the sexual assault victim. Veronen and Kilpatrick (1980a) noted that discussions about treatment issues are likely to be 'heated' and 'full of controversy.' An open debate about conceptual issues is important in that treatment strategies need to be grounded in a theoretical framework so that clinicians do not become lost in surmise and supposition.

Feminist Theory

The increased attention of sexual assault as an area of serious societal concern largely emerged from the grass roots women's movement (Largen, 1976; Resick and Jackson, 1976). Due to pressure from feminists, the psychological community was forced to confront the fact that there were multitudes of women, as well as family and friends, who were victims and 'covictims' of sexual assault in need of clinical treatment (Yassen and Glass, 1984).

The feminist perspective propounds a broad theory of sexual assault that emphasizes sex-role stereotyping and socialization, power relationships between women and men, and political activism (Albin, 1977; Brownmiller, 1975; Griffin, 1971; Vinsel, 1977). Feminist theorists argue for a socio-political-cultural analysis and understanding of sexual assault and stress the need for societal changes in order for sexual assault to be eliminated. Yassen and Glass (1984) state that in our current patriarchal culture 'sexual assault as a societal problem will continue, with a never-ending supply of new offenders and surviving victims' (p. 253).

The feminist approach offers many strengths in that it raises the consciousness of men and women, and avoids the victim-blame common to more traditional conceptualizations of sexual assault by stressing the political aspects of rape. In addition, a strong emphasis on prevention, which is often ignored by other theories, is a major asset of this perspective. The primary weakness of this approach is that it provides limited concrete techniques for helping women to cope with rape-related symptoms.

Crisis Theory

While the feminist movement made clear that the growing problem of sexual assault could no longer be ignored, mental health professionals largely adopted a crisis theory model to guide their conceptualizations and treatment strategies. Based upon the work of several authors (Butcher and Maudal, 1976; Caplan, 1964), crisis theory defines a crisis state as one in which a person is confronted with a problem situation that he or she can neither modify nor avoid by using his or her characteristic means of coping. The person then enters a state of 'dis-equilibrium,' experiencing high levels of subjective distress, in which the person searches for new ways of handling the problem. Crisis theory also asserts that this disequilibrium period is time limited, usually confined to 6 to 8 weeks. This crisis model was originally applied to sexual assault victims by Burgess and Holmstrom (1974). According to these authors, sexual assault fits the criterion for an externally imposed crisis situation that results in disequilibrium for the victims in areas of physical, emotional, sexual, and social functioning.

A major strength of the crisis model of victim reactions is that such a model does not emphasize enduring characterological traits or psychopathology, but rather focuses on the relative normalcy of victims' reactions in a crisis situation. Thus, a crisis model avoids viewing the victim as 'sick' or blaming the victim in some way. However, crisis theory suffers in that it is circular and vague in its conceptualizations and definitions of terms (Kilpatrick et al., 1982). In addition, it does little to account for specific patterns of reaction and recovery that have emerged in the literatue, in particular, the long-term reactions of sexual assault victims (Resick, 1987).

Social Learning/Behavioral Theories

More recently, researchers have advanced behavioral theories to account for the variety of victim responses that have been observed (Holmes and St. Lawrence, 1983). Using two-factor theory, sexual assault is viewed as a situation involving threat or 'felt threat' of being killed or physically injured. In addition, sexual assault involves the experience of loss of control. These experiences become unconditioned stimuli that produce unconditioned responses of anxiety and fear.

Through the process of classical conditioning, any stimuli present during the assault experience may become conditioned stimuli that will evoke conditioned responses of fear and anxiety. In such a situation, any events, objects, or persons present during the assault may elicit fear and anxiety. In addition, events, objects, or persons similar in some manner to the actual conditioned stimuli may also come to elicit fear and anxiety through the process of stimulus generalization. Because of the aversively conditioned reactions, the rape victim then develops escape and avoidance behavior.

In addition to explaining fear and anxiety reactions, social learning theory also provides mechanisms for explaining the development of depression that is commonly found in sexual assault victims. Seligman (1975) proposed a learned helplessness model that explains depression as a response individuals are likely to develop when they are placed in aversive situations in which their behavior has no effect on what happens to them. Sexual assault victims often report feelings of helplessness and loss of control, thus suggesting that depression may develop as a result of learned helplessness. Peterson and Seligman (1983) have applied learned helplessness theory to victims of crime. Another behavioral theory that could account for victims' depressive reactions is that of Lewinsohn (1974). He asserts that depression results from a lowered rate of behavioral response that reduces opportunities for positive reinforcement. Given that sexual assault victims often engage in assault-related avoidance behaviors (to avoid feared conditioned stimuli), this mechanism for the development of depression seems reasonable. Both two-factor theory and learned helplessness theory have been modified in recent years to include the cognitive component of expectancy. This expectancy component is necessary to explain why the anxiety continues in the absence of exposure to the unconditioned stimulus.

Behavioral theories have many strengths in that they adequately account for the development of fear and anxiety (and sexual dysfunctions) through classical conditioning and operant avoidance, and offer some explanation for the development of depression. In addition, they share strengths of feminist approaches and crisis theory in that they focus on the present situation, view the reactions of victims as non-pathological, and avoid victim-blame. However, similar to the criticisms of crisis theory, Resick (1987) noted that behavioral theory also does not account for the full range of reactions and patterns of recovery that are observed in sexual assault victims. Intrusion, the reexperiencing phenomenon associated with PTSD, and problems with self-esteem are better explained by cognitive theory.

Cognitive Theories

Cognitive theories used to explain rape reactions have focused on the depression, problems with self-esteem and fear commonly observed in victims. These theories stress an attribution model of self-blame. After reviewing the literature, Rehm and O'Hara (1979) concluded that blaming the self for negative life events is a major contributing factor in some types of depression. Such internal attributions of blame may thus lead to decreased self-evaluation and subsequent depression in sexual assault victims. Unfortunately, victims, like the general population, may believe common stereotypes and myths about rape, and may exhibit faulty cognitions revealing that they feel they have done something to bring about their assault or are being punished for being 'bad'(Kilpatrick and Veronen, 1984). Janoff-Bulman (1979) delineated two forms of self-blame attributions: characterological and behavioral. Victims who exhibit characterological self-blame attribute the assault to internal, stable personality traits. In contrast, victims who exhibit behavioral self-blame attribute the assault to their behavior.

These cognitive distortions are presumed to serve the purpose of giving the victim a regained sense of control, albeit a false sense, following a traumatic experience of violation and loss of autonomy. For example, if a victim engages in behavioral self-blame, thinking the assault is her fault because she was walking alone, she can gain comfort and an enhanced sense of control by telling herself that as long as she never again walks alone, she will never again be assaulted. Thus, she thinks that by changing her behavior she can avoid future danger (Wortman, 1976). Lerner and Miller's (1978) 'just world' hypothesis also helps to explain the rationale for victim-blame, both by the victim herself, and by those around her. The majority of people tend to view the world as being a place of fairness and justice. If some negative event occurs, there must be a rational explanation; otherwise, the world would seem chaotic and random. Thus, when a woman is sexually assaulted, it must either be due to her behavior or her character. While cognitive/attribution theory does much to advance our understanding of the depression observed in sexual assault victims, its focus is too limited to explain fully the broad range of symptom patterns common in sexual assault victims.

Recently, cognitive theories have been advanced to explain the development of fear and avoidance behaviors. One such theory is expectancy theory (Reiss, 1980; Reiss and McNally, 1985), which moves beyond theories of classical conditioning and operant avoidance. According to expectancy theory, both the level of danger expectancy and anxiety expectancy are important factors in the development of fear and associated avoidance behaviors. Danger expectancies are beliefs that exposure to a certain stimulus (i.e. fear cue) will certainly generate external harm, aversive social consequences, or loss. Anxiety expectancies, also referred to as 'the fear of fear' (Goldstein and Chambless, 1978), involve anticipation that exposure to a fear cue will elicit anxiety, even when the fear cue is known to be benign. Expectancy theory helps to account for avoidance behavior being maintained over an extended period of time. In addition, expectancy theory explains findings in the literature indicating that victims often acknowledge experiencing intense fear of a known non-harmful stimulus.

Emotional Processing Theory is a relatively new theory that has been used to explain reactions to and treatment of sexual assault. In a classic paper on emotional processing, Rachman (1980) wrote that common signals indicating that emotional processing has been inadequate are 'the persistence or return of intrusive signs of emotional activities such as obsessions, nightmares, phobias, or inappropriate expression of emotions . . .' (p. 51). These signs of incomplete emotional processing are the common symptoms of PTSD. Thus, Foa *et al.* (1989) have adopted the concept of emotional processing into their work with sexual assault victims suffering from PTSD. They propose that sexual assault is a major traumatic event that violates previously held beliefs about one's safety and security, thereby making adequate emotional processing difficult.

Foa and Kozak (1986) particularly focus on the fear commonly seen in PTSD, asserting that fear is a cognitive memory structure that contains three interlocking components. These components consist of information about the stimulus itself, about one's behavioral and affective responses to the stimulus, and about the meaning attached to the stimulus and response. Moreover, they assert that the memory-fear structures of people with PTSD contain elements that are pathological, and that treatment should aim to alter these maladaptive elements.

According to this theory, two factors are needed to reduce fear through the alteration of the memory structure (Foa and Kozak, 1986). First, memory of the feared stimulus must be reactivated. Once the memory structure has been elicited, 'information made available must include elements that are incompatible with some of those that exist in the fear structure, so that a new memory can be formed. This new information, which is at once cognitive and effective, has to be integrated into the evoked information structure for an emotional change to occur' (p. 22).

Based upon emotional processing theory, Foa *et al.* (1989) and Stekettee and Foa (1987) suggest that exposure procedures (e.g. flooding) may be useful in treating sexual assault victims with PTSD in that exposure procedures activate the memory structure and provide opportunity for that memory structure to be modified as corrective information is integrated. For example, in treating a sexual assault victim, repeated exposure to the memory of the assault should facilitate the woman's being able to remember the assault without experiencing intense generalized fear reactions. Although the act of sexual assault will continue to be appropriately feared, other non-harmful stimuli associated with the assault (e.g. being at home alone) will cease to elicit fear. Such modification of the memory structure and the resultant reduction in fear is also hypothesized to alleviate other symptoms of PTSD (Foa *et al.*, 1989).

TREATMENT STRATEGIES

Traditional Interventions

Treatment for rape victims has traditionally occurred in rape crisis centers in which crisis intervention and supportive therapy have been the most prevalent treatment modality (Koss and Harvey, 1987). Such intervention typically includes disseminating information and providing the woman with a supportive environment where she can share her feelings about the assault (Forman, 1980; Yassen and Glass, 1984). Although empirical evidence to support the efficacy of traditional treatment strategies is sparse, a recent outcome study that compared the efficacy of supportive therapy, assertiveness training, and stress inoculation training lends some credence to using traditional interventions with sexual assault victims (Resick *et al.*, 1988).

In this study, 37 women who had been sexually assaulted at least three months previously, completed six 2-hour group therapy sessions. Participants also completed assessment sessions pre-therapy, post-therapy, and at 3 and 6 month follow-up periods. A naturally occurring waiting-list control group of 13 participants was also included in the study. The supportive psychotherapy groups consisted of one male and one female facilitator. The group involved an information/education session common to all three types of treatment groups in which a cognitive-behavioral explanation of the development of fear and anxiety following sexual assault was given. This session included information on classical conditioning, operant avoidance, and cognitive and social factors. After the educational session, the participants in the supportive psychotherapy group selected topics for discussion that included not only fear and anxiety, but also a wide range of other issues. Common themes in the groups were the retelling of the rape incident and sharing the reactions they received from other people. The group aimed to normalize reactions to sexual assault and to have group members offer support and suggestions about what they found helpful in dealing with these reactions. The cotherapists occasionally provided information, although no specific training in behavioral procedures was offered.

Results indicated that women in the supportive psychotherapy groups showed significant and lasting reductions in fear and anxiety and increased self-esteem. Depression also diminished, although this finding was not as strong. Although behavioral treatment strategies are currently the most popular, results of this study did not find supportive therapy to be less effective than the more behavioral, stress inoculation training groups. However, the authors suggested that the function of the group may have been to facilitate the emotional processing of the event.

Dynamic psychotherapy has often been recommended as an appropriate treatment following crisis intervention (e.g. Burgess and Holstrom, 1974; Evans, 1978; Fox and Sherl, 1972). However, only a few empirical investigations of dynamic treatment have been conducted. Results from a study employing psychoanalytic therapy (Bart, 1975, cited by Turner and Frank, 1981) indicated that symptoms of sexual assault victims increased. In a study of nine sexual assault victims receiving short-term dynamic group therapy, fear and hostility significantly decreased, even though only four of the seven victims who completed the study reported a change in their overall condition. No control group was employed and the content of the therapy session was not described (Cryer and Beutler, 1980). The impact of brief individual therapy containing both cognitive and dynamic elements was reported by Krupnick (1980). She found that of eight participants who completed 12 weeks of psychotherapy, seven had achieved 'good' outcomes, and one a 'fair' outcome. Outcomes were assessed by the evaluating clinician; no standardized measures were employed; and no control group was included in the study.

Although empirical investigations of dynamic therapy for sexual assault victims have been scant, several authors have proposed dynamic issues to be considered in working with this population (Krupnick, 1980; Ledray, 1986; Metzger, 1976; Notman and Nadelson, 1976). These issues include, but are not limited to, exploring the meaning of the event, addressing the experience of isolation, exploring reactivated dormant images of others, working through disturbing affects, and challenging intensified negative self-images.

Exploring the meaning of the event is often important in conducting psychotherapy with sexual assault victims; the meaning is likely to vary depending upon the individual's previous history and personality structure. Krupnick (1980) cites an example of a 25-year-old woman who was sexually assaulted several years after moving to California against her father's wishes. According to this account the client interpreted the event as a punishment for separating from her parents and for her independence strivings. Although not proposed within a cognitive framework, exploring the meaning of the event is likely to occur within the context of addressing the issue of responsibility. Thus, such therapeutic work fits in well with cognitive/attribution theories of self-blame.

Metzger (1976) addressed the theme of isolation in a personal account of being sexually assaulted. She asserted that one reason sexual assault is such a devastating experience is because it involves total isolation and a complete loss of self. Because sexual assault is an experience of isolation, she feels that the treatment of sexual assault needs to include 'community.' Incorporating a feminist flavor, she recommended that women need to speak out about their traumatic experiences and their oppression, thus revalidating themselves as persons. Along these lines, the benefits of 'community' following sexual assault have been thoroughly documented in the social support literature (e.g. Burgess and Holstrom, 1978; Norris and Feldman-Summers, 1981; Ruch and Leon, 1983).

It has also been suggested that in conducting psychotherapy with victims, the therapist should be alert to the client's dormant images of significant others that may be brought to the surface following the assault. For example, Krupnick (1980) wrote that unconscious images of parents as all powerful and protective caretakers may be rudely altered; such clients may feel they have been abandoned. According to Krupnick (1980), this dynamic is most likely to occur in persons who have previously experienced inconsistent or inadequate caretaking.

Working through disturbing affects is another therapeutic goal that has been advocated by psychotherapists who utilize a more dynamic approach (Krupnick, 1980; Ledray, 1986; Notman and Nadelson, 1976). Anger is a feeling prevalent in nearly all sexual assault victims (Ledray, 1986); however, this anger may not readily be discerned as it is often not expressed directly (Notman and Nadelson, 1976). In addition, they assert that as women have culturally been restricted in the direct expression of anger, these feelings may often be directed inward, leading to a pattern of self-blame. Ledray (1986) also noted that anger may initially be generalized (e.g. to all men), rather than focused on the rapist. Guilt and shame are other common feelings which often emerge in psychotherapy with sexual assault victims. Notman and Nadelson (1976) argued that the victim's guilt is increased by focusing on the sexual aspect of the crime, rather than the violence that is perpetrated. In addition, as many still hold negative sexual attitudes, they assert that even unwilling participation in a sexual act is often held suspect. Furthermore, the traditional expectation that women are to set the limits in sexual situations only contributes to increased feelings of guilt (Notman and Nadelson, 1976).

Another theme that often emerges in psychotherapy with sexual assault victims is intensification of negative self-images (Krupnick, 1980). Common negative images of the self include viewing the self as feeble, frightened, vulnerable, and needy. In addition, PTSD symptoms of fear and anxiety contribute to a self-concept of being out of control. Krupnick (1980) writes that this view of the self as fragile and dependent can be threatening to those whose self-esteem is based on feeling independent and in control. Furthermore, she asserts that this will be particularly true when 'this sense of independence is brittle, unintegrated, and when it serves as a defense against powerful, underlying wishes to be taken care of. In such a case, the intensified need to rely on a temporarily stronger other person may be experienced as a humiliating defeat (p. 349).

Behavioral Interventions

Systematic desensitization

Systematic desensitization (SD: Wolpe, 1958) involves having a relaxed client confront, usually in imagination, a series of increasingly intense anxiety-producing stimuli. In a single case study, systematic desensitization proved effective in treating the fear responses of a woman sexually assaulted seven years prior to treatment (Wolff, 1977). Similarly, Turner (1979) found improvement in measures of fear, anxiety, depression, and social adjustment in a series of nine cases treated with SD.

A recent outcome study (Frank et al., 1988) compared the effects of SD with Cognitive Therapy (CT) in treating both recent sexual assault victims (<4 weeks post-assault) and delayed treatment-seeking victims (>2 months post-assault). Participants were randomly assigned to the two treatment groups. Among the immediate treatment-seekers, 34 participants completed CT and 26 completed SD; among the late treatment-seekers, 14 completed CT and 10 completed SD. The SD protocol began with an assessment of a participant's fears and avoidance behaviors. Next, she was taught progressive relaxation (the alternation of tensing and releasing major muscle groups) following Jacobson's methods (1938, 1970). After relaxation training, target complaints were broken down and assembled into a hierarchy. Then, SD procedures were carried out as designed by Wolpe (1969). Frank et al. (1988) noted that 75% of the SD participants followed a pattern of exposing themselves in vivo to the feared stimuli worked on in each treatment session. This in vivo work was self-directed and spontaneously reported.

Results from the study indicated that victims' targeted fear and anxiety decreased with SD treatment. No differences were found between SD and CT. In their review of the Frank et al. (1988) study, Kilpatrick and Calhoun (1988) note that becuase no control group was employed, observed positive changes could be attributable to factors other than treatment. This is especially true in the early treatment condition as changes may have been due to the naturally occurring pattern of spontaneous recovery seen in many victims 2 to 3 months post-assault. As symptoms have been shown to stabilize following the 3-month post-assault mark, their study provides stronger evidence for the efficacy of SD in the delayed treatment condition. Frank *et al.* (1988) contend that SD was proven effective, even in the early treatment condition, in that comparisons were made between their treated sample and untreated victim samples from other studies. However, Kilpatrick and Calhoun (1988) refute this, arguing that the groups were not demographically equivalent, making comparisons unfounded. In addition, they assert that the rate of symptom change from initial to follow-up assessment between groups was negligible.

Cognitive therapy

Little empirical evidence has been available regarding the use of Cognitive Therapy (CT) with sexual assault victims. Cognitive restructuring and thought stopping was successfully employed in single case studies (Forman, 1980). However, little information has been available on the general efficacy of treating sexual assault victims with CT.

In the Frank *et al.* (1988) comparative outcome study described above, the CT protocol also began with an identification of target complaints associated with the assault. Each of these complaints was collaboratively worked on with the therapist and the participant during three phases of treatment. The first phase of treatment consisted of the participant completing a daily activity schedule, from which the therapist designed homework assignments to increase the level of the participant's activity, enhance the quality of her activities, and gradually involve her in activities that had been avoided subsequent to the assault. The second phase of treatment involved identifying automatic negative thoughts and cognitive distortions. Participants were helped to identify rational responses to these negative thoughts and distortions. Phase three of the CT protocol involved an exploration of the participant's basic assumptions about the world. To provide the rationale for phase three, the authors cite Beck's theory (1972, 1979), which asserts that certain tenacious beliefs may predispose one to depression and anxiety. The authors report that only 20% of the CT participants completed this phase of treatment, as more of their symptoms had already abated prior to this phase. Results of CT treatment gains paralleled those for SD, in that target complaints showed significant improvement. As noted previously, no difference was evidenced between CT and SD and the quasi-experimental design makes interpretation of results, particularly for the early treatment condition, difficult.

Frank *et al.* (1988) attempt to explain the lack of differences found between CT and SD in two ways. First, they acknowledge that their initial expectation was that CT would be effective in treating depressive symptoms while SD would be more effective in treating phobic reactions. However, descriptions of symptom profiles indicate that sexual assault victims experience a unique complex of symptoms that include both depressive and phobic elements. Thus, victims would not be expected to respond differentially to these two treatments. Second, they assert that common to both CT and SD is the facilitation of the client's gaining a rapid increased sense of control. This is important in that primary to the experience of sexual assault is the feeling of complete loss of control.

Flooding

Flooding is another behavioral treatment strategy, which has been used occasionally in treating sexual assault victims. Flooding also has been successful in treating Vietnam veterans suffering from post-traumatic stress disorder (Fairbank and Keane, 1982; Keane and Kaloupek, 1982; Minisek, 1984). Flooding procedures involve prolonged exposure to a moderate- to high-strength conditioned stimulus in conjunction with the prohibition of all anxiety-reducing behaviors. According to behavioral theory, such exposure in the absence of external aversive consequences should result in decreased anxiety related to the fear cue. Such exposure can either occur *in vivo* or in imagination. In one study employing flooding with four physical and sexual assault victims, treatment proved to be effective (Haynes & Mooney, 1975). Flooding procedures have also received clinical support in a case study of an incest victim (Rychtarik *et al.*, 1984).

Currently, Rothbaum and Foa (1988) have been comparing the efficacy of flooding with stress inoculation training (SIT), Supportive Counseling, and a no treatment wait-list. Preliminary examination of their results appears to indicate that flooding and SIT are more effective than supportive counseling or no treatment. It also appeared that SIT produced greater changes at the post-treatment assessment than flooding but that both groups had similar results by the 3-month follow-up. It should be noted that supportive counseling was not the same as reported in Resick *et al.* (1988) or other supportive therapy, in that clients were not given information about rape reactions or counseled about the rape directly. They were taught problem solving and counseled about day to day problems. It should also be noted that this study is still underway and final results have not yet been obtained.

Sexual dysfunction therapy

A behavioral treatment program has been designed to treat sexual assault victims experiencing sexual problems. The treatment package, developed by Becker and Skinner (1983, 1984), contains a detailed assessment followed by 10 group treatment sessions. The assessment included information about the development and maintenance of the problem, outcome of any previous treatment, and the client's treatment goals and expectations. Issues addressed during the group sessions include learning theory as it relates to the development of sexual problems, body image, identification of satisfying sexual fantasies and activities, cognitive restructuring, anxiety reduction, communication skills, and sensate focusing. In a study employing the above treatment package, 80% of a sample of 35 women improved on their target problems. When group treatment was compared to individual treatment, group treatment proved to be more effective. In addition, some participants did not begin the treatment until 10 weeks following the initial assessment. One-half of these delayed participants dropped out of the study. A second treatment package called the 'Sexual Dysfunction Treatment Package' (SDTP) appears nearly identical to Becker and Skinner's (1983) package. In a study employing SDTP, a sample of 43 women demonstrated significant improvement on 92% of their goals. While these programs appear comprehensive in terms of treating sexual problems that may arise subsequent to sexual assault, they do little to address other symptoms and concerns victims may experience (Foa et al., 1987).

Stress inoculation training

Stress inoculation training (SIT) forms the basis of a composite treatment program designed for sexual assault victims by Kilpatrick et al. (1982). The purpose of SIT is to enable the client to cope with intrusive recollections and anxiety engendered by conditioned stimuli in the environment and to help her break up escape and avoidance patterns conditioned following the crime. The original format for the SIT package for sexual assault victims was adapted from the work of Meichenbaum and Cameron (1983) on stress inoculation training. Stress inoculation training consists of three phases. The first phase is educational, consisting of information about the development of fear, sympathetic nervous system arousal, classical conditioning, operant avoidance, the role of cognitions, and the role of conditioned stimuli (i.e. fear cues) in automatic fear reactions, intrusive recollections, and avoidance behavior.

The second phase is one of skill building: progressive relaxation, brief relaxation, thought stopping, guided self-dialogue, covert rehearsal, role playing, and problem solving techniques are taught. The third phase consists of applying newly acquired skills. Fear hierarchies are developed in order to break fear-producing situations into more manageable units, thereby minimizing avoidance behavior. Then, coping skills are employed to tackle each step on the hierarchy. For more detailed information on stress inoculation training procedures with sexual assault victims, the interested reader is referred to Resick and Jordan's (1988) SIT Training Manual.

Stress inoculation training has proved effective in several single case design studies (Kilpatrick and Amick, 1985; Kilpatrick et al., 1982; Pearson et al., 1983) and several comparative studies (Resick et al., 1988; Rothbaum and Foa, 1988; Veronen and Kilpatrick, 1983). In an empirical investigation of stress inoculation training, Veronen and Kilpatrick (1983) offered a choice of 10 sessions of SIT, peer counseling, or systematic desensitization (SD) to sexual assault victims demonstrating elevated fear and avoidance responses 3 months post-assault. More than half of the victims rejected all of the treatments. Of the 15 who agreed to be treated, 11 selected SIT, 3 selected peer counseling, and one subject did not make a choice and was randomly assigned to receive SIT. Given their methodology, no formal comparisons between treatments can be made. In addition, no formal statistical analyses were conducted on the final 6 subjects who completed the SIT treatment. However, the authors indicated they observed improvement from pre- to post-treatment on most measures.

As described earlier, a recent study compared three types of treatment for sexual assault victims: stress inoculation training, assertiveness training, and supportive psychotherapy (Resick *et al.*, 1988). Participants had been assaulted at least 3 months prior to receiving treatment. Common to all groups were a male and female cotherapist team. Resick *et al.* noted that the rationale for the inclusion of a male cotherapist was 'to help participants overcome their avoidance of men and particularly to expose them to warm, empathic male therapists who would be available for role playing when appropriate' (p. 39). In addition, all groups consisted of a common educational session in which a cognitive-behavioral explanation of the development of fear and anxiety following sexual assault was given.

Results indicated that SIT was effective in reducing participants' anxiety and increasing their assertiveness. These gains were maintained through both the 3-month and 6-month follow-up assessments. Improvements were also made in the areas of depression, self-esteem, social evaluation, and failure fears. However, these gains had diminished by the 6-month post-treatment assessment. In addition, no differences were evidenced between the SIT, assertiveness training, and supportive psychotherapy groups. Resick *et al.* (1988) employed emotional processing theory to explain their results. They hypothesized that perhaps the information session combined with the group format was sufficient both to evoke the memory of the trauma and to allow for effective and cognitive corrective information to be integrated into the memory structure. Although the male-female cotherapist team was also common to all three groups, this factor was not analyzed in the present study and deserves further attention. The case study which follows illustrates the implementation of stress inoculation training for rape victims.

CASE STUDY

Katie is a 21-year-old college student who was raped by her boyfriend two years prior to her seeking therapy. Katie's parents were divorced when she was 16, which precipitated a depression. She was on antidepressants for a year at that time. Other than the rape for which she sought therapy, she had no history of victimization. Soon after entering college, Katie became involved with a 19-year-old student who lived two doors away in her dormitory. The relationship was emotionally abusive and Katie again became depressed, resulting in another round of antidepressants in January 1986, her Freshman year. The winter of that year, she began drinking frequently despite the use of medication. In April, one week before the rape, Katie broke off the relationship with her boyfriend. The next weekend she went to a spring festival on campus and had a number of drinks in a short period of time. Her reaction to the alcohol mixed with the medication was so strong that her ex-boyfriend, who encountered her at the festival, took her to a local hospital. Later, he accompanied Katie to her room and helped her to bed. A short while later he returned to Katie's room, told her he was going to give her a shower, took her to a shower stall, and forcibly had sex with her. Although her memories of the event were not distinct because of the inebriation, Katie knew that she had been terrified.

Katie did not label the event as rape but she experienced an emotional shutdown, a numbing of affect, that continued for 18 months. She stopped drinking and phased out the antidepressants, which she felt she no longer needed. In looking back, Katie said she no longer felt depressed; she felt nothing. It took her two more months finally to break off the relationship with the assailant even though she was afraid of him. The first person she told about the assault was her next boyfriend but she still didn't label it as a rape at that time. During the summer and fall of 1986 she received therapy from a female therapist and in the fall of 1987 she received therapy from a male therapist. Although she talked about the incident a lot in therapy, neither she nor the two therapists labeled the event as rape.

During the fall semester, she attended a class in which the professor described reactions to rape and characteristics of rapists. When she finally recognized and labeled her experience as rape, the shutdown of emotions finally lifted and she was overwhelmed with her feelings. Most of her waking time was spent with intrusive recollections of the event, and a roller coaster of emotional reactions including depression, anxiety, self-blame and loss of trust. Her reactions were so strong that she dropped out of school. In November of 1987, she was interviewed and assessed for our research-oriented rape group. While she was on the waiting list, she received counseling from a therapist at another agency, which focused on her writing a letter to her assailant. At the time of the interview, when asked to apportion blame for the incident, Katie said that she blamed herself 70%, the perpetrator 20% and chance 10%. Of the self-blame, she felt that 20% was behavioral and 80% characterological. In April of 1988, Katie participated in a group which received stress inoculation training for eight, 1½ hour sessions. Prior to treatment, Katie was assessed twice, once three months before entering the group when she was placed on a waiting list, and immediately before the group began. She was also assessed the week after the group ended and at three and six months after the group ended.

The first phase of treatment was educational. During the first session group participants were given a cognitive-behavioral model of PTSD and depression in order to normalize their reactions. The rest of the session moved into the second phase of treatment, skill building. Participants were taught progressive relaxation in order to lower their overall level of tension and anxiety.

At the second session, homework was reviewed. Katie did not practice during the first week but began to realize how tense she was most of the time. She did find the explanation of classical conditioning very helpful and began to identify 'cue situations.' The second session was essentially a repetition of the first session to help the clients absorb what they did not take in the first time. The only new material presented was a description of the major channels of fear: physiological, cognitive, and behavioral. A stage model of fear was also presented. They received more relaxation training and were reminded to practice every day. They were also given the homework to observe cues in the environment which trigger fear and were asked to observe their own reactions.

At the next session, Katie reported that she had begun practicing relaxation and that it was helpful. (She later reported that the peer pressure of having other group members practicing successfully goaded her into practicing.) During the third session, group participants were taught two new skills, brief relaxation (the quieting reflex, Stroebel, 1983), and thought stopping. Session four began with a review of homework. Katie practiced and used the quieting reflex a great deal but was having difficulty with thought stopping. She was rather excited by the new relaxation skills and did, in fact, appear more relaxed during the session. The new skills taught during this session were self-instruction (guided self-dialogue) and covert rehearsal.

During the fifth session, role-playing was introduced. Everyone was given the opportunity to role-play in dyads, interpersonal situations in which they anticipated difficulty. These role-play situations often involve telling someone about the rape whom they hadn't told before, for one reason or another. Participants were encouraged to use the coping skills they had learned earlier as part of the role-play situation. Because rape victims may experience learned helplessness during the

Table 11.1   Katie's raw scores on the BSI, TSCS and MFS

Instrument SCL-90	Session				
	Pre1	Pre2	Post	3Mo	6Mo
Somatization	1.5	1.3	.8	.7	.7
Obsessive-compulsive	1.5	1.3	1.9	1.0	.2
Interpersonal sensitivity	1.3	1.8	1.3	1.3	.4
Depression	2.6	2.7	3.0	1.4	.5
Anxiety	2.2	1.7	2.2	1.2	.7
Hostility	1.0	.3	1.0	1.3	.2
Phobic anxiety	1.1	1.1	1.0	.1	.1
Paranoia	1.0	1.3	1.0	.7	.5
Psychoticsm	1.4	1.6	1.5	.6	.2
Tennessee self-concept scale					
Physical	56	55	61	66	72
Moral/ethical	65	60	62	71	75
Personal	56	53	52	61	72
Family	48	64	50	58	68
Social	57	52	62	65	71
Identity	99	96	106	115	122
Self-satisfaction	100	102	89	105	118
Behaviour	83	86	92	101	118
Modified fear survey					
Vulnerability	43	35	24	24	26
Classical	22	19	17	18	16
Sexual	29	32	18	19	15
Social	35	38	27	24	19
Medical	30	16	18	15	14
Agoraphobia	14	16	10	11	6
Loud noises	6	5	3	4	3
Weapons	15	13	15	12	13

crime or may blame themselves and not trust their judgement anymore in other situations, training in problem solving was introduced during the sixth session, based on Goldfried and Davison's model (1976). The seventh session was devoted to describing how to set up a hierarchy.

During the first half-hour of the last session, group members discussed their use of the hierarchy. They were praised for any attempt to confront avoidance situations and were encouraged to continue to use the hierarchy to overcome their avoidance of non-dangerous but fear-producing stimuli. During the remainder of the session all of the concepts and skills that had been introduced were reviewed. Group members were encouraged to continue to practice the skills on a regular basis and were informed that they wouldn't 'own' the skills and be able to use them in difficult situations unless they had practiced them to the point where they were almost automatic.

Table 11.1 and Figures 11.1 and 11.2 depict Katie's scores on the SCL-90, the Tennessee Self-Concept Scale (TSCS), and the Modified Fear Survey (MFS). Katie's scores on the SCL-90 at the two pretreatment sessions were rather elevated. She scored above a t-score of 70 on interpersonal sensitivity, depression, anxiety and psychoticism. Her scores did not improve at the post-treatment assessment except somatization which improved one half standard deviation. However, the three month follow-up, her scores on eight of the nine subscales indicated improvement.

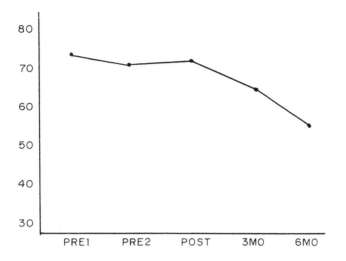

Figure 11.1   Global severity index—SCL-90

Particularly notable were decreases in depression, phobic anxiety, and psychoticism. At the six month follow-up, all nine subscale scores fell within normal limits (below a t-score of 60). Figure 11.1 depicts Katie's total score, the Global Severity Index, across the five assessment sessions.

On the Tennessee Self-Concept Scale (TSCS) Katie scored almost two standard deviations below the mean on overall self-esteem at pre-treatment. She scored particularly low on the identity and behavior subscales. Each of those scales improved approximately one-half standard deviation immediately post-treatment and improved again at each of the follow-up sessions. By six months post-crime, all eight subscales fell at the mean. In fact, two of the subscales, self-satisfaction and personal, fell one standard deviation above the mean. Figure 11.2 depicts Katie's overall TSCS self-esteem score over time.

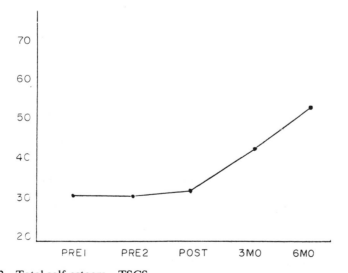

Figure 11.2   Total self-esteem—TSCS

Katie's scores on the Modified Fear Survey were quite elevated pre-treatment. In fact, she scored one to two standard deviations above the mean for rape victims (Resick *et al.*, 1986) on five of the eight subscales: vulnerability, sexual fears, social evaluation and failure, medical fears and weapons. Most of these scales improved markedly by the post-treatment assessment. For instance, on the vulnerability scale she scored one standard deviation below the mean for rape victims and right at the mean for non-victims. Katie continued to score at least one standard deviation above the non-victim mean on sexual fears until the six month assessment. At the six month follow-up, Katie scored within a standard deviation of the non-victim means on all of the MFS subscales except weapons fears which were still elevated one standard deviation.

While Katie reported improvement over the eight weeks of therapy that had not occurred during the preceding year, particularly with specific fears, she felt that her depression was interfering with her ability to utilize the skills she had learned in the group. After the group ended she went to a psychiatrist and was prescribed anti-depressants which she took for almost a year. Looking back from the six month follow-up, Katie wrote:

> When I came into the group I was frightened, depressed, suicidal, and so tense and confused I was beginning to have trouble speaking lucidly, and starting to simply 'phase out,' trancelike, whenever confronted with a conflict, particularly one of a sexual nature, with my current partner. I felt completely desperate and hopeless. At the first meeting, I was actually disappointed that we didn't share our personal stories. At that time, just talking about something that had laid dormant inside of me for two years was a tremendous catharsis. But we didn't commiserate: we got lectured, and then began to learn to relax. Someday, we were promised, relaxation would be our automatic response to stress, if we worked at it. Furthermore, not only could we recover our past level of functioning, we could actually improve it. I was intrigued, but I did not believe it for a minute.
>
> Now six months later, after dropping out of school and out of life, I'm making a new start. I'm back in school and I *have* recovered much of my old confidence and wit. And yes, relaxation has become as much as an automatic-response coping strategy as tension used to be. The areas where group had its profoundest effects on me were these: (1) physical-finding out how tense I'd been, and its effect on my functioning; (2) discovering that my fear and anxiety, which had turned me away from almost everything I enjoyed, was creating a cycle of depression, fear, withdrawal, and more depression; and (3) the therapist's unshakable confidence that we could and would recover and her own strong female personhood that served as a role model for me, demonstrating that a woman *could* be strong and confident, something I thought I'd never be again.

As a parenthitical note, from experience, the therapist did not start these groups with 'war stories' because many women become more frightened hearing how other women have been raped in so many different situations. While relaying the experience is an important part of recovery, it should be done with an individual therapist or much later in the group process. Katie continued to make gains over the six months that followed the group and testing indicated that she fell within normal limits on all of the assessment measures.

While this chapter was being written, Katie was invited back for an interview to confirm the facts in her case. The interview took place one year after she began the group. Katie reported that she had received no more therapy after the stress inoculation group other than the antidepressants. She was not reassessed but did report that she is continuing to do well. She has continued to use regularly the skills that she was taught in therapy and gave specific examples of their use. Katie reported being able to recognize cues in the environment that were triggering anxiety and using her new coping skills to reduce her tension and refrain from escaping from the situation (e.g. tall dark-haired men wearing university jackets, the smell of the dormitory).

She reported using the quieting reflex frequently, covert rehearsal regularly, and thought stopping occasionally. She also described using a hierarchy for dating (first going out for coffee, then with a group in the evening, and so forth). Katie said that she has used the problem solving strategies for a number of major decisions. Finally, when asked to apportion blame for the rape, she said 70% went to the assailant, 20% to the environment (societal socialization), and 10% to herself. Of the self-blame, she ascribed 90% to her behavior and 10% her character.

This case study illustrates how the use of stress inoculation training may be helpful in the treatment of fear and anxiety in victims of rape. It is not a 'clean' case study in that the client also used antidepressants. However, there is no reason to assume that antidepressants would have a pervasive effect on such diverse symptoms as anxiety, specific fear reactions, interpersonal sensitivity, paranoia, and self-esteem. There *is* reason to believe that the skills that she learned, and implemented regularly, would have such pervasive effects. However, it is possible that the antidepressants facilitated the effects of treatment in that she was better able to apply the skills she had acquired with the lessening of the depression. This appears to be the case, because she exhibited gradual and substantial improvement over the 6 months that followed her participation in the group. Furthermore, while this was not a controlled single case design, the length of time since the assault and the length of time between the two pre-treatment sessions indicates that her improvement post-therapy was not merely from the passage of time.

Katie's case is not unusual in that she was an acquaintance rape victim who did not immediately label her experience as a rape. She experienced what appeared to be a delayed reaction because of the shut-down, or massive avoidance response which was triggered as a coping mechanism. While not typical, it is not rare for rape victims to postpone their reactions, particularly acquaintance rape victims who have not accurately labeled the experience and sought help. This type of delayed reaction is also commonly observed in child sexual abuse victims. Finally, this case illustrates an important consideration for therapists; that some clients may have pre-existing problems which may exacerbate their reactions to rape or be exacerbated themselves. Because of her preexisting history of depression, Katie needed more intervention than that which was provided by the stress inoculation.

CONCLUDING COMMENTS

Rape may have profound and longlasting effects on victims. The research which was reviewed in this chapter indicates that many women suffer significant levels of symptomatology for months or years after such an event. While research and development on theories and treatment are quite new, they appear promising. A number of case studies and a few comparative treatment outcome studies have reported significant improvement over fairly brief periods of therapy. However, at this point, there is no one therapy that has been evaluated sufficiently to be called the treatment of choice. In fact, in the few comparative outcome studies which have been conducted thus far, no therapy has been demonstrated to be superior to the others being compared and no one therapy has provided benefits to all clients. It is clear that more research will be needed in the coming years.

It is also clear that more basic research is needed to continue to develop and test theories of victim reactions and recovery. The cognitive information/emotional processing theories of victim reactions have great heuristic appeal and may explain why so many different types of therapy appear to be effective in alleviating the distress of trauma victims. However, these theories have not been evaluated thus far, so their applicability and limitations are not yet known.

All of the therapies which were reviewed have several aspects in common. All avoid victim-blame attitudes. While it may be helpful to consider ways in which the victim may increase safety and crime prevention, it is important for the victim to realize that no matter what she was doing, no one had the right to attack her and rape her and that she did not consciously or unconsciously cause the event to occur. However, it also may be important for the victim to understand the defensive nature of the victim-blame attitudes she is subjected to by significant others.

All of the therapies provide a supportive, yet matter-of-fact attitude in which rape is treated not as a shameful, stigmatizing event, but as a criminal victimization. Such a supportive environment is important for the victim to feel safe in discussing her thoughts and feelings. It also provides the environment in which she can begin to overcome avoidance, both behavioral and cognitive. All of the therapies help the client to integrate and process the event in a more adaptive manner. Finally, all of the therapies provide information and the expectation that the victim's reactions need not be permanent and that she can achieve a full recovery.

As a final note for consideration, all of the therapies which have been developed through research are very brief. It is possible that some clients may need more extensive treatment, or therapy in phases. Occasionally it is not possible to deal with all rape-related issues at once because of environmental or developmental constraints. For example, if a rape victim is not involved in an intimate relationship (or is too young to be in one) therapy for sexual dysfunctions or intimate trust issues may have to be conducted at a later time when it becomes relevant. Furthermore, an unstudied topic is the interaction between developmental and rape-related issues in therapy. Adolescence, a period of important development with regard to identity and independence, is also the period when rape is most likely to occur. How rape affects development and the most important therapeutic interventions for such issues have yet to be explored.

References

Albin, R. S. (1977). Psychological studies of rape. *SIGNS: Journal of Women in Culture and Society*, **3**(2), 423–35.

American Psychiatric Association. (1987). *Diagnostic and Statistical Manual of Mental Disorders*. (3rd edn revised). Washington, DC: American Psychiatric Association Press.

Atkeson, B. M., Calhoun, K. S., Resick, P. A., and Ellis, E. M. (1982). Victims of rape: Repeated assessment of depressive symptoms. *Journal of Consulting and Clinical Psychology*, **50**, 96–102.

Bart, P. (1975, May). Unalienating abortion, demystifying depression, and restoring rape victims. Paper presented at the 128th annual meeting of the American Psychological Association, Anaheim, CA.

Beck, A. T. (1972). *Depression: Causes and Treatment*. Philadelphia: University of Pennsylvania Press.

Beck, A. T., and Emery, G. (1979). *Cognitive Therapy of Anxiety and Phobic Disorders*. Philadelphia: University of Pennsylvania Press.

Becker, J. V., and Skinner, L. J. (1983). Assessment and treatment of rape-related sexual dysfunctions. *The Clinical Psychologist*, **36**, 102–5.

Becker, J. V., and Skinner, L. J. (1984). Behavioral treatment of sexual dysfunctions in sexual assault survivors. In I. Stuart and J. Greer (eds), *Victims of Sexual Aggression*. New York: Van Nostrand Reinhold, pp. 211–34.

Brownmiller, S. (1975). *Against our Will*. New York: Simon & Schuster.

Burgess, A. W., and Holstrom, L. (1974). *Rape: Victims of Crisis*. Bowie, MD: Robert J. Brady.

Burgess, A. W., and Holstrom, I. L. (1978). Recovery from rape and prior life stress. *Research in Nursing and Health*, **1**, 165–74.

Burgess, A. W., and Holstrom, L. (1979). *Rape: Crisis and Recovery*. Bowie, MD: Robert J. Brady.

Butcher, J. N., and Maudal, G. R. (1976). Crisis intervention. In I. Weiner (ed.), *Clinical Methods in Psychology*. New York: Wiley.

Calhoun, K. S., Atkeson, B. M., and Resick, P. A. (1982). A longitudinal examination of fear reactions in victims of rape. *Journal of Counseling Psychology*, **29**, 655–61.

Caplan, G. (1964). *Principles of Preventive Psychiatry*. New York: Basic Books.

Cryer, L., and Beutler, L. (1980). Group therapy: An alternative treatment approach for rape victims. *Journal of Sex and Marital Therapy*, **6**, 40–6.

Dormanen, S. (1980). Statistical Patterns of victimization. *Evaluation*, (special issue), 12–13.

Evans, H. I. (1978). Psychotherapy for the rape victim: Some treatment models. *Hospital and Community Psychiatry*, **29**, 309–12.

Fairbank, J. A., and Keane, T. M. (1982). Flooding for combat-related stress disorders: Assessment of anxiety reduction across traumatic memories. *Behavior Therapy*, **13**, 499–510.

Federal Bureau of Investigation (1986). *Uniform Crime Reports*. Washington, DC: Department of Justice.

Foa, E. B., and Kozak, M. J. (1986). Emotional processing of fear: Exposure to corrective information. *Psychological Bulletin*, **99**, 20–35.

Foa, E. B., Olasov, B., and Steketee, G. S. (1987, September). Treatment of rape victims. Paper presented at 'State-of-the-Art Workshop on Sexual Assault' sponsored by the National Institute of Mental Health, Charleston, SC.

Foa, E. B., Steketee, G., and Rothbaum, B. O. (1989). Behavioral/cognitive conceptualizations of post-traumatic stress disorder. *Behavior Therapy*, **20**, 155–76.

Forman, B. D. (1980). Psychotherapy with rape victims. *Psychotherapy: Theory, Research, and Practice*, **17**, 304–11.

Fox, S. S., and Sherl, D. J. (1972). Crisis intervention with victims of rape. *Social Work*, **17**, 37–42.

Frank, E., Anderson, B., Stewart, B. D., Bancu, C., Hughes, C., and West, D. (1988). Efficacy of cognitive behavior therapy and systematic desensitization in the treatment of rape trauma. *Behavior Therapy*, **19**, 403–20.

George, L. K., and Winfield-Laird, I. (1986). Sexual assault: Prevalence and mental health consequences. Final report submitted to the National Institute of Mental Health.

Goldfried, M. R., and Davison, G. C. (1976). *Clinical Behavior Therapy*. New York: Holt, Rinehart & Winston, pp. 88–92.

Goldstein, A. J., and Chambless, D. L. (1978). A reanalysis of agoraphobia. *Behavior Therapy*, **9**, 47–59.

Griffin, S. (1971). Rape: The all-American crime. *Ramparts Magazine*, **10**, 26–35.

Haynes, S. N., and Mooney, D. K. (1975). Nightmares: Etiological, theoretical and behavioral treatment considerations. *Psychological Record*, **25**, 225–36.

Holmes, M. R., and St. Lawrence, J. (1983). Treatment of rape-induced trauma: Proposed behavioral conceptualization and review of the literature. *Clinical Psychology Review*, **3**, 417–33.

Jacobson, E. (1938). *Progressive Relaxation*. Chicago: University of Chicago Press.

Jacobson, E. (1970). *Modern Treatment of Tense Patients*. Springfield, IL: Charles C. Thomas Press.

Janoff-Bulman, R. (1979). Characterological versus behavioral self-blame: Inquiries into depression and rape. *Journal of Personality and Social Psychology*, **37**, 1798–809.

Keane, T. M., and Kalopek, D. G. (1982). Imaginal flooding in the treatment of post-traumatic stress disorder. *Journal of Consulting and Clinical Psychology*, **50**, 138–40.

Kilpatrick, D. G., and Amick, A. A. (1985). Rape trauma. In M. Hersen and C. G. Last (eds), *Behavioral Therapy Casebook*. New York: Springer, pp. 86–103.

Kilpatrick, D. G., Best, C. L., Veronen, L. J., Amick, A. E., Villeponteaux, L. A., and Ruff, G. A. (1985). Mental health correlates of criminal victimization: A random community survey. *Journal of Consulting and Clinical Psychology*, **53**, 866–73.

Kilpatrick, D. G., and Calhoun, K. S. (1988). Early behavioral treatment for rape trauma: Efficacy or artifact? *Behavior Therapy*, **19**, 421–7.

Kilpatrick, D. G., Resick, P. A., and Veronen, J. J. (1981). Effects of a rape experience: A longitudinal study. *Journal of Social Issues*, **37**, 105–22.

Kilpatrick, D. G., Saunders, B. E., Veronen, L. J., Best, C. L., and Von, J.M. (1987a). Criminal victimization: Lifetime prevalence, reporting to police, and psychological impact. *Crime and Delinquency*, **33**, 479–89.

Kilpatrick, D. G., and Veronen, L. J. (1983, December). The aftermath of rape: A three year follow-up. Paper presented at the World Congress on Behavior Therapy, 17th Annual Convention of the Association for the Advancement of Behavior Therapy, Washington, DC.

Kilpatrick, D. G., and Veronen, L. J. (1984). Treatment of fear and anxiety in victims of rape. (Final Report, Grant No. R01MH2902). Rockville, MD: National Institute of Mental Health.

Kilpatrick, D. G., Veronen, L., and Resick, P. A. (1982). Psychological sequelae to rape. In D. M. Doleys, R. L. Meredith and A. R. Cimminero (eds), *Behavioral Medicine: Assessment and Treatment Strategies*. New York: Plenum, pp. 473–97.

Kilpatrick, D. G., Veronen, L. J., Saunders, B. E., Best, C. L., Amick-McMullen, A., and Paduhovich, J. (1987b, March). The psychological impact of crime: A study of randomly surveyed crime victims. Final report for the National Institute of Justice, Grant no. 84-IJ-CX-0039.

Koss, M. P. (1987, September). Rape incidence and prevalence: A review and assessment of the data. Paper presented at the 'State-of-the-Art Workshop on Sexual Assault,' sponsored by the National Institute of Mental Health, Charleston, SC.

Koss, M. P., and Harvey, M. R. (1987). *The Rape Victim: Clinical and Community Approaches to Treatment*. Lexington, MA: Stephen Greene Press.

Krupnick, J. (1980). Brief psychotherapy with victims of violent crime. *Victimology: An International Journal*, **5**, 347–54.

Largen, M. (1976). History of women's movement in changing attitudes, laws, and treatment toward rape victims. In M. J. Walker and S. L. Brodsky (eds), *Sexual Assault*. Lexington, MA: D. C. Heath.

Ledray, L. E. (1986). *Recovering from Rape*. New York, NY: Henry Holt.

Lerner, M. J., and Miller, D. T. (1978). Just world research and the attribution process: Looking back and ahead. *Psychological Bulletin*, **85**, 1030–51.

Lewinsohn, P. M. (1974). Clinical and theoretical aspects of depression. In K. S. Calhoun, H. E. Adams and K. M. Mitchell (eds), *Innovative Treatment Methods in Psychopathology*. New York: Wiley.

Meichenbaum, D., and Cameron, R. (1983). Stress innoculation training: Toward a general paradigm for training coping skills: In D. Meichenbaum and M. E. Jaremko (eds), *Stress Reduction and Prevention*. New York: Plenum.

Metzger, D. (1976). It is always the woman who is raped. *American Journal of Psychiatry*, **133**, 405–8.

Minisek, N. A. (1974). Flooding as a supplemental treatment for Vietnam Veterans. Paper presented at the Third National Conference on Post Traumatic Stress Disorders: Baltimore, MD.

Murphy, S. M., Amick-McMullan, A. E., Kilpatrick, D. G., Haskett, M. E., Veronen, L. J., Best, C. L., and Saunders, B. E. (1988). Rape victims' self-esteem: A longitudinal analysis. *Journal of Interpersonal Violence*, **3**, 355–70.

Norris, J., and Feldman-Summers, S. (1981). Factors related to the psychological impacts of rape on the victim. *Journal of Abnormal Psychology*, **90**, 562–7.

Notman, M. T., and Nadelson, C. (1976). The rape victim: Psychodynamic considerations. *American Journal of Psychiatry*, **133**, 408–13.

Pearson, M. A., Poquette, B. M., and Wasen, R. E. (1983). Stress-inoculation and the treatment of post-rape trauma: A case report. *The Behavior Therapist*, **6**, 58–9.

Peterson, D. L., Olasov, B., and Foa, E. B. (1987, July). Response patterns in sexual assault survivors. Paper presented at the Third World Congress on Victimology, San Francisco, CA.

Peterson, C., and Seligman, M. E. P. (1983). Learned helplessness and victimization. *Journal of Social Issues*, **39**, 103–16.

Piercy, M. (1976). 'Rape Poem'. From *Living in the Open*. New York: Alfred A. Knopf; Wallace & Sheil Agency.

Rachman, S. (1980). Emotional processing. *Behaviour Research and Therapy*, **18**, 51–60.

Rehm, L. P., and O'Hara, M. W. (1979). Understanding depression. In I. V. Frieze, D. Bar-Tai, and J. S. Carroll (eds), *New Approaches to Social Problems*. San Francisco, CA: Jossey-Bass.

Reiss, S. (1980). Pavlovian conditioning and human fear: An expectancy model. *Behavior Therapy*, **11**, 380–96.

Reiss, S., and McNally, R. J. (1985). Expectancy model of fear. In S. Reiss and R. R. Bootzin (eds), *Theoretical Issues in Behavior Therapy*. New York: Academic Press, pp. 107–21.

Resick, P. A. (1987). The impact of rape on psychological functioning. Paper presented at 'State of the Art Workshop on Sexual Assault'. Charleston, SC.

Resick, P. A. (1988). Reactions of female and male victims of rape or robbery. Final report NIJ Grant no. 85-IJ-CX-0042.

Resick, P. A., Calhoun, K. S., Atkeson, B. M., and Ellis, E. M. (1981). Social adjustment in victims of sexual assault. *Journal of Consulting and Clinical Psychology*, **49**, 705–12.

Resick, P. A., and Jackson, J. (1976, March). The psychological treatment of rape victims: Past, present, and future. Paper presented in a symposium entitled, 'Perspectives on Rape' at the Southeastern Psychological Association Convention, New Orleans, LA.

Resick, P. A., and Jordan, C. G. (1988). Group stress inoculation training for victims of sexual assault: A therapist manual. *Innovations in Clinical Practice: A Source Book* (vol. 7). Sarasota, FL: Professional Resource Exchange, pp. 99–111.

Resick, P. A., Jordan, C. G., Girelli, S. A., Hutter, C., and Marhoefer-Dvorak, S. (1988). A comparative outcome study of behavioral group therapy for sexual assault victims. *Behavior Therapy*, **19**, 385–401.

Resick, P. A., Veronen, L. J. Calhoun, K. S., Kilpatrick, D. G., and Atkeson, B. M. (1986). Assessment of fear reactions in sexual assault victims: A factor analytic study of the Veronen–Kilpatrick Modified Fear Survey. *Behavioral Assessment*, **8**, 271–83.

Rothbaum, B. O., and Foa, E. B. (1988, September). Treatments of post-traumatic stress disorder in rape victims. Paper presented at the World Congress of Behavior Therapy, Edinburgh, Scotland.

Ruch, L. O., and Leon, J. J. (1983). Sexual assault trauma and trauma change. *Women and Health*, **8**, 5–21.

Russell, D. E. H. (1982). The prevalence and incidence of forcible rape and attempted rape of females. *Victimology*, **7**, 81–93.

Rychtarik, R. G., Silverman, W. K., Van Landingham, W. P., and Prue, D. M. (1984). Treatment of an incest victim with implosive therapy: A case study. *Behavior Therapy*, **15**, 410–20.

Seligman, M. E. P. (1975). *Helplessness: On Depression, Development, and Death*. San Francisco, CA: Freeman.

Stekette, G., and Foa, E. B. (1987). Rape victims: Post-traumatic stress responses and their treatment: A review of the literature. *Journal of Anxiety Disorders*, **1**, 69–86.

Stroebel, C. F. (1983). *Quieting reflex training for adults: Personal workbook* (or Practitioner's Guide). New York: DMA Audio Cassette Publications.

Turner, S. M. (1979). Systematic desensitization of fears and anxiety in rape victims. Paper presented at the Association for the Advancement of Behavior Therapy. San Francisco, CA.

Turner, S. M., and Frank, E. (1981). Behavior therapy in the treatment of rape victims. In L. Michelson, M.Hersen and S. M. Turner (eds), *Future Perspectives in Behavior Therapy*. New York: Plenum.

Veronen, L. J., and Kilpatrick, D. G. (1980a, August). Transcending the effects of rape: Towards an integration of behavioral and feminist perspectives. Paper presented at the 75th Annual Meeting of the American Sociological Association, New York City.

Veronen, L. J., and Kilpatrick, D. G. (1980b). Self-reported fears of rape victims: A preliminary investigation. *Behavior Modification*, **4**, 383–96.

Veronen, L. J., and Kilpatrick, D. G. (1983). Stress management for rape victims. In D. Meichenbaum and M. E. Jaremko (eds), *Stress Reduction and Prevention*. New York: Plenum.

Veronen, L. J., Kilpatrick, D.G., and Resick, P. A. (1979). Treatment of fear and anxiety in rape victims: Implications for the criminal justice system. In W. H. Parsonage (eds), *Perspectives on Victimology*. Beverly Hills, CA: Sage.

Vinsel, A. (1977). Rape: A review essay. *Personality and Social Psychology Bulletin*, **3**, 183–9.

Wolff, R. (1977). Systematic desensitization and negative practice to alter the aftereffects of a rape attempt. *Journal of Behavior Therapy and Experimental Psychiatry*, **8**, 423–5.

Wolpe, J. (1958). *Psychotherapy by Reciprocal Inhibition*. Stanford: Stanford University Press.

Wolpe, J. (1969). *The Practice of Behavior Therapy* (1st edn). New York: Pergamon.

Wortman, C. B. (1976). Causal attributions and personal control. In J. H. Harvey, W. I. Ickes and R. F. Kidd (eds), *New Directions in Attribution Research*, vol. 1. Hillsdale, NJ: Erlbaum.

Yassen, J., and Glass, L. (1984). Sexual assault survivors groups: A feminist practice perspective. *Social Work* (May–June), 252–7.

12

Prevention Programs

DEBORAH DARO
Center on Child Abuse Prevention Research, Chicago, USA

OVERVIEW

Over two million reports of child abuse or neglect were received by state child protective service systems throughout the United States in 1986, 200% more than the number reported ten years earlier. Since 1981, the percentage of these reports involving child sexual abuse has dramatically increased, rising from 7% of all reports in 1976 to almost 16% of all reports in 1986. In absolute terms, some 132 000 child sexual abuse cases were identified in 1986, 22 times the number reported in 1976. Of these reports, 42% involve the child's natural or step-parent and another quarter involve other relatives such as siblings or grandparents (AAPC, 1988). Whether this increase represents a real growth in the number of children falling victim to incest and sexual assault or reflects better systematic recognition of an age-old problem, the fact remains that a sizable number of children are experiencing sexual abuse at the hands of those whom society has entrusted with their care.

Intuitively, the notion of preventing child sexual abuse is attractive for reasons of both humanitarian and social cost. Children have a right not to be molested and society as a whole has a responsibility to protect future generations from experiencing such harm. While intervention to remediate the negative consequences of maltreatment can be seen as society's minimal responsibility, policies aimed at avoiding initial abuse are particularly attractive. A child does not have to experience harm before services are available and the society is able to avoid the significant costs of long-term therapeutic interventions. For example, sexual abuse treatment programs for a single family can cost between $50 000 and $93 000 annually and range from simple crisis and casework counseling to weekly individual, family and group therapy sessions for all family members (Daro, 1988).

Clinical Approaches to Sex Offenders and Their Victims
Edited by C. R. Hollin and K. Howells © 1991 John Wiley & Sons Ltd

Child abuse prevention strategies generally have been drawn from broad, causal theories of maltreatment. Common theoretical explanations for child abuse and neglect fall into three categories: *psychodynamic theories* which suggest that parents would be less abusive if they better understood themselves and their role as parents; *learning theories* which suggest that parents would be less abusive if they knew, more specifically, how best to care for their children; and *environmental theories* which suggest that parents would be less abusive if they had greater resources available to them in terms of material support or social support for a given set of actions (Daro, 1988). In articulating a theoretical framework for child sexual abuse, Finkelhor (1984) has identified four necessary preconditions: a motivated perpetrator, an ability to overcome internal inhibitions toward sexual abuse, an ability to overcome external or environmental barriers to sexual abuse, and a victim unable to resist the abuse.

Preventing abuse, therefore, can be seen as a process of altering the potential perpetrator, the potential victim or the environment in which both exist. Responding to the multiple causal theories of maltreatment, the prevention of physical abuse and neglect has focused on altering parental behavior and on providing parents under stress with a variety of programmatic opportunities to ease childrearing burdens. The most common of these strategies include respite care, crisis hot lines, home visitor programs, parenting education classes and support groups (Levine, 1988; Weiss and Jacobs, 1988). Political efforts to improve the social service safety net for families with the fewest material resources and to combat the environmental hazards children face also are viewed as vital and necessary components in any comprehensive child abuse prevention effort (Garbarino, 1988; Gil, 1981; Pelton, 1981).

In contrast, the prevention of child sexual abuse has centered on the provision of child assault prevention instructions in the schools, a strategy aimed at altering the child's behavior. This intervention provides classroom-based instruction for children of all ages on how to protect themselves from sexual assault and what to do if they experience actual or potential abuse. While in most cases these strategies include informational sessions for parents and school personnel, their primary focus is on the last of Finkelhor's four preconditions, that of strengthening the potential victim's capacity to resist assault.

Empowering children so that they are better able to protect themselves from harm has a certain parsimonious appeal. If successful, the approach avoids very costly and often intrusive interventions into the private family. Further, incorporating this strategy in the context of an existing universal service system, namely primary and secondary public education, offers the dual attraction of reaching large numbers of children at very low per-unit costs and avoiding many of the stigmas commonly associated with secondary prevention services. Rather than identifying a specific child or family as being at particular risk of maltreatment, these interventions assume all children are at equal risk and, therefore, in need of the instruction. Also, children who have been mistreated have a safe and supportive environment in which to disclose the abuse and from which to accept assistance.

Despite the laudable goals of this intervention and its intuitive appeal, many have questioned its ultimate utility in reducing sexual abuse rates (deYoung,

1988; Gilbert, 1988; Reppucci and Haugaard, 1989). Others have gone so far as to suggest that sexual abuse may be resistant to any prevention initiative regardless of its scope or content (Melton, in press). The purpose of this chapter is to review the empirical evidence regarding the efficacy of child assault prevention programs and to outline the potential utility of directing prevention efforts toward those adults responsible for a child's safety (i.e. parents and teachers). The chapter concludes with a general framework for building on these initial efforts to create a comprehensive plan for preventing sexual abuse.

STRENGTHENING CHILDREN

Drawing concepts from both the child abuse prevention and rape crisis fields, efforts to strengthen a potential victim's resistance to assault are widespread. A survey of over 260 school districts in the United States found that virtually all schools offer this instruction to both their elementary and high school students and over 40% mandate the provision of a uniform curriculum (Daro *et al.*, 1988). In addition, newspaper articles, television specials and a plethora of comic books, parent guidelines and public service announcements confront children and adults daily with the need to be cautious in their behaviors and to be supportive of victims.

Methods for providing child assault prevention instruction within a classroom setting vary along a number of key dimensions, including the characteristics and background of the instructor, the frequency of the presentations, and the specific content of the message. Most programs, however, share several common goals and objectives:

(1) Direct instruction to the child on the distinction between good, bad and questionable touching.
(2) The concept of body ownership or the rights of children to control who touches their bodies and where they are touched.
(3) The concept of keeping secrets and the importance of the child telling if someone touches him or her even if that person tells the child not to reveal the incident.
(4) The ability to act on one's intuition regarding when a touch or action makes a child feel uncomfortable even if the child does not know why he or she is uncomfortable.
(5) Assertiveness skills, ranging from repeatedly saying 'no' to someone who wants to do something that makes the child feel uncomfortable, to the use of various self-defense techniques (e.g. yelling, kicking, fighting back).
(6) The existence of support systems to help the child if he or she has experienced any form of maltreatment.

In addition, all of the programs include some type of orientation or instruction for both the parents and school personnel. These sessions cover a number of topics including a review of the materials to be presented to the children, a summary of the local child abuse reporting system, a discussion of what to do if you suspect a child has been mistreated, and a review of local services available to victims and their families.

Empirical Evidence

Unlike the relatively rich body of empirical evidence surrounding the development of physical abuse and neglect prevention efforts, relatively few child assault prevention program evaluations have employed experimental or quasi-experimental research designs (Finkelhor and Strapko, in press; Wurtele, 1987). In reporting their findings, the majority of these researchers have compared average performance by groups of children rather than exploring individual performance differences. Further, only a limited number of evaluations have assessed simultaneously two or more methods of providing the information to students (Gilbert *et al.*, 1990; Woods and Dean, 1986; Wurtele *et al.*, 1986). Measuring progress in terms of average group performance and evaluating only a single intervention method offers practitioners limited guidance. While such comparisons are useful in determining if a specific curriculum has any notable impact on a child's attitudes, knowledge or behavior, this type of research is less useful in identifying if one method or curriculum is more successful than another, or if some groups of children are more responsive than others. In addition to these methodological limitations, few studies have systematically assessed key ethical and theoretical questions surrounding these programs, such as the long-term effects of this intervention on a child's attitudes or perceptions of strangers, a teacher's willingness to have physical contact with a child, or a child's fear of being abused by his or her parents or other family members. Anecdotal and descriptive studies regarding specific incidents of success or failure are far more abundant than solid empirical evidence.

While limited in their design and scope, evaluations in this area have become more rigorous over time and have influenced the content and focus of child assault prevention programs. A recent review of 25 such studies indicates that these evaluations consistently report significant learning following the presentations (Finkelhor and Strapko, in press). Participants who have received these instructions demonstrate an increase in knowledge about safety rules and are more aware of what to do and who to turn to if they have been or are being abused. While some of these gains have been noted following repeated presentation of the concepts over a 10 to 15 week period (Downer, 1984; Fryer *et al.*, 1987; Woods and Dean, 1986; Young *et al.*, 1987), the majority of these gains have been realized after less than five brief presentations (Borkin and Frank, 1986; Harvey *et al.*, 1988; Kolko *et al.*, 1987; Nibert *et al.*, 1988; Plummer, 1984; Swan *et al.*, 1986; Wurtele *et al.*, 1986). Garbarino (1987) found that over 90% of his sixth grade sample and 80% of his second grade sample were able to answer correctly six questions about sexual abuse after having read a special Spiderman comic book on the subject developed by the National Committee for Prevention of Child Abuse.

As with all prevention efforts, these gains are unevenly distributed across concepts and participants. On balance, children have greater difficulty in accepting the idea that abuse can occur at the hands of someone they know than at the hands of strangers (Finkelhor and Strapko, in press). Among younger participants, the more complex concepts such as secrets and dealing with ambiguous feelings often remain misunderstood (Gilbert et al., 1990). While most children learn something from these efforts, a significant percentage of children fail to show progress in every area presented. For example, Conte noted that even the best performers in his study grasped only 50% of the concepts taught (Conte et al., 1985). Retention of the gains noted immediately following these instructions also varied. At least one evaluator discovered that while children have been found to retain increased awareness and knowledge of safety rules several months after receiving the instruction, they retain less information with respect to such key concepts as who can be a molester, the difference between physical abuse and sexual abuse, and the fact that sexual abuse, if it occurs, is not the victim's fault (Plummer, 1984).

Significant debate has occurred over the potential of this intervention with a pre-school population. A central feature of this debate has been the finding by several researchers that young children learn significantly less than their older counterparts. For example, Borkin and Frank (1986) found that virtually none of the 3 year olds interviewed retained any of the information presented after only one week and only 40% of the 4 and 5 year olds retained any knowledge over this period. Similarly, Conte et al. (1985) found significant differences in the level of information retained by the 4 and 5 year olds in their sample versus the 6 to 10 year olds. Gilbert et al. (1990) found that between 25% and 65% of the 123 children participating in their evaluation of seven different pre-school curricula remained at risk depending upon the outcome measures of concern.

While apparently learning less than older children, sizable numbers of 4 and 5 year olds do learn as a result of these interventions. A reanalysis of the Gilbert data cited above found that 90% of the participants provided more appropriate answers at post-test in at least one of the areas tested (Daro, 1989). Harvey et al. (1988) found that relative to a no-treatment control group the kindergarten children participating in a child assault prevention education program demonstrated more knowledge about preventing abuse and performed better on simulated scenes involving sexual abuse three weeks and seven weeks after the intervention. Following a five-day, behavioral-based prevention program for kindergarten, first and second graders, Kraizer et al. (1989) found significant improvements in all dimensions tested. Of particular note is the fact that all 33 experimental children indicated they would tell a responsible adult of the incident both when coerced and when asked to keep the encounter a secret. Contrary to what one might expect, kindergartners and first-graders enhanced their scores about equally, with the second grade group having less notable gains.

Learning to tell an adult when confused may be one of the most important concepts to convey to young children. Similar to the Kraizer study, the most dramatic increases in an assessment of seven different programs targeting pre-schoolers was with respect to program recipients, indicating they would encourage a fictional little bunny to tell an adult if something troubled it. Of the respondents, 75% showed improvement or repeated the correct response in this area at post-test (Daro, 1989). This pattern is particularly noteworthy given research on perpetrator behavior. Sexual abuse offenders interviewed by Conte *et al.* (1989) reported that a child indicating he or she would tell a specific adult about the assault does have an impact on their behaviors. Similarly Gilgun and Connor (1989) and Budin and Johnson (1989) report that perpetrators seek out passive, troubled, or lonely children who can be counted on to maintain the secret of an abusive relationship. Regardless of the ability of child assault prevention programs to convey all of the concepts targeted in these curricula, teaching young children the simple task of telling an adult when a situation confuses them may justify retaining these programs.

In addition to having a potential for primary prevention, child assault prevention instructions create environments in which children can more easily disclose prior or current maltreatment. In other words, independent of the impact these programs may have on future behavior, they do offer an opportunity for present victims to reach out for help, thereby preventing continued abuse (Leventhal, 1987). The few studies which have measured the extent to which these interventions result in increased disclosures have been promising. Kolko *et al.* (1989) reported that in five of six schools in which prevention programs were offered, school guidance counselors received 20 confirmed reports of inappropriate sexual of physical touching in the six months following the intervention. In contrast, no reports were noted in the one control school in their study. Similarly, Hazzard *et al.* (1988) found that 8 children reported current sexual abuse and 20 others reported past occurrences within six weeks of receiving a three-session prevention program.

Despite these and similar gains, some have questioned the advisability of raising the sensitive topic of sexual abuse with young children, the majority of whom will not experience sexual abuse by family members, friends or strangers. Several studies which have explicitly looked for increased anxiety or fear on the part of program participants, however, have found very limited overt negative reactions (Hazzard *et al.*, 1988; Kenning *et al.*, 1987; Wurtele *et al.*, 1987). Others have found more disturbing trends: Garbarino (1987) found that over one-third of the second, fourth and sixth graders who participated in an evaluation of the National Committee for Prevention of Child Abuse's Spiderman comic book reported being worried or anxious after completing the two stories on sexual abuse. Interestingly, girls were more than twice as likely as boys to express these fears, perhaps reflecting the fact that very few girls reported prior experiences with Spiderman comics in general.

While no study completed to date has documented any lasting increased anxiety as a result of child assault prevention instruction, several have found children exhibiting some behaviors that suggest caution is warranted in developing these programs. Swan *et al.* (1985) noted that, following a presentation of the play *Bubbylonian Encounter*, 93% of the children recognized the potential within their own families for a coercive (i.e. nonviolent) episode of child sexual abuse, and 88% saw the potential for violent sexual assault. One interpretation of this finding is that the children successfully grasped one of the program's key concepts: sexual abuse is not something that only involves strangers. On the other hand, the finding also suggests that a large number of children are now questioning, perhaps unnecessarily, the safety of their own homes. Similarly, Gilbert *et al.* (1990) noted that a greater number of pre-school children participating in their study had more negative attitudes toward not only clearly negative touches (e.g. hitting) but also toward rather benign or natural touches (e.g. tickling and bathing). Whether this finding represents a significant and permanent shift in these children's perceptions of touching or an artifact of this particular methodology, the issue of impact and the manner in which young children generalize the concepts they are presented with in these classes both need further study.

Programmatic Reforms

In addition to documenting the initial and longer term impact of child assault prevention programs, evaluations of this intervention have identified several ways to enhance program performance. These suggestions fall into two major categories.

(1) *Changes in program content*
   —Providing children with behavioral rehearsal or prevention strategies and offering feedback on their performance to facilitate a child's depiction of their involvement in abusive as well as unpleasant interactions.
   — Developing curricula with a more balanced developmental perspective, and tailoring training materials to a child's cognitive characteristics and learning ability.
   — For young children, presenting the material in a stimulating and varied manner in order to maintain their attention and to reinforce the information learned.
   — Teaching generic concepts such as assertive behavior, decision-making skills, and communication skills which children can use in everyday situations, not just to fend off abuse.
   — Repeatedly stressing the need for children to tell every time someone continues to touch them in a way that makes them uneasy.
   — Emphasizing those situations in which adults may be disobeyed and promises broken.
   — Distinguishing between sexual abuse and physical assault.
   — Stressing that abuse, if it does occur, is never the child's fault.
(2) *Changes in program structure*
   — Developing longer programs which are better integrated into regular school curricula and practices.
   — Creating more formal and extensive parent and teacher training components.
   — Offering booster sessions to reinforce the concepts presented.
   — Creating strategies to develop more positive and supportive relationships among parents, teachers, and students.

— Expanding current efforts to include extended after-school programs and more in-depth discussion opportunities for certain high risk groups (e.g. former victims, teen parents) in those communities requiring additional support.
— Involving all significant adults (e.g. teachers, parents, extended family, communmity leaders) in learning about sexual abuse and how to respond to reports.

Many of these recommendations have influenced the refinement of existing curricula and the development of new initiatives. For example, the Seattle-based Committee for Children revised their pre-school materials to de-emphasize a child's need to rely upon his or her own feelings. Instead, the most recent version of 'Talking About Touching: Personal Safety for Preschoolers and Kindergartners' establishes specific rules for children to apply to various situations. A long-term comprehensive program involving 27 lessons presented over a 12-month period, the curriculum extends the types of rule-oriented guidelines provided to children with respect to fire and traffic safety (e.g. do not play with matches, look both ways before crossing a street, etc.) to areas of personal safety. Children learn to determine 'safe' and 'unsafe' touch based upon simple, straight-forward guidelines such as 'No one should touch your private parts and if someone does you should tell an adult.' In this way, the burden of deciding an appropriate versus inappropriate touch is placed on adults, not on a child's intuition.

One of the most consistent recommendations from the evaluations completed to date is the need to provide children with opportunities to utilize the concepts they are being taught through role-play by simulating at-risk situations (Borkin and Frank, 1986; Kolko *et al.*, 1989; Stillwell *et al.*, 1988). Wurtele *et al.* (1987) found role-playing and participant modeling a more effective method for teaching safety concepts than experimenter modeling of prevention skills. In response to these and similar findings, child safety programs are increasingly utilizing this technique. For example, the 'Children Need to Know Personal Safety Program' developed by Sherryll Kerns Kraizer relies upon role-play to teach children the following concepts:

(1)   Your body belongs to you.
(2)   You have a right to speak up anytime someone touches you in a way that you don't like, that makes you feel uncomfortable, or in a way that you think is wrong.
(3)   Speaking up effectively includes using your words, body language and eye contact.
(4)   If a person doesn't stop after your first request, say 'I'm going to tell if you don't stop.'
(5)   Tell and keep telling until someone listens and helps you.
(6)   Touch should never have to be a secret.

Critical to this 10-session program is the repeated application of various role-plays in which childen are given an opportunity to respond to the range of ploys frequently used by perpetrators to engage their victims, such as bribery, emotional coercion, indifference, intimidation and threats.

Evaluations of this approach have found it to be effective in strengthening a child's ability to resist abusive situations. Fryer *et al.* (1987) documented a significant change in a child's behavior toward strangers following receipt of this intervention. Unique to the evaluation was the staging with each child of an actual situation the day before and the day after the classroom program. This simulation was comprised of the child's encounter with a member of the research team in an isolated setting in the school. The research assistant, posing as a stranger, requested the child's assistance in the performance of a task which entailed their leaving the school building together. Prior to the program, 13 of the 23 children in the experimental group and 10 of the 21 children in the control group failed (i.e. they agreed to leave the building with the researcher). Following the presentation, only 5 of the experimental children again agreed to leave the school building, a rate of change not noted among the control children. While the methods used in this evaluation have been questioned (Conte, 1987), the technique does serve to demonstrate the utility of a behavior-based curriculum.

Both the content and the structure of child assault prevention programs and the methods used to assess their effectiveness are under constant revision. Underscoring all program changes must be a commitment to evaluate the relationship of these programs to later learning and to study how children, parents and teachers are coping with the increasing references to sexual abuse and child abductions in all aspects of their lives. Model curricula that place greater emphasis on the role of parents and day-care providers in conveying safety concepts to children as well as creating safer environments for children need to be developed, implemented and evaluated.

Further, child assault prevention programs need to expand their explicit outcomes. Knowledge regarding child sexual abuse, the need for a child to tell an adult if he or she is threatened or abused, and the need for a child to avoid risky situations are all important messages. Equally important, however, is the need to continue to develop accurate measures of the ability of these programs to enhance positive self-awareness and solid decision-making skills. Research on young adults involved in various problem behaviors such as teen pregnancy, drug use and delinquency suggests that these individuals frequently share an inability to cope effectively with the demands of modern living. A common set of skills has been identified by educators as essential for rejecting these behaviors in favor of more appropriate, healthy and productive life choices. These attributes include communication skills; problem-solving and planning skills; assertiveness skills; negotiated conflict resolution; friendship skills; peer resistance skills; low-risk choice-making skills; stress reduction skills; self-improvement skills; consumer awareness skills; self-awareness skills; critical thinking skills; and basic academic skills (Benard, 1989). To the extent that child assault prevention programs mature into curricula which offer explicit opportunities for this type of skill building, they become programs which prevent not only child abuse but also a host of other dilemmas children face.

STRENGTHENING PARENTS AND CARETAKERS

Children, as dependent members of a society, require the support and care of adults. Throughout a child's development, he or she will draw intellectual stimulation from and be protected by a wide range of informal and formal caregivers. Initially, a child's parents, extended family members and an assortment of other adults, such as babysitters, child care providers and health care professionals, will shape their universe. As children mature, educators become a critical force in a child's intellectual and social development. The education of all professional groups working with children and the enhancement of parenting skills have been central tenets in the creation of comprehensive prevention systems targeting physical abuse and neglect. Until recently, few of these efforts explicitly addressed sexual abuse. The purpose of this section is to summarize the initial work done in this area with educators and to outline aspects of parenting education programs that offer the most promise in reducing intrafamilial sexual abuse.

Working with Educators

As discussed above, virtually all child assault prevention curricula include a teacher training component. The majority of these efforts involve brief, one to two hour sessions on curriculum content, indicators of sexual abuse, and responding to disclosures. Depending upon the school's policy, these sessions also may include an overview of local child abuse reporting laws and procedures. In a few cases, teachers are provided with more elaborate training programs lasting one to several days and offering more in-depth training on curriculum presentation and responding to suspected cases of maltreatment.

While information on child abuse reporting laws and requirements is found in virtually every school district in the United States (Daro et al., 1988), corresponding training on how best to handle suspected cases and to present any type of prevention education is far less common. A 1983 survey of 104 elementary and junior high teachers in a major metropolitan area found that over two-thirds had received three or fewer hours of child abuse education (Hazzard, 1984). More recently, less than half of the 550 elementary school teachers participating in a national survey reported that their schools provided in-service workshops on child abuse and neglect-related topics. Over two-thirds of the respondents felt that the child abuse education provided by their school districts was insufficient given the complexity of the problem (Abrahams et al., 1989).

This lack of training is held by many to account for the very low rate of abuse and neglect cases teachers observe which actually result in formal investigation by child protective services. The most recent federally-funded National Incidence Study found that only 23% of the cases identified by teachers were also found on child protective service caseloads (Westat, 1988). To some extent, this discrepancy reflects the policy in many schools for teachers to report suspected cases of maltreatment to their principals or school counselors rather than to child protective service workers. However, the size of the discrepancy and the lack of training in this area suggest that many teachers are operating with less than ideal information in confronting child maltreatment.

Comprehensive training regarding child abuse in general and child sexual abuse in particular has demonstrated changes in teachers' knowledge levels, comfort and confidence in conducting child assault prevention classes, and their abilities to identify abuse incidents. Hazzard (1984) found that a one-day training workshop on child abuse increased teacher knowledge about child abuse and developed more sympathetic attitudes toward the abusive parent. While the training did not result in increased reports of maltreatment, the treatment teachers were significantly more likely than an untrained control group to talk with individual students to determine if abuse was occurring, to give class presentations on child abuse and to talk with their colleagues about the topic. Similar findings were noted by the author when the training was limited to the issue of child sexual abuse (Kleemeier et al., 1987).

Extensive teacher training in preparation for presenting or following up on child assault prevention programs has been found in at least one instance to enhance child outcomes. In a federally-funded study conducted jointly by the City of Seattle's Department of Human Resources, Childhaven, and the Committee for Children, researchers found that children learned a good deal more when teachers received at least minimal formal training on the curriculum. While children receiving the program from teachers who had minimal training did not perform significantly better at post-test than children who had received the program from teachers receiving more enhanced and comprehensive training, the additional training had significant impacts on the teachers' comfort and perceived competence with the topic (Young et al., 1987).

Similar to the contributions research has made to enhancing the content and structure of child assault prevention classes, suggestions have emerged with respect to the content of teacher training. The collective message from these and other studies is that training teachers must be an essential component of all prevention education. Further, such training should go beyond the content of the curriculum and child abuse reporting procedures. Essential topics to cover include alternative methods for presenting the various lessons based upon the unique needs of a given classroom; parent involvement and awareness issues in normal sexuality development; feelings of ambivalence and anger toward abusive parents; and coping with a teacher's own victimization or abusive behavior (Hazzard, 1984; Miller-Perrin and Wurtele, 1988; Young et al., 1987).

In addition, at least one research team has emphasized the need to provide explicit, technical guidelines for teachers and school counselors covering how to discuss confidential disclosures with children and parents and when to report such discussions to local child protective service agencies. Kolko et al. (1989) offered this suggestion after noting that of the 20 confirmed cases of sexual touching reported during the six-month period following the presentation of a safety program, only two of the cases had been formally reported. The most common response to these disclosures involved discussing the episode with the child's parents. The information provided by the authors makes it impossible to determine the appropriateness of these procedures. However, the findings do underscore the variety of situations teachers and school administrators face in dealing with disclosures.

Working with Parents

Strengthening a parent's capacity to care better for his or her child is a common focus among child abuse and neglect prevention programs (Daro, 1988; Kagan *et al.*, 1987; Weiss and Jacobs, 1988). While the content and structure of these programs vary, critical service goals include:

(1) Increasing the parent's knowledge of child development and the demands of parenting.
(2) Enhancing the parent's skill in coping with the stresses of infant and child care.
(3) Enhancing parent-child bonding, emotional ties and communication.
(4) Increasing the parent's skill in coping with the stress of caring for children with special needs.
(5) Increasing the parent's knowledge about home and child management.
(6) Reducing the burden of child care.
(7) Increasing access to social and health services for all family members.

On balance, programs which incorporate these objectives rely upon a mixture of therapeutic and supportive services. Common service elements include routine health screening and developmental testing for the child, instruction in or modeling of basic child care techniques either through clinic-based classes or regular home visits, identification and enhancement of the parent's system of formal and informal supports, and, if appropriate, case management and advocacy services at the client and system levels.

Traditionally, parent education and enhancement services have not been viewed as methods for preventing sexual abuse. However, a certain degree of education for parents regarding this topic has been woven into the child assault prevention curricula. As cited above, the majority of these efforts include at least one informational meeting with parents, on a voluntary basis, prior to the classroom presentation. The most consistent finding from evaluations of these efforts is that they successfully encourage parents to talk with their children about sexual abuse (Daro *et al.*, 1987; Kolko *et al.*, 1987; Swan *et al.*, 1985; Wurtele *et al.*, 1986). More limited gains have been observed in a parent's understanding of the dynamics of child sexual abuse, and in the fact that the vast majority of such abuse occurs at the hands of individuals known to the child. The tendency of parents to be more fearful of this notion than their children has been suggested by Garbarino (1987) in his evaluation of the impacts on elementary school-aged children from reading a comic book on this topic. Of the fourth grade children who read this book with their parents, 80% reported feeling scared or worried afterwards, a feeling expressed by 50% of the children who read the comic alone.

These and similar findings suggest that enrolling parents as full partners in child sexual abuse prevention efforts requires more intensive programs than are currently in place. Brassard *et al.* (1983) have suggested the development of unique parent education programs which would be sponsored by local Parent-Teacher Associations and open to all parents in a community. The topics covered by such a course might include the definition, description, prevalence and consequences of incest; information on the intergenerational transmission of abuse; sources of help for incest abusers and victims; recognizing signs of abuse in one's own children or other children; and the responsibilities and rights of parents and children.

Effectively utilizing general parenting education and home visitor services as a vehicle for preventing child sexual abuse will require some shifts in the conceptualization and delivery of these service modalities. To date, the vast majority of these programs have targeted their services to mothers, a decision reflective of the sizable number of families headed by single mothers. Also, even in two-parent families, the mother usually retains primary if not sole responsibility for infant care. Consequently, most of the gains noted by these programs have reflected changes in a mother's behaviors or attitudes. However, research on this population, particularly teenage mothers, suggests a high percentage have been victims of sexual abuse. For example, the Ounce of Prevention in Illinois surveyed 445 pregnant or parenting teenagers throughout the state, asking them whether they had ever been asked or made to have an unwanted sexual experience. Almost two-thirds of these young women indicated that they had experienced such an event (Ounce of Prevention Fund, 1987). In response to this finding, the Ounce established a model program, Heart to Heart, to strengthen the adolescent parent's ability to protect herself and her child against sexual abuse. The 10-session program has three goals: to increase knowledge of child development issues related to sexual abuse; to increase positive parenting skills; and to help the teenage parent draw on community resources.

Those few programs which have successfully engaged fathers in their services report generally positive outcomes. Compared to similar fathers not receiving services, those involved in time-limited parenting education programs are found to be better in anticipating their infant's needs, and to respond better to their infant's cues (Dickie and Gerber, 1980). Similar educational efforts for fathers with older children (i.e. 6–12 years of age) have resulted in an increase in communication with and sensitivity toward their child (Levant and Doyle, 1983). Finally, Larson (1980) noted that fathers were more easily engaged in a home visiting program when such visits were initiated prior to rather than at the time of birth.

In their review of the literature, Williams and Finkelhor (1990) cite a number of factors associated with an elevated risk for incest. Three of the problem areas cited by this review—a lack of empathy for the child, a lack of involvement in child care responsibilities, and an inability effectively to utilize social supports—are areas amenable to improvement through the consistent application of new parent programs. New parent programs interested in expanding their efforts to address incest might well begin by enhancing service components in each of these areas, as discussed below.

First, incestuous fathers consistently and widely demonstrate difficulties in empathy, nurturance and caretaking. As a group, these fathers are not very involved in the early care of their children and at least one study notes that these fathers report spending very little time with their children during their first three years of life (Parker and Parker, 1986). In some cases, these patterns reflect personal functioning difficulties stemming from an abusive or neglectful childhood. As with many abusive parents, incestuous fathers can present problems of low self-esteem, poor impulse control, distorted dependencies, immaturity, and feelings of helplessness and isolation.

Because the majority of new parent programs place special emphasis on improving parent-child bonding and enhancing the capacity of parents to meet the emotional and physical needs of their infants, such programs offer an excellent method to decrease the risk for incest associated with this factor. To fulfill this potential, however, new parent programs need to be much more aggressive than they have been in engaging fathers in their services. Program administrators need to expand their conceptualization of the at-risk population to include those fathers who show an unusual disinterest in their child's birth or who seem to distance themselves from all child care responsibilities. Further, specific support groups led by fathers for fathers need to be incorporated into the service structure. Existing bias toward viewing childrearing as 'women's work' or embarrassment over their lack of knowledge regarding parenting skills may make it particularly difficult for men to participate in bisexual parenting education or support groups.

Second, because of their abusive history, incestuous fathers often carry with them very poor models of parenting. Some incestuous fathers fail to become involved in child care simply because they do not know how to care for their children, or they have a limited repertoire of discipline, or child care techniques that are either harmful or ineffective. Parenting education programs are well suited to filling this type of informational gap either through written material, group presentations, or individual home instruction. In many respects, conveying this type of basic knowledge to parents may be the easiest task in improving parenting potential.

Beyond providing parents with general information, however, lies the more difficult task of helping parents translate knowledge into behavior. For some parents, this transition will be a natural extension of having received the information or of having observed appropriate caregiving. For other parents, particularly males, the transition may be significantly more difficult. Parents who experienced healthy care as children or who observed or perhaps assisted their parents in the care of younger siblings will have less difficulty making use of the knowledge parenting education resources offer than will parents who lack concrete, positive experiences. For the latter group of parents, identifying and addressing the barriers they face in meeting their child's needs can be a complex and time consuming task for practitioners. Service providers may need to spend several sessions simply modeling the implementation of basic parenting information or assisting parents in securing necessary support services such as medical care or day care.

Finally, incestuous fathers, like many child abusers, are not well integrated into a positive formal or informal support system. This isolation precludes them

from seeking support when the stresses of daily life overrun their fragile resistance. Parenting programs, either through instruction or by example, teach participants how to make better use of formal and informal supports. Again, the most
serious challenge facing new parent programs in their efforts to offer this type of
support to potential perpetators is engaging fathers in service. For many fathers,
a singular emphasis on parenting skills or parent-child bonding may not make a
compelling case for enrollment. Additional services which might offer greater
attraction to fathers include job counseling or employment assistance, a method
found particularly useful in engaging teenage fathers; support groups around the
issues of adult relationships and sexuality; and support groups for men who have
a history of maltreatment.

A COMPREHENSIVE STRATEGY FOR PREVENTING SEXUAL ABUSE

Program effectiveness aside, it is clear that a more expansive prevention policy is
in order to insure a reduction in the number of sexual abuse cases. In developing
an effective approach to preventing child sexual abuse, it is critical to begin with
an overall model which highlights those personal and environmental factors
which contribute to an increased likelihood for maltreatment. Such an approach
has two advantages. First, it protects program planners and policy makers from
vesting too much in one specific prevention strategy. Because child sexual abuse
stems from multiple causes, it would be unrealistic to expect any intervention, no
matter how well designed, effectively to prevent abuse on its own. Success in
preventing this type of abuse, as well as other major types of maltreatment, rests
on the development of a coordinated effort including numerous programs, each
addressing a specific aspect of the problem. Second, the development of an
overall model helps identify the breadth of actors and conditions one needs to
consider in designing prevention strategies.

What would a comprehensive approach to preventing child sexual abuse include? With this question in mind, the National Committee for Prevention of
Child Abuse, along with a number of practitioners and policy makers working in
the area of sexual victimization, outlined a plan for preventing adults from
becoming child sexual abusers (Cohn *et al.*, 1985). The plan rests on eleven
assumptions regarding the nature of the sexual abuse problem and the maturity
of the current response system.

(1) Child sexual abuse is a very complex problem with causal roots in a host
     of personal functioning problems and social conditions.
(2) Current knowledge as to the causes of sexual abuse, the charactcristics
     of offenders, the characteristics of victims, and the most appropriate
     response system is imperfect. While much more is known today than ten
     or even five years ago, program planning continues to occur with less
     than ideal information.

(3)   There is no profile of the average sexual abuse offender. Identified perpetrators come from all walks of life, all income groups, and all races. Similarly, there are no consistent features found in all victims. This reality underscores the need to allocate some resources toward blanketing the entire population.

(4)   Offenders are not limited to adults. Research shows that perpetrators with the largest number of victims begin these behaviors as young adolescents. Frequently, this pattern follows their own sexual victimization.

(5)   Sexual fantasies and thoughts often precede behaviors, suggesting that a critical opportunity for prevention is when those fantasies begin.

(6)   Sexual abuse is not strictly a power issue. It involves sexual ideas, beliefs and preferences and, in some instances, confusion over appropriate sexual touching.

(7)   In certain cases, sexual abuse occurs because children do not resist advances, often because they do not know that they have the right to say no or how best to exercise that right.

(8)   Some sexual abuse exists because children are not in a safe environment. Parents or adult caretakers have not insured that those adults having contact with their children are committed to treating them in a positive and non-abusive manner.

(9)   Sexual abuse exists in part because of values and messages transmitted through the media. Violence, particularly against women, and the sexual dominance of men send a message that such behavior is not only appropriate but that it is essential for sexual fulfillment. Further, in a society which lauds individual freedom, there is a reluctance to articulate in clear and unambiguous language the inappropriateness of certain sexual behaviors, such as the use of children for sexual gratification.

(10)   Sexual abuse is deeply embedded in our society, in our values and in the way families are structured. American society values the private family above all else and has established legal principles and normative values which limit the capacity of the state to intervene in the raising of children. Children are very much the property of their parents rather than a collective treasure for the entire community.

(11)   Recognizing the limitations of the current knowledge base, any plan to prevent child sexual abuse needs to be flexible so as to maximize the opportunities to adjust the plan in light of emerging clinical and non-clinical research findings.

With these parameters defining the planning framework, it becomes clear that a multifarious approach to preventing child sexual abuse is needed, one which simultaneously targets the potential victim, the potential perpetrator and those aspects of the social fabric which nurture abusive behaviors. At a minimum, the approach should include six elements.

First, beginning where the field is at, it remains important for children to receive quality prevention education at regular intervals. While this education can most efficiently be presented through the schools, all children and youth groups should offer their members opportunities for this type of education. Rather than focusing solely on child sexual abuse, this education should cover all forms of abuse and neglect. For example, children should be made aware of the fact that they do not deserve to be belittled, yelled at, or emotionally ignored. If they are experiencing this behavior they need to talk to a trusted adult. Schools and organizational leaders need to create an environment in which a child feels comfortable talking about these experiences. Further, these programs need to insure that when a child does disclose abuse, he or she will be treated in a fair and appropriate manner.

Second, all adolescents need to receive education about healthy sexuality and appropriate displays of affection. Teenagers need to be made aware of what is normal and what is not and whom they can talk with if they have questions. All adolescents, teenage and pre-teenage, need to have access to 'well adolescent' clinics where identifiable or predictable sexual conflicts can be flagged and addressed.

Third, comprehensive training programs need to be developed for all professionals who work with children. Such training should cover, among other things, the identification of abuse, how to report abuse, how to teach children to protect themselves, how to help parents better educate their children regarding sex and potential abusive situations, how to screen and train staff and volunteers, and what is appropriate and inappropriate touching. As part of licensing requirements, professionals should be tested on these topics to determine if their knowledge is current and accurate.

Fourth, parents need to be educated not only about sexual abuse but also about broader parenting responsibilities, beginning with early attachment and bonding between parent and child. Fostering this bond may be the best protection children can be offered against all forms of abuse. As the child matures, parents need assistance on how to talk with their child about sex in general and about child sexual abuse in particular. Parents need to be given information on how to deal with a disclosure of sexual abuse in a manner which does not further complicate the treatment process. This is particularly important if the offender is a member of the child's family or the parent's spouse or partner. Parents, like child professionals, need to know how to make a report and how to detect potential abuse in their children.

Fifth, institutional changes will be required within child service and child welfare agencies to prevent initial and subsequent victimization. All child-serving organizations need to make a commitment to training children regarding self-protection and to involve parents in this training. Further, administrators have a responsibility to insure that no one on their staff has a prior record of victimization or behaves in a manner detrimental to a child's well-being. Reforms in the formal legal and treatment responses to sexual abuse disclosures are necessary so that children are not revictimized by society's quest for justice.

Finally, public awareness efforts regarding sexual abuse and its magnitude need to be expanded. A message needs to be given to the general public that preventing child sexual abuse, like all forms of maltreatment, is everyone's responsibility and everyone's problem. Specifically, all adolescents and adults need to know that child sexual abuse is a crime; that there is help out there if they need it; that abusive behavior is chronic unless you get help—no one cures themselves; that child sexual abuse hurts children; and that children can never consent to abuse. Likewise all children need to know that it is 'OK' to say no to touching that makes them uncomfortable, that it is not their fault if abuse occurs, that they need to reach out and tell someone if they are being victimized, and that help is available.

While common sense may suggest that this plan, if fully implemented, will move the field in the right direction, research findings supporting this approach are less clear and less available. A clear companion to the diversification of the child sexual abuse prevention package is the expansion of applied research and program evaluations. Among other questions, further research is needed to determine the extent to which individual behavior and attitudes can be altered as a result of various early intervention efforts, and the extent to which any of these changes result in less vulnerability for children and less proclivity toward sexual abuse among adults. Attention also needs to be paid to determining if increased awareness regarding sexual abuse causes individuals any lasting discomfort or impinges upon healthy parent-child relationships or child development.

Over and above these empirical concerns is a broader philosophical question regarding the overall advisability of prevention. It can be argued that prevention is extremely problematic within any reasonable scope of fiscal effort and within the values of a free society that gives people the right to be left alone. Also, to promote an appropriate level of sexual contact or define, explicitly, what constitutes 'correct' and 'incorrect' sexual touching is dangerous in that it requires practitioners and policy makers to make value judgements as to what constitutes approved sexual conduct. Despite these difficulties, responding only after the fact insures the continuous need for society to deal with the victims' dysfunctional families, individuals, and the social policies this will inevitably produce. Just as the hallmark of good leaders is the ability of their followers to operate efficiently without them, one might argue that the best child welfare system will be one that eventually is able to reduce its overall size and scope not by definition (i.e. by ignoring the precursors of specific social ills), but rather by reducing the number of sexually abused children through thoughtful and coordinated early intervention.

References

Abrahams, N., Casey, K., and Daro, D. (1989). *Teachers Confront Child Abuse: A National Survey of Teachers' Knowledge, Attitudes and Beliefs*. Chicago, IL: National Committee for Prevention of Child Abuse.

American Association for Protecting Children (1988). *Highlights of Official Child Neglect and Abuse Reporting, 1986*. Denver, CO: American Humane Association.

Benard, B. (1989). Life skills for children and youth. Paper presented at the Children's Trust Fund Forum II, Austin, Texas.

Borkin, J., and Frank, L. (1986). Sexual abuse prevention for preschoolers: A pilot program. *Child Welfare*, **65**, 75–82.

Brassard, M., Tyler, A., and Kehle, T. (1983). School programs to prevent intrafamilial child sexual abuse. *Child Abuse and Neglect*, **7**, 241–5.

Budin, L., and Johnson, C. (1989). Sex abuse prevention programs: Offenders' attitudes about their efficacy. *Child Abuse and Neglect*, **13**, 77–87.

Cohn, A., Finkelhor, D., and Holmes, C. (1985). *Preventing Adults From Becoming Child Sexual Molesters*. Chicago, IL: National Committee for Prevention of Child Abuse.

Committee for Children (1988). *Talking About Touching: Personal Safety for Preschoolers and Kindergartners*. Seattle, WA: Committee for Children.

Conte, J. (1987). Ethical issues in evaluation of prevention programs. *Child Abuse and Neglect*, **11**, 171–2.

Conte, J., Rosen, C., Saperstein, L., and Shermack, R. (1985). An evaluation of a program to prevent the sexual victimization of young children. *Child Abuse and Neglect*, **9**, 329–34.

Conte, J., Wolf, S., and Smith, T. (1989). What sexual offenders tell us about prevention strategies. *Child Abuse and Neglect*, **13**, 293–301.

Daro, D. (1988). *Confronting Child Abuse: Research for Effective Program Design*. New York: Free Press.

Daro, D. (1989). When should prevention education begin? *Journal of Interpersonal Violence*, **4**, 257–60.

Daro, D., Abrahams, N., and Robson, K. (1988). *Reducing Child Abuse 20% by 1990: 1985–1986 Baseline Data*. Chicago, IL: National Committee for Prevention of Child Abuse.

Daro, D., Duerr, J., and LeProhn, N. (1987). Child assault prevention instruction: What works with preschoolers. Paper presented at the Third National Family Violence Research Conference, University of New Hampshire.

deYoung, M. (1988). The good touch/bad touch dilemma. *Child Welfare*, **67**:1, 60–8.

Dickie, J., and Gerber, S. (1980). Training in social competence: The effects on mothers, fathers and infants. *Child Development*, **51**, 1248–51.

Downer, A. (1984). An evaluation of talking about touching. Unpublished manuscript available from author, PO Box 15190, Seattle, WA 98115.

Finkelhor, D. (1984). *Child Sexual Abuse: New Theory and Research*. New York: Free Press.

Finkelhor, D., and Strapko, N. (in press). Sexual abuse prevention education: A review of evaluation studies. In Willis, D., Holder, E., and Rosenberg, M. (eds), *Child Abuse Prevention*. New York: Wiley.

Fryer, G., Kraizer, S., and Miyoski, T. (1987). Measuring actual reduction of risk to child abuse: A new approach. *Child Abuse and Neglect*, **11**, 173–9.

Garbarino, J. (1987). Children's response to a sexual abuse prevention program: A study of the Spiderman comic. *Child Abuse and Neglect*, **11**, 143–8.

Garbarino, J. (1988). *The Future As If It Really Mattered*. Longmont, CO: Bookmakers Guild.

Gil, D. (1981). The United States versus child abuse. In Pelton, L. (ed.), *Social Context of Child Abuse and Neglect*. New York: Human Services Press.

Gilbert, N. (1988). Teaching children to prevent sexual abuse. *The Public Interest*, **93**, 3–15.

Gilbert, N., Duerr Berrick, J., LeProhn, N., and Nyman, N. (1990). *Protecting Young Children from Sexual Abuse: Does Preschool Training Work?* Lexington, MA: Lexington Books.

Gilgun, J., and Connor, T. (1989). How perpetrators view child sexual abuse. *Social Work*, **34**:3, 249–51.

Harvey, P., Forehand, R., Brown, C., and Holmes, T. (1988). The prevention of sexual abuse: Examination of the effectiveness of a program with kindergarten-age children. *Behavior Therapy*, **19**, 429–35.

Hazzard, A. (1984). Training teachers to identify and intervene with abused children. *Journal of Clinical Child Psychology*, **13**:3, 288–93.

Hazzard, A., Webb, C., and Kleemeier, C. (1988). Child sexual assault prevention programs: helpful or harmful? Unpublished manuscript, Emory University School of Medicine, Atlanta, GA.

Kagan, S., Powell, D., Weissbourd, B., and Zigler, E. (1987). *America's Family Support Programs*. New Haven, CT: Yale University Press.

Kenning, M., Gallmeier, T., Jackson, T., and Plemons, S. (1987). Evaluation of child sexual abuse prevention programs: a summary of two studies. Paper presented at the Third National Conference on Family Violence, University of New Hampshire.

Kleemeier, C., Webb, C., Hazzard, A., and Pohl, J. (1987). Child sexual abuse prevention: Evaluation of a teacher training model. Paper presented at the meeting of the American Psychological Association, New York City.

Kolko, D., Moser, J., and Hughes, J. (1989). Classroom training in sexual victimization awareness and prevention skills: An extension of the Red Flag/Green Flag people program. *Journal of Family Violence*, **4**, 25–45.

Kolko, D., Moser, J., Litz, J., and Hughes, J. (1987). Promoting awareness and prevention of child sexual victimization using the Red Flag/Green Flag program: An evaluation with follow-up. *Journal of Family Violence*, **2**, 11–35.

Kraizer, S., Witte, S., and Fryer, G. (1989). Child sexual abuse prevention programs: What makes them effective in protecting children? *Children Today*, **18**, 23–7.

Larson, C. (1980). Efficacy of prenatal and postpartum home visits on child health and development. *Pediatrics*, **66**, 191–7.

Levant, F., and Doyle, G. (1983). An evaluation of parent education programs for fathers of school-aged children. *Family Relations*, **32**, 29–37.

Leventhal, J. (1987). Programs to prevent sexual abuse: What outcomes should be measured? *Child Abuse and Neglect*, **11**, 169–71.

Levine, C. (ed.) (1988). *Programs to Strengthen Families*. Chicago, IL: Family Resource Coalition.

Melton, G. (in press). The improbability of prevention of sexual abuse. In Willis, D., Holden, E., and Rosenberg, M. (eds), *Child Abuse Prevention*. New York: Wiley.

Miller-Perrin, C., and Wurtele, S. (1988). The child sexual abuse prevention movement: A critical analysis of primary and secondary approaches. *Clinical Psychology Review*, **8**, 313–29.

Nibert, D., Cooper, S., Fitch, L., and Ford, J. (1988). *Prevention of Abuse of Young Children: Exploratory Evaluation of An Abuse Prevention Program*. Columbus, OH: National Assault Prevention Center.

Ounce of Prevention (1987). *Child Sexual Abuse: A Hidden Factor in Adolescent Sexual Behavior*. Chicago, IL: Ounce of Prevention Fund.

Parker, H., and Parker, S. (1986). Father-daughter sexual abuse: An emerging perspective. *American Journal of Orthopsychiatry*, **56**, 531–49.

Pelton, L. (1981). *Social Context of Child Abuse and Neglect*. New York: Human Services Press.

Plummer, C. (1984). Preventing sexual abuse: What in-school programs teach children. Paper presented at the Second National Conference on Family Violence, University of New Hampshire.

Reppucci, N., and Haugaard, J. (1989). Prevention of child sexual abuse: Myth or reality. *American Psychologist*, **44**, 1266–75.

Stilwell, S., Lutzker, J., and Greene, B. (1988). Evaluation of a sexual abuse prevention program for preschoolers. *Journal of Family Violence*, **13**, 269–81.

Swan, H., Press, A., and Briggs, S. (1985). Child sexual abuse prevention: Does it work? *Child Welfare*, **64**:4, 395–405.

Trudell, B., and Whatley, M. (1988). School sexual abuse prevention: Unintended consequences and dilemmas. *Child Abuse and Neglect*, **12**, 103–13.

Weiss, H., and Jacobs, F. (eds) (1988). *Evaluating Family Programs*. New York: Aldine de Gruyter.

Westat Associates (1988). *Study Findings: Study of National Incidence and Prevalence of Child Abuse and Neglect*. Washington, DC: US Department of Health and Human Services.

Williams, L., and Finkelhor, D. (1990). The characteristics of incestuous fathers: A review of recent studies. In Marshall, W., Laws, D., and Barbaree, H. (eds), *The Handbook of Sexual Assault: Issues, Theories and Treatment and Offenders*. New York: Plenum.

Woods, S., and Dean, K. (1986). *Community-Based Options for Maltreatment Prevention: Augmenting Self-Sufficiency*. Prepared under contract to the US Department of Health and Human Services, National Center on Child Abuse and Neglect.

Wurtele, S. (1987). School-based sexual abuse prevention programs: A review. *Child Abuse and Neglect*, **11**, 483–95.

Wurtele, S., Marrs, S., and Miller-Perrin, C. (1987). Practice makers perfect: The role of participant modeling in sexual abuse prevention programs. *Journal of Consulting and Clinical Psychology*, **55**, 599–602.

Wurtele, S., Saslawsky, D., Miller, C., Marrs, S., and Britcher, J. (1986). Teaching personal safety skills for potential prevention of sexual abuse: A comparison of treatments. *Journal of Consulting and Clinical Psychology*, **54**, 688–92.

Young, B., Liddell, T., Pecot, J., Siegenthaler, M., and Yamagishi, M. (1987). *Preschool Sexual Abuse Prevention Project: Executive Summary*. Report prepared under a research grant funded by the US Department of Health and Human Services, Office of Human Development Services, Washington, DC.

Sex Offenders and Victims: Overview and Conclusions

Kevin Howells

and

Clive R. Hollin

A large and increasing number of practitioners devote their professional lives to working with the perpetrators and victims of sexual abuse and offending. The range of ways of working, of assessing the relevant variables and of producing change, is reflected in the preceding chapters of this book. The diversity of professional and academic contributions masks what appears to us to be an underlying unifying objective. The majority of workers in this area can usefully be construed as engaged in the task of *preventing* the suffering and distress engendered by abusive sexual behaviour.

Prevention, at this broader level of victim distress, can be achieved either by reducing the incidence of abusive behaviour itself (see Daro's chapter) or by modifying victims' psychological reaction to abuse. Abusive behaviour (including both rape and child sexual abuse) needs to be the subject of a *functional analysis* (Owens and Ashcroft, 1982; Slade, 1982) before programmes to reduce or eliminate it can be undertaken. Functional analysis stresses that behaviour is a function of both antecedents and consequences and that both need to be addressed in an attempt to produce changes.

CHANGING ABUSIVE BEHAVIOUR

Work reviewed in previous chapters suggests that abusive behaviour can be seen as a function of three broad classes of antecedent—of perpetrator, situational, and victimological variables. This analysis has many similarities to the four

Clinical Approaches to Sex Offenders and Their Victims
Edited by C. R. Hollin and K. Howells © 1991 John Wiley & Sons Ltd

preconditions model of child sexual abuse described by Finkelhor (1984), although Finkelhor's model is more specific in attempting to delineate preconditions (necessary conditions) for child sexual abuse to occur. Preconditions are an important subset of a more general category of causal influences. Thus, for example, aggressive impulses or anger may be important instigators of sexual abuse (particularly of rape) but they are not *necessary conditions* for sexual abuse in that abuse can occur without aggressive or angry feelings being present in the perpetrator.

It has become unfashionable to value interventions and preventive measures at the level of the individual perpetrator. Indeed the series of books of which the present volume is a part was undertaken to reassert the need to include perpetrator characteristics in explanatory and therapeutic models (see Preface). The work reviewed in previous chapters by Conte, Lanyon, Murphy, Haynes and Worley, and Perkins, and in a previous review by Marshall and Barbaree (1989), clearly shows the necessity and value of interventions with perpetrators. These reviews suggest that the targets for interventions are complex and wide-ranging. Deviant sexual arousal itself is a major target but deviant arousal appears to be neither a necessary not a sufficient cause of sexual offending (chapter by Murphy, Haynes and Worley; Blader and Marshall, 1989). The evidence that individual perpetrators are often responsible for large numbers of abusive acts (see the chapter by Conte) further reinforces the utility of continuing to direct some preventive efforts towards clinical interventions with perpetrators.

Preventive measures with perpetrators will be secondary rather than primary in that they can be implemented only after an abusive act has been perpetrated. The emphasis of programmes will, therefore, be on preventing recidivism. It is noteworthy that primary preventive programmes for potential perpetrators are largely undeveloped. These would need to take the form of educational programmes directed at men and male adolescents, focusing perhaps on teaching the risks attached to particular forms of sexual fantasy, attitudes and cognitions (see Lanyon's chapter).

So far we have emphasized the necessity for prevention programmes to tackle intra-perpetrator variables, such as deviant arousal, aggressive impulses and abuse-promoting cognitions. Each of these components, in turn, needs to be the subject of a functional analysis. What are the antecedents and consequences that lead to the development and maintenance of deviant arousal or deviant cognitions, for example? Such analyses would quickly require us to consider socio-cultural, historical and systemic factors and are beyond the scope of the present book.

Clearly, the likelihood of abusive acts occurring is a funtion of variables other than those within the perpetrators' psychology (see Finkelhor, 1984). As Finkelhor has pointed out in relation to child sexual abuse, a strong interest in and predisposition towards deviant sexual behaviour may be suppressed, or alternatively facilitated by the situational context. Opportunity factors, particular family constellations (see Bentovim's chapter), and situational influences such as stress, alcohol or poor supervision or protection may make it likely that an abusive act will occur. Clinical work with families such as that described by

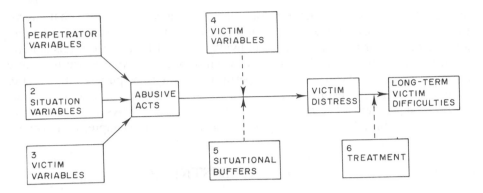

Figure 1   Antecedents of victim distress following sexual abuse. Numbered boxes indicate variables that might serve as targets for prevention and intervention

Bentovim, and broad preventive programmes as described by Daro, reflect attempts to modify the contribution of situational factors both in primary and in secondary ways.

To point out the victimological contribution (see Figure 1) to the abusive act does not, in any way, imply ascription of moral responsibility for the abusive act to the victim. As Finkelhor (1984) has pointed out, perpetrators need to overcome the potential resistance of victims and it is likely that potential victims vary in their ability to recognize dangerous situations, to notice and understand sexual cues in the environment, and in their capacity for effective assertiveness and other deterring behaviours. Indeed, it is this very kind of individual difference that provides the rationale for preventive programmes intended to provide women and children with skills to prevent them becoming victimized. Daro's review indicates the considerable progress made in this field although a range of methodological and theoretical problems needs to be addressed (Reppucci and Haugaard, 1989). Once again, the victimological variables that may contribute to the occurrence of abusive acts, such as ineffective assertion or lack of sexual information in children can each become, in turn, the focus for further functional analyses. Assertiveness and sexual knowledge, for example, are likely to be functions of patterns of socialization, which in turn are a function of broader societal beliefs about children and about male–female differences. To summarize our discussion so far, a comprehensive prevention programme would attempt to diminish the probability of abusive acts occurring by intervening with all three classes of antecedent – perpetrator, situational, and victimological variables. Further functional analyses of these 'proximal' variables would identify 'distal' antecedents, often of a systemic nature, which would also need to become targets for change.

The type of functional analysis we have just described is of abuse as a general phenomenon. In clinical work this analysis would need to be paralleled by a similar functional analysis of the individual case. Thus, for example, although aggressive motivation, deviant arousal, disinhibition, expectations of 'getting away with it' and faulty cognitions might all be perpetrator variables that need investigating, a particular perpetrator will show only some of these characteristics. Similarly, only very particular situational and victimological 'releasers' of abusive behaviour may apply in the individual case. It follows from this general point that it would be possible to have two instances of sexual abuse that were *topographically* similar (e.g. both perpetrators fondled pre-pubescent girls) but functionally entirely distinct, the two abusive acts being the product of entirely different antecedents. The need for individual functional analysis is an important feature of the broad therapeutic approach described in the chapter by Perkins.

REDUCING DISTRESS

The second broad class of preventive strategy is to prevent victim distress by intervening therapeutically with victims themselves. A distinction needs to be made between short- and long-term distress and disturbance. Work described in several of the chapters (West, Berliner, Jehu, Resick and Gerth Markaway) suggests that whether or not major distress follows abuse is a function, in part, of the nature and circumstances of the abusive act, the degree of relationship between victim and perpetrator, the extent of violence, and other factors. It is likely (see Figure 1) that pre-existing dispositions of personality, attitude, cognition and affect in victims will influence the extent to which abusive acts create major short- or long-term disturbance. Equally it is likely that situational 'buffers' exist which may facilitate coping with the trauma of some assaults. Social support has been shown in some studies to provide a buffering effect, as does family cohesion (see chapter by Berliner).

The detailed accounts of therapeutic programmes provided by Berliner, Jehu, and Resick and Gerth Markaway suggests that psychologists, doctors and social workers now have available to them a substantial array of therapeutic measures with considerable potential for the prevention of psychological distress. Although prevention of this sort is *secondary* prevention, it is also feasible that knowledge of the impact of abuse on victims could be used to 'immunize' potential victims. Knowledge about the high probability of harmful and unrealistic internal attributions (self-blame) for abusive incidents, for example, ought to prepare people for, and even undermine, this particular psychological reaction.

CONCLUSIONS

We should like to conclude this book by making some general points about clinical practice and research in the area of abusive sexual behaviour and sexual offending.

Theory

The first relates to the role of psychological theory. Lanyon makes the point in his chapter that much work in this area has been empirical and data-driven rather than theory-driven. The expansion of empirical information has been one of the strengths of work in the area of sexual abuse in the last decade. On the other hand, research findings are often difficult to interpret in the absence of an integrative theory or model. Two types of theory or model-building seem to us to be desirable. Firstly, there is a need for integrated models of sexual abuse itself. These should have both an explanatory and a therapeutic function. Such models will need to incorporate both interpersonal, situational, and victimological variables (see above). We see Finkelhor's (1984) pioneering effort to provide such a model as being an important step forward. Although it is likely to need revision in the light of new research information, it remains a useful integrative framework for understanding and modifying abusive sexual behaviours. The incorporation of rape within this model would be a useful step forward.

The second kind of theory-building we advocate is the attempt to relate concepts and theories in the area of sexual abuse to *general* psychological theories and frameworks. The acquisition of deviant sexual interest leading to abuse is, after all, part of a much more general process of the learning of sexual preferences. Sexual interests leading to abuse need to be understood in terms of the general processes involved in the acquisition of many types of sexual diversity (Howells, 1984). The recent attempt by Laws and Marshall (1990) to describe a more general theoretical account of the learning of deviant and non-deviant preferences is an example of the sort of work we see as useful.

There are other areas where the need for a general theoretical base is apparent. We are encouraged by Davies's attempt in his chapter to relate child witness research to psychological theory concerning memory and other processes and the base that provides for practice (see Vizard's chapter). We would argue also that work on children's reactions to sexual victimization must, eventually, be linked to mainstream developmental psychological theory. To understand how children respond to sexual trauma we need to know how non-abused children understand sexuality and interpersonal relationships in general. Similarly, family adaptation to sexual trauma needs to be located within a general account of family functioning and adaptation. Bentovim reveals a clear attempt to relate clinical work to family and systems theory in his chapter. This seems to us to add considerably to the findings and clinical methods he reports.

Integration

It is our experience that clinical research and practice in the area of sexual abuse and offending is fragmented. Clinicians' and researchers' activities and interests are often shaped by the particular settings in which they work and by whom is defined as the 'client'. The range of activities and clients is wide and this range is reflected in the diversity of the chapters in the present book. Some professionals work exclusively with perpetrators, often in a penal or forensic psychiatric setting. Naturally, the focus of attention for such workers is often the psychology of the perpetrator. Perpetrators may be assessed only in the institutional setting and the investigator has limited excess to the context in which the offending behaviour occurred. Additionally, the perpetrator group studied is likely to be highly unrepresentative of the general population of perpetrators. They are the survivors of a series of filters which have biased the group characteristics in ways that are largely unknown.

At the other extreme a child or adult victim of sexual abuse may be seen in a community setting. The victim herself and (in the case of children) the family context are the focus of attention, as the perpetrator may be unknown, detained in custody or unwilling to attend for assessment or treatment. There is a temptation, particularly in the case of incestuous abuse, to play down the role of within-perpetrator factors and to emphasize family or systems pathology as the major actiological variable (see Conte's discussion of incestuous offenders).

Other professions work purely in a primary prevention capacity with parents, teachers and other groups, and may have relatively little direct contact with either victims or perpetrators. It seems to us that there is a need for increased communication between these various groups of workers and for the integration of ideas and findings. Conte, in his chapter, refers to the unfortunate schism between offender and victim work and offers various suggestions for 'shared data collection and dialogue'. A broad-based societal approach to prevention will require that such a dialogue be maintained and extended.

Objectivity versus Engagement: a Middle Path?

Sexual abuse and offending pose a particular and distinctive challenge for the practitioner. The challenge lies in trying to balance the affective reaction to abuse with the need for objectivity and detachment. Emotional reactions to abuse, even in professionals, are not to be entirely discounted as unhelpful. It is likely, for example, that the mushrooming of research, clinical intervention and even resources devoted to sexual abuse has been instigated, in part, as a result of angry reactions by practitioners and others. Indignation about the scale of sexual abuse and about the neglect of victims and their needs has almost certainly been an energizing and activating force for research and clinical work.

Conversely, emotional reactions are discernible in those who, as Conte suggest, have a sense of disbelief and irritation because of the excessive 'hype' associated with sexual abuse. Such reactions, again, are not necessarily entirely destructive in their consequences; they may engender a commendable scepticism and methodological rigour in both clinical practice and research.

As we see it, what is required for the psychologist, doctor or social worker is the capacity to tread a middle path between blinkered 'engagement' and excessive detachment. Complete detachment about sexual abuse is probably neither possible nor desirable. On the other hand, the capacity for cool appraisal, the willingness to conduct clinical work on a scientific and empirical basis and the ability to accept that a favourite assumption has been proven false are virtues indeed.

References

Blader, J. C., and Marshall, W. L. (1989). Is assessment of sexual arousal in rapists worthwhile? A critique of current methods and the development of a response compatability approach. *Clinical Psychology Review*, **9**, 569–87.

Finkelhor, D. (1984). *Child Sexual Abuse: New Theory and Research*. New York: Free Press.

Howells, K. (ed.) (1984). *The Psychology of Sexual Diversity*. Oxford: Blackwell.

Laws, D. R., and Marshall, W. L. (1990). A conditioning theory of the etiology and maintenance of deviant sexual preference and behavior. In W. L. Marshall, D. R. Laws and H. E. Barbaree (eds), *Handbook of Sexual Assault: Issues, Theories and Treatment of the Offender*. New York: Plenum.

Marshall, W. L., and Barbaree, H. E. (1989). Sexual violence. In K. Howells and C. R. Hollin (eds) *Clinical Approaches to Violence*. Chichester: Wiley.

Owens, R. G., and Ashcroft, J. B. (1982). Functional analysis in applied psychology. *British Journal of Clinical Psychology*, **21**, 181–9.

Reppucci, N. D., and Haugaard, J. J. (1989). Prevention of child sexual abuse: Myth or reality? *American Psychologist*, **44**, 1266–75.

Slade, P. D. (1982). Towards a functional analysis of anorexia nervosa and bulimia nervosa. *British Journal of Clinical Psychology*, **21**, 167–9.

Author index

Subject index

Indexes compiled by John Gibson